Practicing Theory in Introductory College Literature Courses

COLLEGE SECTION COMMITTEE

Practicing Theory in Introductory College Literature Courses

Edited by

James M. Cahalan and David B. Downing
Indiana University of Pennsylvania

National Council of Teachers of English
1111 Kenyon Road, Urbana, Illinois 61801

Staff Editor: Robert A. Heister

Interior Design: Tom Kovacs for TGK Design

Cover Design: Robin Loughran

NCTE Stock Number: 36659–3050 (hardcover)
36532–3050 (softcover)

It is the policy of NCTE in its journals and other publications to provide a forum for the open discussion of ideas concerning the content and the teaching of English and the language arts. Publicity accorded to any particular point of view does not imply endorsement by the Executive Committee, the Board of Directors, or the membership at large, except in announcements of policy, where such endorsement is clearly specified.

Library of Congress Cataloging-in-Publication Data

Practicing theory in introductory college literature courses / edited by James M. Cahalan and David B. Downing.
p. cm.
Includes bibliographical references and index.
ISBN 0–8141–3665–9 (hardcover)
ISBN 0–8141–3653-2 (softcover)
1. American literature—History and criticism—Theory, etc. 2. English literature—History and criticism—Theory, etc. 3. American literature—Study and teaching (Higher) 4. English literature—Study and teaching (Higher) 5. Literature—Study and teaching—Theory, etc. 6. Literature—Study and teaching (Higher). I. Cahalan, James M. 1953– . II. Downing, David B., 1947– .
PS25.P7 1991
807.1'1—dc20 91–29051
CIP

Contents

Preface ix

1. Introduction 1
   James M. Cahalan and David B. Downing

I. Orientations toward the Student: Reader Response and Psychoanalysis 17

2. Reading from Inside and Outside of One's Community 19
   David Bleich

3. Combining Personal and Textual Experience: A Reader-Response Approach to Teaching American Literature 36
   Patricia Prandini Buckler

4. From Clinic to Classroom while Uncovering the Evil Dead in *Dracula*: A Psychoanalytic Pedagogy 47
   Mark S. Paris

II. Orienting the Reader: New Historicism, Reception Theory, and Marxism 57

5. "Text," "Reader," "Author," and "History" in the Introduction to Literature Course 59
   John Schilb

6. In Search of Our Sisters' Rhetoric: Teaching through Reception Theory 72
   Louise Z. Smith

7. The Historical Necessity for—and Difficulties with—New Historical Analysis in Introductory Literature Courses 85
   Brook Thomas

8. The Reader and the Text: Ideologies in Dialogue 101
John Clifford

III. Confrontational, Collectivist, and Feminist Alternatives 113

9. Confrontational Pedagogy and the Introductory Literature Course 115
Ronald Strickland

10. The Walls We Don't See: Toward Collectivist Pedagogies as Political Struggle 131
C. Mark Hurlbert

11. Feminist Theory, Literary Canons, and the Construction of Textual Meanings 149
Barbara Frey Waxman

12. Coyote Midwife in the Classroom: Introducing Literature with Feminist Dialogics 161
Patrick D. Murphy

IV. Curricular Alternatives: Multicultural and Theoretical Transformations of Classroom Practice 177

13. A Multicultural Introduction to Literature 179
Phillipa Kafka

14. "Who Was That Masked Man?": Literary Criticism and the Teaching of African American Literature in Introductory Courses 189
Pancho Savery

15. Less Is More: Coverage, Critical Diversity, and the Limits of Pluralism 199
Douglas Lanier

V. Dialogue and Deconstruction in the Classroom 213

16. From Discourse in Life to Discourse in Poetry: Teaching Poems as Bakhtinian Speech Genres 215
Don Bialostosky

17. Teaching Deconstruction: Theory and Practice in the Undergraduate Literature Classroom — 227
    Lois Tyson

18. Reading Deconstructively in the Two-Year College Introductory Literature Classroom — 239
    Thomas Fink

VI. Poststructuralism, Postmodernism, and Computer Literacy — 249

19. Practicing Textual Theory and Teaching Formula Fiction — 251
    M. H. Dunlop

20. Theory as Equipment for (Postmodern) Living — 261
    Thomas McLaughlin

21. Students as Theorists: Collaborative Hypertextbooks — 271
    James J. Sosnoski

VII. Bibliographic Essay and Comprehensive Works Cited — 291

22. Selected Further Resources for Theory and Pedagogy: A Bibliographic Essay — 293
    James M. Cahalan and David B. Downing

Works Cited — 335

Index — 367

Editors — 379

Contributors — 381

Preface

As we enter the 1990s, few would disagree that the past twenty years have witnessed a tremendous explosion of theoretical work in the humanities and social sciences. The recent proliferation of theoretically informed programs in higher education, such as cultural studies, women's studies, interdisciplinary studies, American studies, semiotics, discourse analysis, and others, has often been cited as the most noticeable sign that there is a "crisis in the profession" of the teaching of literature and the humanities. As Robert Scholes, Nancy Comley, and Gregory Ulmer point out, the "whole conception of literary study is heavily influenced by recent developments in literary theory" (1988, iii). Cary Nelson notes that "the rapid theorizing of the humanities and social sciences in the last twenty years may seem a single, unified, almost willed event" (1986, ix). Moreover, developments in literary theory in recent years are ones that ought to be particularly empowering for teachers of introductory literature courses. As diverse as theoretical developments have been, they share a common emphasis on the centrality of readers and their culture in interpreting literary texts.

Despite these transformations, however, we continue to find reproduced a tremendous institutional gap between the scholarship of "high" theoretical study at prestigious graduate institutions, on the one hand, and the actual effect that scholarship has on curricular designs and classroom practices in introductory courses at the vast majority of two-year and four-year colleges and universities. As we argue in our introductory essay, while many contemporary theories ostensibly call for radical social change, a rejection of the separation of theory and practice, and alternative pedagogical as well as disciplinary practices, what we most often find is in fact a perpetuation of the gap between scholarly theoretical discourse and the teaching of those disciplines and texts that constitute the humanities. As Charles Moran and Elizabeth Penfield note in *Conversations: Contemporary Critical Theory and the Teaching of Literature* (1990), "In the past two decades literary theory has emerged . . . as a vigorous and exciting field. Yet the vigor and excitement have not inspired widespread conversation about the teaching of literature. Unlike composition theory, contemporary literary theory has remained somehow remote from our talk about classroom practices" (1). This is particularly the case in the introductory, nonmajor, "service-oriented" segment of our professional lives that remains dominated by primarily formalist, New Critical doctrines, despite the more noted curricular changes at some of the better-known research institutions.

We envision this book as contributing to what will have to be a much larger project shared by all those critical of academic hierarchies. These hierarchies have allowed even those theories ostensibly calling for the most radical social change to have a minimal effect on the material practices of introductory literature courses. Indeed, we have begun to see signs that the next decade will witness a great deal of effort devoted to the pedagogical assimilation of literary theory in introductory courses. Our contributors' essays, our own final bibliographical essay devoted to further resources on theory and pedagogy, and the large unified list (at the end of the book) of the works cited by the authors all reflect the burgeoning nature of this project. Our central aim is to help develop and deepen a strong working relationship between teachers of introductory literature courses and those who specialize in literary and cultural theory.

We wish to acknowledge and thank some institutions and people who aided us in crucial ways without which we could not have completed this book. We are grateful for the support of the Faculty Professional Development Council of the Pennsylvania State System of Higher Education as well as the Senate Fellowship Program of Indiana University of Pennsylvania, both of which provided us with grants that made it possible for us to finish this project. Gerry Stacy, former IUP Associate Graduate Dean for Research (now Graduate Dean at Central Washington University), was instrumental in our securing both of these grants. John D'Ambrosio, our graduate assistant, provided significant help in identifying and collecting the large number of sources to which we refer in our bibliographical essay; his successor, Mark Crilly, helped fill in some missing references; and our doctoral student, Dallas Dillon, put us on to a few other sources. Carol Connell, IUP librarian and English bibliographer, contributed pivotal assistance in tracking down several of the most recent books we cite, even rush ordering a few of them. Without the work of Catherine Renwick, IUP Graduate English Office secretary, on correspondence and typing, we could never have gotten this project off the ground, let alone complete it. Blake McCully, systems analyst for IUP's College of Humanities and Social Sciences, reformatted and printed two earlier versions of our manuscript, and members of IUP's Micro-Computer Support Office converted many of the disks that contributors sent us. At NCTE, Charles Suhor gave us initial encouragement to propose this book; Michael Spooner has been a constant source of support, help, and insight from beginning to end; and Robert A. Heister has served as our perceptive, efficient, and patient manuscript and project editor. We dedicate *Practicing Theory* to our fellow teachers and students.

—J. M. C.
D. B. D.

Practicing Theory in Introductory College Literature Courses

1 Introduction

James M. Cahalan and David B. Downing
Indiana University of Pennsylvania

The 1990s promise to be an exciting time in college English in the wake of recent developments in the field. Ten years ago, Gayatri Spivak outlined some "of the complicated organizational" transformations that the profession of literary studies faced in the 1980s: "faculty development, fundamental curricular revision, overhauling of disciplinary lines until the term 'English literary studies' changes drastically in meaning" (1981, 35). Spivak is one of the more influential proponents of the last three decades' social activist "theory movement," which would do much to bring about such changes. As we enter the 1990s, we find that many of these predicted changes have, in fact, now materialized in those universities that have adopted the curricular rhetoric of "textual studies," "cultural studies," or "rhetorical and discourse studies." These are changes that all the contributors to this volume would, for the most part, welcome. With some notable exceptions, however, we find that most such "liberalizing" curricular changes have taken place primarily in major research institutions where such timely innovations have often been sought out by administrators attempting to acquire the "comparative advantage" for universities competing for prestige, money, and resources in the academic marketplace. This historical condition is, of course, neither new nor surprising, but we mention it as one sign of an important but complex institutional problem that this book addresses. The essays that follow all speak to college English teachers in every kind of institutional setting (from the two-year college to the large university), seeking to help bridge the apparent gap between theory and practice in our discipline.

Developments in literary and cultural theory should be empowering in new and alternative ways for both teachers and students, and many contemporary theorists have called for and have been invoked in pedagogical as well as curricular changes. Yet so far, the actual effect on classroom practice has been much less than one might suspect, given the intensity of the theoretical debates. We agree with Bruce Henricksen and Thaïs E. Morgan who, in the preface to their recent book *Reorientations: Critical Theories and Pedagogies* (1990), maintain that "to teach literature and writing is to be involved in a social and instititutional critique, and the intense theoretical activity of recent years (maligned by the likes of Allan Bloom and William Bennett) has contributed greatly to this project" (ix). However, the project remains quite remarkably incomplete with respect to its own "pedagogical imperatives" (in Barbara Johnson's phrase). The usual explanation for the gaps between theoretical discourse and classroom practice typically hinges on the assertions of the difficulty of the theories, the abstruseness of their "jargon," or the simple impracticality of the ideas. Following this argument, the NEH Director, Lynne Cheney, voices the traditional antitheoretical complaint "that much new research in the humanities is esoteric and overly professionalized and has no applicability to what is taught in literature or history classes" (quoted in Coughlin 1989, A14).

Hostility to theory is dangerous and illusory, however, for as Terry Eagleton stresses, "hostility to theory usually means an opposition to other people's theories and an oblivion of one's own" (1983, viii). We do not see this book as an effort merely to "simplify" the difficulties of theory (although that remains a necessary phase of the project) since, in one very important sense, "theory" may be no more difficult than any other complex social problem. And that is just the point: the impact of theory on the classroom will not come about merely by asking scholars and theorists to be "clear and applicable" in their writing. We must first recognize as a social problem the production of theory within the hierarchies of academic institutions. It is necessary to come to grips with the politics of the teaching of literature. Those who pretend that teachers of literature (or anyone else) can or should be "above" politics delude themselves; Kenneth Burke reminds us (as Barbara Frey Waxman notes in her essay in this book), "whenever you find a doctrine of 'nonpolitical' aesthetics affirmed with fervor, look for its politics" (1969, 28).

We need to recognize the gap between theorists at large research universities who write about literature and literary theory but who rarely teach introductory literature courses (especially to nonmajors) and all those instructors at the vast majority of two-year and four-year colleges and universities for whom such teaching is a daily duty and devotion. We should note that, as members of an English department at a medium-sized state university with a doctoral program in literature and criticism but who also teach a heavy load of introductory "service" courses, the two of us are positioned in an intermediate institutional setting. We sit on the fence observing both the heated theoretical debates (which are of deep interest to us) at larger research universities and the difficult teaching loads (which we understand and empathize with out of our own experience) at other teaching institutions. The professional and institutional structure of the literary discipline amply rewards scholarly research through conferences, journals, and books. In contrast, few institutional structures reward pedagogical practices or answer the educational needs of teachers. These diverse structures of reward and prestige function, as Evan Watkins explains, to control "the social circulation of people" (1991, 217), or, in short, to limit our mobility. The national scope of this problem is reinforced for us every year by the stories we hear from our doctoral students, most of whom are experienced faculty members who come from teaching institutions all over the country to study with us in our summer doctoral program.

The divergent interests of theorists at research institutions and instructors at teaching institutions were also evident at the NCTE Summer Institutes for Teachers of Literature to Undergraduates that were initiated at Myrtle Beach in the late 1980s. At these stimulating four-day events, the teachers (many of whom were enjoying brief respites from heavy teaching loads) listened to and questioned the presenters (each of whom was a well-known theorist at a prestigious research university). The teachers frequently wanted to know more about how the theories presented could be applied in the introductory classroom than the theorists tended to address or sometimes seemed able to say. *Conversations: Contemporary Critical Theory and the Teaching of Literature* (1990), edited by Charles Moran and Elizabeth Penfield, is a valuable book which resulted from the first two Myrtle Beach institutes and which we discuss further in our bibliographic essay. In it, Bobby Fong, a teacher and administrator from a small college who attended the institute, reminds us that doctoral departments represent only six percent of the English departments in the United States. Fong cogently explains why the nationally and internationally aimed concerns of the theorists whose presentations he heard failed in many respects to address the specific local needs of small regional colleges with student populations differing in respect to age, class, ethnicity, educational preparation, and life experience.

The hierarchy of advanced research versus introductory teaching is deeply embedded in the higher-education system of this country, which in turn is deeply embedded in the ideological differences of race, class, gender, and ethnicity of U.S. social life, so we must recognize that it will take much more than simply "writing about pedagogy" to bring about the kinds of curricular and social change being advocated by most contemporary theories. Moreover, even those publications that have specifically called for applications of theory to pedagogy tend to be subsumed by dominant scholarly models of interpretation and modes of discourse. As Gerald Graff develops at length in *Professing Literature* (1987), most theorists and critics have learned an approach to research that is derived from the "positivism" of the powerful natural sciences. They focus on producing more and different kinds of interpretations, while attending to texts (like a biologist looking through a microscope) with little or no specific discussion of the classroom practices available for teaching those texts.

Thus, even in an important recent book like Cary Nelson's *Theory in the Classroom* (1986), most essays (authored by writers at research institutions) are devoted to problems of meaning and interpretation. Such problems have, no doubt, provoked much recent theoretical debate, but (with the exception of Paula Treichler's essay on feminist teaching) the underlying assumption is that such debates will have necessary and inevitable consequences for the classroom. To some extent, this is not a false assumption: if we interpret a given literary text in a new way, we will undoubtedly teach it in a different way. But important questions (to name a few) about how we specifically go about teaching the new interpretations, what our role as authority figures to our students may be, what particular new activities we may initiate in the classroom, what kinds of texts we assign, what kinds of writing tasks we assign, what kind of media we address—these questions tend simply not to have a place in the scholarly debates, even when they ostensibly focus on pedagogy. Consequently, as Heather Murray argues, "the institutionalization of theory has led, against the hopes and labors of many, to a teaching of theory rather than a theorized teaching" (1991, 187). "Theory" is then just one more subject to be "covered" according to the "field coverage" principles which Gerald Graff and others have described. In short, the traditional scholarly models still operate as powerful constraints on the dissemination of the very pedagogical alternatives being recommended by those authors.

One further example may illustrate how these disciplinary constraints operate even in an important text aimed at disseminating theory to a wider audience and advocating pedagogical changes that we too wish to advocate. In *Tracing Literary Theory* (1987), Joseph Natoli confronts the seemingly impossible task of trying to provide a narrative framework for such an inexhaustible terrain as contemporary theory. His solution is to deploy Mikhail Bakhtin's conception of dialogics to present "a heterogeneous image of theory in which the theory body of interconnected and interrelated discourses draw [*sic*] upon each other in differing fashions and with differing, often contrary, results" (5). Natoli stresses one consequence of his engagement with theory:

> Theory is wrapped inextricably around and through and in other discourses, is both a product of them and a creator of them. This world of interaction between literary theory and other discourses is unamenable to pedagogy in the present because it challenges the very foundations of traditional conceptions of learning, of pedagogy, disciplines and departments. (8)

We agree with this general assessment of the multiple dimensions of theoretical writing and practice and the challenges to "traditional conceptions," but the actual consequences of this belief in the "unamenable" relation of theory to "pedagogy in the present" have often led to the implicit reproduction of the professional hierarchies that sustain "theory innovation" at the major research institutions, where privileged and relatively high-paid faculty have opportunities in graduate courses to be relatively less constrained "by departmental and disciplinary boundaries" (8). Again, the production of theory proceeds with great claims for pedagogical transformation but with little material evidence of such change in the classroom. Natoli's book, for example, either omits or rarely mentions many of the more specific pedagogical works that we have sought to highlight in our concluding bibliographic essay. In contrast, those teachers whose professional lives involve a much greater commitment to teaching undergraduates generally find themselves in departments that constrain institutional and disciplinary innovations.

Our concern for those of us who teach in such institutions is not then to acquiesce to the powers that be, and certainly not to patronize those not in positions of academic power, but, rather, to provide resources attentive to the needs of those teachers throughout the academic world, to listen to their needs for transforming their teaching rather than provide unrealizable goals of curricular and institutional transformation. Again, this does not mean we should neglect the big picture: we need such broad-based social and curricular changes in American education. As Donald Morton and Mas'ud Zavarzadeh have argued, we must "understand pedagogy not commonsensically, as classroom practices or instructional methods as such, but as the act of producing and disseminating knowledge in culture, a process of which classroom practices are only one instance" (1991, vii). Nevertheless, such broader perspectives should include increasing attentiveness to the voices of teachers and students who have been too easily excluded from the "theory body."

Natoli's articulation of the changing conditions of knowledge provides a point of departure common to most contemporary theories. Reader-response critics, feminists, poststructuralists, Marxists, and others share an emphasis on the conditional, situational, and therefore provisional nature of what counts for knowledge. By rejecting the traditional positivist notions of "objectivity," these theorists challenge not only the New Critical sense of a relatively objective and determinable meaning "in the text," but also any stable and authoritarian position for the teacher as a "knower" of an objective body of knowledge, field, or canon. As Eagleton points out, over the years literary criticism has gradually shifted its focus from the author (in Romanticism and old historicism) to the text (in Russian formalism and New Criticism) and more recently to the reader (not only in reader response but contemporary theory in general) (1983, 74). The very language in which we speak, read, and write what we know can no longer be said to refer to or represent unproblematically the outside, "objective" world or text. Traditional disciplinary boundaries become more suspect than reassuring, and we are led then to reconsider the social and political consequences for teaching, reading, and writing about the "intertextual" social, political, and literary environments that we inhabit.

In contrast, traditional epistemological models reinforce what Paulo Freire (1970) called the "banking" model of education, according to which the authoritative teacher deposits bits of information in passive students. When one rejects this epistemological model, one likewise opens to question the social hierarchy in which the teacher is positioned "above" the student. The New Critical obsession with studying the text "in itself," independent of the culture that produced it and the culture which produced the reader, can then be seen as clearly adaptable to the banking model of education. New Criticism was attractive for teachers because once its method (involving the preeminence of the textual form and the literary devices within it) was "mastered," classroom teaching became an art at which teachers enjoyed being better "bankers" than students and could avoid doing much extratextual homework. One could spend considerable time on short, complex texts, with students struggling to emulate the teacher's expertise at explicating them. But students quickly learned that they were mostly incapable of playing the interpretive game as well as their professors and that their own responses were very often "wrong" (even if that word was not used in class). From the instructor's point of view, this was an efficient way to teach, especially when faced by multiple sections of courses filled with many students, as was the case after World War II when New Criticism achieved its dominance. The problem, as we perceive it, is that introductory courses are still often taught in this fashion even by teachers who have not read New Critics in years, or have not needed to read them because the New Critical doctrines have been so deeply naturalized as the professional "unconscious" of literature departments.

The scarcity of theoretically informed textbooks and anthologies (some of which we mention in our bibliographic essay) may discourage even those instructors seeking to retheorize their own teaching. As William Cain notes in *The Crisis in Criticism*:

> In part the New Critics succeeded in revolutionizing English studies because their methods were teachable, but even more because they devoted themselves as much to pedagogy as to criticism and scholarship. They wrote textbooks, handbooks, and rhetorics; they secured their techniques (and stabilized their revisions of the canon) not only in monographs and professional journals but in the classroom as well. Today the situation is different: the major theorists and critics and the writers of textbooks and pedagogical materials often seem to form two distinct populations who rarely come into contact with each other. Whatever their errors and misplaced emphases, the New Critics can still teach us certain lessons, the most important of which is the need to incorporate theory and practice, criticism and pedagogy. They saw, in a word, the urgency of an integrated approach to the reform of English studies. (1984, 276)

As much as we disagree with the now very old New Critics, we need to devote ourselves to pedagogy as they did, or else introductory literary pedagogy will continue by default to follow New Critical methods or be left to the major commercial presses (or, as James Sosnoski warns us in his closing essay in this book, to software and computer companies) who will produce the means by which literature can be taught according to their own devices.

Ironically, the radical challenges of contemporary theory have typically been voiced through institutional channels that implicitly sanction academic hierarchies: the expert knower of theory can tell the nontheorists what is good for them. As Sosnoski points out in his article "Why Theory? Rethinking Pedagogy" (1990), it is no wonder that many experience the impact of theory as threatening, painful, and anxiety-ridden, even when they might otherwise be sympathetic to new theory and practice. In short, the conditions of exclusion do not necessarily go away when one critiques the principles of exclusion.

In this book we do not offer easy answers to these complex social and institutional problems. What we do intend is to provide a resource for teachers of introductory and survey literature courses. Our focus on introductory courses is necessary for several reasons. For one thing, they have been most neglected by recent theorists. Yet "service" courses for nonmajors contain one of the most tangible audiences—and certainly the largest—by which the profession reaches beyond itself in everyday practice. Business majors are, after all, public citizens who may well have far more influence on the directions our future takes than even the most prolific and influential theorists. We must attend to the needs of this audience with respect to our own interests and hope for, as our friend and colleague Mark Hurlbert states in his essay, "a different America, a more radically democratic one." Second, whereas a teacher can safely assume some level of interest among English majors, this is, of course, not always the case with nonmajors. Consequently, these circumstances pose difficult challenges in terms of the impact any contemporary theory might have.

For these reasons, the essays in this book include student voices, and the authors themselves represent a variety of institutional settings ranging from large research universities to medium-sized, four-year universities, liberal arts colleges, and two-year colleges. Several of our essayists describe writing assignments (inspired by composition specialists such as James Moffett and William Coles) as well as literary teaching practices. We have imagined our audience as being composed of two different groups: (1) teachers of undergraduate introductory literature courses who are seeking ways of altering their classroom practices in light of critical theories that have remained abstruse and scholarly, and (2) theorists looking for theoretically informed and specific, concrete ideas and further resources for the teaching of introductory courses as well as discussions of how such teaching in turn illuminates theory. The constant focus of the essays is on addressing the possibilities for changing the concrete, pedagogical needs of the undergraduate literature teacher. We expect that such an audience will include those who teach at two-year as well as four-year colleges and universities, and we intend the book to be accessible to all those for whom there is considerable need to engage with those issues that are changing the shape of literary and humanities study today.

In particular, we have designed the book to include essays drawn from the perspectives of reader-response criticism, psychoanalysis, reception theory, New Historicism, Marxism, feminism, African American and multicultural perspectives, dialogics, deconstruction, post-structuralism, and computer-cybernetic theory. This "pluralist" inclusiveness, however, should not obscure our political intention to include those essays that demonstrate a consensus that we need to transform all those structures of domination and exclusion that inhibit social and pedagogical liberation. As Gregory Ulmer remarks, "The principal lessons to be learned from much contemporary theory go beyond any particular critical technique" (1985b, 38). In this sense, then, our book is not a "neutral" compendium, despite the wide diversity of particular vocabularies and methods found in it; the essayists share a belief in the necessity of new and liberating pedagogical strategies.

The first section, "Orientations toward the Student," suggests a pedagogical focus sustained through all the essays, despite their differing theoretical perspectives. All the contributors share a belief in the need to reorient students from passive consumption of authoritarian teacherly meanings to active involvement and participation in meaningful activities. Since reader-response criticism has frequently promoted such a reorientation, we begin with David Bleich's account of his engagement with the reader/student in the context of his own culturally defined personal responses to Kafka and Morrison. Drawing on his previous work on literacy and social relations, which he developed at length in *The Double Perspective* (1988), Bleich focuses in this essay on the ethnic "multiple belongings" of the classroom as community, and he offers a critique of the entire rhetoric of the "introductory" class as an ideology that patronizes students since the teacher occupies the privileged position of the "expert" who knows. In contrast, Bleich proposes that we engage students in the classroom as a community of readers, fostering discussion of personal, emotional reactions to the assigned readings as well as social and collective discussion and negotiation of those meanings and feelings. The political implications of his pedagogy are pursued in some of the subsequent essays, such as John Clifford's, and the reader may also want to follow up Bleich's essay by reading our bibliographic essay's section on reader-response theory and pedagogy.

Patricia Prandini Buckler develops those dimensions of reader-response criticism that help create "a link between real-life experience and the work—helping students to connect" what they read to what they live in ways outlined by Louise Rosenblatt. Focused on responses to short fiction, her examples come from introductory literature students in a medium-security prison in Indiana as well as on campus. She demonstrates the importance of combining personal, textual, and social dimensions of reading so that "students can gain confidence in their own critical faculties." The psychoanalytic focus of Mark Paris's essay draws on feminist and Lacanian theorists such as Shoshana Felman and Jane Gallop, who offer powerful critiques of the unconscious privileging inscribed in traditional pedagogies. But Paris insists that such psychoanalytic theory cannot afford to retreat from the classroom into an "ivory tower" obscurity. Following Felman's lead, Paris argues "that the teacher must become a student not in the traditional sense of a learner of a larger body of received knowledge, but a student of one's own students." But in order to do this so as to expose "inherently oppressive social structures," one must bring the "curative potential of psychoanalytic theory" to the "educational maladies" of rigid authority and text-based formalism in order to engage the deeper personal and social dimensions of reading and teaching. Paris provides specific examples of how he has engaged first-year literature students in their own psychic and social unconscious by reading *Dracula*. The reader can compare Paris's employment of psychoanalysis with its applications in the essays by Ronald Strickland and Douglas Lanier.

As Steven Mailloux explains in *Rhetorical Power* (1989) (and as reflected particularly in Bleich's essay), much contemporary reader-response theory treats readers not as isolated individuals but emphasizes instead their rhetorical, sociohistorical, and cultural contexts. Our second section includes essays that further develop these historical dimensions of the reading and teaching of literature. More specifically, all our efforts to empower the reader/student require reevaluations of our most basic pedagogical vocabulary. As John Schilb points out, terms such as "the text," "the reader," "the author," and "history" have "at one time or another . . . guided entire critical movements." From both a theoretical and a practical perspective, however, these terms are not esoteric, but neither are they unproblematic. Schilb argues that because these terms are so accessible to first-year students, they provide a good focus by which to "provisionally acknowledge each term while investigating them all," and he suggests how such investigations can be pursued in a number of literary texts. Schilb's recommendations for how to "inform students of a work's varied reception" without reverting to "uninvolving lectures" leads us to the reception theory presented by Louise Smith. Since traditional "thematic approaches underplay the situatedness of readings—the roles that a reader's own gender, race, ethnicity, class, religion, politics, previous reading experience, and so on play in interpretation"—Smith offers a critical version of reception theory that, unlike many reader-response theories, does not replace the "idealized text" with some kind of "idealized reader." As her case study, she focuses on the students' and teacher's pursuit of the reception history of Alice Walker's essay "In Search of Our Mothers' Gardens."

The sociohistorical focus of reception theory is complemented by the concerns of new historical analysis, which Brook Thomas demonstrates can be effectively brought into the introductory literature class. Thomas directly confronts the usual objection that New Historicism is simply too time-consuming for first-year students. In contrast, Thomas suggests that literature's complex relation to history provides a perfect occasion to confront the historical "amnesia" that plagues our culture and thus our students and ourselves. New Historicism (which Schilb and Lanier also draw on in their essays), he argues, suggests ways in which we can begin to "teach historically in an ahistorical culture." Thomas demonstrates with specific and well-known examples from Shakespeare and Keats that by treating works of literature as "social texts" rather than "verbal icons," we can begin to engage our students in developing a sociohistorical awareness that current educational systems have tended to neglect, so that students may better be able "to have some say in what sort of future they will have." John Clifford similarly proposes a self-consciously political pedagogy that combines the student orientation of reader response (inspired by his former teacher Louise Rosenblatt and linking him with Bleich's and Buckler's essays) with recent post-Marxist insights. In particular, Clifford offers ways in which we can effectively combat the Althusserian insight that "teachers and students pass on the dominant ideology, replicating ideas that could be inimical to the possibility of a democratic renaissance of what goes on in the classroom." Since our own and our students' subjectivities are "not hegemonically ordered," it is possible to create spaces for resistance, "space for students and teachers to help each other respeak their subjectivities through an exploration of the intellectual and emotional landscapes on which we hope to build a literate and democratic symbolic order." His pedagogical examples focus on essays by Maxine Hong Kingston and E. B. White.

We then turn in the third section to the more explicitly political pedagogies that emphasize various kinds of confrontational, collaborative, and feminist alternatives to traditional teaching models. Ronald Strickland's basic assumptions tend to be shared by all the contributors: we must challenge "the traditional assumptions of canonical knowledge and pedagogic authority." By combining the insights of poststructuralist psychoanalytic theory with an explicitly Marxist oppositional pedagogy, Strickland confronts "the individual student's resistance to knowledge as analogous to the repression of the unconscious." More specifically, Strickland confronts students' desires to reproduce the dominant "neoconservative and corporate-sector" ideology that merely trains them "to fit the needs of a capitalistic and patriarchal society." Ranging in his pedagogical examples from Sophocles and Milton to contemporary film, Strickland argues that teachers must "avoid posing as mentors to their students and champions of their subjects." They must become willing to critique the liberal humanist versions of the "free individual," the rational subject relatively unconstrained by history and culture. Mark Hurlbert shares Strickland's assumptions about the connections between knowledge and power relations, and his critique of the ideology of individualism. However, the shift from Strickland's confrontational practices to Hurlbert's collaborative ones leads to quite different kinds of intervention. Rather than directly confronting student resistances, Hurlbert follows the lead of a group of Soviet socialist theorists who explore the possibilities of actually changing in the classroom the social hierarchies that have produced these resistances in the first place. Hurlbert's is an ambitious project consisting of "nothing less than the transforming of competitive, oppressive, and male social relations in our classrooms and in our society into cooperative, collective, and diagendered relations." In his more personal narrative of his classroom experiences, he directly confronts the limitations of his collectivist teaching of contemporary fiction through his own pedagogical/political struggles to make our work in the classroom "part of a larger movement toward cultural change."

Likewise, Barbara Waxman places her feminist pedagogy "within a wider social community" and follows Henry Giroux's sense that "teachers are 'transformative intellectuals'" engaging students in the production of critical knowledge in the classroom. Feminist emancipatory strategies focus on transforming patriarchal relations and questioning underlying assumptions about gender relations in the texts they read and the classrooms where they discuss them. Following Strickland's mode of questioning institutional authorities and expectations, and focusing on poems by e. e. cummings and Nikki Giovanni, Waxman suggests specific ways students can learn to become "resisting readers" through collaborative interpretations rather than authoritarian demands. Patrick Murphy combines feminist, Bakhtinian, and Native American beliefs so as to decenter traditional educational models and produce an "open-ended, self-correcting" pedagogical program. In his teaching of a variety of contemporary poems and works of fiction, the "coyote midwife" serves as an image or trope for the teacher as an assistant in "giving birth" to dialogue in an ongoing process of mutual understanding, exchange, and critique as opposed to the mere "fathering" or authorizing of an objective knowledge.

The three essays in section four then focus on multicultural and theoretical transformations of the curriculum and the classroom. Phillipa Kafka provides an account of her own experience working to transform the overwhelmingly white, male list of authors stipulated for a traditional "Landmarks of World Literature" course at Kean College of New Jersey into a multicultural and more egalitarian curriculum. First, she offers a critique of the traditional assumptions of the Western canon. She then provides a critique of, on the one hand, any effort to merely "tokenize" what we call "ethnic" or "minority" writers in a revised syllabus and, on the other, any effort to provide conveniently "unifying" or "universalizing" themes to bring an ahistorical coherence to historically different and ideologically conflicting readings. She suggests in concrete ways how Buchi Emecheta, Alice Walker, and *The Tale of Genji* can be taught in pointed comparison with and contrast to, for example, Homer's *Odyssey* and plays by Shakespeare and Ibsen. Pancho Savery directly confronts the issue of whether contemporary literary theory can be helpful in teaching African American literature. Savery follows Henry Louis Gates, Jr., in suggesting the ways that "the black vernacular meets poststructuralism" through the "uniquely black rhetorical concept" of "'signifyin(g).'" As a figure for the intertextuality of African American texts, this concept enables us to view "African American literature from principles derived from the literature itself." Savery shows how this concept can be put to work in specific teaching strategies for introductory courses, drawing his examples from Frederick Douglass, James Weldon Johnson, Zora Neale Hurston, Ishmael Reed, and others.

Douglas Lanier proposes alternatives to the "coverage model" of most traditional introductory literature courses. He suggests that in the paradigm shift from teaching discrete texts to the sociohistorical dimensions of interpretive processes, one cannot simply replace New Criticism with a single "other" critical orientation because doing so tends to leave the coverage model still in place. Instead, Lanier demonstrates why offering students a range of critical strategies (while avoiding a "facile critical pluralism") highlights theoretical and practical differences from the beginning so that they can develop their own "critical self-awareness rather than mastering a kaleidoscope of minimally contextualized anthology selections." He describes in detail how he taught *Frankenstein* from a variety of critical perspectives—formalist, historical, psychoanalytic, and feminist—within the introductory curriculum at Allegheny College.

Since all of these theoretical alternatives depend on rhetorical and linguistic effects, the next section demonstrates how Bakhtinian and

Derridean perspectives on language may affect our teaching practices. Don Bialostosky confronts the "notorious pathologies" and the difficult "conditions of communication in the introductory literature classroom" insofar as they point to the lack of shared experiences of teachers and students. By drawing on Bakhtin's notion of "speech genres," Bialostosky provides models of how students' own tacit and explicit knowledge of such socially common speech genres as the apology can provide the beginnings of a commonality of repertoires. In this way, the "estranged" world of literature proves less initially esoteric and not so tied to a special "literary" language familiar only to the teacher. Focusing on poems by Milton and William Carlos Williams, he shows how students can learn to "expand, enrich, and reflect upon their discursive repertoires and improve their verbal performances."

With a similar goal of building upon what students already know, Lois Tyson dispels the notion that deconstruction is merely "a superficial analysis of word play." Deconstruction sees literary tension not as part of an "organic whole" but rather as the "product of ideological conflict." In contrast to the New Critical principles implicitly operating in many undergraduate classrooms, in deconstruction "literature loses its privileged status." Through the specific assignments (of texts by Blake, Whitman, Frost, and Judith Minty) and strategies described by Tyson, students are encouraged to "develop critical thinking skills transferable to other domains." Likewise, Thomas Fink claims that "there are various divergent purposes for deconstruction," and he allies his own teaching with those forms of "deconstructive investigations" intended "to serve the critique of socially oppressive institutions." Fink develops specific examples of how to employ deconstructive activity in the teaching of a "specimen text" (a sonnet by Shakespeare) to first-year literature students at a two-year college. This essay provides a good rebuttal to the notion that deconstruction is so esoteric as to be of practical value only to advanced students.

Our concluding section on "Poststructuralism, Postmodernism, and Computer Literacy" includes three essays that incorporate many of the premises developed in the previous sections. The poststructuralist textual theory engaged by M. H. Dunlop emphasizes a refusal to honor the "old hierarchical divisions among literary, nonliterary, and subliterary texts." Students can then become "producers who may write along with a text" rather than mere passive consumers of the teacher's authoritative knowledge, since they no longer need to defer to an elusive and privileged meaning. Dunlop shows the value of formula fiction—Horatio Alger, Raymond Chandler—in the classroom since, by its very premises, it circumvents any consideration of its originality and uniqueness. Questions about the "correctness" of the codes and formulae which students can easily recognize can then lead to more subversive cultural questions that may resist the formulae themselves. Thomas McLaughlin then emphasizes the ways in which "theory is unavoidable" in the classroom, especially when one's interest is in teaching students to understand and even to resist the "ideological manipulation" that has inevitably shaped their lives in a postmodern culture. McLaughlin's special claim is that "today's students are ready to use those strategies," if only because they have "been brought up in the same culture of the sign that accounts for the very existence of poststructuralist models." The central task in the introductory course, then, is to devise ways to make it "possible for students to transfer their ability to 'read' nonverbal languages to the activity of reading written texts" (Katherine Anne Porter's "The Grave," in this case). McLaughlin demonstrates such examples whereby students' "competence in nonverbal semiotic systems can be turned into knowledge" so that they can learn to "read culture more carefully than it desires to be read."

Finally, James Sosnoski addresses the possibility of students "as theorists" in the postmodern electronic environments that will play an increasingly more powerful role in education in the coming years. Sosnoski recognizes the tremendous potential and capacity of electronic introductions to literature and cultural studies currently being designed, but he also emphasizes a need to critique the often-concealed "hidden agendas" of the structuralist and formalist models used in the programming of elaborate databases. The intertextual arena of hypertexts (programs allowing readers to examine together several interrelated texts) is less decentered than many of its advocates claim, since its multiple links are possible only along the lines for which the system has been programmed. Sosnoski then proposes an alternative way for students to engage hypertext databases in more critical and self-reflexive ways. He describes a project in "student librarying" whereby students design, theorize, and anthologize "their most valued cultural items." Sosnoski's conclusion is that students "like us . . . are theorists." He thereby registers the shared concern of all our contributors for enabling students to become stronger readers of the cultural life of the past and present, so that they may also become more active participants in the production of less oppressive and more egalitarian social relations in the future. His student anthology project is similar to Hurlbert's.

As a guide toward further resources for theory and pedagogy, we have included a bibliographic essay that also serves to position our book in relation to other works that are available in theory and pedagogy. The essay is divided into several parts—reader response, psychoanalysis, cultural theory and pedagogy (reception theory, New Historicism, and Marxism), feminism, African American and multicultural theory and pedagogy, and dialogic, deconstructionist, and poststructuralist theory and pedagogy—that follow roughly the sequence of essays in our book, as outlined above. The reader can therefore follow up an essay of particular interest in our book by examining the related section in our bibliographic essay or may prefer instead to read the bibliographical essay as a whole as an overall guide to the field. The single, unified list at the back of the book of the works cited by all of our essayists is a convenient and extensive, if not definitive, bibliography of theory and pedagogy (as well as the diverse literary texts cited as pedagogical examples by our essayists). This project has truly been a collaborative one, just as the larger project of teaching in theoretically informed and committed ways must be a collaborative and ongoing effort throughout our profession.

I Orientations toward the Student: Reader Response and Psychoanalysis

2 Reading from Inside and Outside of One's Community

David Bleich
University of Rochester

When I first started teaching I accepted the almost universal belief that education first begins in college and that the first (previously called "freshman") year was the foundation of all other learning. I also had thoughts of a "new beginning" when I started going to college as well as to high school. As I reconstruct these distant memories, it looks, still today, as if part of the institution of school, as well as the institution of the classroom, is founded on a "born again" social psychology. On the one hand, both schools and teachers feel, deep down, that they wish to "make over" students into something the schools, administrators, and teachers imagine students should be, and on the other, students, like the rest of us, wish to have another chance. At least two values are the casualties of this perspective—the effect of history and the sense of community. If we really think we can (and sometimes should) start over at any point in school, this also means that we are no longer responsible for understanding what led us to this point—no longer responsible for integrating our personal and collective histories into our decisions for the present and future. At the same time, if we can start over in the sense of being "reborn," we do this as individuals, and it does not matter what other individuals and what other groups we find ourselves in class with, much less if and whether these other people also have starting over on their minds.

As you can probably tell, I have come to reject the "new beginning" attitude in my approach to school, to teaching, and to first-year university students. My teaching of literature and literacy, through its characteristic emphasis on responses to and in languages of all kinds, urges and encourages students to include their past experiences in and out of school to help enlighten all classroom inquiries. At the same time, I have come to believe that no student or teacher can work alone, no matter how we may try to isolate ourselves and our studies. This attitude casts doubt on the idea itself of an "introductory" course.

Rather, work in the first year, as in any other year, is a continuation of previous work, a working through of previous relationships, even as new work is read and written, even as new work relationships are formed.

Of course, distinctions can and should be made between students of eighteen and those of twenty-six, for example. But these distinctions show less about how much knowledge people have already acquired than about what styles of learning and thinking are characteristic of people of different ages. Looking at teaching in this way, we find that other distinctions of style are also needed, regardless of age. These other distinctions have to do with culture, community, and history—categories which now commonly include considerations of gender, race, and class. Thinking about these more politically alert categories leads us to see that they may not be used to separate students into learning groups, but, rather, that they must be integrated into the techniques of treating the subject matter of our courses. These new categories are themselves in the midst of change, a situation which must be considered as we plan any new courses and university experiences. When I was fourteen, very few people used the word "gender" except perhaps in French class. When I was twenty-one, there were "two cultures," science and humanities—and, no question, physics, in Chomsky's words, was "the best" science. Today, genders, cultures, and disciplines can vary within each community and among many. And not only is there no "best" science anymore, but some people are asking whether any form of knowledge is inherently more certain than any other form and whether, in any event, certainty should be the main feature of knowledge. There is doubt about whether knowledge is a noun, and there is doubt that "truth" is the same thing for all people.

These changes are related to how politics and language have broadened their relevance. Politics now includes the attention to individual personal lives, while the study of language no longer looks only at the behavior of the individual speaker. The individual has become more important to politics, the community more important to language. It is becoming ever more difficult to teach literature and other English courses without calling attention to these subjects.

At the same time, no category of thought that I can remember has disappeared. Categories have changed in the sense that none can be considered permanently fixed and none considered most fundamental "in all possible worlds." For example, hierarchical thinking, while not out of the picture, is now considered just one of many possibilities of thought; some are saying that thinking in terms of intersubjectivity, collaboration, and mutual relatedness is a style we ought to follow, rather than one that leads to the truth. People have been suggesting that how we think is a choice to be governed by a variety of considerations of how responsible we are, to whom, to what extent, and for how long.

I like these changes because they address questions I had throughout my development as a student. At age fourteen I asked, why don't I understand or like Shakespeare, while other Jewish boys in my school seemed to know and understand many of his plays? At twenty-one I wondered, why don't I like Ezra Pound and T. S. Eliot, while the Jewish professor in graduate school taught them as if they represented an eternal standard of literary achievement? Why do I think Kafka is funny, while the Jewish professor who taught him wanted me to "deduce the narrator" from the given text? As you can see, these questions concern, at the same time, my sense of membership in my own community, as well as the values of the community at large. Shakespeare, Pound, and Eliot are "received" figures whose works bear received values. Members of my own culture and ethnic group accepted what they "received" in high school, college, and graduate school. In earlier parts of this century, in order for Jews to become literature professors, to begin with, they learned, taught, received, and accepted what the Christian, Anglo-Saxon intelligentsia considered its own. Even Kafka, an Eastern European German-speaking Jew, was taught by American Jewish scholars in terms that derived from the study of British and American Christian writers—Dorothy Richardson, Joyce, Woolf, James. I think that in many cases, women and minority group members feel today, in some ways, what I felt in my later years of schooling. Discussions arise within today's politically active communities about whether to teach "one's own" literature, whether "the academy's choice," whether both or neither. And there are further questions about whether there is a "one's own" literature at all, whether all literature really belongs to all people, regardless of political and cultural memberships. These are some of the issues I want to think about now, and particularly about how they affect the teaching of language and literature. I also want to remember that whether I address first-year university students or fourth-year graduate students, it is the membership of these students in various communities that is most pertinent to their studies of language and literature, rather than what formal sorts of knowledge they have already been exposed to before they entered my classrooms. If we acquire the courage to eschew our patronizing task of "introducing" students to "our" style of study, and instead ask all our students, younger or older, to introduce their own ways and thoughts for mutual sharing, we will have begun a productive response to the many voices now seeking to educate for an authentically just society.

In my classrooms, I have used literary response projects to pose questions of community and societal membership. Over the past fifteen years or so, students of reading and literary response have been contributing to the categorical changes of thought I mentioned before. Response processes have begun to change how we think about literature and how we make decisions about what to read, what to teach, and who is choosing what to read and teach in the first place. In the discussion that follows, I would like to share a few instances of literary response which raise these questions and to think about how the study of literary response in politically conscious ways can contribute to our search for new understandings among the genders and cultures among us. I especially want to know more about what it means to be a member of one or more communities and yet feel a part of literature that emerges from others' communities.

I think it is essential for teachers of all students, including those in middle and secondary schools, to find ways of "introducing" themselves while they introduce their subjects, to show how the subject "lives" in them, thus identifying more explicitly what they as teachers are bringing to the classroom. Let me start by commenting on my own reading and my own sense of community. I will then discuss how I and others in my class and classroom approached "joining" Toni Morrison's communities. Here is a short work of Kafka's called "The Vulture" that I find particularly winning and which calls up a response which helps to identify some of my senses of communal membership.

> A vulture was hacking at my feet. It had already torn my boots and stockings to shreds, now it was hacking at the feet themselves. Again and again it struck at them, then circled several times restlessly round me, and then returned to continue its work. A gentleman passed by, looked on for a while, then asked me why I suffered the vulture. "I'm helpless," I said. "When it came and began to attack me, I of course tried to drive it away, even to strangle it, but these animals are very strong, it was about to spring at my face, but I preferred to sacrifice my feet. Now they are almost torn to bits." "Fancy letting yourself be tortured like this!" said the gentleman. "One shot and that's the end of the vulture." "Really?" I said. "And would you do that?" "With pleasure," said the gentleman, "I've only got to go home and get my gun. Could you wait another half hour?" "I'm not sure about that," said I, and stood for a moment rigid with pain. Then I said: "Do try it in any case, please." "Very well," said the gentleman, "I'll be as quick as I can." During this conversation the vulture

> had been calmly listening, letting its eye rove between me and the gentleman. Now I realized that it had understood everything; it took wing, leaned far back to gain impetus, and then like a javelin thrower, thrust its beak through my mouth, deep into me. Falling back, I was relieved to feel him drowning irretrievably in my blood, which was filling every depth, flooding every shore.†

As I mentioned earlier, in graduate school, for a similar first-person narrative, the professor, a man I respected and admired, asked us as a class assignment to infer what sort of person the narrator is. I did this with enthusiasm, riddling my analysis with psychological speculation, writing an essay twice as long as was assigned, and, imagine, I got an A-. What I suppressed in this essay, however, was what I try to express now, rereading this piece in a way that lets my "blood" fill "every depth" and flood "every shore."

Something I have felt for a long time, but never dared speak or write about in "criticism" or even in response essays, was that the act of "speaking" Kafka's literature—as opposed to simply reading it—lets me bring out feelings of my own about my community membership (an American Jew from New York) and my professional membership (a faculty member whom society generally views as "an academic"). Consider the latter membership first. Since I have become a senior faculty member, I have taken the liberty to speak to department chairs and deans about the larger problems of teaching and academic life. "A vulture is hacking at my feet," I said, and gave them an account of how the vulture would have gone right for my head but that I decided to sacrifice my feet instead. The chairs and deans said, yes, we can help, but can you give us a half an hour to get our "guns." My requests were then reviewed by three or four committees, finally to be turned down or so altered that the vulture went for my head after all. When I read this account of the vulture, my identification of the gentleman merged with my identification of the bureaucratic hacks who I thought were making it impossible for me to move. My conversations with the hacks were civil and decent, even serious and respectful. But the message of my thoughts—to eliminate grading in my course for one year on an experimental basis—was the equivalent of the vulture, gun, and blood, which are the main terms of this parable. People said, yes, that makes sense, let me help, and proceeded to help in just the way to defeat my project and draw "blood" from me personally. As an academic professional, I follow the rules of

† From *Parables and Paradoxes* by Franz Kafka. Copyright 1946, 1947, 1953, 1954, © 1958 and renewed 1975 by Schocken Books, published by Pantheon Books, a division of Random House, Inc.

conversation; in a polite and civilized way, I present my "narrative" in the same calm that the narrator of "The Vulture" presents his. Do I need to "deduce" or infer this narrator? What a false project that is, since I am already this narrator as soon as I start reading this text. My voice comes alive because, before I was born, another Eastern European Jew had already recorded the conversational structure, depicted its results in the very terms that describe my feelings as I talk with department chairs and deans about how teaching is being hacked to death daily, now, in the most respected universities in this country.

Now I feel certain that a good percentage of you who are reading this are thinking that "he is going too far; teaching is not really being 'hacked to death.' In any event, Bleich is not being hacked to death, since he would not be writing this essay if that were the case." Maybe so. But here is also where my communal membership as the first-generation offspring of Eastern European Jews is at work. Kafka's vocabulary and style of speech were present in my childhood household, not as his, but as my parents'. My friends and I made the same kind of jokes. As far back as I can remember there has been a conversational leitmotif in which real, or dangerous, or intolerable circumstances of life are routinely described in these deadpan metaphors of violence and death. My mother was a genius at spontaneously thinking up devastating epithets to describe villains or others who, in her judgment, behaved badly, and sometimes I was the one who got the metaphor. (For example, will you understand me if I refer to someone I don't like as "a cholera"?) So when someone says, "a vulture was hacking at my feet," I recognize it immediately, without analysis, and I feel its meaning by virtue of my membership in that community of discourse. I don't analyze its existential meaning; I don't go digging for Kafka's Oedipus complex; there is no literary riddle for me to solve. In my world, now as then, the "gentleman" who offers to save my life in such a way that will actually do me in is recognizable as the well-dressed evangelist coming to my door offering me the good news about God's love for me.

At an early age I learned to speak two languages at once—not just my parents' language, Yiddish, and my community's language, English, but within my English I included the vocabulary of the Yiddish culture, the East European culture in which both my parents and Kafka lived, the culture which was already used to external hostility. My parents' culture had already begun to respond to an environment whose German-speaking descendants finally did try to do us all in through a well-organized, civilized operation of humiliation and murder. To read Kafka not only reestablishes these historic fears and dangers in my mind, but articulates my own culture's ways of naming and dealing with them through a kind of intrapersonal wit and dramatic metaphorical initiative that we Jews from New York in my generation recognize as "our language."

The fact is, when I claim that bureaucratic hacks are hacking teaching to death in major universities, it seems to me like ordinary, rather than dramatized, discourse. If my discourse seems strange to you, you need only question it, so that, as I have tried to do now, I may explain and share it, then learn what others and authors think, and then what these voices, strange and familiar, represent as cultural and political forces. Without presenting my participation in Kafka's work, from within, so to speak, I would be discoursing here—haranguing you, really—on a "received" author without accounting for my implication in this essay. I am not implicated in Kafka's language just because I like this author, but because I feel that his voices within me represent a way of speaking and knowing that play a role, now, in these universities, in this country, in this mix of cultural interests. It matters to me to know whether and to what extent I am reading and thinking "from within" because I draw emotional, cultural, and intellectual sustenance from my historic communal memberships.

But then I read the work of Toni Morrison and, without warning, something very similar happens. In spite of every expectation to the contrary, her language has a similar effect on me. On the one hand, I approach her work as an academic: I want to know the literature of other cultures; I want to hear about the heritage of slavery in today's United States. But instead I become caught up in her voice in ways quite similar to how I was involved in Kafka's. Here is a group of characteristic passages from *Beloved* that had Kafka-like effects on me.

> When the four horsemen came—schoolteacher, one nephew, one slave catcher and a sheriff—the house on Bluestone Road was so quiet they thought they were too late. Three of them dismounted, one stayed in the saddle, his rifle ready, his eyes trained away from the house to the left and to the right, because likely as not the fugitive would make a dash for it. . . .
>
> Inside, two boys bled in the sawdust and dirt at the feet of a nigger woman holding a blood-soaked child to her chest with one hand and an infant by the heels in the other. She did not look at them; she simply swung the baby toward the wall planks, missed and tried to connect a second time, when out of nowhere—in the ticking time the men spent staring at what there was to stare at—the old nigger boy, still mewing, ran through the door behind them and snatched the baby from the arch of its mother's

> swing. . . . Right off it was clear, to schoolteacher especially, that there was nothing to claim. The three . . . pickaninnies they had hoped were alive and well enough to . . . take back and raise properly to do the work Sweet Home desperately needed, were not. Two were lying open-eyed in the sawdust; a third pumped blood down the one he said made fine ink, damn good soup, pressed his collars the way he liked besides having at least ten breeding years left. (1988, 148–49)

This is one of the three (or more) accounts of the event around which this novel turns. Beloved is the ghost of the infant daughter Sethe murdered as she tried to kill all her children to avoid their being taken back to Sweet Home by the four horsemen of slavery. As I, the narrator, get into Schoolteacher's head, I feel that same outrageous Kafka-like irony in the evocation of the slaveowner's unabated wishes for fine ink, good soup, and pressed collars even as he watches the infant's blood "pumped down" her mother's dress. Every name, practically every word, is loaded with the same bitter double voice: Sweet Home, the site of slavery and torture; Schoolteacher, the fascist dispenser of sadism and violence; Beloved, the incomplete inscription on the gravestone as the name of Sethe's murdered child, yet living in the novel as a mature, beautiful young woman, the invincible object of Paul D's sexual license; Paul D, the weak, cowardly, apostle of male sexuality.

Here too, somehow, I don't need formal analytic techniques to feel this language inside me. If this work is an outraged account of the history of a people, it is also a celebration of the freedom to speak, to speak out, to shout, in fact, that "a vulture is hacking at my feet." Does it make sense at all, in fact, to "analyze" this text without a means of discovering how we as affective and historical figures are implicated in it? Doesn't historical and communal belonging provide the translation of this novel's languages into the terms of our daily lives? Let me continue with my own translation.

When I responded to this novel last November in my introductory course, I cited the following passage:

> And the Germans who flooded southern Ohio brought and developed swine cooking to its highest form. Pig boats jammed the Ohio River, and their captains hollering at one another over the grunts of the stock was as common a water sound as that of the ducks flying over their heads. (55)

Here is what I wrote:

> I think this was the only mention of Germans in this book, though they are the ones I thought of throughout much of my reading. . . . I thought it was noteworthy that the Germans were associated with

> swine—here mainly as consumers of swine, I think, where Paul D was a worker in a swineyard, and it tells how he had to wash pigshit and other offal from all over his body. When Paul D was in Delaware the first bit of food he got was pork sausage. Six went on the path toward being shot when he took a shoat. . . .
>
> I never read anything about how women lived in a world of Nazis but this novel told about it and that is what I learned, in some ways, for the first time. I have seen countless films of the death camps in Europe, countless tellings of naked people marching to be gassed, countless narrations of how it was. Here is the same story stretched out, dedicated to the "sixty million" (instead of the familiar six million). The story seems the same because it was the group of men [the four horsemen] that brought out the truth of the atrocity that millions of people collaborated in creating, in this free country over a period of two hundred years—a mother running a handsaw over the throat of her nine-month-old child.
>
> The cancerous mentality infiltrated the being of these women, and still their only recourse is to harm their own, to become insane (like Pecola in *The Bluest Eye*), and, in a miraculous way, to continue to live. The usual story is how the man, Paul D, survives the programmatic animalization. But here when he sees his own fate in Sethe's—asks her to count her legs—as a result of Stamp Paid informing him of just who Sethe is, man and woman are separated as different beings, the man's feeling and desire separate themselves from the woman he loves and in this way collaborates in her terrible degeneration. . . .
>
> My mother is about ninety years old. I visit her about five or six times each week and help her to eat dinner. I usually make sure the food is firmly on the fork so she can transport it to her mouth. I notice myself taking extreme pleasure in her simply eating most of the food on her plate. Because she had gastric lymphoma three years ago, she seemed to have lost most of her real-life memory during the treatment. . . . Sometimes I think she got sick only because she was lonely, and when one is sick one *gets* more attention. That's just what happened. She *got* so much more attention from me when she was sick and now she still does.
>
> Of course, I don't feel like a villain. But since I am a man who has a career . . . I am, inescapably, part of the "conspiracy" of men who depended on women without understanding just what their lives meant to them. I feel sort of like Paul D, returning with understanding at a point when it seems too late.

As is usually the case in close examinations of literary responses, I arrive at less-than-pleasant self-perceptions. I can leave off reading Kafka with a sense of pleasure and triumph; it took my reading of his biography to contemplate the frequent narcissism and sexist dependencies of his thought, life, and work. Because of my sense of belonging to the Jewish aspect, his community, another community we are both in—the community of men—does not quite emerge in consciousness. And yet the same thing almost happened in reading Morrison: we Jews can easily identify with those who were once slaves, those who were victims of fascism. But it is harder and much less reassuring to perceive myself as a member of the hegemonic masculine community, those in power, those partially responsible for Sethe's relationship with a ghost. Yet what else can I conclude as I reread and rethink my response to *Beloved*? If I understand Paul D, if I feel his betrayal of Sethe, and if peremptorily and without calculation I tell a similar story about myself and my mother, I think I have seen the sense in which I am in a different community from Toni Morrison.

The terms and style of otherness will vary from person to person, culture to culture. In my white, mostly female class, the responses show that all readers are emotionally caught up in this tale, and none even suggests that this was not a worthwhile reading experience. Three readers, one male, introduced their responses with the same word.

> Wow! I think that sums up my reaction pretty well, but I think you're expecting me to elaborate on that. I enjoyed reading *Beloved* for many different reasons. It was a pleasure book instead of a methods book. . . . It gave me a different perspective on life . . . and it made me realize how lucky I am. I couldn't help thinking about my life and how different it was from the characters'. This may seem odd, but it really struck me. (Ms. D)

> Wow! I was very spellbound by the book. I loved the characters, especially, the slow pace with the development of character. The dialogues felt very real. I am impressed with the writing style and strength of Morrison. I do see the reason why it won the 1988 Pulitzer Prize. (Mr. L)

> Wow! What a book. The way Toni Morrison quietly unravels such horror and pain. But she does it slowly, nonchalantly, letting a line drop here and there that reveals a glimpse of yet another horror, yet another atrocity. The effect is amazing. It conditions us to the events. They become hidden in our minds amongst all the new happy things that are happening to the characters, the same way they become hidden in the characters' minds. We keep pushing the events behind us, not daring to feel the true impact of them, not daring to understand them, until they force themselves to the surface, and we must face the horror head on, somehow deal with it and make sense of it. (Ms. R)

I consider that for all three of these readers to feel "wow" is to remain detached, in the responses, from their actual implication in this novel. They are willing to report that they felt moved, but by and large, the people in this novel are "others." ("I couldn't help thinking about my life and how different it was from these characters.") Of the three, Ms. R is the most articulate and most alert to the conventional literary statements one could make about the reading. Yet throughout the three or four pages of each of these responses, none of these readers could find a way to identify with any character, as they are wowed as if this were an adventure and the reading was the occasion to learn of the occult happenings in the enslaved zone of American history. After observing that "it's unbelievable what happened to these people" and listing some of the novel's atrocities, Ms. R writes:

> Finally, a woman driven to kill her own baby rather than give up that baby to the system of the white slave owner. A woman who feels that she is nothing but that her children can be something. A race of people forced to deny love, hope, or any other emotion, because such an emotion can be torn into bits at any moment.

In spite of the fact that Ms. R is an eager, sincere, and inquiring student of history on this occasion, she seems to write as if she were reading about "these people" or "a race of people" rather than people who are connected to her in some way. When speaking of modern times, she mentions lynchings in the South and white gangs in the North. In the last sentence of her response she observes that the only way out of this history is "if we on the other end stop acting in ways for which we will always have to make amends." Although I do not fault this response as a contribution to our class, I feel it showed some stake in the otherness that the novel and the author are trying to change. These "wow" feelings are the first line of resistance to the voices of this novel in that they represent an American male tradition of detached innocence well documented in works like "Benito Cereno" or socially ignorant guilt represented in works like *The Scarlet Letter*. Although I am not sure, I think these two female readers did not participate in the novel's prominent exploration of motherhood and female bonding because, due to their own good circumstances in life, they perceived more in the reading about the history of African American people than about the history of women.

This was not true of all readers, however. Ms. N writes, for example,

> Sethe killed her daughter to spare her from the abuse she herself has suffered from. Is this a justification and a rationalization of a murder: Is a murder ever really the proper course of action? I, as a reader, sympathize with Sethe while, simultaneously, feel a

> conflict because I cannot imagine what could bring a mother to kill her own child.

Although Ms. N also did not bring her own history to bear on this response, she does bring herself to question the premise of this work: that history and society seemed to have forced a mother to kill her infant, the question similarly raised by Mary Wilkins Freeman in her story, "Old Woman Magoun," and similarly greeted with disbelief by many young women (and men) today. The nub of the matter is for Ms. N, as it is for me, that "I cannot imagine what could bring a mother (or a father) to kill her (his) own child." Kafka did not write about such issues, and careful scrutiny of his work shows that he rarely wrote about women and that none narrated his stories. For my part, I was not in the death camps, and I don't know what my relatives and ancestors did do or would do in order to face down the four horsemen.

Ms. G's response explores the matter somewhat further. Ms. G wonders why she did not notice the premise of the novel:

> When I realized that Sethe had killed her baby to keep her free from slavery I was totally overwhelmed. I hadn't had a clue that this was how she had died. As I look over passages in this book, though, I think that I should have at least suspected that this was what had happened. . . . I think the reason I didn't suspect Sethe of murdering her own daughter is because it is so contrary to my idea of motherhood. Mothers nurture their babies—they don't kill them. Sethe's actions are very much like the grandmother's in Freeman's "Old Woman Magoun." Both women believe that death is better than living a life they have no control over.

Discovering a key feature of accurate reading, Ms. G realizes that mistakes are made when the author is speaking the language of a different community, one which has values different from the reader's. She obviously understands, in an intellectual way, what happens in this work (and in Freeman's) but she does not see how to bring more than an intellectual understanding since she sees that would mean rethinking her sense of what motherhood is. Her response shows, however, two other elements which suggest why this value holds up many readers. They appear in the two paragraphs that follow the one I just cited.

> I was uncomfortable with the relationship that developed between Sethe and Beloved at the end of the story. It seemed more like they were best friends or even lovers, rather than mother and daughter.
>
> For example on page 241, "She played with Beloved's hair . . . They

> changed beds and exchanged clothes. Walked arm in arm and smiled all the time." This relationship is too intimate for me. I'm close to my mother, but I'm not that open with her and so I have a hard time understanding this kind of mother/daughter relationship.
>
> I don't particularly like Paul D. He's a real weak-kneed creep when it comes to women. He sleeps with Beloved although he claims he doesn't want to and when he finds out the truth about Sethe, he runs. Beloved first appears in the flesh after Paul D has moved into 124 and she disappears while he is gone. Only after she's gone does Paul D go back to Sethe and 124.

These passages suggest Ms. D's image of the family: mother and daughter close, but not too close, with mother's partner loyal and respectful of mother and daughter; we need not be great analysts to notice a somewhat indirect portrayal of the archetypal nuclear family. Other readers have noticed Morrison's portrayal of special closenesses between women in this and other of her novels. My own negative response to Paul D may represent the same value as it does for Ms. G. In my readings and in my responses, I virtually ignore the relationship of Beloved and Sethe, and I feel I have no language to say what it is or what it means. (I think, do people really relate to ghosts?) So would it be fair to say that Ms. G and I share some allegiance to the archetypal, and shall we also say, patriarchal, nuclear family?

In the light of Ms. G's responses—and mine and the others—we might want to say that Sethe's killing of her infant daughter on one level makes sense to us as an escape from slavery, but we sort of hesitate about it because of our continuing allegiance to traditional family life. One can say, as Ms. G did, that under slavery, there can be no family, and so maybe I can sympathize with what Sethe did. But how many of us will challenge the premise of the family itself, and how many of us will entertain the thought that this premise is also the premise of slavery? How many of us are willing to believe that the premise of slavery is the same as the premise of the family?

One reader in my class was interested in entertaining this thought and here is some of her response.

> Even though *Beloved* is set a century ago, in a culture that outwardly seems totally alien to anything I know—I found myself being reminded of pieces of me and my life as I read. Unfortunately for my mom, Sethe and she have a lot in common. Sethe is defined by, and she found her self-worth in, those she took care of. . . . Mom talks about us [five] kids like we are reflections of the kind of person she is. There is that blurring of boundaries between mother and child that Sethe speaks to when she talks about one of her girls, "She was my best thing." . . . My

> brother . . . an alcoholic . . . died in an alcohol-related accident. My mother . . . blames herself for my brother's horrible death. There must have been some inherent flaw in her mothering skills, or she would have been able to save him. Ironically, Sethe caused the death of her daughter to save her from a life that she believed would have been much worse than death and she still was plagued with guilt. Women have carried what seems like the guilt of the world on their shoulders for so long—as bearers of humankind they are tied to a yoke of guilt and unfulfillment.
>
> In a sense, all women who are solely homemakers are slaves. . . . My mom, like Sethe, when we all grew up and left, felt like she had nothing . . . she had denied selfhood in order to be a "good" mother. Like Paul D told Sethe, I try to tell my mom: "You are your best thing." And she answers, "Me?" like the thought of a "me" never occurred to her. I can't fathom the idea of not tending to my personal needs, of denying that I even have needs, of being scared to live on my own for fear the community would ostracize me like Grandma Baby's "friends" did to Sethe. One hundred years later, I live on my own and I feel the same pressure to get a man and "settle down," like until I find a man and get on with what life is "really" about, I'm some sort of whirling dervish wild woman who is somehow apart from everybody else. . . . [My mom] talks like I would have withered and died if she wasn't there every second to watch over me, feed me, love me. Mom wanted us kids to feed off her love, that's what she thought a "good mother" meant. . . . I feel for Sethe and my mom, and all the women like them who give and give and give and in the end they find themselves old, lonely, and staring into a mirror where they can't even see their own reflections.
>
> I'm glad I'm not my mother I'm glad I am my mother.

Ms. S poses a problem that is one step beyond the enigma of a mother killing her child to stay out of slavery: Why does Sethe nevertheless feel guilty? That is, the novel, being actually taken up with Beloved's long stay with Sethe, is an extended metaphor of maternal guilt. Ms. S's answer, that this is the historic lot of women, also seems to say that this novel, for her, is about the lot of women, and that slavery as we know it—racial slavery—is a subcategory of the universal slavery of women who are associated only with domestic life and children.

Now think for a moment of Ms. S's formulation: "All women who are solely homemakers are slaves." The radical and shocking simplicity of this statement, something many people and many women included would dispute, is of a piece with "A vulture is hacking at my feet." One feels the unusual daring, the pugnacity of both statements, yet their literal immediacies are compelling in both cases. In ordinary situations, Ms. S's view is commonly cited: "I work like a slave in this house," I have heard my mother say, repeatedly; "I am not your slave,"

Ms. G reported having informed her fiancé. In a literary formulation, Ms. S's no less than Kafka's and Morrison's, we may tie together human physical pain with the authentic sense that a feature of society is responsible, here and now, for this pain, and we see this responsibility because we are inside and not outside of society.

After reading Ms. S's response, there is a sense in which some of the other readers' hand wringing about how foreign this black community is can be seen as a callous trivialization of Morrison's repeated shouting that there is a fire in the house and we are all in danger of perishing. I too may seem too academic in aiming to make distinctions—to compare and contrast Black history and Jewish history—the sixty million and the six million, when, from Ms. S's perspective, a fundamental condition of slavery now exists in the human race, has existed at least as far back as eight thousand years ago through the present, has characterized almost every human society ever known, and shows signs of abating only in the small corners of rich and privileged societies, and perhaps not even there either.

Neither Ms. S nor others who have thought like her are either wringing their hands or rejecting the need to distinguish one's own interests, one's own community, from those of others we meet in a fluid society. Ms. S believes in families and rejects slavery. Yet she suddenly saw, in response to this reading, to this suffering mother Sethe struggling with an intolerable memory, to her own mother with a similarly intolerable sense of failure in spite of a lifetime of self-denial, that slavery is the predictable result of living in a patriarchal family and that her own life and the lives of fellow students and fellow teachers are similarly planted in that history.

In Ms. S's response we find a new challenge to politics and to language. She writes: "I'm glad I'm not my mother I'm glad I am my mother." Ms. S, without using a period or other punctuation, is a part of her mother and not a part—the same as mother, yet not the same; part of a traditional family yet not a part. This "blurring of boundaries" is the new phenomenon, since it is decidedly not the elimination of boundaries that we are considering. Other respondents, myself included, show this element in their discourse—the declaration of simultaneous membership in several communities, participation in several societies, being a product of several histories. Our language begins to accommodate contradiction, the condition of being in and out, something and not something at once. In reading Kafka and Morrison, I experience the simultaneity of multiple belongings, the depth of several perspectives. I suppose this pluralization of our familiar categories of thought complicates our lives even more, since we need now examine our patterns of membership rather than just whether we are in or out.

This means not only that "introducing" should take place in any classroom, but that it is a mutual obligation, and that it refers to the mutual introduction of people to one another rather than to the one-way introduction of a subject matter to a set of "blank slate" minds. If we are specifically thinking of first-year college or university students, we should be persuaded that they come to their new readings with a culture and an ideology already well in place. The task of reading necessarily uses each reader's preexisting structures of value and style. It is not just a technique of collaborative study that needs "introduction." It is, rather, the feeling that all readers enter the classroom with something to introduce to others as well as the expectation that others—not mainly the teacher—will also be introducing things to collective attention. The foregoing responses that I cited and discussed were read and discussed by their authors with one another. Ms. G learned about the novel and about her reading of the novel at once as she became engaged in the readings of others. None of the readers were called upon to announce "what I learned." Yet it was clear from the developing relationships among the students that they were learning to read other people's readings, as well as change their own styles and standards in response to what others were contributing.

Furthermore, this way of reading in university classrooms is something that needs to be recovered rather than introduced or reintroduced. Habits of sharing and relating to others found in early childhood and in the early grades of primary school are replaced by the school system with the habits of individualism, with "looking out for number one." When children learn to read, they are inexorably urged to read privately and to "report" their reading to the teacher. Comparing readings and considering their distinctiveness is far in the background to creating a self-contained skill at "accurate" and politically inert analysis. However, in view of what can be achieved by eager university students, I imagine that a title like "recovering language and literature" might be a better title for first-year English courses than "introduction to literature." "Recovering" is what I and my students did in reading Kafka and Morrison.

If I think of the teaching of language and literature in this way, I imagine I can be more forgiving toward my fellow Jews who taught Eliot and Pound, though I doubt I will teach their work except as they represent values I reject. I can then also admit that I am glad I know Shakespeare's work, though I advocate having a nationwide academic moratorium on the teaching of Shakespeare and Milton. I can expect to continue to enjoy reading Kafka, even though his obsessive self-involvement is often overwhelming to me. And I know I will watch for what comes next from Toni Morrison even though I am not likely to master her work in some scholarly way.

I think my long-standing communal allegiances have been mostly to students, classrooms, schools, and to the hope they give for changing and making history. In the classroom, the vulture stops its hacking, and the boundaries of my communal memberships are brought out for review by those in other parts of society and in other generations. It is here where the categories of thought start to change, where all of us class members can recover our own best things and participate in continuous mutual introduction.

3 Combining Personal and Textual Experience: A Reader-Response Approach to Teaching American Literature

Patricia Prandini Buckler
Purdue University North Central

> When this course first began, I wondered if I hadn't errored by taking it. I surely didn't know what was expected of me. In a math class, I know that I am there to learn math. In an accounting class, I know that I am there to learn accounting, but what was I supposed to learn in a literature class?
>
> —Victor

Many students taking their first literature class share the sentiment expressed in Victor's reading journal. They do not know what to expect or what is expected of them. Inexperienced in the formal study of literature, they overlook the clues necessary to interpret a piece of writing according to established codes, so their efforts are frustrating and often counterproductive. They begin to tune out discussions that seem to be conducted in a foreign language within a strange culture. Resentment of the class follows and soon resentment of literary study.

Their predicament can be eased considerably, however, if teachers lead them to dig into their own experiences and find there a matching context for the events of the story, poem, or play. By using reader-response techniques, such students can learn to integrate their knowledge of life with literary texts, opening up for themselves a rich, new understanding of literary art. As Victor explained later: "It is easy not to care for other people or their plight until their humanity is understood, or better said, until their life's circumstances are equated with our own." Yet, when guided carefully through a series of tasks that incorporate reading, responding, and writing, the beginning literature student can develop interest, confidence, critical ability, and writing skills. Experienced literature students also benefit from the reader-response approach because it reawakens their ability to embrace a work fully, with more than their conscious minds. It reminds them that "there is a shape to the experience of art . . . not reducible to any propositional content that the text might convey or even to the formal features of the text itself" (Rabinowitz 1989, 89).

The description of reading and writing activities that follows uses reader-response criticism and writing to achieve just such a goal. Louise Rosenblatt's ideas of transactional reading as set forth in *The Reader, The Text, The Poem* (1978) are merged with James Moffett's writing stages from *Active Voice* (1981). The way these critical reading and writing tasks can work with introductory-level students is illustrated through the use of two short stories set in the American West, Stephen Crane's "The Blue Hotel" and Louise Erdrich's "Lulu's Boys." The classes described below generated the student responses quoted throughout this essay.

"The Blue Hotel" was the first story that I covered in an introductory literature course taught as part of the Purdue University North Central college program in the Westville Correctional Center (WCC), a medium-security facility for men in Indiana. The last work of the semester was devoted to "Lulu's Boys," a very different Western tale. I used the same materials and approach with students in the same course on the Purdue University North Central campus. Enrollment in this "regular" class included a couple of English majors, but it was mainly comprised of general education students taking their first college literature course. Although the two groups of students brought vastly different life experiences to bear on the readings, they were able to move from highly individual initial reactions to quite similar aesthetic analyses. Ultimately the immediacy of experiencing the texts was subsumed by the larger concept of the works as literature.

Louise Rosenblatt's *The Reader, The Text, The Poem: The Transactional Theory of the Literary Work* presents a utilitarian approach to reading a *poem* (her word for any literary text) which encourages students to bring their own life experiences to bear on their interaction with the text, while at the same time leading them to a more objective, aesthetic view. Rosenblatt sees the act of reading literature as a real experience "generated by the words" (1978, 31) that occurs in at least two simultaneous streams: the ongoing evocation of the literary work and a "concurrent stream of feelings, attitudes, and ideas . . . aroused by the very work being summoned up under the guidance of the text" (48). The poem must be thought of as an event in time that becomes part of the reader's ongoing stream of life experience, to be reflected on from any angle important to a human being (12).

Rosenblatt concurs with psychologists' views of human perception—that the way an individual sees an object or environment is determined by past experience and habits and is colored by interest, expectations, and anxieties (19). ("Oh no!" a WCC student wrote. "Not Stephen Crane right from the start. Crane and his *Red Badge of Courage* were the source of a bad grade in high school twenty-eight years ago.") Students whose experiences do not include much formal study of literature find fresh and unexpected interpretations of the poem, or sometimes see nothing in it at all. "'The poem,'" Rosenblatt writes, "comes into being in the live circuit set up between the reader and 'the text'" (14).

The most valuable pedagogical application of reader-response criticism creates a link between real-life experience and the work—helping the student to connect—and then builds on that connection. Once the reader evokes the poem, it can be synthesized with preexisting concepts and then distilled, analyzed, and critiqued.

Rosenblatt identifies two primary approaches to reading a text—efferent and aesthetic. In the efferent stance, the reader concentrates on information to be gleaned, problems to be solved, ideas to be carried away from the text (23). The aesthetic stance, on the other hand, centers directly on what the reader is living through during this relationship with that particular text (25).

The teacher of an introductory literature class must show students how to read aesthetically. An illustration of this challenge shows up in the journal of a third student, Bill, a WCC student who intially resisted moving beyond efferent reading. Early in the course, he wrote about "The Blue Hotel": "The story rambled on for eighteen pages talking about different characters in a Nebraska hotel during the late 1800s and that is about all that I can say for the story." This student was beginning to read aesthetically, however, because a little further in the same entry, he wrote, "In the second [to the] last paragraph, he [the Easterner] compares the gambler to the adverb in a sentence. . . . I thought that this comparison was sort of out of place for a cowboy or a rugged western story."

Unlike the efferent stance, the aesthetic requires an awareness of words and a consciousness of the text that Bill was just beginning to develop. An important quality of the transactional view of reading is this close attention to the words. It differs from New Criticism, however, in that it assumes "an equal closeness of attention to what that particular juxtaposition of words stirs up within each reader" (Rosenblatt 1978, 137). Reader-response critics ground their arguments "in the reader as a perceiving subject rather than in the text as an autonomous object" (Rabinowitz 1989, 81). The words are important, but so are the responses. Peter Rabinowitz describes Roland Barthes's view of texts as "unlimited opportunities for orgasmic free play" (81), but students should not be encouraged to believe that any interpretation at all is legitimate because they must learn the parameters of the literary discourse community—how to "talk literature."

Once students have begun to read aesthetically, a sequence of writing tasks modeled after those proposed by James Moffett in *Active Voice* can mobilize them to recognize and articulate their responses to the poem. Moffett's approach meshes effectively with Rosenblatt's because both theorists base their work on a psychological model that sees the human intellect as an entity that actively tries to synthesize and organize perception around some rational framework. The mind uses language to create meaning from experience; students get more out of reading when they talk and write about it.

Moffett's sequence is broken into three groups that run "parallel more than lying end to end." These are *revising inner speech, dialogues and monologues,* and *narrative into essay* (5).

The first type, *revising inner speech,* is basically a recording of inner speech that can lead to many different sorts of finished products and consists mostly of note taking to capture material for later development (5–6). This mode, consisting mainly of prewriting activities, is the externalized equivalent of Rosenblatt's first stream when the reader is involved immediately with the text. In the account below, this stage is labeled "reader-focused."

Moffett's second group, *dialogues and monologues,* moves from inner speech to external language experience, building on the ability to sustain continuity of a monologue (writing in a single voice) out of the give-and-take of conversation (6). Rosenblatt's second stream is equivalent here—the mind tries to distance itself from and organize the first set of impressions it receives. The immediate interaction of reader and text is replaced by a more reflective reading (and consequently writing) stance. Below, this stage is labeled "subject-focused."

The third, even more distant type of reaction to the original experience, *narrative into essay,* enlarges the space between author and subject, resulting in essays and articles of generalization and argumentation (6). This kind of writing flows naturally from the reader's evaluation and analysis of a work after it has been completely recreated and seen as a discrete experience. Below, this stage is labeled "text-focused."

I chose to start with Crane's short story because I knew it would appeal to the Correctional Center students, who love to read books with male protagonists and lots of action. The works of Louis L'Amour are popular there. The second reason for starting with Crane was that the relatively short piece would hold up well under close scrutiny while allowing an introduction to concepts of short-story form. The third reason was that "The Blue Hotel" would inherently challenge student misconceptions about literature as something stuffy and elitist, an important consideration with introductory classes. Fourth, the story works against the stereotypical Western narrative, a fact that I hoped would provoke the students more quickly into looking directly at the work itelf rather than through the lens of preconception. Finally, I felt that this story would be accessible to both classes, allowing them immediate success in a course that they found intimidating.

Ending with "Lulu's Boys" made sense for all the same reasons, with some additional formal concerns. Although written about a hundred years apart, "The Blue Hotel" and "Lulu's Boys" bear some striking similarities that students can readily recognize. Both narrate the conflict experienced by an outsider between his fantasy of life in a particular Western community and his actual experience of it. Both stories undermine American cultural stereotypes—one, the cowboy, and the other, the Indian. Both explore the communal nature of human experience. "The Blue Hotel" shows the destructive power of a community's act of exclusion, while "Lulu's Boys" reveals the healing force of inclusion, the benefits of "Love Medicine."

The students themselves discovered even more common ground when they wrote about the two stories together at the end of the semester. They were struck by the similar yet contrasting uses of death in both tales, they perceived significance in the semicivilized state of both communities, and they were intrigued by the conflict of fate versus will. More of their insights will be recounted later.

Combining Personal and Textual Experience

The reading and responding sequence breaks roughly into three stages, although the stages are recursive rather than linear. The first group prepares students to perceive cues triggered by their own experiences (reader-focused). The second set helps students look for patterns of cues (subject-focused). The third encourages students to move from understanding meaning to conceptualizing significance (text-focused).

In designing similar activities, the teacher should think about what experiences students might have had that would help them read the piece and then use those experiences to spark the connection between reader and text. What feelings associated with those experiences might the act of reading bring to the surface? What discussions or writings would be most effective in helping students combine personal experience with textual experience? How can the students learn to merge personal and textual cues into a pattern that represents objective knowledge? What activities will move the students into symbolic-level operations, where they deal with more abstract questions of meaning and significance? How can they be led to appreciate the single work as part of the universe of literary discourse?

The Reader-Focused Stage

The teacher looks for common ground between the student readers' experiences and those represented in the text. In the case of "The Blue Hotel" and "Lulu's Boys," I tried to tap into the impressions of cowboys, Indians, and the Old West that students already possessed from books, movies, and television. Discussion preliminary to "The Blue Hotel" focused on the typical Western showdown and shootout tale—what a reader might expect to find in such a story and how true to history that notion might be. The students immediately realized how much Crane's story differed from the common image. "I never thought in a million years that a Swede could represent a cowboy," commented Jack, a WCC student. "The place where the story happened didn't seem like your regular traditional cowboy town." Relying on their own knowledge of the Western, the students could confidently comment on the story's use of the stereotype. They already had a basis on which to build a more sophisticated interpretation of the work.

When preparing for "Lulu's Boys," the Correctional Center students sympathized most vocally with the oppression of the Indians, and they seemed well informed about some of the Native American cultural and political issues. Campus students, however, also related personal experiences such as visits to Indian reservations: "Isolated from our 'free enterprise system,' and our society, [Indians] have a hard time fitting in outside their groups. Very proud—should be" (Wanda, campus). Patsy mentioned that her "stepfather is 100 percent Blackfoot Indian and I feel he suffers emotionally due to the treatment of his 'kin.' He takes it personally when he sees something on TV about the Indians." Once again, images from their own experience grounded the readers in familiar territory from which they could explore Erdrich's representation of Native Americans.

The "outsider" status of the Swede in the Crane story and of Beverly in Erdrich's tale provided the students with a chance to associate a different set of experiences with their reading. Although the inmate-students understood the role of the outsider most keenly, members of both classes had known the pain of exclusion. "Both Lulu's and Beverly's life seems to be on the outskirts and momentary. . . . Each are near outcasts of their own realms. Lulu the whore, Beverly the out-of-place Indian," wrote Victor (WCC), while a foreign student, Zuhair (campus), compared his experiences as an outsider in American culture to those of the Swede. Several women mentioned how isolated and alienated they had felt when first returning to school after years in the workplace or the home. Even though these "outsider" experiences were varied on the surface, the core of feeling the students shared offered a quick connecting point with the stories. Just as with the Western stereotypes, the students already knew something about the situation in the stories. They readily recognized that in the Twin Cities, Beverly was an outsider because he was an Indian, and on the Reservation he was an outsider because he had abandoned his Native American culture.

The Subject-Focused Stage

The next stage should move students from simple emotional or experiential reactions to more complex, thoughtful responses to the story's subject matter. By looking not only for single clues but for patterns of clues, they begin to comprehend larger chunks of the work's meaning while at the same time exploring such issues as character, setting, heroism, fate, intention, and community.

In "The Blue Hotel," for example, my students defined character as they examined the variety of persons gathered in the inn. They formulated their own concepts of hero as they tried to understand Crane's and to match his up with the stereotype. Implications about fate, will, and individual responsibility are particularly cogent in this story and readily accessible to readers who know how to look for them. Such questions as "Who is the hero?" and "Who was responsible for the Swede's death?" triggered an avalanche of mordant responses. "Swede . . . is savage on one hand and a nobleman on the other. This guy has conflict with everyone . . . with himself . . . with the town . . . with the hotel owner . . . also has a certain insolence toward everyone he meets" (Jack, WCC). "Crane had me . . . re-defining my perceptions about the attributes that I gave certain characters in the story" (Paul, WCC).

Perhaps the most startling example of the interweaving of a reader's life with the Crane story came from my Correctional Center student Victor, who wrote many pages on the themes of death and violence as viewed by those who have committed murder or other violent crimes:

> What is this thing, violence? I've known a violent life. Until recently violence seemed a natural thing to me. . . . I'd worked hard to become callous and uncaring, thinking that cruelty was strength, thinking meaness was wisdom. My opinion today is that fear is the seed of violence. . . . A scared man is a dangerous man. He will over react. He can kill before he knows what it is that he has done. . . . The Swede's fear is what killed him. His paranoia caused him to fear. I think he tried to confront his fear in a fool hardy way by pressing the issue of Johnny's cheating at the card table. As a scared man he over reacted to the situation.

Although I expected strong differences between the campus class and the prison class in their responses to Lulu, I did not get them. While Jonathan (WCC) called her "The town tramp that flirted with every Tom, Dick, and Harry that seemed interested," Marian (campus) wrote, "At first I thought of her as sad, now I think of her as cheapened. I'm being judgmental." Jerome (WCC) did not euphemize: "Lulu is a *sex freak*!" When asked to point to evidence from the stories to support their opinions, the students noted Lulu's advances to Beverly upon his return to the Reservation, her very cool way of appraising the sexual prowess of both her late husband Henry and of his brother Beverly before deciding which one to marry, her sexual encounter with Beverly on the night of Henry's funeral, and her reputation. In other words, the readers took their own knowledge of human behavior, applied it to the subject, and demonstrated the validity of their intepretation. They could support their responses through referencing the text.

Furthermore, the students could see how the nature of one character revealed facets of another. They found parallels between Lulu and Elsa: "Elsa and Lulu both utilize sex as a way to control Beverly. . . . Elsa gave sex sparingly . . . Lulu gave sex liberally" (Frederick, WCC). They contrasted Lulu and Beverly: "Lulu does not deny her heritage and feels a comfort in the country, a closeness of ancestral spirit. Beverly turns his back on all that was and tries to be what he is not in a world he doesn't belong" (Larry, WCC). By the time they had gotten to "Lulu's Boys," they could interpret the story and draw conclusions like these without much coaching. They were no longer reading "for possession," as Victor put it, but for understanding.

The Text-Focused Stage

While the reader-focused responses concentrate on the immediate emotional impact of the poem on the reader, and the subject-focused activities expand and objectify the reader's understanding of the poem, the text-focused exercises engage the higher critical faculties of the reader, asking questions about form and style, meaning and significance.

In this phase, then, the students extend without abandoning their original, experiential responses to the poems and begin to operate more fully as members of the discourse community outside the small, classroom group. They strive to see the big picture while becoming more conversant with conventional literary language and concepts. In the stories under discussion, text-focused issues included the significance of the titles, the character's relationship to American stereotypes of cowboys and Indians, themes and motifs, symbolism, similarities and differences between the stories themselves, and the larger meaning of the two interpreted together. Many college teachers present these interpretive approaches through lectures or outside reading assignments. Readers who apply their own critical faculties and experience to the text, however, become better believers with deeper understanding of, commitment to, and appreciation for the study of literature.

For starters, my students noted that both writers included the outsider-insider theme, described fictional communities that existed on the edges of "civilization," included significant suicidal acts, and turned certain pivotal scenes around card games, thus highlighting the themes of chance and fate. They contrasted Crane's normal chronology with Erdrich's flashback technique and compared the respective authors' opposite uses of women: In "The Blue Hotel," women are marginal, functioning as mothers and nurses, while in "Lulu's Boys," the women are central—strong, influential—and Lulu is virtually Mother Earth herself. The comparatively frank references to sexual activity in the Erdrich piece were not lost on them either:

> Elsa is cold, self-centered, and in control. She dislikes kids. Lulu loves kids and is adored by her own children, she is a take-charge sort of person who claims what she wants. . . . Elsa has classic beauty, while Lulu is earthy and human in her open display of desire. (Jack, WCC)

Patrick (WCC) was able to discuss the paradoxes of the two stories with remarkable insight and precision:

> It is rather ironic that this similarity . . . of the protagonist fulfilling his fantasy . . . is also a complete contrast. The Swede left every-

> thing he knew and died as an unloved outsider at the time he fulfilled his fantasy. . . . Beverly left the city where he was essentially an unloved outsider and started a new (and probably happier) life at the time he fulfilled his fantasy.

The most panoramic vision came from Paul (WCC):

> To return to a story as similar to "The Blue Hotel" as "Lulu's Boys" really brings all the things that were done in this class into focus as a single experience, as opposed to many small fragments spread over the semester.

Paul's remark is particularly gratifying because it demonstrates that he has integrated the reading of American literature into his life experience, envisioning it now both as an entity and as a part of himself. Likewise, the other Correctional Center students were able to connect with American literature, with themselves, and with a larger community of readers simply by interacting with texts. They shared experiences with students on campus and others on the "outside" without ever leaving the confines of their institution. This capacity for expansion by moving one's mind alone is truly a benefit of reading literature.

Some years ago when I taught at a large, boys' private high school, I decided against using Virginia Woolf's "Death of a Moth" because I wanted to spare myself the unnecessary anguish of watching a crowd of unappreciative teenage boys crush this exquisite and fragile sensibility. I withheld this essay because I didn't know quite how to empower those students to relate it to their own experiences. Today, I would devise a reader-response approach to this work that would enable my students to move from initial, idiosyncratic responses to more informed and skilled appreciation of this text.

By learning to value their own experiences and to validate their personal responses, introductory-level students can gain confidence in their own critical faculties. Through the teacher's appropriate intervention, reading "for possession" becomes reading for pleasure and appreciation—the nature of the experience itself changes. Evoking a poem becomes as valid an experience as eating a meal, nurturing the intellect as the food does the body.

Furthermore, the inductive process required by reader-response techniques not only guides students through the world of the text, but it draws from them a fuller commitment to their own learning. It stimulates an organic understanding of the intertextual relationship between literature and life. Once this connection between the reader, the text, and the poem is created, other critical approaches may be added. The historical background of a work, its place in its author's life, its conventions and counterconventions simply enhance its future evocations by the reader. It can be deconstructed, viewed from Marxist, feminist, or historical perspectives, analyzed rhetorically, or explicated word for word. Students can dramatize it, videotape it, write music about it, dance it, or create new works based on it. As Louise Rosenblatt says:

> Much, much else can flow from the literary experience, many further benefits may be derived from reflection and criticism. But the intrinsic value of a literary work of art resides in the reader's living through the transaction with the text. (1978, 132)

Literature is about people and their experiences, about the ways they think and act and grow and change. As human beings, we all possess the urge to make sense out of life through the use of language. By reading, talking, and writing, students can intertwine their life experiences, the experiences in the text, and the experiencing of the text in order to comprehend the reading and to understand their own lives as well. The reader-response approach quickly empowers introductory literature students to participate both individually and communally in this great conversation.

4 From Clinic to Classroom while Uncovering the Evil Dead in *Dracula*: A Psychoanalytic Pedagogy

Mark S. Paris
University of California at Riverside

The initial threads of psychoanalytic literary theory are easily enough grasped, but further unraveling exposes a multiplicity of meanings, issues, applications and implications. Sigmund Freud's observation that the artist is essentially a neurotic, "who turns from reality because he cannot come to terms with the demand for the renunciation of instinctual satisfaction . . . and who then in phantasy-life allows full play to his erotic and ambitious wishes," opened the way to a (re)examination of the artistic impulse and its relation to literary criticism (1911, 19). Thus biographically certifiable neuroses were seen reflected in the texts of, for example, Shakespeare or Dostoyevsky. But such a definitive birth contrasts markedly with the cloudy genesis of psychoanalytic theory. From Freud, psychoanalytic literary theory traversed the European intellectual landscape to Otto Rank and C. G. Jung, both of whom concentrated on the artist as the conscious or unconscious purveyor of social and personal values. The advent of the New Critical mode of interpretation witnessed the movement away from the practicing clinical psychoanalysts and toward more accomplished literary theorists, including Lionel Trilling, Alfred Kazin, and W. H. Auden. The New Critics' formalist emphasis did not obscure psychoanalysis's questioning of authorial dominance; rather, it caused a new examination of character motivation. Early Marxist and feminist critics, such as Gilles Deleuze and Felix Guattari in *Anti-Oedipus* (1977) and Kate Millett in *Sexual Politics* (1970), tended to view Freud as espousing a patriarchical social structure and thus an innately repressive ideology, but more recent theorists in this field, such as Juliet Mitchell, Jane Gallop, and Shoshana Felman, have found psychoanalytic theory—often a Freudian reinterpretation à la Jacques Lacan—a useful tool in exposing inherently oppressive social structures.

In one sense, Lacan's (re)reading of Freud, based on the poststructuralist doctrine of a coauthored text, is an inviolable "end" to psychoanalytic literary theory. Lacan's belief in the priority of psychic combat with the Other and his Saussurean-derived emphasis on signifiers and the signified as structures within the unconscious are as definitive in the study of the psyche and its relation to literary texts and textual creation as Freud's parallel theories on the tripartite structure of the human mind, conflict, and repression. Future study of the interaction between art and psychoanalysis cannot fail but to (re)address Lacanian notions. But in true poststructuralist fashion, Lacan has split the thread into innumerable fibers. The infinitely diverse nature of poststructuralism should allow for further explorations in reader-as-created-text theory. In regard to the implications of this concept for psychoanalytic theory, psychoanalysis presents a prime inroad to discovering/recovering the Self as text.

But strangely enough for a theory of literary criticism supposedly based on intensely human dialogue, psychoanalysis—like many of its theoretical cohorts—has left the realm of the dialogue, the classroom, and retreated to an ivory tower safety and obscurity. This is especially impoverishing in the case of psychoanalytic theory, for the further from practice it moves, the further from practicality and thus theoretical advance it grows. In another trait shared by its colleagues, psychoanalysis' decline as a critical tool can be traced to the apparent impenetrability of the latest texts. In a great understatement, Shoshana Felman refers to Lacan's writings as "stylistically demanding" (1982a, 507).[1] But there have been other problems. Felman points out that issues of privilege and classism surface even during a simple consideration of the combination of psychoanalysis and literature, noting that this was once and often still remains "a relation in which literature submitted to the authority, to the prestige of psychoanalysis" (5). Even noting an existing identity between the two is not enough, for we must ask, along with Peter Brooks, "what does one want to claim in showing that the structure of a metaphor in Victor Hugo is equivalent to the structure of a symptom?" (1987, 8). Felman solves the dilemma by calling for the psychoanalytic interpreter to

> act as a go-between, to *generate implications* between literature and psychoanalysis—to explore, bring to light and articulate the various (indirect) ways in which the two domains do indeed *implicate each other*, each one finding itself enlightened, informed, but also affected, displaced, by the other. (1982a, 9)

Felman reformulates the relationship between literature and psychology to encompass a conjunction of the two, a theoretical stance she expands into a pedagogical one in *Jacques Lacan and the Adventure of Insight* (1987). Here Felman notes that the teacher must become a student not in the traditional sense of a learner of a larger body of received knowledge, but a student of one's own students: to be their unconscious in a reflective manner.

> [T]he analyst . . . must be taught by the analysand's unconscious. It is by structurally occupying the position of the analysand's unconscious, and by thus making himself a student of the patient's knowledge, that the analyst becomes the patient's teacher—makes the patient learn what would otherwise remain forever inaccessible. (83)

Thus psychoanalysis becomes more than a tool with which to analyze texts and their spaces; the emphasis moves to the classroom itself, the relationship of teacher/student to student.

But in a work geared toward other ends—namely making Lacan more accessible to the American educational system—Felman leaves us pretty much in the theoretical wilderness as to the specifics of application. In order to create the analysand-analyst relationship that Felman requires, we must begin by noting the current roles of both students and teachers and build from that base. Having experienced the American educational system's primary reliance on the New Critical method, the first-year college student's interpretative skills lie essentially in the identifications of character, plot, and theme. Building on these skills to create not a universal "best text" but a self-relevant, self-revealing reading for the individual student is the chief goal of a psychoanalytically founded literary theory. It is Julia Kristeva who points to this remediative function, noting that psychoanalytic literary theory "is not solely a means of rendering our phenomenological description of [a] symptom more penetrating; by the interpretation that this knowledge allows us to elaborate, by a verbalization as exact as possible of destructive affects, it can also be an essential therapeutic measure" (1987, 122). It is precisely this curative potential of psychoanalytic theory which should most concern teachers of introductory literature courses, noting particularly the transformation of clinic into classroom.

The more psychically and physically damaging neuroses should certainly be left to the professional, yet there exist educational maladies effectively ameliorated by theory and its classroom applications. Perhaps the most prominent of these neuroses seen in the everyday world of the introduction to literature classroom is the students' apparent inability to read beyond the superficial texture of a work. *Hamlet*, for instance, often emerges as little more than the confused drama of a confused man without ever entering the realms of psychological causality—or any number of equally viable pedagogical/theoretical approaches which tend to create Shakespeare's work on a more significant level. To promote such levels of understanding beyond that of which New Criticism is capable, *Hamlet* must be taught in such a way that answers the systematic inculcation of this neurosis.

The use of the word "neurosis" in a classroom context brings up the question of signification. "Neurosis," for Freud, connoted an ego-based problem, a breakdown in the dynamic process of ego-id/world relations. If we can simplify this to mean a reflection of our unconscious desires' inability to function in healthy conjunction with the reality organ (or ego), the problematic signifier "neurosis" can take on a pedagogically practicable signification: neurosis, in the classroom sense, means an inability to come to grips with the subtextual level of interpretation. The students' concentration on personality as a result of self-inflicted actions, their desperate need for autonomy, and concurrent rejection of Other forces parallels their inexperienced reading practices. In the same way that they tend to see themselves as solely self-directed because they deny or repress the influence of both environmental and hereditary factors, students tend to "miss" larger contextual realities. In Kristeva's meaning, psychoanalytic theory performs a curative function of exposing disparate realities of both text and self.

The pedagogical practice that allows such revelations involves formal features of the text at hand, its historical circumstances, and more traditional psychoanalytical applications—all of which retain the essential purpose of creating within the student a larger awareness of Self. As object text, Bram Stoker's *Dracula* (1897) serves as a fine example of the sort of attributes which can lead students to this exploration of the unconscious/conscious dichotomy. Simply put, everything that Count Dracula stands for—unadulterated evil, sin, death, Satan, the incursion of Eastern European/"barbaric" modes of thought, irrationality, and especially sexual licentiousness—can be seen as symbolic of our unconscious. The repression of sexuality was an ingrained Victorian moré, leaving Dracula and his overt sensuality a dire threat to the orderly Victorian social structure. Dracula must be suppressed because, as Deleuze and Guattari point out, "every position of desire, no matter how small, is capable of bringing into question the established order of society" (1977, 116). The response to this threat is in turn the repression of Dracula effected by Dr. Van Helsing and his avenging crew of *fin de siècle* warriors. Van Helsing, Jonathan Harker, Dr. Seward, Quincey Morris, Lord Arthur Godalming, and of course, the group's spiritual leader, Mina Harker, are not a plain substitution for the conscious, but their actions illustrate both the

Victorian mode of dealing with sexuality—repression—and the interactive relation of the conscious to the unconscious.

Yet it is not necessary to select a text which carries such an immediacy of repression as the Victorian novel. The forces of social repression lie within both texts themselves and the context that in large part creates the text: whether of contemporary or historical nature, all societies have their rules and evince varying degrees of repression. Greek tragedy has at its base the rejection and punishment for violation of religious doctrine; the *Beowulf* poet wreaks havoc on transgressors of the Anglo-Saxon heroic ideal; in "Howl," Allen Ginsburg attacks the "one eyed shrew of the heterosexual dollar" (1956, 40) in twentieth-century America; all texts provide fertile ground for exhibiting repression in terms of prevalent values and the codified versus illicit responses to the obfuscation of desire.

Our discussion of *Dracula* begins with a brief look at Stoker's life, not with the objective in mind of forging biographical links with the text or its "meanings" but in order to recover the historical context. Thus Stoker's early childhood illness and his father's apparent absence from Stoker's life reflect not merely Stoker's desire for a powerfully signified leader, but society's desire as a whole. In the same vein, Stoker's sexual experiences become a metaphor for Victorian sensual repression. Stoker's sex life apparently took a turn toward connubial quiescence as he and his wife evidently broke off sexual relations for the last twenty years of their marriage, a deprivation which led biographer (and Stoker's grandnephew) Daniel Farson to conclude that Stoker's death from tertiary syphilis was due to several visits to French prostitutes (1976, 234–35). Florence Stoker's frigidity, real or imagined (by Stoker or subsequent biographers), mirrors the prevailing Victorian sensibilities on the subject of sex: it simply didn't exist in either the public or the private sphere. A discussion of this aspect of his world can result in a profitable exploration of the sexual morés of and pressures on the contemporary college student.

Since the forces that create a novel are neither fully a contemporary reflection nor solely some sort of supernatural nocturnal visitation, the genesis of the vampire figure in both literature and history becomes important to a revealing rendition of Dracula. Early vampire myths, such as the 1500 B.C. Babylonian accounts of succumbi or the ancient Greek lamia myths, eventually become the stuff of Gothic novels (specifically the works of Ann Radcliffe and Matthew Lewis) and thus exhibit a wealth of both acknowledged and unacknowledged influence. Under the former category, Stoker's mining of Carpathian folklore for his version of the "Vlad the Impaler" story serves as a valuable means of questioning the derivation of the artistic impulse.

Once this requisite historical grounding has been accomplished, we are ready to enter the formal aspects of Dracula, beginning with the Count himself. I ask students to list the characteristics and abilities of the vampire as they know it, a twentieth-century phenomenon, and Stoker's Count (paying particularly close attention to the opening physical description of the Transylvanian nobleman). Beyond the shared characteristics of bloodsucking, fangs, immortality, fear of garlic and crosses, the prevalent focus which emerges from their lists is the physical and particularly the sexual attractiveness of the vampire. In one memorable class discussion, George Hamilton—the tanned bloodsucker of Susan Saint James and love nemesis of Richard Benjamin in *Love at First Bite* (1979)—became our immediate frame of reference. The chief discrepancy between Stoker's Count Dracula and the most widely held perception was one of appearance; Stoker's Count is a rather hideous, reeking old man, while George Hamilton is youthful, urbane, and sexy. This last feature becomes a constant theme of our study with the novel: Stoker's reworking of the vampire myth to include an overt sexuality.

The novel itself offers a wide variety of sexual values, holding up a usually taboo region for inspection and criticism. The "rape" of Jonathan Harker at the hands (and lips) of Dracula's three succumbi introduces the issue of role reversal in sexual standards (Jonathan Harker as passive male versus the active females). This is often a fruitful subject of discussion, for by illuminating Jonathan Harker as a typical Victorian gentleman who must assume a sexually and socially dominant position, Stoker might have been bringing subconscious erotic desires to bear on the public domain of the novel. On an unconsciously reflective social level, the repressed Victorian males (with Jonathan Harker as literary purveyor of established morality) wanted what they could not have—sexually aggressive females.

Reactions vary as to what students feel is a sexual impingement on the meaning of this novel. "Reading too much into it" is the oft-heard accusation, but this reaction can evoke a discussion of the nature and purposes of interpretation: Is there any such thing as a "bad" meaning? Such a reaction also provides the opportunity for the students to come face to face with repression on both a personal and social level. There is usually a great moment of suspended silence followed by a good deal of tittering when I mention that Dracula's final attack on Mina Harker is an act of forced fellatio.[2] But verbalization is an opening to further Self-awareness, for as Lacan notes, the unconscious is linguistically structured and expression necessitates a confrontation with the conscious/unconscious dynamic. Certainly it may not be socially healthy to publicly parade one's entire unconscious, but in order to combat some of the more stultifying ingrained morés we must treat them in an open and honest manner.

Because few students want to uncover their own repressions in full view of their peers, the primary impact of this approach becomes the more immediate liberalizing of the classroom. Simply by using terms that do not belong to the traditional conception of what goes on in a literature (or any other) classroom, the conventional wall that separates and distances students and teachers begins to crumble and in its place stands a bridge of knowledge. As one student put it, "*Dracula* allows the reader to experience these forbidden pleasures without fear of social or legal disgrace." The overall impact of reforming the learning situation, whether by questioning sexual morality or any other Other-established principle in our society, lies within the reformation of exactly these values.

Other formal aspects of a text might serve this end equally well, not merely as representative of conscious and unconscious desires but in differing psychological spheres as well. Setting, for instance, has been shown by a number of critics to be reflective of differing states of consciousness. Charlotte Perkins Gilman's *The Yellow Wallpaper* (1892) is an excellent example of this. Confined to a bedroom (which quickly becomes her prison) by her husband's diagnosis of "a slight hysterical tendency" (10), Gilman's protagonist eventually falls victim to the therapeutic efforts of an outside world bent on her "cure." The text as a whole serves as a particularly stark illustration of the sexual forces inductive of female subjugation, while the scenario of the bedroom/cell and the view of the outside world implicate a social repression based on gender.[3]

Rooms function in much the same manner in Charlotte Brontë's *Jane Eyre* (1847). Quite early in the novel Jane learns the punishment for defying the laws of a patriarchy: "imprisonment in the 'red-room' where the principle of irrationality is given concrete form" (Moglen 1976, 110). By way of comparison, Jane's stay at Thornfield Hall represents hope and a belief that "a fairer era of life was beginning" (*Jane Eyre*, 95). Here Jane is "free," yet controlled by the Other, Mr. Rochester, who has ordered her conscious world in a mode of his choosing. The openness and light which come to her in this space at Thornfield Hall sharply contrast with both her own childhood experience and that of Bertha Mason. The Other Mrs. Rochester is sequestered in a "cell" (*Jane Eyre*, 406), far removed from the rest of

Thornfield's inhabitants, suggesting that Bertha's abode represents the ostracism of the dark unconscious. Jean Rhys's *Wide Sargasso Sea* (1966) provides a perfect counterpoint to Brontë's text, showing as it does Bertha's marginalization at the hands of two very different cultures. Not only do the morés of gender socialization appear in both novels, but a comparison of the two reveals varying ideas on the correct treatment of both the conscious and the unconscious as exemplified by spatial relations.

In *Dracula,* it is this sort of sociological examination that draws us into an exploration of what we want as human beings as opposed to what we are told to want. In class, I explain, as best I can, Freudian theories on repression and early psychical formation (the Oedipus crisis as pivotal event), opposing Freud with Lacan and psychical formulation due to responses to the created Other. I then outline what I perceive as the objective of this section of the course: to apply psychoanalytic theory in a "clinic-as-classroom" sense in order for them to achieve a better understanding of the nature of the forces which constitute Self; to break down the imprisoning force of "autonomy," which is but a twentieth-century sign for either narcissism or selfishness, and perhaps bring them to a recognition of empowerment—the ability to change the world at large by recognizing the social and psychological forces at work. There is a great deal of initial resentment at the idea that an individual lacks absolute control, yet first-year college students are also quick to notice their own burgeoning sense of freedom in light of their own very recent experiences in the peer group pressure cooker of the contemporary high school. In *Dracula,* the symbolic associations assumed by the Count all become reflective of Victorian societalwide fears and desires, fears and desires common to our own world. As Deleuze and Guattari point out, that which we fear is usually caused for a reason: "psychic repression is a means in the service of social repression" (119).

The novel's *dénouement,* the staking of Dracula, is rather anticlimactic, but the characters' feelings about the Count's death as well as the oft-paralleled class's opinions can illustrate the variety of available responses to social and psychical repression. Mina's belief that Dracula's demise is an ascension (*Dracula,* 367) portrays the spiritualization of the many Dracula representations: the unconscious is not destroyed but altered to an acceptable state. All the unknowable is relegated to a single sphere. Contrasted with this view of the proper placement of the unconscious is the desire of Jonathan Harker to "send [Dracula's] soul for ever and ever to burning Hell" (*Dracula,* 368), an obliteration of the "evil" side of the human being. Though students generally agree with the necessity of his death, there is extreme disagreement over the ultimate nature of the novel as influenced by the ending. Some students view Dracula as the embodiment of Victorian repression, holding pretty much to the "Jonathan Harker-as-hero" line. Others interpret Dracula's death as an integration of the unconscious, that the text is a call for comprehension as seen in the novel's rather overt display of normally hidden desires. Yet the point here is not to inculcate Lacan's conviction in the need for a recognized Other (or alternately, Freud's belief in "health" as a smoothly operating system), but to simply allow the students to recognize a subtext that involves the unconscious/conscious dichotomy embedded in the text, its spaces, and its audience: to see the larger issues at work not only in *Dracula* or any other text, but themselves and their world as well.

One student noted that much of Dracula's power stemmed from his noble lineage, adding that "the upper class usually get what they want" and "they tend to have a domineering effect over other social classes." She saw an egalitarian effort on Stoker's part: "Since the middle class [Van Helsing et al.] attacked the aristocracy and won . . . Stoker was trying to make the differences between the social classes less." In class, she went on to parallel the Victorian situation with her own thoughts on Eastern Europe, commenting that in both cases it is the power of the group that overthrows the dictatorial class claiming to hold the power of the people. The reaching of such a stage of textual- and Self-examination is the aim of the "classroom-as-clinic" psychoanalytical approach.

I have referred to the educational maladies of our students, their unwillingness or inability to see outside the superficiality of either "autonomy" or a text, and the possibility of resuscitation through the generation of implications among Self, literature, and psychology. Yet the "clinic-as-classroom" approach equally—and perhaps in an even more pressing manner—requires the discernment of a teaching neurosis as well. "To learn from our students" is an oft-repeated phrase telling us to beware a too-firm belief in our own mastery, so much so that it has assumed the status of cliché. But the problem is not an overuse of the phrase, but its underutilization: only when the cliché becomes an axiom will we have reached the stage of education which empowers all the players in the education game.

Notes

1. Felman's description of the "and" in this relationship in "To Open the Question," her introduction to *Psychology and Literature: The Question of*

Reading: Otherwise (1982a), is not to be missed: "(a) misleadingly innocent, colorless, meaningless copulative conjunction" (5).

2. For a fuller discussion of the sexual symbolism of Dracula, see C. F. Bentley (1972), "The Monster in the Bedroom: Sexual Symbolism in Bram Stoker's *Dracula*."

3. Sandra M. Gilbert and Susan Gubar (1979), *The Madwoman in the Attic*, 89–92.

II Orienting the Reader: New Historicism, Reception Theory, and Marxism

5 "Text," "Reader," "Author," and "History" in the Introduction to Literature Course

John Schilb
University of Maryland

How Introduction to Literature Can Introduce "Theory"

In a sense, "Introduction to Literature" courses have always introduced "theory" as well. Even when they claim to consider just primary texts, they still entail "theory" by tacitly endorsing certain works and methods. As Gerald Graff observes, "any teacher of literature is unavoidably a literary theorist. Whatever a teacher says about a literary work, or leaves unsaid, presupposes a theory—of what literature is or can be, of what literary works are worth teaching and why, of how these works should be read and which of their aspects are most worth being noticed and pointed out" (1989, 250). Indeed, determining what to include in an introduction to literature course usually requires many "theoretical" decisions, given all the texts and approaches the field presently encompasses.

Nevertheless, if teachers of the course did address the field's current interest in "theory," they would not associate the word with their bedrock premises and proceed with business as usual. Instead, they would recognize how principles they may have taken for granted are now explicitly contested. That is, they would incorporate "theory" in another sense Graff proposes, "as a discourse that is generated when assumptions and concepts which once went without saying have become objects of discussion and dispute" (254). The concepts he specifically mentions include "text," "reader," "author," and "history" (254). At one time or another, each has guided entire critical movements. The present discourse of "theory," however, has complicated how to define and connect them. I want to propose, then, an introduction to literature course that also introduces "theory" by having students explore how these four terms relate.

Some might fear that such a model could displace "literature" altogether, robbing students of reading pleasures that the course and the discipline it introduces have usually offered as their rationale. My version would, in fact, preclude relegating "literature" to the allegedly autonomous, disinterested realm of "aesthetics." "Literature" would emerge instead as a culturally produced category for texts, thus provoking questions of history, philosophy, and politics, too. Yet the inquiry I envision can continue to dwell upon works that instructors have long valued. Although I will suggest expanding the kinds of works usually dealt with in the course, it can still build upon students' intimate experiences of texts it has included. Instructors hardly need to inject actual works by professional "theorists" in order for their classes to analyze the four key terms.

A course probing "text," "reader," "author," and "history" might also concern instructors not used to privileging each of these words. Reader-response enthusiasts, for example, might wish to bar the "author" and "history" from class, whereas adepts of the New Criticism might prefer to invoke just the "text." Obviously, students could not experiment with these terms if the instructor dogmatically ranked them. Again, the idea would be to recognize how the current discourse of "theory" complicates their relations. In my next section, I will suggest how the class can, indeed, provisionally acknowledge each term while investigating them all. More precisely, I will explain how even though distinct critical movements have coalesced around each, they can all shed light upon one another.

Some might fear that my course will bewilder students, for literary theorists often traffic in jargon and difficult concepts. As with any subject matter, though, teaching the discourse of "theory" means deciding which of its terms, texts, concepts, and scholars might reach students. It also means translating for them at times, gradually expanding their vocabulary and thinking. I suggest focusing upon the words "text," "reader," "author," and "history" because they are accessible to begin with, even if the course then emphasizes their complexity. In any event, students need not emulate the verbal pyrotechnics of a Jacques Derrida. They can be encouraged instead to develop a hybrid discourse, one that blends whatever "theory-talk" they can assimilate with languages more familiar to them.

Actually, rather than baffle students, an introduction to literature that investigates the terms I have cited might prove easier for them to grasp. In reviewing transcripts of literature classes, George Hillocks has noted a disturbing pattern: "There is little attempt to use one work as preparation for reading the next. The focus tends to be on the content of individual works with the teacher providing explanations of that content" (148–49). Introduction to literature seems especially disposed to this pedagogy, considering the abundance and variety of works it usually tries to cover. Far from offering a precise sequential logic, anthologies designed for the course organize masses of texts simply by genre or conventional literary period. The alternative of consciously, steadily exploring a set of critical terms might better enable students to integrate their reading experiences—helping them develop the "schemata" Hillocks feels they need for processing each text they encounter (149–50).

Hillocks also worries that instructors dominate class discussion, and those who would introduce "theory" do need to guard against this habit. Teachers already immersed in the professional debates that "theory" has stirred might feel tempted to flood their classes with their own sentiments and background knowledge, especially if they consider their uninformed students guilty of "false consciousness." A course built around "theory" or anything else should observe two principles of active learning formulated by the educational researcher Alexander Astin: "First, the amount of student learning and personal development associated with any educational program is directly proportional to the quality and quantity of student involvement in that program. And second, the effectiveness of any educational policy or practice is directly related to the capacity of that policy or practice to increase student involvement" (1985, 36). The field of literary studies now questions itself through "theory" partly because it has found involving today's students difficult. They often challenge traditional pedagogy with their sheer demographic range, varying in gender, ethnicity, social class, age, academic background, and career aspiration. An introduction to literature course pondering "text," "reader," "author," and "history" also risks alienating them if it deems its content intrinsically compelling. The teacher needs to plan events and projects that can genuinely elicit inquiry. In my third part, therefore, I will suggest how certain principles of text selection can spur it, and in my last I will indicate how certain kinds of writing assignments can as well.

"Text," "Reader," "Author," and "History": Some Possible Relations

The course I propose sets out to reflect how current "theoretical" debates have made the status of its four central terms unstable. More precisely, it encourages the class to intermingle them, considering the perspectives that emerge when they get exchanged or linked. The class should keep these terms in dynamic interplay, gradually discovering for itself how they might connect. Yet because certain movements have given these terms varying priority, let me note what issues can surface in juxtaposing them. Rather than try to spell out all the ways they might relate, I will simply identify some, pivoting around the word "text" while moving through the others.

"Text" remains associated mostly with the New Critics, who called for "close reading" of the literary work itself. Some feel this mission continued with deconstruction, although it found textual disunity where wholeness and balance loomed for New Criticism. The latter dominated the postwar era partly because it served new student constituencies unfamiliar with literary history. Supposedly it plucked "texts" out of rhetorical contexts and settled for analysis of their intrinsic design.

But "textual" study has increasingly felt pressed to acknowledge the "reader." For one thing, developments in science, philosophy, and the social sciences have underscored that our "subjective" human perceptions shape our experience of supposedly "objective" phenomena. Although even reader-response theorists differ over just how much interpreting a "text" entails "subjectivity," they challenge us to consider its role when we analyze how the "text" works. Furthermore, critics of the literary canon have pointed out how it often presumes a "reader" affiliated with dominant groups and ideologies. Judith Fetterley (1978), for example, has suggested that women actually need to become "resisting readers" of male-oriented works like *A Farewell to Arms*. Even if they wish to "resist" her own stance, students can ponder how certain "readers" get solicited and others marginalized as the "text" passes through various settings and eras. The class can analyze, too, how literary studies as an institution socializes critics and teachers to view certain "texts" in particular ways—certifying them as skilled "readers" by leading them to apply particular terms, methods, bodies of scholarship, and professional goals. Whether it studies past or current audiences, though, the class should consider how "readers" are themselves "texts," in the sense that their reactions need to be interpreted rather than uncritically accepted as transparent data. As I will elaborate later, the class's own responses can lead to collective analysis of the ideas, feelings, and background circumstances informing them.

When it privileged the "text," New Criticism officially slighted "the author" as well, declaring biographical approaches "the intentional fallacy" in one famous manifesto. More recent theorists also challenge "authorial intention" as an organizing principle for "texts" and for literary studies as a whole. Deeming the "text" unstable, many deconstructive critics, for example, question appeals to "the author" as a controlling intelligence. Feminist poststructuralists such as Toril Moi (1985) associate "the author" with a patriarchal humanism that limits the actual diversity of "textual" meaning. In turn, other theorists such as E. D. Hirsch (1976) strongly defend "the author" as ultimate arbiter.

Steven Knapp and Walter Benn Michaels (1982) have persuasively argued, however, that even "text"-oriented critics assume an "author," in the sense that they implicitly posit some mind behind the work's meaning. In fact, often such critics tag a "text" with the "author's" name, invoke the "author's" body of work, and even teach a "major author" course. Students might discuss, then, how attention to the "text" relies upon what Michel Foucault (1977) called "the author-function" even when it tries to rule out biography. But I depart from Knapp and Michaels, as well as from Hirsch, in suggesting that we need not credit "authors" with utter sovereignty over the "text" in order to grant their aims a role in its reception. Derrida has noted that from his own deconstructive point of view, "the category of intention will not disappear; it will have its place, but from this place it will no longer be able to govern the entire system of utterances" (1982, 326). His position can lead students to investigate just how much the "authors" of particular "texts" have controlled their reception. With Moi's claim in mind, the class can also examine just how authoritarian (or subversive, for that matter) particular appeals to "the author" have proved to be. It can consider, too, how "authors" have acted themselves as "readers"—weighing, for example, Harold Bloom's (1973) claim that "great" poets strongly "misread" their predecessors, or Henry Louis Gates's (1988) argument that black writers respond to a uniquely African American literary tradition. Of course, students should recognize that "authors," like "readers," are "texts" requiring interpretation rather than transparent beings.

I have already intimated that questions of "history" emerged when New Criticism's "ideal" reader was increasingly felt to be the product of particular contexts (or "interpretive communities," to use Stanley Fish's [1980b] phrase). Moreover, just as New Criticism actually tolerated institutional structures that recognized the "author," so it accepted a curriculum divided into historical periods, and more or less acknowledged them even as it explicated "texts." Actually, this movement began as a deliberate intervention in the culture of its day, even if it officially challenged critical approaches devoted to "historical" context and claimed that literature ultimately transcended time. Besides considering how New Criticism did operate with notions of "history," the class can ponder how current advocates of "textual" study nevertheless encourage research into the past. Though accused of insufficiently recognizing "history," deconstruction at least broaches it by claiming that "texts" unsteadily echo, rework, and displace other "texts." Mikhail Bakhtin (1981a) has inspired several accounts of "the dialogic imagination" through which "texts" respond to other "texts." Similarly, Julia Kristeva conceives the "text" as a site of "intertextuality" that borrows from other works and sign-systems (59–60).

Of course, "history" has become more than just another term of literary studies. Many theorists now virtually exalt it, in effect adopting Fredric Jameson's slogan "Always historicize!" (1981, 9). While still concerned with "texts," they emphasize how discourse gets produced, classified, and circulated in various contexts. Often they focus upon gender, ethnicity, class, and sexuality, explicitly affiliating themselves with movements such as feminism, civil rights, Third World struggles, Marxism, and gay liberation.

To be sure, issues remain even for those now committed to "historical" analysis, and students can ponder them throughout the course. Scholars have had to figure out just how to link a "text" with its social background, especially if they want to avoid the classic Marxist habit of seeing culture as merely reflecting economic circumstances.[1] The question of what constitutes "historical evidence" in the study of "texts" thus takes on new force. How variables like gender and ethnicity relate to one another also needs to be pinpointed. Still another issue is whether "authors" and "readers" of "texts" have enjoyed significant degrees of agency or succumbed to larger forms of power.[2] Given that recent scholarship has excavated "noncanonical" works and challenged the "universality" of the canon itself, English departments on the whole need to decide whether a bounded notion of "literature" can still serve as a basis for curriculum.

"History," too, then, has emerged as a "text." Not only does it require interpretation; it proves accessible only through "textual" records, and historians apply their own "textual" strategies to it when they write about it.[3] If "history" must be filtered through contemporary lenses, though, it can still amount to more than subjective fiction. Cultural historian George Lipsitz suggests an attitude toward "history" that students can adopt as they explore this term along with the others:

> Knowing subjects (themselves shaped by historical contingencies beyond their control) construct the periodizations and cause-effect relationships characteristic of historical narratives, but they do so with a commitment to come as close as possible to an inclusive and collective truth. They do not presume the disinterested objectivity that blinds traditional historians to their own ideologies,

> nor do they let the fact that history appears in story form convince them that history is just stories. Instead, they accept retrospective narratives as useful tools, as ways of organizing and understanding evidence about experiences with change over time. (1990, 31)

In emphasizing "retrospective narratives" as "useful tools," Lipsitz acknowledges them as human constructs while pointing out that they can be tested according to criteria such as inclusiveness. Overall, the course I propose examines all four of its key terms "as useful tools, as ways of organizing and understanding evidence about experiences with change over time." To use I. A. Richards's (1955) similar phrasing, it compares them as "speculative instruments," even as it applies them to the students' experience of particular works.

Selecting Works That Stimulate Inquiry

Teachers of introduction to literature have drawn from a range of works, and the "theoretical" inquiry I propose would not reduce their options. But the instructor needs to choose and arrange works so that students can enthusiastically, coherently explore what "text," "reader," "author," and "history" mean. This aim would preclude treating the instructor's favorite works atomistically or relying upon the loose format of an anthology. Instead, the texts could be chosen to generate interesting conceptual problems, each of which moves the class along in its study of the central terms. To use Richards's language again, the texts might constitute "assisted invitations" (1968, 97) that help students reflect upon the terms as "speculative instruments." Consider the following two possibilities.

First, the instructor might juxtapose works that deal with roughly the same subject but differ crucially in certain ways. In various courses, I have paired "canonical" texts with "noncanonical" ones on the same theme. Often I have brought works by famous white male writers together with ones by lesser-known black women: for example, Benjamin Franklin's *Autobiography* with Maya Angelou's *I Know Why The Caged Bird Sings* (the theme of self-development), poems of William Butler Yeats with Audre Lorde's *The Black Unicorn* (the uses of mythology), F. Scott Fitzgerald's *The Great Gatsby* with Zora Neale Hurston's *Their Eyes Were Watching God* (the romantic dreamer), Arthur Miller's *Death of a Salesman* with Lorraine Hansberry's *A Raisin in the Sun* (materialism and the American family), D. H. Lawrence's *Women in Love* with Toni Morrison's *Sula* (art and sexuality), and John Steinbeck's *Of Mice and Men* with Alice Walker's *The Color Purple* (same-sex relationships). Each pairing has led students to ponder how gender, ethnicity, and other factors have produced different works with different fates, even if they deal with similar topics. Invariably classes find themselves discussing terms like "text," "author," "reader," and "history" as they compare the works' form, content, production, and reception.

Take the case of Steinbeck's *Of Mice and Men* and Walker's *The Color Purple,* paired as treatments of same-sex relationships. Because these are accessible works, and because they strikingly differ even as they address a similar theme, students feel moved to investigate them through the frames of reference the four terms provide. Students quickly note, of course, that Steinbeck's novel emphasizes relationships between men, while Walker's novel affirms relationships between women. They recognize that even though Steinbeck's protagonists come from a marginalized class, Walker's must also cope with discrimination based upon gender, race, and sexual preference. While both works present an American vernacular, students like to analyze how their versions of folk speech differ, with Walker showing the expressive power of Black English (consciously emulating her literary predecessor Zora Neale Hurston as she does so).[4] Students are interested to see, too, that Steinbeck imitates drama and Walker produces an epistolary novel—although they will probably need help discovering that she revives an early form of the genre, one that also addressed female victimization. Furthermore, students inevitably compare the classic status of Steinbeck's work with the burgeoning popularity of Walker's, analyzing what shapes reputations in general and what might influence the future of these specific novels. In particular, they consider whether Steinbeck's characters will seem more "universal" than Walker's, given invidious hierarchies of gender, race, and sexual preference. Not uncommon is the student who reported to me that although she was initially disquieted by *The Color Purple*'s affirmation of lesbianism, she eventually wondered whether the male bonding in Steinbeck's novel is necessarily more "normal." She came to sense, that is, that contingencies of "history" can affect how "text," "reader," and "author" are perceived. Throughout the class discussions, students find themselves elaborating these concepts even as they examine their concrete responses to specific works. An instructor can ask them to note how they are in fact relating these terms at various moments, especially when they are about to pass from one set of works to another.

Inquiry into the terms can be spurred by a related situation: when students encounter not just "the text itself," but the ways in which different audiences have found different meanings and values in it. With this situation, the class again finds itself considering why certain works get canonized and others do not. But the instructor can underscore how even works now widely taught have been variously perceived. Shakespeare's plays are an obvious example, and the class can be invited to trace how they have been reinterpreted and actually revised through the centuries. Students can even examine how the modern institutionalization of Shakespeare as "high culture" and school subject has already affected their responses to his works. Most of us have encountered students who hate Shakespeare's plays because they have found them intimidating in previous English classes; instead of deeming this attitude a barrier to leap over, why not use it to probe how the "interpretive communities" that students historically pass through shape their understanding of Shakespeare as an "author," of his plays as "texts," and of themselves as "readers" of his texts? The class can also consider how the plays' durable status has not allayed the fear of their being potentially scandalous, and thus prone to bowdlerizing by eighteenth-century impresarios as well as twentieth-century school authorities.

Indeed, the "classic" work with traces of "scandal" can nicely foreground how "texts" and "authors" get differently construed by "readers" throughout "history." I have found three novels from the period of American realism quite useful in this respect: Kate Chopin's *The Awakening*, Theodore Dreiser's *Sister Carrie*, and Mark Twain's *Adventures of Huckleberry Finn*. To be sure, Chopin's novel was long neglected, and students might analyze why. They might ponder, for example, how the male professoriate slighted the tradition of women local colorists when establishing "American Literature" as a field. Today, though, survey courses regularly include *The Awakening*. Given its new status, and the modern feel of its heroine's quest for fulfillment, students may fail to recognize how its apparent endorsement of female sexuality has previously bothered some readers. They may even blame the heroine for not pursuing her desires enough. As I have related elsewhere (Schilb 1985b), a student of mine stimulated lively classroom debate when she asserted this position, for she raised the issue of just how much Edna Pontellier faced certain constraints of era and social milieu. When I reminded her that *The Awakening* itself was banned from the public library in Chopin's own hometown of St. Louis, she took this information into account by modifying her disapproval of Edna; more important, she found herself having to consider how "historical" circumstances affect our notions of "text," "author," and "reader." Dreiser's *Sister Carrie* also provokes this sort of inquiry when students learn how it was severely edited and scarcely promoted by its publisher, again because the theme of female sexuality was threatening.

Twain's novel can prove especially valuable if the class is encouraged to study how various audiences have found it troubling in various ways. Scholars and teachers are likely to consider Twain's novel a mature expression of themes central to American literature: innocence versus experience, and individual versus society. At the same time, they may brood about a perpetual issue in Twain studies: whether there is any way to justify the last part of the novel, where Tom and Huck revert to tricking Jim. Many students, however, will not approach the book through this disciplinary framework. When I ask mine to identify how they have contextualized it beforehand, they often respond that they know it simply as an entertaining story for young adults, because they have read it in high school and/or seen a film version of it. Members of these "interpretive communities" may or may not know that various people today find the novel racist, with some even seeking to expunge it from curricula. They may or may not know that the Concord Free Public Library did ban the book when it first appeared. Even if they have heard of this event, they may not know what Steven Mailloux discovered: that the library feared the book would encourage juvenile delinquency, not certain racial attitudes (1989, 104–29). Investigating these "scandals" aroused by Twain's novel or other works, students also undertake the "theoretical" analysis of terms I have proposed as an agenda for an introduction to literature course. For example, after one of my classes discussed the *Huckleberry Finn* scandal, a student wrote in her journal that she had gained "historical" perspective on herself as a "reader" of the novel: having previously categorized it as a "children's book," she now saw how people of another era could damn it as anything but.

A cautionary note is in order, though. Needing to inform students of a work's varied reception, teachers might resort to uninvolving lectures. I suggest they try to present materials that help students figure out on their own what the heritage of a work might be. These documents could certainly include accessible examples of current literary criticism. Yet they might also include reviews and newspaper accounts from various stages of the work's existence, as well as excerpts from anthologies and syllabi that have contextualized it in certain ways. Students could analyze how still other discourses have affected people's sense of what constitutes appropriate "literature." In discussing *Huckleberry Finn,* for instance, they might look at the editorials, speeches, and tracts against "bad boys" that Mailloux found to have influenced its reception.

The Uses of Writing

I see writing in the course as a crucial way of exploring composing's "theoretical" issues. Above all, the act of composing can help students actively review how their thinking about the course's terms has proceeded. In other words, the writing assignments can also be "assisted invitations" to reflect upon the course's "speculative instruments."

Instructors should realize, though, that certain kinds of assignments traditionally favored in introduction to literature may not produce the motivated, self-reflective inquiry I advocate. It is not necessarily propelled, for instance, by the formal *explication de texte* geared solely to the teacher, or the research paper marshaling citations for the same audience. To be sure, I would not dismiss these modes altogether; with some modification, they can indeed encourage the class to explore issues I have raised. Often students fear the first kind of paper because they have little background for discussing the text in question and suspect the teacher knows much more about it. If they see their analysis of the text as emerging from, and feeding back into, the whole class's examination of certain terms, they can better sense the paper's nature and value. If "research" comes across not as a mere accumulation of data from the library, but as a step in the class's inquiry, students can better understand and appreciate it as a project. With both modes, then, I am suggesting that class discussion be the origin and destination of the student's writing. Instructors can reinforce this framework by even allowing collaborative authorship at times. Note how the following kinds of writing help, too.

Many teachers have recognized that journals enable students to record and analyze their experience in a course. One form especially suitable for this one is Ann Berthoff's "dialectical notebook," where a student writes down observations on one side and then analyzes them on the other.[5] In this course, students can record their immediate responses to the texts and class discussions, and then place these responses in the context of their inquiry into "text," "reader," "author," and "history." Students can take turns contributing to a notebook for the whole class, and indeed, each class period can begin with particular students reading aloud their latest entries.

Another possibility is the sequence of short, frequent writing assignments described by William Coles in books such as *The Plural I* (1978) and *Teaching Composing* (1974). Briefly, Coles devises assignments inviting students to explore various aspects of one or two key words, such as "amateur" and "professional" or "teaching" and "learning." Any or all of the central terms I am proposing for an introduction to literature course can serve as the basis for a similar sequence.[6] For example, students can be asked on one assignment to explain how a discussion of Shakespeare affected their sense of the term "author," and they can then be asked to explore how "author" relates to "text" when they move to a case like Twain's. They can exchange and discuss their responses to these assignments in class, thus contributing to a group dialectic as well as their personal understanding.

I see these Colesian assignments as calling for tentative reflections, not crisp judgments, upon the course's terms. Naturally, the sequence allows students to express firmer stands when they can. But in contrast to many other courses, the one I am proposing explicitly encourages writing that seeks out qualifications and nuances rather than definitive positions. With such an end in mind, the students can test their developing thoughts by writing to people outside their classroom. For example, they can exchange letters with another section of introduction to literature exploring the same issues. They can even correspond with a "theorist" at another institution. At the end of the course, they can publish their reflections or even present them in a departmental symposium, inviting other students and faculty to serve as respondents. Experiences like these not only expose the class to additional points of view, but also make students feel part of wider, ongoing scholarly research.

I want to conclude by pointing out still another benefit of circulating the students' writing beyond the instructor's eye. It allows them to sense how the questions they are grappling with apply not just to works by professional authors, but also to their own. When the students can observe how various audiences interact with what they themselves write, they are in a better position to grasp how "text," "reader," "author," and "history" can get complicated as terms. The teacher who fears that "theory" will overwhelm students might not be used to circulating their work so that issues of "theory" naturally arise for them. The introduction to literature course can be an inspiring introduction to "theory" if it not only presents certain terms, texts, and assignments but also treats students' own writing as worthy of the class's "theoretical" discussion.

Notes

1. In the last two decades, some of the best critiques of materialistic reductions of "culture" have come from within the Marxist tradition itself. See in particular Raymond Williams's *Marxism and Literature* (1977).

2. "Power" has become a key term for the group of scholars known as the New Historicists, whose conception of it is heavily influenced by Michel Foucault's. Focusing mostly upon the English and American Renaissances, they find overwhelming forms of "power" operating in these periods. For a good overview of their work, see H. Aram Veeser's anthology *The New Historicism* (1989). For a sharp critique of it, see Carolyn Porter's "Are We Being Historical Yet?"

3. Hayden White has extensively analyzed the "textual" strategies of historians. See, for example, his book *Metahistory* (1973).

4. Henry Louis Gates concludes his book *The Signifying Monkey* (1988) with an interesting analysis of the relationship between Walker's novel and Hurston's *Their Eyes Were Watching God* ([1937] 1978, 243–58).

5. Berthoff has long sought to bring I. A. Richards's ideas into composition and construes her writing assignments as "assisted invitations" to reflect upon "speculative instruments."

6. A writing sequence can be built around other terms that come up in the course. In a women's studies course, for example, I myself had much success with a sequence pivoting around the word "power."

6 In Search of Our Sisters' Rhetoric: Teaching through Reception Theory

Louise Z. Smith
University of Massachusetts at Boston

> Much of my scholarly and critical work has been an attempt to learn how to speak in the strong, compelling cadences of my mother's voice.
>
> —Henry Louis Gates, Jr., "The Master's Pieces"

Whether we are teaching a contemporary work like Alice Walker's "In Search of Our Mothers' Gardens" (1973) or an older work, there is more to teaching it historically than providing information about its cultural milieu. Of course, information is important. When my introductory course includes *Pride and Prejudice,* I have to explain why the Bennets, in students' parlance, are "so stressed out" about marrying off their daughters; a respectable middle-class woman in Austen's day had three choices, marry, live with relatives as a fifth wheel, or, still worse, live with strangers as a governess. These young women could not, as students recommend, "wait for true love" or "just move to London and get jobs." And students tire of Austen's nattering on and on about houses and landscapes. How can they realize what her original readers knew: that Rosings's many windows displayed its owners' wealth (they could afford a hefty window tax) and that Pemberley's graceful landscape betokened Mr. Darcy's gracious sensibility? No wonder such arcane facts escape all but the very "good" readers if most need explanations of the basic historical facts of life.

But that is not all. With each new audience, rhetorical relationships perforce change. *Pride and Prejudice*'s first words, "It is a truth universally acknowledged," evoke "Yes, go on," from an eighteenth-century rationalist, but "Are you kidding?" from a twentieth-century relativist (which is not to call all the former rationalists or all the latter relativists). These audiences' differing responses show why "teach[ing] historically in an ahistorical culture" (see Thomas's chapter in this book) has rhetoric at its heart; hence, why it is important for today's readers to meet readers from the past.

Students reading contemporary works also need to meet other readers, people whose pragmatic and reading experiences differ from theirs. When in *Hunger of Memory* Richard Rodriguez (1981) names a chapter "Aria," he addresses a readership that excludes most of my students. His implied readers know that an aria is an elaborate melody for a single voice, as in an opera or oratorio, often with an instrumental accompaniment; they can then interpret the recurrent motif of the "single voice"—isolated linguistically, socially, and psychologically—throughout the book. As book reviews show, some real readers resented the book's stylistic and thematic elitism, and others praised its candor. When my students read some original readers' responses to bilingual education and affirmative action, in general and in *Hunger*, they understand these issues much better than if I simply explain them.

That is because experience is a better teacher than explanation. When we teach writing, we know this. Instead of exhorting student writers to "analyze your audience," we use workshops where students read each others' drafts and ask questions that make a writer's tacit knowledge explicit for the real audience sitting in the next chair. But when we teach literature, we forget. We exhort student readers to "read historically," which usually means to imbibe our explanations of what Austen's or Rodriguez's original readers knew. Most students quickly forget these passively acquired facts, however: easy come, easy go. In turn, we divide the class into the good, the bad, and the ugly: the "good" (vigorous, alert, empathic) readers who—as lifelong readers grubbing for their own facts about others' worlds—so easily slip into original readers' shoes and "get" how a well-landscaped estate and its owner's character, or a "single voice" and an "achievement of desire" for one's family, could be related; the "bad" (lazy, inattentive, hostile) readers who, hopelessly confined to their own little worlds, never really "get" why Charlotte Lucas marries Mr. Collins or why Rodriguez turns down a tenure-track job offer; and the "ugly" who will do anything to avoid reading, period. There is, I believe, no substitute for lifelong reading. But there is a better way for us to help all our student readers meet "others," a way shown by reception theory.

The most historically oriented of reader-response theories, reception theory introduces present readers to readers in the past. (Confusingly, some use "reader-response" and "reception" interchangeably [e.g., Eagleton 1983, 74–90; McCormick, Waller, and Flower 1987, 260].) All reader-response theories reject the New Critics' notion of "the text" as an unchanging, "idealized" entity that can be objectively observed and correctly interpreted no matter who does the reading. Instead, they agree, it is "realized" in readings that vary with readers' experiences and expectations. Some reader-response theorists, however, replace the idealized text with an idealized, imaginary reader. For example, Michael Riffaterre's (1966) composite "superreader," Stanley Fish's (1980c [1970]) "competent" or "informed reader," and Wolfgang Iser's (1974; 1976) "implied reader" all in one way or another follow the cues and reading strategies a text evokes. These imaginary readers constitute a normative range of response. But they are ahistorical constructs, and they supplant "the text" as an idealized entity. By contrast, psychologically oriented reader-response theorists like Norman Holland (1975a) and David Bleich (1975a) deal with real readers: themselves and their students. These theorists' by now classic studies pay little attention to the role of history and culture in producing psychological responses. Moreover, neither invites present readers to consider how past readers might have experienced a text (though, as his essay in this volume illustrates, Bleich has more recently turned to the role of culture in reader response).

Reception theory (*Rezeptionsästhetik*) does. Its manifesto was Hans Robert Jauss's inaugural lecture, "Literary History as a Challenge to Literary Theory," given at the University of Konstanz in April 1967. This lecture has been translated into fifteen languages and now appears, along with an elaboration, as "History of Art and Pragmatic History" (1970), in *Toward an Aesthetic of Reception* (1982; henceforth cited as *TAR*). Jauss looked at what our rhetoric textbooks call the "rhetorical triangle" of author, work, and audience. Authors, he noted, were being studied; humanists compared authors' lives, gathered parallels in a "composite historical picture of a periodic recurrence of the golden age" ("History," *TAR*, 47), and produced histories of ideas and genres (*Geistesgeschichte*). Works, too, were being studied; philologists traced "sources" and "influences" that followed an "already sanctioned canon" ("Literary," *TAR*, 3–4). But audiences were ignored: "the question of the third party, the reader or public, was not expressly posed or was relegated to the 'unscientific' field of rhetoric" (1989, 117).

"Unscientific" or not, rhetoric's hour had come. Heisenberg and Kuhn were beginning to reveal the rhetorical aspects of science: the very questions scientists dared ask depended upon other scientists' doubting an existing explanation enough to seek a new one. Research depended on the scientific audience's receptivity, and a "paradigm shift" took place through rhetoric. Hans George Gadamer (1960) had dared to doubt whether readers could ever escape their own historical standpoint, their "situatedness" in time, place, and culture. Could they really recreate the artist's mind, as the humanists claimed to do, or reconstruct a work's original purpose and meaning once-and-for-all, as the philologists claimed to do? "No way! [*Keineswegs*!]" said Gadamer: readers could, at best, embrace their own historical standpoint and examine its interactions with earlier historical moments as seen from the present (146–50). Jauss then dared to suggest that by reconstructing the "horizon of expectations, in the face of which a work was created and received in the past," we both can discover "how the contemporary reader could have viewed and understood the work" and can examine the interaction of that reader's understanding with our own ("Literary," *TAR*, 28–29). Jauss now sees the response to his new question as a Kuhnian paradigm shift (1989, 116–17), played out before American readers primarily through the pages of *New Literary History* since 1969 (see Holub 1984). Three features of reception theory are of primary interest to teachers of introductory literature courses: its capacities to integrate formal with social analyses, to construct an intergenerational chain of receptions based upon real readers' experiences, and to reveal the socially formative nature of literature.

Integration of Formal and Social Analyses Tests "Classics" and Canons

By studying a work's historical readers, reception theory integrates formal with cultural analyses to "obtain a history that has the character of a *process*" ("Literary," *TAR*, 5; my emphasis). ("Process" invites a comparison I cannot resist: just as researchers study "the composing process" through successive drafts of a student's essay, so reception scholars study "the literary-historical process" through successive readings of an author's work.) In this process, "the succession of works is mediated not only through the producing subject [the author] but also through the consuming subject [the reading public]" within history (both literary and pragmatic). A scholar asks how a work challenges and changes its original readers' expectations and compares their responses with her own to determine the "aesthetic distance" (understood qualitatively, not measured quantitatively) (*TAR*, 15–19).

For example, in 1857 French readers of *Madame Bovary* expected a narrator to condemn the adulterous characters, as had narrators in earlier classic novels; they were shocked to find instead a formal innovation, *impassibilité*, in which the narrator merely observes without comment. In overturning ("negating") readers' formal and moral expectations based on earlier classics, *Madame Bovary* became itself a classic, distinguishable from the day's equally provocative confessional novels which faded into obscurity because they merely satisfied readers' expectations as "culinary" art. Reception theory helps modern readers, who take impersonal narration for granted, to notice differences between Flaubert's readers' formal and moral expectations and their own ("Literary," *TAR*, 25–28).

Our beginning students, of course, know very well what a "classic" is. It's whatever we put on the syllabus. Our authority substitutes for their acquaintance with a "classic" work's original readers, who valued its formal and moral challenges enough to recommend it (through their conversations, correspondence, book reviews, critical commentary, and artistic responses) to later readers. Jauss, though, knows the value of this intergenerational chain: the first reader's understanding "will be sustained and enriched in a chain of receptions from generation to generation; in this way the historical significance of a work will be decided and its aesthetic value made evident" ("Literary," *TAR*, 20). Hoping to acquaint students with at least a few "great" works, we choose *Pride and Prejudice* as a "classic" surviving many generations of readers, instead of *Mansfield Park*, whose "negation of expectations" continues to produce critical debates more suited to English majors and graduate students than to beginners. The more contemporary the work, the more our authority counts: when we tell beginners in African American studies, women's studies, or American studies that Alice Walker's "In Search of Our Mothers' Gardens" is worth reading, fewer generations of readers are there to back us up. Frequently cited and anthologized, the essay may be entering the canon. But is it "classic" enough to be included in the forthcoming *Norton Anthology of Black Literature*?

That will depend, according to reception theory, on the essay's "negation" of readers' formal and moral expectations. Readers who know Walker, if at all, through Steven Spielberg's film *The Color Purple* (1985) are in for a surprise. His emphasis on Mister's transformation and his neglect of the novel's African and feminist aspects runs entirely counter to "In Search of Our Mothers' Gardens," which says little of men's roles and emphasizes women's—as mothers, daughters, lovers, workers, artists, and spiritual beings. Rhetorically, the film addresses an Oprah Winfrey talk show audience, but the essay addresses an elite audience about whom I will say more below.[1]

If we begin exploring expectations by asking, "What social expectations does Walker challenge?" students identify "the black woman as suppressed artist," a theme so pervasive in black women's writings that Mary Helen Washington opens her course with the essay (1982, 209). "*Whose* expectations, then, does the essay challenge?" we ask. We can tell students that on the bases of race, gender, and political stance, Calvin Hernton identifies two audiences for black women's writings, "a large popular audience, . . . comprised of both blacks and whites, women and men," and within it a "subpopular audience" of "conscientious feminist black and white women, and a few men" who read writings by feminists, lesbian-feminists, and theorists (Hernton 1984, 142). Students readily see that the "subpopular audience" is not challenged: it already knows "the black woman as suppressed artist." The challenged audience is the "large popular" one that thinks women's everyday work of gardening, sewing, and quilting cannot be Art, an assumption explored in Walker's story about quilting and heritage, "Everyday Use" (1973).

So far, so good, but now comes the hard question: "How does the essay's form challenge readers' expectations?" Asking this is like leading students blindfolded to the *smörgåsbord*: they wonder, "what is form, and what forms have you got?" Most have never analyzed the form of any writing (well, maybe the Shakespearean sonnet), let alone essay forms. So I offer them a four-step sequence of short, informal writing assignments (the kind of "speculative instruments" John Schilb mentions in this book). First, I ask them to say what the essay's parts seem to be and how they are connected; their responses provide a benchmark of present readers' reception. Next we focus on forms Walker mentions: the blues and the crazy quilt (that "follows no known pattern of quilt-making"). I play Bessie Smith's "Special Delivery" (though any blues would do), and ask students to describe the stanzas they hear and to write their own blues. Most describe a three-part form (two parallel parts and a third contrasting part that "turns" and ends the stanza). This exercise enables them to discover—instead of being told—not only the blues form, but the notion of form itself. Third, I ask them to write about how this form "fits" the essay. They typically note the essay's alignment of comparable stories about suppressed black women artists, named and nameless, and the "turn" (the paragraph beginning "How they did it . . .") leading into Walker's discovery of Art in her mother's garden, Art reflected in her own writing. Walker's "re-reading" of her essay in 1983 (Tate 1983, 176) shapes the last assignment:

> In an interview, Alice Walker compared her stories to quilts. She said, "A crazy-quilt story is one that can jump back and forth in time, work on many different levels, and one that can include

> myth." After that interview, scholars often analyzed Black women's writing in terms of quilting. How might someone compare "In Search of Our Mothers' Gardens" with a quilt? How might it *not* be a quilt?[2]

This series of assignments certainly does not qualify students to claim Walker's essay is a "classic" because "quilting" alters essay form as Flaubert's *impassibilité* altered narrative form. (Many other essays, indeed, take this form.) It does, however, enable them to integrate formal with social analyses in ways that would be less accessible without reading the essay through "others": the rhetoric of the blues, of Walker in 1983, and of the semiotically inclined readers of African American "signifying systems."

These assignments also help students become better judges of value, knowing not only what they like, but why. When students call a work we treasure "boring," they often mean that it is too different from what they are used to, that it asks too much of them. Instead of blaming themselves, they blame the "boring" work, thus permitting themselves to withhold their attention from it. (In truth, each of us also has a secret list of unread "classics" for the same reasons.) When I have paired *Pride and Prejudice* with Zora Neale Hurston's *Their Eyes Were Watching God*, students have tested the extent to which a reader's comment on the former (such as Charlotte Brontë's charge in 1850 that Austen's village manners provide too narrow a scope for realistic portrayal of passions) can be applied to the latter, or to neither. Such questions help students decide for themselves whether—and why—a work belongs in the canon.

Real Readers' Experiences Form a Chain of Interpretations

Reception theory's intergenerational chain also reminds us that authors did not write for students in classrooms—as John Clifford also reminds us (in his essay in this book) regarding the original audience for E. B. White's essay "Once More to the Lake." Walker's essay is about the same age as 1990s freshmen, who cannot live through their experience of reading it as their parents did, nor as we do today through memory. The essay had two very different early audiences. The first, whom Walker later described as "the *crème de la crème* of black educated women in America" (1983, 316), included some two hundred participants in a Radcliffe symposium on "The Black Woman: Myths and Realities," held May 4–5, 1973, where Walker gave the keynote address. The symposium was, in part, a response to the bitter debate occasioned by

Daniel Patrick Moynihan's *The Negro Family: A Case for National Action* (1965), which maintained that women played "unnaturally dominant" roles in the "Black matriarchal family" (Scott 1982). Walker's listeners (few of whom were male) included community activists, program administrators, social scientists, historians, and other academics.[3]

Two assignments (each written by half the class and then compared) reveal Walker's double voice. Some students write about how Walker, a sharecropper's daughter turned celebrated novelist, builds solidarity with this elite audience. They note her appeals to professional expertise and her "academic moves": the accumulation of evidence (from Toomer, the African poet Okot p'Bitek, blues singers, black women writers); the metacommentary on her title and references to poems by "Anon."; the posing of contrasts (Virginia Woolf's and Phillis Wheatley's "necessities" for literary production); and the paraphrase in African American terms of a passage from *A Room of One's Own*. Other students, to whom I give Toni Cade Bambara's introduction to Walker's address as defining "what makes being Black, being Black" (Mitchell and Bell 1975, 24), note rhetorical features that create solidarity with a wider community of black women: the call-and-response opening of epigraph and comment that fuses creative with destructive "myths" of black women, the "secret" known only to black women, and the rolling cadences addressing the "congregation." In other words, rhetoric mediates between art and history as Walker's double voice speaks historical and social realities in personal terms, and personal realities in mythic terms.

The second audience,[4] a "popular" one in Hernton's sense, read Walker's essay in *Ms.* (May 1974). The keynote address (as reprinted in the symposium proceedings edited by Mitchell and Bell) ended with Walker's poem "Women" (*sans* title, from *Revolutionary Petunias & Other Poems* [1971]), followed by a single-sentence paragraph. But the version in *Ms.* adds three short paragraphs. I ask students to write about why differences between a listening and a reading audience might have made Walker want a new ending. They speculate that in spoken delivery, the poem's rhythms, followed by the single amen-like sentence, end powerfully, making additions anticlimactic. In writing, the seven-fold repetition of "perhaps" and the uses of parallel structure and of series retain the address's sermonic cadences. But the added references—to Africa, to Phillis Wheatley, to painting and weaving, storytelling and song—recapitulate earlier exposition, encouraging readers to reread and reflect. And the added reemphasis on writing—"signed" and "signature" have nearly the last word—plays on voice and sign, presence and absence, to emphasize the roles of duration and name in identifying artists. Since we lack any real map of *Ms.*-reading in the form of letters to the editor, though, we are in this assignment leaving reception theory behind as we imagine an idealized reader *à la* Fish and Iser.

Nevertheless, we are meeting reception theory's charge to recreate the "historical moment" in which a work first appeared. Microfilm enables students to see what a "popular audience" might have had in mind while reading the essay in *Ms.* Many more assignments suggest themselves than I can describe here. The May, 1974, cover subtitles Walker's essay "A Creative Legacy of the Black South," supplying for American studies courses a new regional context for readers' responses.[5] This issue of *Ms.* provides two ironic contrasts to Walker's themes and rhetorical stance: several articles on "The Fathering Instinct" and Anaïs Nin's reflections on why "we may not care to live in the house of . . . our grandparents" (59). It also presents "Black Feminism: A New Mandate" (97) by Margaret Sloan, chairwoman of the National Black Feminist Organization, who denies that black feminists are creating a division in the black movement and affirms they are part of the women's movement. These articles raise important issues for introductory women's studies courses: how readings of "In Search of Our Mothers' Gardens" might shape and be shaped by these interpretations of fathers' roles, child and grandparent relationships, and the relationships of black feminists to black men and to non-black feminists. We can infer how *Ms.*'s contributors might have read Walker's essay and how their articles might have influenced the popular audience's readings of it.

Literature Forms Social Praxis

A strong incentive for students to "read historically" is their discovery that, as reception theory holds, literature not only represents but also forms social praxis ("Literary," *TAR*, 45). Jauss's vision of this "socially formative" function implies interdisciplinary study of literature because literary works, unlike historical documents that "simply document a particular time," remain "'speaking' to the extent that they attempt to solve problems of form or content, and so extend far beyond the silent relics of the past" ("History," *TAR*, 69). Deliberations on what is a "classic" and what belongs in the canon are, then, socially formative.

To reveal how literature forms social praxis, I like to make an assignment calling upon students' knowledge of economics and social policy. I ask students to write an imaginary dialogue between Minnie

Lou Walker (Alice's mother) and the black woman pictured in an NAACP ad that seeks $10 donations enabling people to buy $240 in food stamps. The ad is captioned "Call It Backbone":

> She's held her head high for 78 years. She's managed and done and somehow made ends meet. But nowadays, on her backroad in Alabama, there just isn't anything to make do with. . . . She's never asked for help and she's not going to start now. (*Ms.*, January 1974, 13)

Some students see the essay as reinforcing the ad's message; they imagine Mrs. Walker comparing notes with the woman on ways to "make do" and offering her neighborly help. More often, students see the essay and ad as working at cross-purposes; they imagine Mrs. Walker asking the woman, and implicitly the NAACP, "what's the difference between accepting food stamps and asking for help?" One student even had Mrs. Walker donating her $10 to the United Negro College Fund's campaign ("A mind is a terrible thing to waste") instead, so as to enhance the woman's grandchildren's education, hence their ability to care for her. Follow-up discussion of these dialogues reveals students' assumptions about gender, race, and class vis-à-vis those in Walker's essay and the NAACP's ad. Each person considers, "If I read the essay and then the ad, would I donate?"—a question about how literature forms social praxis.

Comparable assignments could be based on articles in *Ms.* for August 1974: a critique of the 1965 Moynihan Report and the Nixon administration's erosion of black employment (16–18); a profile of Cicely Tyson's career and her role in the film *Sounder* (46 ff.); excerpts from Harriet Jacobs's "Incidents in the Life of a Slave Girl" (68 ff.); and a children's story about Rosa Parks (71–74). When students look at these microfilms, they *experience* primary historical research, not only on Walker but on whatever catches their curiosity as they browse, and they notice reader responses they might otherwise miss (what can Minnie Lou Walker tell us about Rosa Parks?) or take for granted.

Walker refuses to limit her audiences to the "*crème de la crème.*" She observed in 1983 that black writers "don't have a large black readership; I mean, black people, generally speaking, don't read. That is our main problem" (Tate 1983, 182; see Hooks 1985). She hoped that Spielberg's film would reach blacks who might not read *The Color Purple*: "So much of my constituency just doesn't read. . . . I knew that people in my own hometown might not read the book. But I knew they would see the film. . . . I wanted it to be there, to appear in the villages" (quoted in Dworkin 1985, 95). The novel, of course, hinges on Celie's developing literacy, and literacy is of growing concern to Walker. Her essay collection, *In Search of Our Mothers' Gardens* (1983), is subtitled *Womanist Prose,* where "Womanist is to feminist as purple is to lavender" (xii; see Ogunyemi 1985). Womanists value "the Folk," wholeness of the self and the community of black sisters, mothers and daughters, whereas mere feminists overlook or appropriate black women's experiences. Walker argues that black authors need support from a community that rejects not only sexism, racism, and intraracism but also classism and heterosexism, and that includes Africa, Latin America, and the Third World. She would concur, I believe, with Joyce Joyce's view (1987a) that African American critics, by guiding the black community in understanding the subtleties of its texts, can help it escape white domination. Students can explore a "womanist" reading of Walker's essay, considering what rhetorical features make it accessible to the widest audience, thus forming social praxis by promoting Black, Latina, and Third World literacy.

Conclusion

Assignments on the reception of contemporary works offer students a taste of historical scholarship which most find irresistible. I often ask beginning composition students to look up the *New York Times* for their birth dates and write about how some event affected their own or their families' lives. This assignment works because it joins the personal with the historical, the anecdotal with the scholarly. Among University of Massachusetts at Boston students, whose average age is twenty-seven and whose ethnic, racial, religious, and social backgrounds are very diverse, it yields particularly rich responses and discussions. But I believe it would appeal as well to younger, more homogenous groups of students. In literature courses, the more homogenous the class, the more reception theory can contribute by introducing the contrasting points of view of "others," the past readers.

It is easier than it may look for students to find early readers' responses. Norton Critical Editions of various "classics" include selected comments by writers and scholars who read the work when it first appeared and by subsequent critics. An author's collected correspondence indexes the names of other authors and works; students can find out what Scott wrote to his friends about Austen, for instance. Biographies of authors, too, often include their reactions to what they read. *Book Review Digest,* which began in 1905, summarizes reviews appearing in seventy-five British and American periodicals, most of which are on microfilm. Most students know how to use the *Reader's*

Guide to Periodical Literature and are happy to find that the *Social Science Index* and the *Humanities Index*—in fact, all the Wilson indexes—are set up the same way. People with access to research libraries can use the *Arts and Humanities Citation Index*, which began in 1976, to find out where a work is discussed and/or footnoted; they should bring a magnifying glass.

Reception theory offers several advantages. It engages students in their own primary research. Just as it helps them find their way around a library, and want to, so it helps them read historically, and want to. The most foot-dragging student I ever taught, whom I nearly strangled when she sighed, "Can't we take the elevator?" one floor from the periodical indexes to the microfilms, asked at the end of her first hour of research on *Hunger of Memory*, "Is this how I can find stuff for my other courses, too?" She reminded me that foot-dragging can be anxiety and despair in disguise. So can refusals to read at all, or to read historically; in part, they betoken students' anxiety about all there is to know and despair at how long it takes to learn it: *ars longa, vita brevis*. I can't claim that my assignment converted my foot-dragging student into a doctoral candidate in English; like many eighteen-year-olds, she stopped out to earn money and motivation. But when she joins our older and wiser "returning" students, her having actually done a bit of scholarly digging—instead of being explained-to and pep-talked-to—will count.

Reception theory also sets students face to face with other readers, thus illuminating rhetorical and thematic features of a work that they might otherwise miss and reminding them that all readings, even theirs, are historically situated. In teaching *Hard Times*, for example, one can use microfilms of the *Edinburgh Review*, the *Westminster Review*, and others or, if those are not available, can draw upon the Norton Critical Edition and George Ford's *Dickens and His Readers* (1965) for nineteenth-century British authors' and reviewers' readings of the novel. Victorian readers—particularly those for whom novel reading was a family activity—were shocked to find "damn," a very strong oath, in *Hard Times*; on the advice of the censor, John Forster, Dickens revised it in other novels (Ford and Monad 1966, 30–31). Our students, whose Walkmen may contain X-rated rock music tapes, at first find such responses merely quaint. But reception theory encourages them to ask more questions. What might justify, for Dickens's original readers, the inclusion of such an oath? To what extent did such represented speech, negating readers' expectations, make *Hard Times* a step toward social realism despite its plentiful elements of fantasy? What is the role of censorship in creating a "classic"? Students can follow the intergenerational chain of readers into the twentieth century: 1950s readings revealing inside jolly Pickwickian Dickens a somber novelist of "the grotesque"; 1960s readings discovering Dickens the existentialist; 1970s readings of Dickens the Foucauldian Marxist. By showing how and why differing formal and moral expectations—as well as differing theories of reading—come into fashion and then fade as the chain of readers lengthens, reception theory helps student readers become more self-conscious of the bases for their own responses to reading and more willing to read historically.

Notes

1. John Clifford (1986) notes that "*The Color Purple* is now fairly canonical, at least in progressive classes, but [Walker's] powerful nonfiction is rarely encountered, which is too bad. In reading selections from *In Search of Our Mothers' Gardens*, my students were genuinely engaged by these narratives" (55).

2. I stopped giving students Walker's next sentence: "It is generally much more evocative of metaphor and symbolism than a [patchwork] novel that is chronological in structure, or one devoted, more or less, to rigorous realism," when too many became entangled in "metaphor," "symbolism," and "realism." The scholars of the quilt as a "signifying system" include Christian (1984; 1986), Ogunyemi (1985), Pryse (1985), Marcus (1989), and Perrin (1988).

3. I wish to thank Ms. Jane Knowles of the Radcliffe Archives, Schlesinger Library, for providing materials from the Radcliffe Symposium of May 1973, and to thank Ms. Geraldine Griffin for her intelligent, energetic research assistance.

4. Two other receptions may be of interest. Mitchell and Bell, who edited the symposium's proceedings, stressed the audience's democratic composition and unity, whereas Walker recalled its elite composition and discord (Walker 1983, 313–19). Alumnae readers of the *Radcliffe Quarterly* (June 1974) received Walker's essay about nameless artists in utter silence, but they—and Walker—wrote letters to the editor about using their own or their husbands' surnames.

5. This context was reinforced when the essay reappeared in "Generations: Women in the South" (special issue), *Southern Exposure* vol. 4, no. 4 (Winter 1977).

7 The Historical Necessity for—and Difficulties with—New Historical Analysis in Introductory Literature Courses

Brook Thomas
University of California at Irvine

Given general agreement that the assumptions of the New Criticism are outdated, it is surprising how widespread support remains for the pedagogical principles associated with it. Listen, for instance, to Jonathan Culler. While he blames the New Critics for our present problems in criticism, Culler praises their influence on teaching, going so far as to call the New Critics' "commitment to the autonomy of the literary text, a fundamental article of faith with positive consequences for the teaching of literature" (1981, 4). Culler reconciles this seeming contradiction by arguing, "But what is good for literary education is not necessarily good for the study of literature in general, and those very aspects of the New Criticism which assured its success in schools and universities determined its eventual limitations as a program for literary criticism" (4). On the contrary, I argue that what is good for the study of literature in general is good for literary education. One of the most exciting developments in the study of literature has been the rise of new historical analysis. The question remains as to how we will use that analysis to vitalize literary education. My essay will briefly try to explain why, at this moment, there is such a need for historical analysis and to suggest how we can introduce such analysis into the classroom, especially where it is needed most: in our introductory courses for the general student population. In making my point I confront a problem familiar to all teachers: the constraints of time. Interrelating history and literature takes time, time all too often sacrificed in the classroom. In this essay the constraints of time dictate that I conduct my argument more by polemic than by detailed historical analysis.

The problem with American culture is not, as Christopher Lasch (1978) argues, narcissism, but amnesia, although the two are related. More than any debate taking place between poststructuralist theorists

This chapter appeared in somewhat different form in *College English* vol. 49, no. 5 (September 1987): 509–22. Used with permission.

and literary historians, America's cultural amnesia is a precondition for what has been called a New Historicism, for it indicates the need to rethink how we relate to our cultural tradition. The amnesia is so widespread that many using the label New Historicism seem to have little awareness of the history of the term, which to European ears recalls a discredited mode of historiography dominant in the nineteenth century, especially in Germany.[1] Whereas the New Historicism could perhaps most succinctly be defined as the renewed interest in the historical analysis of literature in the wake of the poststructuralist attack on traditional historical criticism, we should not forget that the call for a New Historicism was first made in the 1960s before the poststructuralist "theoretical" revolt took place in this country. Nor should we forget that there is nothing new about calling movements concerned with the study of history new. History departments have their new New History to distinguish it from James Harvey Robinson's (1912) New History at the beginning of the twentieth century. In turn, Robinson's New History was a self-conscious effort to break with the methods of the old-fashioned nineteenth-century historicism of Leopold von Ranke, which itself had been considered a new history for breaking with even older methods.

This persistent call for new histories seems to guarantee that shortly the New Historicism will seem old, just as the New Criticism does today. But this built-in antiquarianism is not the problem it might seem to be, because, if the rallying cry of the New Historicism is truly successful in awakening a historical consciousness, historical approaches will always be made new. If it is unsuccessful, the label will not exist as an embarrassment to the new historians, but to those who fail to understand this aspect of the New Historicism. A new history should never be old. Study of the past starts with a present situation that is always changing, and yet that present situation cannot be understood without an understanding of the past. A New Historicism responds to a cultural amnesia that has left us with no perspective on the present, thus making it more difficult than ever to shape the direction of the future. Alienated from history, our students are confined to a series of fragmented, directionless presents.

Of course, our students' lack of historical awareness is not the fault of literature courses. To think that changing the way we teach literature will drastically alter the historical conditions leading to that lack would be naive. A complex set of cultural conditions has led to our cultural amnesia. To take one minor example, regular television series set in the past are almost nonexistent. Television does not expose students to even a simplified view of, say, the American West or Robin Hood's

England that teachers could complicate. Nonetheless, it is not a credit to our profession that, rather than combating the lack of historical awareness our students have, many of our approaches to teaching literature, especially introductory courses, succumb to them.

To find ways to teach literature that will combat these conditions is not easy, however. How does one teach historically in an ahistorical culture? That question leads us on a circular investigation from which there seems no escape: what seems to be the most obvious solution—to add a little history to our instruction of literary texts—is itself a symptom of our problem. Students will read literature historically only when they are historically aware. To think of history as some *thing* that we can add to literary texts is the very opposite of historical awareness. Yet how can our students, raised in a culture that suppresses their contact with history, develop a historical awareness unless we expose them to some history in our classrooms?

The only way out of this dilemma is to confront it historically. It is, after all, true that in our culture history has come to be considered something that we add to the study of literature. Any historically aware teaching of literature must start with that situation and use it to move toward a more genuine historical awareness.

The ahistorical approach to literature can in part be attributed to the increased specialization of knowledge in the twentieth century. Of course, literature and history have been considered separate disciplines since Aristotle at least. But the rise of disciplinary specialization in the late nineteenth century greatly increased the gap between the two. We can trace the widening of that gap by examining two movements that started in the first half of this century: Robinson's New History and the New Criticism.

For Robinson the rise of disciplinary specialization was an exciting development. In *The New History* (1912) he was especially interested in the newly established professional social sciences. Robinson felt that histories written in the nineteenth century were too narrowly political, telling the story of great leaders and wars while neglecting other areas of human life. He demanded that historians draw on the social sciences to give a fuller account of change, an account that covered economic, psychological, and social life as well as political life. He wanted more inclusive histories that told the lives of all humankind, not just an elite few. Recognizing the potential of the new disciplines to fragment knowledge, Robinson saw history as the discipline that could draw from them all. To the objection that if, as he urged, each discipline would adopt a historical model of knowledge there would be no need for the discipline of history, Robinson replied that the task of history is to unite these separate histories.

There were two disciplines, however, that Robinson felt necessary to exclude: literature and philosophy. Aware that history had long been considered a branch of literature or moral philosophy, Robinson felt it needed to break from both. The historian, he argued, "is at liberty to use his scientific imagination, which is quite different from a literary imagination" (1912, 52). For Robinson, "the conscientious historian has come to realize that he cannot aspire to be a good storyteller for the simple reason that, if he tells no more than he has good reason for believing to be true, his tale is usually very fragmentary and vague. Fiction and drama are perfectly free to conceive and adjust detail so as to meet the demands of art, but the historian should always be conscious of the rigid limitations placed upon him" (51). The "literary" historian is too prone to "yield to the temptations to ignore yawning chasms of nescience at whose brink heavy-footed History is forced to halt, although Literature is able to transcend them at a leap" (55).

A generation later the New Critics accepted the split between literature and science, but used it to argue that literature, not scientifically based history, was the discipline that could combat the fragmentation of the modern world. Whereas other disciplines confined themselves to specialized types of knowledge, literature's special quality was that it resisted the fragmentation accompanying specialization. Literature, we were told, is organic and whole. Engaging the entire person, its special qualities are accessible to everyone—not just specialists. Literature's claim to universality and nonspecialization is what helps justify requiring all undergraduates to take a course in it. The special knowledge it brings transcends major, class, race, gender. In short, literature humanizes. Since the special knowledge of literature humanizes in and of itself, there is no need to supplement it with knowledge from other disciplines. To do so is to risk reducing its unity and wholeness to a narrow, more specialized knowledge. This includes history. If Robinson wanted to free history from literature, the New Critics wanted to keep literature separate from history. After all, the knowledge we gain from literature transcends the confines of history.

So long as we think of literature in this way we will have two different goals for teaching introductory literature courses. On the one hand, we want to teach students the reading skills they need to gain access to the humanizing knowledge contained in the literary work. On the other, we want to make them read the greatest works of literature, since these contain the fullest expression of the human condition. The first goal leads to courses such as "Introduction to Fiction" or "Introduction to Poetry and Drama," the second to "Masterpiece" courses. Organized to emphasize the techniques peculiar to literature—point of view, plot, atmosphere, imagery, and so on—the first very often completely ignores historical considerations in selecting works to read. The second often seems to consider history because frequently works are organized in chronological order, but that chronological ordering is only superficially historical. Works are chosen because of their intrinsic merit, their value as autonomous works of art. Although a teacher is not forbidden from doing so, relating each work to its historical situation is not necessary because each stands on its own. The humanizing experience comes in the reading of individual works, not in relating one work to something outside of itself.

From this overly simplified sketch of the assumptions underlying the organization of many introductory courses, a contradiction becomes apparent. The notion of a piece of literature as an organic, autonomous whole that combats the fragmentation of the modern world can easily lead to teaching practices that contribute to the fragmentation our students experience in their lives—a fragmentation confirmed in their educational experience. At the same time that sophomores take a general studies literature course, they might also take economics, biology, math, and accounting. There is nothing, not even the literature course, that connects the knowledge they gain from these different courses. For although literature is supposed to offer unified knowledge, its special brand of knowledge has been defined against the other types of knowledge they are exposed to. Whereas Robinson tried to combat the fragmentation of knowledge by using history to unite the various disciplines, the New Critics tried to combat it by excluding other disciplines. Furthermore, because each work students read in a literature course is an organic whole that stands on its own, there is really no reason why they should relate one work to another taught in the same course. As they read one work, then another, then another, each separate and unique, each reading can too easily contribute to their sense of education as a set of fragmented, unrelated experiences, in which wholeness and unity are to be found only in temporary, self-enclosed moments (see Graff 1986).

My (too symmetrical) comparison between the New History and the New Criticism emphasizes that the separation of literature and history cannot be blamed on literary critics alone—especially one school of critics. But if my brief history reminds us that historians share some of the responsibility for the separation, it also gives a different perspective on the New Critics' powerful argument that a historical approach would assimilate literature to another discipline and thereby destroy students' appreciation of literature's special humanistic qualities. Rather than counter the fragmented spirit of the age as they thought, the New Critics fostered pedagogical practices that contributed to it. What I propose is that we can make a step toward countering our students' sense of a fragmented education by learning from the New History, but correcting its mistake of separating history and literature. We can do so by thinking of a historically based study of literature as a discipline that can relate separate realms of knowledge. Rather than retreat to literature as the last outpost of humanism in a dehumanized world, we might start using literature to combat the fragmentation our students sense by making connections with other human activities they experience.

If at this point I seem to be arguing more for interdisciplinary approaches to literature than new historical ones, it is because an important characteristic of the New Historicism, like that of Robinson's New History, is its openness to other disciplines. Once we break down disciplinary boundaries we question the criteria used to establish "literary" evidence. New historicists not only call on evidence that the New Critics labeled extrinsic but also that which many traditional literary historians would have suspected as having little bearing on the noble production of art—evidence from social and economic history as well as intellectual history. As a result, we have a different concept of what constitutes a history of literature. The new histories produced no longer consider literature as a timeless space of order in an unstable world nor as a world elsewhere allowing the free play of the imagination. Instead, literature is seen in constant relation to the world around it, not so much reflecting its historical situation as responding to it. Because that historical situation is so complex—because there is an overdetermination of defining forces—we will never be able to have a total understanding of literature. Nonetheless, since both individual texts and literature as an institution are defined by their response to their historical situation, we cannot attempt to understand them in isolation from it. This refusal to study literature in isolation from other fields of knowledge opens up new teaching possibilities. Precisely because they interweave evidence previously compartmentalized, the new histories of literature can help combat the fragmentation our educational system unsuspectingly fosters.

The fragmentation of knowledge that our students experience is so ingrained within the institutional structure of our universities, which in turn is so vitally linked to our culture's social structure, that it would take a radical restructuring of our society to combat fully our students' lack of historical consciousness. Nonetheless, if we consider the goal of general education courses in literature as helping students connect different realms of knowledge rather than as introducing students to yet one more isolated realm of knowledge, some practical, if not revolutionary, possibilities present themselves. My suggestions will be sketchy and require elaboration and adjustment to local circumstances, but they are a start. First of all, we can change our general education program so that the holy trinity of humanities, social science, and natural science requirements are interrelated by paired courses. Students can be required to take world literature in conjunction with world civilization or American literature in conjunction with American history. Students could fulfill both social science and humanities requirements by taking a course on the family as an institution at the same time that they take a course on the family in literature. A course on the history of science could be paired with a course on metaphor and narrative as modes of knowledge.

If institutional bureaucracy makes even these minimal changes impossible, the English department still has options. Many departments have established writing-across-the-curriculum programs. Is not a literature-across-the-curriculum program also possible? Literature courses can connect with almost any discipline offered at the university: law, science, economics, and so on. A business major who wrestles with *Merchant of Venice* and *Death of a Salesman* may have a different perspective on the role of commerce in the present world, just as the English major in such a course might develop a different perspective on literature's connections to business.

As minor as these institutional changes are, they are bound to be resisted. With all of my talk about the restrictions of disciplinary boundaries, most of us still teach in institutional settings where those boundaries are, if anything, more solid as budgetary cuts force departments—especially humanities departments—to protect their institutional turf. The New Historicism offers some practical suggestions on how to deal with this dilemma. Since for the new historians literature is always produced within a system of constraints, the institutional constraints on teaching literature can be used as a teaching principle. By reflecting on what we are doing and the constraints that arise from that activity, we can raise important historical questions that evolve from our students' (and our) concrete situations.

The most obvious constraint our students confront is the requirement that they take a general studies literature course in the first place. The least we can do (and it continues to surprise me how often this is *not* done) is to explain to them the institutional—and social—reasons for their humanities requirement. An answer to that question requires reflection upon the function of literature at the present time, a reflection impossible without comparison to its function at other historical moments.

Another constraint a college situation imposes on reading is a required syllabus. Sharing with students the criteria of selection and organization of the syllabus would not only help combat any sense they might have that works are randomly chosen and thus unrelated, but it would also force us to raise the question of the canon that is so important in today's theoretical debate. Indeed, many issues debated in the rarified realm of theory have direct bearing on teaching practices.

One of the most important debates in terms of efforts to teach historically is over what we mean by a historical consciousness itself. If, as I would argue, it involves not only a knowledge of the past, but also the use of that knowledge to create a sense of the present as the history of a possible future, then a historically organized syllabus need not be chronological. Disruptions of chronology through juxtapositions of past and present texts can at times be extremely effective in letting students see the radical otherness of the past, an insight that can make it easier for them to view their own present as potential other, a distancing necessary for critical analysis of their situation within history. This is not to say that a chronologically ordered syllabus could not produce similar effects. The point is that current debates about the nature of historicity itself have consequences for how we organize our courses so as to teach historically. Not only should we be aware of the terms of such debates in formulating our syllabi, we should consider sharing the terms of them with our students, since, after all, those debates theoretically affect them.

I am not arguing that an introductory course should turn into a course on "theory." Our awareness that all reading takes place within a system of constraints should not lead to a situation in which we spend more time discussing those constraints than reading. When the New Critics advocated close readings of texts, they responded to a real historical need. Students still need to develop a sensitivity to the nuances of a work's language, its patterns of imagery and metaphor, and its structures. To teach historically is not to abandon these already existing ways of reading but to use them to move towards a fuller historical reflection.[2] This insight has practical consequences for the classroom because it means that, when teaching an individual work, we can often start much as we always have. We just cannot stop where we normally have. Just when we used to conclude by tying all the threads of the text together and demonstrating its organic unity, we need to unwind a loose thread to open it to its historical situation. To do so is to alter what it means to read closely.

No matter how constrained teachers of literature are by institutional practices, we still have a certain amount of freedom when it comes to how we teach students to read and how we define the activity of reading. No essay on new historical analysis in the classroom can neglect how we read works of literature. For examples I have chosen two short poems from historical periods outside of my own area of specialization. I chose poems intentionally, because they seem least likely to lend themselves to historical analysis. Yet one strength of the New Historicism is its demonstration that we cannot read a work's language closely without a historical awareness and that a close reading of a work's language can alter our sense of history. I will start with Shakespeare's "Sonnet 87."

> Farewell, thou art too dear for my possessing,
> And like enough thou know'st thy estimate.
> The charter of thy worth gives thee releasing;
> My bonds in thee are all determinate.
> For how do I hold thee but by thy granting,
> And for that riches where is my deserving?
> The cause of this fair gift in me is wanting,
> And so my patent back again is swerving.
> Thyself thou gav'st, thy own worth then not knowing,
> Or me, to whom thou gav'st it, else mistaking;
> So thy great gift, upon misprision growing,
> Comes home again, on better judgment making.
> Thus have I had thee as a dream doth flatter,
> In sleep a king, but waking no such matter.

A love poem relying heavily on legal terminology—"estimate," "charter," "releasing" (with the pun on lease), "bonds," "determinate," "granting," "patent," "judgment"—this sonnet can sensitize students to different types of diction. It also illustrates how the Shakespearean sonnet form lends itself to a reversal or change of tone in the final couplet. Drawing upon these two formal elements, we can remark on how both help the poet to accomplish a very difficult task in the highly emotional moment of the breakup of a love affair. They allow him to praise his beloved and also to maintain his self-worth. On the one hand, the legal language distances the poet emotionally. On the other, when contrasted with the language of the couplet, it convinces the reader of the poet's emotional involvement. For while the couplet compares the affair to a dream, the legal language confirms its actuality. Read this way, the poem can be said to transcend time and speak to anyone who has experienced or can imagine experiencing the breakup of a love affair.

To historicize the poem is to let it speak more poignantly to our students. One of the commonplaces of Renaissance studies is that the Renaissance coincided with the discovery of the modern interiority of self. As Anne Ferry (1983) has argued, one amazing aspect of the sonnets is Shakespeare's ability to express inner feeling at a historical moment when our modern vocabulary for the inner self was lacking. What Ferry does not note is that the "private" language of the inner self develops simultaneously with a public language of the law. This concurrence happens because the notion of an autonomous, independent self capable of private interior feelings is in part the result of the legal definition of self developing in the Renaissance as feudal social relations transformed into capitalist ones—in other words, as the very notion of possession changed. In feudalism the self is not constituted as an independent, autonomous subject; instead, mutually dependent human beings are connected in hierarchical relationships of servitude and mastery. Under capitalism humans are constituted as independent agents who freely enter into contractual relations. In describing his relation to the lover in the legal language of contract, the poet implies his status as a free agent capable of freely entering into and out of human relations. Thus, we can better understand how the poet's use of legal language allows him to maintain his self-worth while heaping praise on his beloved. At the same time we can detect a nostalgia for a different relationship not so freely entered into and dissolved. For in the poet's flattering dream in the couplet he reverts to the language of feudal relations—"In sleep a king"—implying that bonds cannot be broken. The cost of that eternal bond, however, is a relationship of subservience and mastery. To conclude, the play between the poem's amorous subject and its legal language, between the first twelve lines and the couplet, is one between different historical concepts of social relations, concepts in severe tension in Shakespeare's England, a tension that persists today, as even our postindustrial society retains residual elements of feudal relations. In fact, I can guarantee that students will share the tension the poem dramatizes between the contractual and eternal notion of a love relationship. Reading the poem historically, they will be in a better position to understand the historical forces leading to the tension they feel and thus be better able to understand the costs involved in both sorts of relationships as well as some of the reasons contractual relations have increasingly dominated the world in which they live.

I have proposed teaching "Sonnet 87" by looking at how a noticeable quality of its language registers historical change. By turning to another poem frequently taught—Keats's "Ode on a Grecian Urn"—I want to suggest other ways to teach historically. The traditional reception of the poem invites a discussion of its implied aesthetic. The poem's aesthetic is, however, intricately linked to its attitude toward the past. The urn is, after all, Keats's "sylvan historian." To ask what sort of history a piece of art presents to us is, of course, to raise one of the central questions of historical criticism. It also opens up a variety of directions to take in historicizing the teaching of literature. Most likely no one would want to follow all of these directions with any one class on Keats's "Ode," but I will pursue them because they provide examples of how to historicize other texts.

To ask what history the urn relates to the reader easily leads to a discussion of how much our sense of the past depends upon art and the consequences of that dependency. These are important questions, because even if our students have little knowledge of the past or even interest in it, they do have an attitude toward it. A poem like Keats's "Ode" can help them reflect upon what that attitude is and on how it has been produced.

Such a discussion also offers a way to raise what critics have traditionally seen as the poem's central conflict: that of the temporal world of man versus the atemporal world of art. The urn records two different visions of the past, both at odds with what we normally associate with historical accounts. On the one hand, it preserves a beauty that resists the destructive force of time. On the other, it records a quotidian scene populated by nameless people rather than the account of "famous" personages and "important" events our students often associate with traditional histories. Art, Keats seems to suggest, both keeps alive a sense of beauty in a world of change and gives us a sense of the felt life of the past. But in its search for a realm in which truth and beauty coexist, art risks freezing the "real" world and becoming a "cold pastoral," cut off from the very felt life it records. In dramatizing this conflict Keats's "Ode" allows students to see both art's power to keep the past alive and its tendency to distort it.

Chances are, however, that not all students share Keats's sense of the relationship between art and history. Rather than demonstrate their lack of "aesthetic appreciation," this difference can open up another direction to pursue in discussing the poem. To acknowledge a difference between our present attitude and the one embodied by Keats's poem is to call into question the conditions that have contributed to the changed attitude. Thus, if the first approach to the poem aims at having students reflect generally upon the influence art has on our attitude toward the past, this approach demands that we look at the specific historical conditions that help shape our general attitude toward both art and the past. In the case of the "Ode," this can lead to a discussion of the economic and political conditions of early nineteenth-century England that helped shape Keats's image of ancient Greece. On the one hand, there was England's self-image as the inheritor of ancient Greece's republican institutions and, on the other, a nostalgia for a harmonious pastoral world in contrast to the present state of industrialized, fragmented British society. Thus, the two versions of the past offered by Keats's sylvan historian—the aesthetic one in which harmony and beauty are preserved and the democratic one in which the life of everyday people is recorded—are related to specific historical conditions at the time Keats wrote. The challenge for our students (and for us) would be to speculate on how our attitudes toward art and history are shaped by our historical moment—how that moment is different from and similar to Keats's.

A third way to teach the poem historically is to concentrate on the urn itself as a historical as well as aesthetic object. "Where," we might ask our students, "would Keats have seen such an urn?" Most likely someone will respond, "A museum." If so, we are ready to discuss the phenomenon of the rise of the art museum in eighteenth- and nineteenth-century Europe, how cultural artifacts from the past were removed from their social setting and placed in museums to be contemplated as art. Seemingly taking us away from Keats's poem, such a discussion might be the best way to help our students understand Keats's aesthetic, for they will clearly see that in Keats's poem an urn that once had a practical social function now sparks aesthetic contemplation about the nature of truth, beauty, and the past. If we ask why the urn takes on this purely aesthetic function in a society that was increasingly practical, our students might start to glimpse how our modern notion of art has been defined in response to the social order.

To consider the urn a historical as well as an aesthetic object is also to raise political questions. For how, we might ask, did a Grecian urn (or the Elgin marbles, if we were to teach another Keats poem) end up in England in the first place? Such a question moves us from Keats's image of ancient Greece to a consideration of Greece in the early nineteenth century, and to how a number of Englishmen who sympathized with its struggle for liberation at the same time pillaged its cultural treasures and set them on display in London to advertise Britain's "advanced" cultural state. Thus, a very simple historical question about Keats's urn can force us to consider the political consequences of our cultural heritage. As Walter Benjamin warned, the cultural treasures that we so love have an origin we should not contemplate without horror: "They owe their existence not only to the efforts of the great minds and talents who have created them, but also to the anonymous toil of their contemporaries. There is no document of civilization which is not at the same time a document of barbarism" (1969, 256).

If we consider the task of historical scholarship to recreate the conditions of the past so that we can recover the author's original intention, the questions I have asked about Keats's "Ode" are not valid ones to ask. Clearly my questions are not primarily directed at recovering that intention. Instead, I am treating Keats's poem as social text, one that in telling us about the society that produced it also tells us about the society we inhabit today. This approach is not to say that we should completely abandon the effort to recover Keats's intention, but that, as in the case of formalist criticism, we need to go beyond the traditional historical scholar's efforts. We need to try both to reconstruct the author's intention—for instance, what Keats thought about art and history—and to read against the grain of his intention.

As I indicated, no one teaching Keats's "Ode" in an introductory course would likely raise all three questions. Nonetheless, I do think that they should be posed at different times in the course. Furthermore, the course should be organized so that at some time the three questions can be posed in relation to one another. Pondering a situation in which art helps shape our attitude toward history at the same time that our attitude toward art is shaped by historical conditions (conditions that impart political consequences to our attitudes toward both art and the past) our students might start to see literature as a way to explore the complex interrelations among art, society, politics, and economics that have helped to shape their particular place in history.

Of course what I am proposing demands much from general education teachers. In addition to knowing literary works, they will have to be familiar with the history of various ages and have the ingenuity to relate the two. The demands such analysis places on teachers present real problems. Certainly, one reason why other forms of analysis seem to have a better chance of institutionalization in this country is that they do not make similar demands. For instance, many of the analyses that present themselves as alternatives to the New Criticism do not really ask teachers to move beyond the framework it established. The major skill they demand is one the New Critics taught so successfully—a sensitive reading of language. The New Historicism demands that and more.

In a 1961 address with the ominous title "Is Literary History

Obsolete?," Robert Spiller asked why New Critical analysis had "taken over from history in the academic study of literature?" He found his answer in the simple "realization, a few years ago, that Johnny can't read—Johnny in this case being Professor X, Ph.D., of the English Department of University of Y." New Criticism, Spiller admitted, triumphed because it "sent us back to the text and taught us again to read" (348). The New Historicism reminds us that the text we need to get back to is much larger than we thought and that our lesson in reading is not yet over.

Describing his desire to find "a historical approach to literature, but an approach that would be or include a genuine history of literature, and not the assimilating of literature to some other kind of history," Northrop Frye argues:

> Criticism will always have two aspects, one turned toward the structure of literature as a whole and one toward the other cultural phenomena that form its environment. Together, they balance each other; when one is worked on to the exclusion of the other, the critical perspective goes out of focus. If criticism is in proper balance, the "centrifugal" tendency of critics to move from critical to larger social issues becomes more intelligible. Such a movement need not, and should not, be due to a dissatisfaction with the narrowness of criticism as a discipline, but should be simply the result of a sense of social context, a sense present in all critics from whom one is in the least likely to learn anything. (1973, 57)

That sense of social context is something we teachers must cultivate if our students are going to learn anything from us. But there are serious consequences for our students if, as much of the profession has, we adhere to Frye's simple story of how a narrow critical reading of literature-as-such moves to a consideration of larger social issues. According to Frye this move occurs naturally so long as critics possess a sense of social context. Certainly, for those with a developed sense of social context, close critical reading will always already have larger social implications. But what about those with an atrophied sense of social context? Does the centrifugal tendency Frye describes occur for them automatically? My experience as a teacher would tell me, no. The problem with Frye's simple narrative when it comes to our role as teachers of introductory courses is that it fails to tell the story of how a sociohistorical awareness develops in the first place and how the study and reading of literature might contribute to that development.

The danger in teaching literature is not, as so many teachers of literature fear, that a historical approach will subordinate the special qualities of literature to another discipline, thus turning teachers of literature into second-rate historians who have abandoned their role as teachers of the humanities. Instead, it is that in demarcating a special territory for literary studies we save literature as an academic institution at the cost of reducing it to a specialized discourse related only extrinsically to human society and history. Indeed, at this specific historical moment, the special quality of literature may well be its historicity, a historicity that gives it the potential to develop the sociohistorical awareness lacking in so many of our students. But that potential will not be activated so long as we assume that reading literature will somehow automatically produce such an awareness or when we assume, as someone like Stanley Fish might, that students are not lacking in a sociohistorical awareness—they just have a different awareness. Both assumptions help maintain an ahistorical teaching of literature because they rule out the need to teach literature self-consciously in such a way as to activate its potential to increase our students' historical consciousnesses.

One of the New Critics' major complaints against traditional literary historians was that in placing a work in the context of its times they denied us a ground from which to judge the aesthetic value of each work. This failure to judge, they felt, succumbed to the modern era's widespread relativism. Thus, they demanded that we turn from history to criticism and establish criteria of literary greatness that transcend history. As our present situation illustrates, however, separating literature from history did not provide more solid ground for judgment but led to the deconstruction of all ground for judgment. Not to teach historically is to deny our students the very possibility of reading critically. Immersed in the immediacy of one present after another, students lack a sense of otherness necessary to start a dialogue with a text that allows their position in turn to be judged and altered. Tapping the historical quality of literature, the New Historicism attempts to provide a perspective from which we can judge the very conditions of our judgments. A product of the past, forever capable of reproduction in the present, literature can help create a historical consciousness that reflects upon and judges our present situation, a reflection and judgment that can increase our students' potential to have some say in what sort of future they will have.

Notes

1. On the history of the term "historicism," see Iggers (1968). On the use of the term in literary history, see Morris (1972). On the present New Historicism, see Greenblatt (1985); Howard (1986); Jameson (1979); Lindenberger; McGann (1981); and Montrose.

2. See Fredric Jameson's claim that the answer for a historical critic is not to turn "away from the formalizing kinds of criticism to something else, but rather of going all the way through them so completely that we come out the other side" (1976, 32).

8 The Reader and the Text: Ideologies in Dialogue

John Clifford
University of North Carolina at Wilmington

Aside from trying to rewrite our cultural values, one of my less utopian goals is to problematize reading, to encourage students to look self-consciously at this seemingly natural process with a jaundiced eye, to make them suspicious of the commonsensical, ordinary ease with which they read texts. Actually, I am hoping that the two are related, that our society can become more humane, more ecologically rational and less exploitative when the people who act in that world become more conscious of their own sociopolitical context and more sensitive to the cultural implications of their own values. More concretely, when the readers in my introductory literature class come to see that since their interpretations of essays and poems reflect the ways in which they have been continuously and unconsciously constructed to see the world, they will realize it is also possible to reconstruct themselves, to consciously revise their values, their way of being in the world. And so, regardless of the texts or the class, my topic is always the same—always the dialectic between the reader and the text, always the contradictory and conflicting visions of social reality that emerge from frank discussions even in a fairly homogenous class.

I realize this sounds rather blatantly political. Perhaps you hear echoes of Marx's famous injunction that while philosophers try to understand the world, the real challenge is to change the world. In principle, I agree with him, certainly not about the possibility of a proletarian revolution, but about an ethical imperative to make our work count for more than socialization. Perhaps John Dewey would be closer to my meaning here. Like him, I think the purpose of a literary education is to reform our flawed society, to make it more democratic, more sensitive to injustice, more equitable. That is the basic theme that informs my teaching of reading and writing. Although I think a concern for reform has been a motif in my approach to reading texts since the late 1960s, my pedagogy has certainly been influenced by the thinking of my profession over the past twenty years. As necessary background for my current teaching strategies, I want briefly to weave together two influential theoretical strands, reader-response and Marxist criticism. Like so many of today's literary theories, the narrative gets interesting long ago and far away in the late 1960s.

In 1968 New Criticism was still the influential approach to reading literature, even if its hegemonic grip on the profession was clearly weakening. Professionally and pedagogically, rigorous close reading of canonical poems still seemed the right thing to do. However, this was a time of intellectual and political unrest, and eventually alternative voices were heard within the dominant critical conversation. Under pressure from the anti-Vietnam War and civil rights movements, there was a general loosening of confidence in authorities of all sorts. Literary studies and the reading of texts eventually felt the contradictory shock waves of theoretical uncertainty and personal assertiveness. I no longer felt comfortable being told that meaning was in the text, divorced from the passionate inner lives of readers, removed from the commitments to peace and equality that motivated so many. In the heady atmosphere of participatory democracy and personal fulfillment, the domination of the text gave way to readers too involved in a tumultuous world to accept the quietism and refined tastes of textual exegesis.

It was inevitable that readers would assert their right to create meaning against a formalism that seemed aloof from ordinary life, wedded instead to the sensibilities and experiences of the privileged. One long-standing ally of the active reader was Louise Rosenblatt, whose revised *Literature as Exploration* (1938) resurfaced in 1968. Rosenblatt asserted that a spontaneous, emotional reaction to literature was, far from being self-indulgent or solipsistic, necessary, sound, and in keeping with a democratic ethic. For me the insight that reading texts was analogous to reading the world was empowering, and still is. The ideas that my students found in texts could now be put into dialogue with their own diverse voices. Suddenly the artificiality of cordoning off school from the real world became obvious. Literature is in the world in the same way that students are in the world; the responses of my students demonstrated the cogency of this insight every day. And so the structure of my classes changed, from lecture to discussion, from exploring texts to dialogues between students' lives and the text, from literary analysis to a careful look at the cultural values that are foregrounded when text and reader confront each other. I have tried to explain this approach in several published essays, using fiction by John Updike ("Beyond Subjectivity"), nonfiction by Alice Walker ("Response Pedagogy") and

Loren Eiseley ("Using Intuition" and "Reader's Text"), and a poem by William Stafford ("Enacting").

In this essay I want to use an excerpt from Maxine Hong Kingston's imaginatively autobiographical text *The Woman Warrior* (1975) to describe my current pedagogical thinking. But another critical strand needs to be woven into the pedagogical fabric. Over the last twenty years or so I have rather eclectically blended post-Marxist insights into my teaching. During the sixties, contrary to the prevailing conservative paranoia, the Left was unimpressed with and uninfluenced by conventional Marxist dogma. Respected critics from the thirties such as Granville Hicks and Vernon Parrington were accused by the New Left of "vulgar Marxism" for attaching too much significance to the power of economic determinism, the classless state, and a workers' uprising. Courting oversimplification, I would like to mention a few ideas I have adapted from three post-Marxist thinkers as a way to bring us to the present.

Richard Ohmann's *English in America* (1976) and his recent *Politics of Letters* (1987) reflect his ongoing struggle to demonstrate that reading is not neutral, not value-free, and certainly not apolitical. Any criticism, especially that asserted under the guise of professionalism, reflects the values of the critic while it subtly teaches us to take a certain stance toward the world, toward knowledge, and toward the significance of the self. For example, Ohmann analyzes criticism of *The Catcher in the Rye* during the 1950s and finds that ideas about privilege, class injury, competitiveness, and stunted human possibilities are completely repressed in popular and academic scholarship in favor of themes of adolescent nonconformity, hypocrisy, and spiritual questing. Politics and history are largely ignored, subsumed under the universal and timeless concerns of the human heart. Ohmann's crucial move here is rejecting the literary work as either a reader's private experience or a writer's unique expression in favor of treating the text as a social performance situated in our collective cultural and social history. To treat *The Catcher in the Rye* with a serious sense of social consciousness is to be enmeshed in a text written in a specific, historical moment and read by a fully contextualized reader. It is not to be involved in some transhistorical aesthetic process. Ohmann wants readers to discuss Holden's sadness at the loss of human connectedness in the context of the power of his social class rather than in familiar ahistorical psychological and moral terms.

Frank Lentricchia's *Criticism and Social Change* (1983) is a good example of what I have been calling post-Marxism. Lentricchia directly connects teaching literature with the social world. Literature is social;

teaching is political. Our profession is an integral part of an institution intertwined with other institutions in the reproduction of specific values and assumptions as well as in the creation of a particular slant on what counts as authentic knowledge and culture. This is the crucial conceptual linchpin in recent Marxist thinking: the argument that ideas and values are subtly and effortlessly reproduced within society's institutions through our efforts as literature teachers. Working from Antonio Gramsci's study of ideology, Lentricchia wants to encourage teachers to oppose the uncritical dissemination of the dominant ideology. This can be done effectively only by teachers who are suspicious of discourses that "claim privileged access to truth" (Merod 1987, 127). Teachers as intellectuals are always alert to the relation between truth and power, especially in the classroom doing what they do best—teaching lyric poetry, narrative writing, or language theory.

Louis Althusser, the post-Marxist philosopher, is my last strand in the theoretical tapestry I have been trying to weave as a backdrop for a critical pedagogy. Althusser also argues that the traditional Marxist notion of an economic base inexorably determining the cultural and institutional superstructure is flawed. Instead, he sees ideology as the motor generating the asymmetrical replication of class values, assumptions, and cultural perspectives. Althusser holds that ideology permeates everything we do, especially the material practices of reading and writing. We absorb its principles through specific discourses. Literary studies, history, and educational management all have their own discursive rules and values, as do specific religions, parenthood, advertising, television news, specific newspapers, and so on. Within their language behaviors, all these discourses contain values that affect us when we take part in those discourses' conventions, especially when we read and write. When we read these discourses in the ways in which we have been taught, we are not only assimilating values; we are also being called upon to take up the limited and predetermined roles or subject positions that these discourses make available. In the traditional classroom, for example, the subject who knows is clearly demarcated from the subject who does not. In the courts and in penal institutions, rigid positions are assigned to judges, defense lawyers, prisoners, guards, and inmates, all of whom have little chance to assert alternatives.

Classrooms are more flexible, but Althusser still sees the discourses that circulate within schools as inevitably imbued with the dominant ideology, inevitably proscribing power relations between teacher and students that can be altered only slightly. Consequently, we are all governed by the rituals of the discourse that we are both using and being used by. If it is particularly strong, as in religious fundamentalism or scientific empiricism, a given discourse will overshadow all others, eventually cutting us off from alternative visions, from the contradiction which can lead to growth. The Althusserian insight that seems most provocative is that the good subjects, those who are able effectively to internalize the rules of scholarly literacy, will assume they have decided to do so, believing that they have learned the normal method for dealing with texts. It is the nature of ideology always to disguise the arbitrariness of reading and writing. In this way good teachers and students pass on the dominant ideology, replicating ideas that could be inimical to the possibility of a democratic renaissance, under the guise of a commonsensical apolitical reading process. This, it seems to me, raises the cultural and political significance of what goes on in the classroom. Without our oppositional intervention, the status quo will be endlessly privileged over the possibility of an evolving present, and students will be socialized to adjust uncritically to their future institutional subject positions. If we allow this to happen, I think we will have failed in our responsibility to educate citizens who are aware of the complex struggle necessary to maintain a democratic critical and cultural consciousness. And for those perceptive students who do see the specific social work that literature teaching does in the world, and have therefore adopted a stance of cynical pragmatism, we will have demonstrated either our political myopia, our ethical passivity, or our intellectual blandness.

The following approach is offered as a representative anecdote, one specific attempt to enact a response pedagogy sensitive to our sociopolitical context. In a recent introduction to literature course, I assigned Kingston's "No Name Woman," a haunting and provocative account of a Chinese American's struggle both to exorcise and to empathize with the ghosts of her parents' culture. The author relates the story, told to her by her mother when she was a teenager, of her Chinese aunt who is beaten and harassed by her neighbors because she has become pregnant outside of marriage. In a violent and highly symbolic destruction of her house and all her possessions, the offending woman is rejected by the community whose ideology she has tried to rewrite. Depressed and with no prospects, she drowns herself and her infant in the community well in an equally symbolic spite-suicide.

I almost always have a general sense of the direction I hope the discussions will take, so I ask specific questions before the reading, hoping to create a conducive atmosphere for the students to encounter the issues that invariably arise. I ask them to describe aspects of their personalities or identities: "What is it about you that makes you who you are? Jot down anything that comes to mind, significant or trivial." Typically their first responses are cautious: "My sense of humor," someone will answer. But they will soon venture into deeper waters, noting intellectual commitments and cultural affiliations. Then I ask them where they think these identities and the values they imply come from and what factors seem most salient. Can they, for example, remember a family injunction or tradition that seemed to have as its purpose the shaping of certain attitudes? What personality traits or inclinations did their parents object to or encourage the most and why? What were they rewarded for most in school? Students write these responses in a double-entry journal, with their initial speculations on the left-hand side, leaving two or three inches on the right for later speculation, for metacommentary following group discussions. I then ask that the students use these journal entries to write a brief narrative about the experiences that shaped their consciousness. The point here is to create a parallel text to be set against Kingston's.

That informal, first-draft narrative becomes the basis for a class discussion that I begin simply by asking seven or eight students to read selections for a minute or so. The resulting discussion gives me an opportunity to offer history, race, class, and gender as umbrellas for their random comments. Although their inclination is to resist seeing themselves as overly influenced by parents and institutions, the momentum of the discussion invariably forces them to see that no person is an island.

This text-specific frame enables students to read "No Name Woman" with a certain sociological awareness of the dubiousness of the notion of the autonomous, self-created individual touted by traditional humanism. The students then read the selection and freewrite on three or four specific passages. The following are two representative excerpts from Kingston:

> Whenever she had to warn us about life, my mother told stories that ran like this one, a story to grow up on. She tested our strength to establish realities. Those in the emigrant generations who could not reassert brute survival died young and far from home. Those of us in the first American generations have had to figure out how the invisible world the emigrants built around our childhoods fits in solid America. (1975, 5)

> Chinese-Americans, when you try to understand what things in you are Chinese, how do you separate what is peculiar to childhood, to poverty, insanities, one's family, your mother who marked your growing with stories, from what is Chinese? What is Chinese tradition and what is the movies? (5)

Essentially, I make the same inquiries about Kingston's passages as those I use to generate the students' own narratives. This is a crucial move in helping them to see that both are interested constructions of reality, that both are open to scrutiny and interpretation. And since both accounts are ostensibly nonfictional, the counterintuitive point can also be made (if not accepted) that all texts are rich sources of investigation, that the very notion of textuality, in fact, renders all discourse fictive.

Student responses to the selected passages are best discussed first in small groups and then in a large one. At first many students feel some experiential distance from what they see as a tragic tale of cruel retribution. However, the discussion usually evolves from "the weird customs of the Orient," to an empathetic "everybody has to deal with parental craziness growing up," to more specific ways in which childhoods are framed by local ideology. "I was told not to play with the Catholics down the street," one student wrote in her journal. In discussion this elicited agreement from other students who substituted Blacks, Italians, and Indians. "I thought everybody in America was middle-class and went on vacations, got braces at thirteen, and lived in nice houses in the suburbs. I never came in contact with anyone else," another student commented in a large-group discussion. It was not difficult for the class to begin to see parallels between Kingston's narrative and the ways particular discourses, whether in China or America, can build walls against difference.

The force of these insights builds naturally as the specific student anecdotes accumulate. This specificity leads to generalizations which lead to further variations on the theme. "I was raised to get successfully married," one young woman claimed. "I was never given the kind of encouragement my brothers got," another quickly asserted, followed by agreement, some disagreement, and animated discussion about the validity of the evidence used to support their interpretation of their own autobiographical texts. I am eager during these discussions to keep moving between Kingston's passage and their texts. I want to demonstrate that their ability to make meaning out of Kingston's text is strongly connected to their own lived narratives. It is not long before few of us are certain whether we are critiquing Kingston's text or the texts of our own lives, or if it matters.

Thus I have two sets of responses dialectically set against each other. One is grounded in the textuality of an exotic narrative, the other in the emotional familiarity of the students' own experience. Both are open to critique, and at this point in our discussions students are aware that both are ultimately grounded in an ideology constrained by specific historical, cultural, and economic forces. That is really the topic here—the exploration of the ideological situatedness of both Kingston's aunt and the students as revealed in their responses. Students see the desperation and courage of Kingston's aunt more clearly because they can relate her act to their own contexts: "It seems a question of degree," one student noted. "In my own life I felt I had some options, but I knew someone in high school who did commit suicide. I think I now understand better, why." As readers of both texts they are processing through cultural filters, initially responding with disdain for the primitive and brutal superstition of the Chinese villagers, but then with awareness of the commonalities in cultural difference. Only through discussion can their early ethnocentricity become apparent. The only effective rhetorical strategy is to allow the insights about cultural relativity to emerge naturally and slowly. I see myself creating a context in which students can more easily understand how their deeply held opinions are only partially theirs. To belabor this point is only to encourage a natural defensiveness about their cultural milieu. A delicate balance must be established among a respect for the vulnerability of students, an awareness that such insights can be emotionally destabilizing, and encouragement for those for whom the arbitrariness of cultural norms is already accepted and nonthreatening. Of course, the actual content of "No Name Woman" reinforces the post-Marxist point about the multiple ways in which culture writes us all, but under investigation all texts will reveal specific ideologies since all readers in their responses will expose their communities' values. All reading is interested because all responses can be traced to a variety of discourses situated in a particular historical moment. Reading then becomes something the students must do for themselves; no one can read for you.

For example, in another of the selected passages explaining why adultery in economically desperate and politically unstable times was such a forbidden passion, Kingston writes:

> In the village structure, spirits shimmered among the live creatures, balanced and held in equilibrium by time and land. But one human being flaring up into violence could open up a black hole, a maelstrom that pulled in the sky. The frightened villagers, who depended on one another to maintain the real, went to my aunt to show her a personal, physical representation of the break she had made in the 'roundness.' Misallying couples snapped off the future, which was to be embodied in true offspring. The villagers punished her for acting as if she could have a private life, secret and apart from them. (12–13)

Most of my students focus immediately on the idea of privacy, contrasting their culture's commitment to privacy with the public interference of a rural village. The familiar and ubiquitous refrain, "That doesn't happen here any more," insulates them from any identification with the peasants.

Although a reader-response pedagogy encourages students to react in this spontaneous way, to openly give their opinions on textual events, this can only be an initial critical move. What students say is and should be valued as significant, but why they are responding in this way seems more significant, more critically and culturally relevant. In the discussion following the readings of their responses, I want to interrogate their remarkably similar views on privacy: "Privacy is having one's own room"; "being able to choose one's friends"; "being able to live apart from unwanted neighbors on private property." Coincidentally, all believe they have decided on the value of these ideas individually, holding that their version is transculturally and transhistorically the most desirable. Only in a collective public discussion could these similarities illuminate how subtly Althusser's concept of the dominant ideology works, constructing these subjects to think of themselves as choosing autonomously. The fact that advanced consumer capitalism dictates and thrives on the implications of this kind of privacy goes unnoticed. The notion that they and the Chinese peasants are comparably written by economic and cultural forces seems, at first, perverse. To encourage indirectly the kind of creative and skeptical intelligence that would be suspicious of such myopia is one of my responsibilities as a university instructor who also lives in a culture desperately in need of critical thinkers. Students can be helped to engage such counterintuitive ideas in an environment that is supportive as well as challenging.

In the typical heterogeneous introductory literature class, reading responses to texts in groups demonstrates to students that they are written not only by a dominant ideology, but also by many diverse, even oppositional, discourses. I expect students to restate the major tropes of our culture, including their belief in personal freedom and the power of the individual, but they can also be expected to offer contradictory testimony when allowed to speak from their specific subject positions within the discourses of race, class, gender, ethnicity, sexual orientation, religious persuasion, and age. When students are encouraged to bring their own experiences to the class as a critical tool, their similarities and differences can be seriously interrogated. When I ask them why the villagers were "frightened" and why the "real" needs to be maintained, an opportunity has been created for them to see that the "real" very much depends on whose discourse is privileged. For within the complexity of their own lives there are many "reals," each one repressed as they are required to assume another position. This is especially dramatic when working-class ethnic students encounter alien academic values for the first time. My hope is not to offer these students yet another submissive position that once again asks for repression of experience. I want them instead to experience the contradictions of their various discursive selves through reading and discussing texts in the hope that on such contested ground a critical and self-assured intelligence can be asserted.

I also want to encourage students to read against the grain, against the ostensible intention of the text. To do this it is necessary to look at texts unlike *The Woman Warrior,* which clearly reinforces my contention that cultural values strongly shape our sense of self. E. B. White's "Once More to the Lake" (1941), for example, appears to students to be simply about growing old, about memories of childhood and clearly not about race, gender, or class. Again my approach is to ask students to write before they read, responding in their double-entry notebook to a series of questions about childhood vacations, about fishing with dad, about "the American family at play" (200). These responses again form a parallel narrative, dialectically in counterpoint to White's essay.

In a typical class there will be varied responses to my inquiries since the kind of summer interlude described by White in this frequently anthologized essay is not common, especially if we include women, the urban working class, and most ethnic minorities. The disparity becomes obvious when the students read the essay and respond in their journals to selected passages, including the one where White refers to "the American family at play, escaping the city heat, wondering whether the newcomers in the camp at the head of the cove were 'common' or 'nice.'" Intentionally, I am directing readers to places they might not ordinarily go. And unlike the Kingston piece, where the influence of a radically different cultural context was foregrounded, White's essay appears to be written in a cultural vacuum. Certainly it was not his intention to have his reminiscence characterized as typical white, upper-middle-class male obliviousness. But readers must assume some subject position in reading, and certainly an ideologically engaged position is preferable to a formalist repression of history. During the discussion, my questions about race, class, and gender cannot help but situate most students outside the privileged and homogeneous *New Yorker* audience that White envisioned. They can ignore that reality and read only "what's in the text," or they can focus on what's not there, on what is so glaringly absent. This power to choose one's reading stance is intellectually stimulating for students long accustomed to thinking of reading as a standard technique one must master to be among the initiated. Students routinely complain that, "My teacher had a way of making me feel we were always wrong, never different, just wrong." Students begin to see that they are not wrong; they are just different readers, with different ideologies.

To read against White's assumed intentions by focusing on absence—on the issues of race, class, and gender not confronted in this 1941 essay—is to shift critical attention from the syntactic and structural elements of a canonical text to the experiences of real readers alive to history. Students will begin to sense their own power as readers and will see that the authority critics have previously claimed is arbitrary and oppressive. They see that they can choose instead to write about class privilege, about the repression of the social struggle, about an offensive masculine viewpoint. "I always disliked Hemingway and his macho hunting," a male student noted. "I sure would like to be able to rewrite my paper on Francis Macomber." Students need not be confined to the isolated subject position that most anthologies and traditional literary ideologies suggest, focusing on White's specific details and his crafted sentences. Eastman's *Norton Reader* (sixth edition), for example, asks how the "boats of the past and the boats of today relate to or support the point of [White's] essay" (83). In the approach I am suggesting, the point of the essay is not an a priori entity, but can only be created by reader and text, by the ideological configurations of specific readers with the multiple discursive selves set against a text with its own ideological inclinations and absences. White's essay allows for a limited number of subject positions for its readers if one goes with the thematic flow and focuses on mortality. But reading against the grain allows for innumerable subject positions, each one created by students in dialectical tension with the actual text and their lived experience.

Reading is a discursive ritual that constructs us in culturally specific ways. But our subjectivity is not hegemonically ordered. Unless we join a monastery or convent, we are only partially written by the discourses we inhabit. There are always opposing voices that create contradictions for our sense of self. Within literary studies there is clearly space for resistance, space for students and teachers to help each other respeak their subjectivities through an exploration of the intellectual and emotional landscapes on which we hope to build a literate and democratic symbolic order. Reading provides just such a problematized space.

III Confrontational, Collectivist, and Feminist Alternatives

9 Confrontational Pedagogy and the Introductory Literature Course

Ronald Strickland
Illinois State University

In this essay, I will outline a strategy of confrontational pedagogy which uses the key concepts of resistance and opposition as they function in both psychoanalytic and politicized critical theories. Confrontational pedagogy is premised on two assumptions that may not be accepted by all literature teachers. First, it assumes that students are qualified, conscientious intellectuals, in the sense in which Antonio Gramsci argued that each social group produces its own "organic intellectuals" (1971, 6). Therefore, I would argue, students must be confronted as intellectuals, rather than patronized as inferiors. Second, confrontational pedagogy assumes that students come into the course with established positions on the most fundamental question which must be answered: Why study literature? That is, I assume that the student knows why he or she is taking the class.

This latter assumption, I admit, may not always be warranted, but I think it is a necessary pedagogic strategy. It is necessary, that is, to require the student to think about why he or she is taking a literature course. A student who cannot think of a good reason may decide to drop the course, saving everyone concerned a good deal of time and effort. Other students will simply state that they are required to take the course, or that they are particularly fond of literature. From these simple responses more complex questions follow. On the one hand, why should it be so important for the university to require unwilling students to study literature? On the other hand, why should the student who reads for pleasure gain college credit for this leisure activity? By virtue of our institutional authority, we teachers find ourselves at odds with both the unwilling and the too-willing student—often we are caught in the uncomfortable position of justifying the study of literature to those who do not like it, and of censoring the

This chapter appeared in somewhat different form in *College English* vol. 52, no. 3 (March 1990): 291–300. Used with permission.

reading lists of those who do. By confronting students openly with these fundamental questions, we can turn these silent power struggles into productive critical engagements.

At some point, all students are resisting students. Even the eager student who enjoys reading and discussing literature may suddenly seem to have a mental block when it comes to studying the finer points of prosody or psycholinguistic theory. It is an unfair oversimplification to label such students "ignorant," "stupid," or "insensitive," though the obvious alternative—admitting that we are dull, boring, or insensitive as teachers—is not very pleasant, either. But as long as we accept, as given, the privileged inviolability of both the "knowledge" to be imparted (literature or literary theory) and the conventional methods of imparting it (including all of the institutional and personal apparatuses and methods by which authority is vested in and deployed by the teacher), there appears to be no other way to recognize opposition and resistance in the classroom.

Fortunately, we do not have to accept the privileged inviolability of the "knowledge" we are teaching or the conventional methods of teaching it. There are at least two currents of recent pedagogical theory which suggest new models of teaching precisely by challenging the traditional assumptions of canonical knowledge and pedagogic authority. Psychoanalytic critics have rethought the traditional opposition of "knowledge" and "ignorance" by seeing "ignorance" as an active form of resistance to knowledge and by identifying the individual student's resistance to knowledge as analogous to the repression of the unconscious. In a more directly political vein, Marxists and feminists have called for an oppositional pedagogy which can understand the way the concept of knowledge is implicated in the reproduction of the dominant ideology, and which can empower students to resist the neoconservative and corporate-sector demand for an educational system that shapes students to fit the needs of a capitalist and patriarchal society. These theories demand, it seems to me, a radically unconventional orientation for the teacher. The teacher of literature should adopt a confrontational stance toward students, and a critical, skeptical stance toward the subject matter; teachers should avoid posing as mentors to their students and champions of their subjects.

In a seminal essay on psychoanalysis and pedagogy, Shoshana Felman has argued that the single most important contribution of psychoanalysis to education is that psychoanalysis reveals "the radical impossibility of teaching" (1982b, 21). The "teaching" Felman refers to is the conventional notion of teaching as the transmission of existing knowledge from an authoritative, "knowing" teacher to an "ignorant" student who desires to know. What psychoanalysis calls for, instead, is a radical rethinking of the concepts of knowledge and ignorance. Traditional theories of pedagogy implicitly assume the existence of a substantial, fixed, and absolute body of "knowledge" which can be "mastered" by the student. But when knowledge is conceived as an absolute category, teaching can only be indoctrination; there is no discursive space in which new knowledge can be produced. The notion of absolute knowledge is exploded, as Felman points out, by the Lacanian conception of the unconscious, "the discovery that human discourse can by definition never be entirely in agreement with itself, entirely identical to its knowledge of itself, since, as the vehicle of unconscious knowledge, it is constitutively the material locus of a signifying difference from itself" (28).

This critique of the positivist conception of knowledge, of course, casts new light on the concept of "ignorance" as well. Ignorance may be seen as the dominant order's term for the suppressed "other" against which it defines itself. Or, as Constance Penley has observed, ignorance may represent unconscious resistance to the dominant order: "Ignorance is not a passive state but an active excluding from consciousness (that is, repression) of whatever it does not want to know" (1986, 135). The point at which the student's "ignorance" manifests itself, the point at which the student "desires to ignore" the knowledge proffered by the teacher, is precisely the point at which any real learning has to take place. It is the point at which minds are changed. The difficulty comes in flushing out this resistance and confronting it in the classroom. Students are conditioned, by traditional patterns of pedagogy, as well as by the conventional structures of society, to defer, as "unknowing" subjects, to the teacher as a "subject who is supposed to know," in Lacan's phrase (1978, 230–43). But insofar as this deferral goes unchallenged, students are not really learning anything new. They are only adding to, reinscribing, and reaffirming what they already know: the "truths" of the dominant ideology of our society.

Psychoanalytic critics have generally viewed the student's "passionate ignorance" as a barrier to self-knowledge (see Jay 1987). But in calling attention to the subject's refusal to acknowledge his or her own implication in knowledge—or, one might say, in the particular configuration of discourses which produces an academic discipline—psychoanalysis offers a glimpse of a politicized understanding of the opposition of ignorance and knowledge. In a move reminiscent of Louis Althusser's rethinking of ideology in terms of Lacan's theory of the unconscious, the problem can be restated as that of the subject's refusal to acknowledge his or her implication in ideology (Lacan 1978, 170–83).

As Marxist critics have demonstrated, conventional literary studies has been more complicitous, perhaps, than any other academic discipline, in the (re)production of the dominant ideology. According to this critique, the traditional literature course operates as what Terry Eagleton has called a "moral technology," producing—or, in Althusser's term "interpellating"—individual students as liberal humanist subjects (Eagleton 1985/86, 96; see also Morton and Zavarzadeh 1991). The liberal humanist conception of subjectivity is that of a unitary, constant entity, originating from a rational individual consciousness which is relatively unconstrained by sociohistorical forces. Traditional English studies helps to maintain liberal humanist individualism through its emphasis on authorial genius (focusing on "great men," such as Milton, to the neglect, for example, of the sociopolitical determinants of textual production and reception) and through its cultivation of "original," "individual" response to literature in students. By representing individual genius as the essence of literature, and by granting literature a privileged role as the prime repository of human experience, the traditional curriculum represents liberal humanist individualism as the "natural" and "universal" mode of human subjectivity. But this particular construction of the "human" is itself the product of a specific sociohistorical framework. Postmodern critical theory has radically problematized the idealist-humanist conception of consciousness as prelinguistic and of the individual subject as an originator of language rather than as an effect of language.

The "common sense" readings of texts favored by traditional literary studies are revealed, then, as unselfconsciously biased ideological effects. They take for granted an unproblematized relationship between author and reader as two autonomous, individual, self-present consciousnesses in communication. There is a specific political imperative to resist the privileging of individualism in this practice, for, as Terry Eagleton has demonstrated, it amounts to a form of ideological coercion in the interests of a conservative, elitist politics (1985/86, 102–4). Yet, notwithstanding the current prominence of critical theory, the study of English literature remains deeply implicated in perpetuating liberal humanist individualism. Precisely on this point the discipline of English most strongly resists criticism and change: it is almost unthinkable to suggest an anti-individualist approach to literature because individual genius is seen as the fundamental ground of literature. An oppositional pedagogy would reveal the literary canon and the familiar landmarks of the curriculum—the core curriculum course for nonmajors, the major figure course, the period survey course—as constructions of critical and pedagogical apparatuses, rather than distinct and substantial bodies of knowledge which exist independently of our work as scholars and teachers. As Gerald Graff has reminded us in *Professing Literature*, the familiar subjects and methodologies of our curricula are themselves products of historical conflicts which have been systematically forgotten (1987, 247–62). Of course, this critique of conventional pedagogy would apply to most alternative courses as well. One cannot do away with critical and pedagogical apparatuses—or, to paraphrase Voltaire, if there were no canon to teach, the teachers of literature would have to invent one. What the teacher can do, however, is to acknowledge his or her implication in the institutional assumptions and conceptual frames which produce our particular constructions of "knowledge." This acknowledgment in turn calls for a questioning of those intellectual boundaries and opens up the possibility for alternative knowledges produced in other cultural sites to contest the social values implicit in the institutionally supported curriculum.

In fact, I would suggest, such an oppositional strategy is the only way to achieve an intellectually responsible pedagogy. Any "knowledge" which is not self-conscious about its enabling assumptions and conceptual frames can only reproduce itself, can only adduce new data and win new converts to support what it already knows. Such teaching is inherently limited to the passive transmission of known information as "knowledge" and can only stumble upon new ways of understanding by accident, when the system breaks down, when someone misunderstands and others happen to recognize the misunderstanding as a viable alternative. Much is to be gained, therefore, from a pedagogy which systematically focuses on misunderstanding.

To illustrate some of the advantages of a radically oppositional pedagogy, then, I would like to offer some specific strategies for fostering self-conscious misunderstanding, or the production (as opposed to the "reproduction") of knowledge in literature classes. My strategies can be grouped under three broad headings: identifying and confronting the subject positions of students and acknowledging resistance between teacher and students; resisting cultural hegemony and developing oppositional reading strategies; and resisting individualism.

Confronting Students

In order for knowledge to be produced, rather than merely reproduced, the teacher must resist the students' attempts to defer to the teacher as the authoritative dispenser of absolute knowledge—as, in Lacan's phrase, "the subject who is supposed to know." The way to resist this deference and transference is not to deny the teacher's authority, but rather to acknowledge and demystify the institutional function which this authority is constructed to serve. Above all, the teacher should avoid the pretense of detachment, objectivity, and autonomy. To this end, I see the teacher's role as divided among three functions: convener, archivist, and adversary. First, as convener, empowered and somewhat constrained by the authority of the institution, the teacher is responsible for setting the topic of the course, writing the syllabus, and preparing the list of readings. As archivist, the teacher should provide extensive bibliographies which enable students to develop strongly situated positions on the issues which arise in class. By providing access to these materials, one gives the students access to the sociopolitical and institutional discourses of the discipline. The positions that students will occupy in their readings of texts for the course will be identifiable as positions produced in relative degrees of alignment or contestation with various positions already shaping the disciplinary struggle over knowledge and values. As such, these student positions will be available for the critique of all participants in the class, including the teacher. Thus, at this stage, the teacher can best facilitate the production of knowledge by adopting a confrontational stance toward the student, and by avoiding models of assimilation and apprenticeship.

I require students in my classes to produce several one-to-two-page critical response/position papers on issues concerning the structure, content, and practice of the course. Each week I reproduce a packet of eight or ten of these texts, along with position papers that I write against some of them, for distribution to the entire class. In this manner a considerably larger proportion of the class discourse is textualized than would be the case in a traditional lecture/discussion course. The position papers produced in the class become part of the general text to be studied, decentering the institutionally authorized content of the course and producing alternative centers of meaning (on the margins of the discipline) where readers situated differently in relation to class, race, gender, and other culturally significant discursive categories engage the official texts. Through this practice of publishing the texts of students and teacher, positions are occupied in a way that makes them much more accessible for critique than in the traditional classroom discussion. Increased textualization also produces some welcome practical side effects. For one thing, it encourages students to give more carefully considered thought to their responses to the issues raised in the course. Though many teachers use reading journals to achieve this purpose, I think the response/position paper has considerable advantages over the journal. As an ostensibly "private" mode of writing, the journal is unavailable as a source of knowledge and as a target of criticism for other participants in the class. Thus, the journal cannot contribute directly to the productive conflict that I seek. Another useful side effect results from the attention focused on students whose papers are circulated to the entire class. This attention, I have observed, is inevitably perceived as a mark of distinction, even when the students' positions are subjected to the critical attacks of the teacher and other students. Thus, the response/position paper functions as a sort of reward, allowing a relatively large proportion of the work produced in the course to remain outside the institutional sphere of the grading system.

The conventional letter-grading system, as I see it, is an unjustifiably reductive evaluation which pretends to represent the student's work for an entire semester in a one-letter text. In addition, as David Bleich has argued, the grading system "promotes the attitude that the sharing or negotiation of knowledge among students must finally be subordinated to the student's performance as an individual" and thereby discourages the open exchange of ideas necessary for knowledge to be produced (1988, 4). I am not well acquainted with the experience of those universities which have abandoned letter grades in favor of alternative systems, but I would like to suggest my own alternative to letter grades: at the end of the semester the teacher would give the student a one-to-two-page evaluation of the student's work to which the student could write a response or rebuttal. Both texts should be made part of the student's permanent record. Some might object that such a practice would be impractical; that it would require too much sifting through evaluations by prospective employers and graduate school admissions committees. Nonetheless, I think it would involve both students and teachers in a productive continuation of the learning process. For the time being, I conform to my institution's requirements (and my students' insistent demands) by submitting letter grades for each student. However, I also make longer evaluations available to students and invite them to respond. I require students who are dissatisfied with their grades to submit position papers detailing their arguments. I answer these in writing, and verbal discussions begin only after this written exchange. This process discourages shot-in-the-dark complaints about grades, but some students actually go through the end-of-the-semester exchange with me just for the learning experience it provides.

As students often remind me, the authority to assign grades gives me the upper hand in our classroom debates. One might expect that the fear of grade retribution would intimidate them. In actual practice, however, the collective awareness produced by the position papers works to offset the imbalance of authority; students assume authority through discursive alliances with other writers in the class. In addition, my well-publicized policy for negotiating disagreements over grades quells fears of retribution. I acknowledge that my grading may be biased and depend on the negotiation process to correct unfair grades.

Adopting a practice of contestation between the student and teacher and between the reader and the text disrupts the traditional pedagogical model which aims for the unquestioned transmission of information as knowledge. In the traditional model, the teacher/text is positioned as the authority on the subject, and the student passively receives his/her/its wisdom. The common practice of close reading supports this authoritarian model in its privileging of the text. The close reading, by definition, attempts to occupy the same epistemological frame as the text it reads. Ungrounded by a theorized position, it can only reproduce the institutionally authorized "meaning" of the text, which is, like all meaning, ideologically and discursively constituted, though it usually does not acknowledge itself as such. To counter this reproduction, I advocate a practice of "strong reading" (reading that acknowledges the discursive subject position of the reader in its interrogation of the text) and "symptomatic reading" (reading that attends to the symptoms of disorder within the constructed order of the text). In contrast to close reading, strong/symptomatic reading deliberately violates the presumed authority of the text. But this is not a random act of violence—the strong/symptomatic reading asserts the reader's discursive subject position against the position of "reader" proffered by the text in its social and institutional context. The acknowledged conflict between these different centers of meaning is the focus and impetus of the strong/symptomatic reading. Thus, unlike close reading, the strong/symptomatic reading strives for an epistemological break between the reader and the text. It is in this space of rupture that knowledge can be produced, and not merely reproduced.

Resisting Cultural Hegemony

The effects of cultural hegemony can be resisted by making the course itself an indictment of the conditions behind its institutionalization. The literature course should be subjected to a critique which reconstructs the ideological conditions in which the course is situated and makes them available as part of the text of the course. The introductory course for nonmajors is a particularly inviting subject for this sort of ideology critique. Such courses are often a mandatory requirement for students in technical and professional fields for which literary education is hard pressed to demonstrate its usefulness. But, as teachers of introductory courses, we do not have to be apologists for literature. We have a responsibility, rather, to be critical of its institutional effects.

In a somewhat paradoxical but not entirely surprising way, the fact that I often take a critical position against the value of studying the designated subject matter of the course places many students in the unfamiliar position of arguing for the value of the course. These students may complain, in position papers, that they have enrolled in a course in "literature," not "theory," and that we should neither be questioning the literature nor reading the theory. Sometimes I am able to persuade such students that such an unquestioning reverence for "literature" and "tradition" has dangerous moral and political implications, and sometimes they force me to rethink my self-consciously marginal positions. In either case, this kind of conflict is always more intellectually stimulating than discussions which assume literary appreciation as the common, unquestioned goal. Furthermore, I find in each class that there are always some usually detached backbenchers for whom my iconoclastic positions represent an unexpected breath of fresh air. It is particularly gratifying to see such students become involved in the class discussions.

Ideology critique requires a considerable allotment of class time to theoretical, historical, and other contextual and "countertextual" texts. I introduce the issue of the ideological effects of literary study with one or more assigned readings—usually Althusser's essay "Ideology and Ideological State Apparatuses" (1971b) and Eagleton's "The Subject of Literature" (1985/86)—at the beginning of each semester. In addition to texts which raise larger institutional questions about literary study, literary texts can be "expanded" in ways which enable larger social questions to be raised around them. For example, I often teach the *Cliffs Notes* or *Monarch Notes* for a literary work alongside the work itself. This produces several interesting effects. Since many students see these study guides as aids for cheating, they are surprised to find them on my syllabus, and this can lead to productive considerations of what it means to "read" or to "know" literature. As condensed (often reductive and mechanistic) readings of literary texts packaged for the student/consumer who is "too busy" to read for him- or herself, the study guides promote the most pernicious aspects of the "cultural literacy" approach to education: they encourage readers to memorize disjointed facts at the expense of critical thinking, and they present a body of mostly centrist-to-conservative values and opinions as the authoritative interpretations of literary texts. But they are useful as teaching tools precisely because of these shortcomings. One brief example will suggest the kind of opportunity for critical reading which these texts offer. A sample test question taken from a *Monarch Notes* study guide for *Oedipus Rex* asks the student to "Compare Jocasta's moral integrity and strength of character with Creon's. Give examples from the play to support your statements." As many students are quick to notice, this question displaces our attention from the protagonist's highly problematic moral status (too ambiguous for students to deal with?) and invites a comparison of two supporting characters in what will be represented as a neatly defined opposition of moral strength/Creon (male) versus moral weakness/Jocasta (female). The study guide then provides a sample answer to this question, beginning with a definition of moral integrity:

> Moral integrity implies wholeness, perfect condition, and uprightness of principles in a person. Honesty and sincerity are associated qualities. . . . Unlike Teiresias, [Creon] does not lose his temper when Oedipus falsely accuses him but remains moderate, reasonable and equable. Such behavior indicates that he is at peace with himself, is confident of his rightness, and perhaps has even a certain faith that he will be vindicated before it is too late. Of course, it might merely indicate a sophistic skill in argument and great self-possession unless it were confirmed by other evidence, such as comes in the last scene. There he is clearly intended to be seen as the person in supreme control.

Perhaps what is most interesting is the way this structural homology of composure, authority, moral strength and Creon is defined not in relation to Oedipus, but to Jocasta:

> Jocasta, on the other hand, exhibits neither high principles nor consistent principles. . . . In comparison to Creon . . . Jocasta cannot be considered to have great moral integrity, nor can her strength of character be said to approach his. This is best seen in her suicide; she flees the reality of her situation shortly after learning what it is. (Walter, 106–7)

Here, I might call students' attention to the way the question of Oedipus's response to the reality of his situation is curiously elided (if they do not quickly notice it on their own), and to the fact that the whole exercise avoids the obvious comparison of Oedipus and Creon. In this reading, Oedipus's tragedy of intellectual hubris and rashness is replaced with a gratuitously misogynist comparison of two supporting characters.

Whatever the class makes of the study guide, it offers an opportunity to examine the economic and cultural conditions subventing a particular transmission of cultural values. In one sense, the Monarch study guide for *Oedipus Rex* is extremely authoritarian—the sample question and answer offers to usurp the teacher's authority (in setting the question) and the student's authority (in providing an answer). Yet, in another sense, such texts are marginalized, since most faculty discourage students from reading them. It is this paradoxical combination of authoritative voice and marginal status, I think, that makes these study guides especially useful teaching tools. They offer students opportunities to do critical, symptomatic readings of ostensibly authoritative texts with fairly obvious ideological biases.

In addition to the commercial study guides, I use film adaptations and parodies of literary texts, advertisements, music videos, scholarly journal articles, and introductions to literary textbooks as "contextual" texts available for symptomatic reading by students. Often it is the peripheral material associated with a literary text that provides the loose thread which will unravel an ideologically oppressive construction of the work. For example, when the British Broadcasting Corporation Shakespeare plays were aired by the Public Broadcasting System, several of the plays were accompanied by short introductions and closing interviews featuring executive producer Jonathan Miller and, occasionally, one of the actors from the production (John Cleese, who played Petruchio in *Taming of the Shrew*, and Warren Mitchell, who played Shylock in *The Merchant of Venice*). Miller's comments on the controversial plays reveal a concern to forestall criticism of Shakespeare as sexist, racist, or anti-Semitic. Miller acknowledges, for example, that modern viewers may be offended by the apparent sexism of *The Taming of the Shrew*, but he urges us to bear in mind the historical context of the play. In the case of *Othello*, Miller opines that the key element of the tragedy is Othello's jealousy, not his race, and that the play could be produced with a white actor portraying a white character with no loss of tragic power. In an interview with Warren Mitchell, who played Shylock in the BBC's *The Merchant of Venice*, Miller fends off an anticipated charge of anti-Semitism with a preemptive red herring—noting that the production is unique in that it had a Jewish producer (Miller), a Jewish director (Jack Gold), and a Jewish actor (Mitchell) playing Shylock, he expresses a passing concern that the play may be taken as anti-Christian. I provide transcripts of these introductions and interviews for students to critique in position papers, and I focus paper topics and class discussions on the issues of sexism, racism, and anti-Semitism in relation to the BBC productions and to Miller's comments.

In other cases, the contextual text I use will have no direct connection with the literary text being studied. One textual juxtaposition which students find particularly provocative is a familiar television commercial for Brut cologne and the description of Eve's first moments of consciousness from *Paradise Lost,* Book IV. The Brut commercial opens with soft light filtering through venetian blinds onto a young woman lying on a brass bed. As a sultry clarinet yawns in the background, she rises, stretches, and goes to the closet. Instead of choosing something from her wardrobe, however, she reaches for a man's shirt. She slips it on, turns to view herself in a mirror, then repeats this action with his necktie and his hat. Finally, just as she is splashing on some of his Brut, the phone rings. She is startled—a look of panic flashes across her face—then the commercial cuts to a shot of her sitting on the bed, twirling the phone cord around a finger, and saying, "Honey! I was just . . . thinking of you!" The pause before "thinking" emphasizes the slightly illicit status of her cross-dressing, but we are, of course, encouraged to view it as cute, not perverse. Indeed, students often see the commercial as a harmless romantic fantasy. If no one in the class is disturbed by the commercial, I usually do a walk-through of the scene with gender reversed. This never fails to generate energetic discussions about advertising's role in the social construction of gender.

I then move from the commercial to Book IV of *Paradise Lost.* As Christine Froula (1983) has demonstrated, Eve's description of her first moment of consciousness provides a lever with which the poem's patriarchal hierarchy can be deconstructed. The scene also offers an interesting gloss on the Brut commercial. Eve recalls awakening on a soft bed of ferns, then going over to look into a clear pool of water. She is entranced by the image which stares back at her:

> . . . there I had fixt
> Mine eyes till now, and pin'd with vain desire,
> Had not a voice thus warn'd me, What thou seest
> What there thou seest fair Creature, is thyself,
> With thee it came and goes: but follow me,
> And I will bring thee where no shadow stays
> Thy coming, and thy soft imbraces, hee
> Whose image thou art, him thou shalt enjoy
>
> (IV: 465–73)

In class discussions I focus on the structural parallels in these two scenes—the moment of "self"-contained rapture before the mirror/ pool which is interrupted by the phone call or male voice. The two scenes also fairly closely fit Jacques Lacan's "mirror stage" description of the subject's entry into consciousness (1977, 1–7), and, perhaps more closely, Althusser's model in "Ideology and Ideological State Apparatuses," adapted from Lacan, of the subject's interpellation into the social order. Eve and the woman in the Brut commercial are each hailed from a moment of narcissistic self-absorption into a recognition of woman's subordinate status in relation to man by the intervention of a male voice—the voice of patriarchy. I would suggest that the close structural parallel between the two historically distant texts occurs not as a result of direct or indirect literary influence, nor as an expression of a universal paradigm of gender relations, but as a historically distinct yet related manifestation of the political logic of patriarchy which informed Milton's society and still informs ours.

There are many other psychoanalytic and feminist implications to be drawn from this Brut commercial, though, of course, the focus of interest will vary from class to class. Like the study guides, the advertising text provides an opportunity to examine the ways cultural (political) values are implanted in subjects under the ostensibly apolitical and "free" system of capitalist production and free-market consumption.

In a scene from the film *Dead Poets Society*, Robin Williams, playing a prep-school English teacher, shocks his students by asking them to rip out the pages of the introduction from their literature textbooks. The implication is that the introduction contains merely the bothersome and reductive musings of some crotchety old schoolmaster who probably doesn't understand poetry at all. However widely this view is shared, introductions to literary anthologies and textbooks constitute a powerful theoretical influence on the reading of literature. In some sense the introductions themselves invite our contempt, since they often assume rhetorical postures of abject deference toward the literary texts they introduce. Of course many introductions are quite useful for students. In my pedagogy, however, I am most particularly interested in getting students to read these introductions critically and symptomatically. This practice can be facilitated by having students read one introduction against another to compare how two different introductions treat the same literary material. Or I will ask students to consider how adequately a general poetry introduction describes some random selection of poetry for which it was not specifically intended. One contextual text which I have found useful for this kind of juxtaposition is Ron Mann's film *Poetry in Motion*, a documentary which features a relatively wide range of contemporary poets reading and performing their works. Though this film generally shares the romantic view of poetry found in most of the poetry textbooks, some of the poets in the film push the limits of poetry far beyond those found in the textbook definitions.

Though some introductions are much more deserving of critique than others, any introduction can be read from a critical perspective. Jordan Miller's preface to the *Heath Introduction to Drama* (1976), for example, offers the reader a very accessible summary of dramatic conventions based mainly on Aristotle's *Poetics*. When I ask students for a critical reading of the introduction, however, several students usually identify a fundamental ambivalence in Miller's text. Though Miller is concerned to give students some cursory background in the specific, historical conventions of Western drama, he also is at pains to present that history as transhistorical. Thus, he begins with a prehistoric anecdote:

> Ever since Og returned to the cave and, for the benefit of Zog and his friends, elaborated on the size of the saber-tooth tiger that got away, the human animal has delighted in putting on a show. . . . The essence of the theatre has been with us in tribal dance or religious ecstasy from far back in human time, whether we have shaken the rattle and sung the songs ourselves, or have witnessed the proceedings in awed fear or happy delight in the give and take which is the fundamental nature of the art. (1976, 1)

From this grandly transhistorical beginning, Miller moves to a description of post-Renaissance Western drama with one swift move. "Everything that follows in this volume," he writes, "is a direct descendent of the show that Og probably put on for Zog." Students familiar with the "Flintstones" television cartoons will recognize the anachronism-as-sleight-of-hand at work here. In class discussions we explore the conditions which enable the anecdote to pass as authoritative discourse and we consider some of the consequences of that passing. In addition to enabling a critique of the representation of a particular literary canon as transcendent and universal, this introduction offers a practical opportunity for students to try their hands at a Derridean deconstruction of a posited "origin" as an authoritative source of meaning.

These few brief examples will, I hope, suggest the range of possibilities for resisting cultural hegemony and promoting critical thinking in introductory literature classes. The contextual texts may be drawn from the most unlikely sources, though some of the most successful texts will be those the students have some familiarity with, such as movies, television commercials, and music videos. Such contextual texts are useful for giving students a critical perspective on canonical texts, and for engaging students in the project of understanding how highly politicized meanings and values are promoted by the various institutional apparatuses through which literature and literary appreciation are produced.

Resisting Individualism

Traditional literary study has had the effect of "centering" the student and the teacher as liberal humanist subjects reaffirming the dominant ideologies of our society. The literature student is commonly expected to produce "unique," "original" readings of literary texts. But if one takes seriously the postmodern claims of intertextuality and intersubjectivity, this ideal of originality evaporates. It is revealed as merely a mechanism for keeping the individual-as-autonomous-self in place. An oppositional pedagogy should strive to displace the traditional model of the individual scholar/critic and to replace it with that of the interrogating intellectual who could recognize his/her subject position as the product of discursive conflict.

The critical response/position paper facilitates this kind of intellectual work in two ways: it depersonalizes the student's position, makes it public and available for critique and symptomatic readings from other students and the teacher, and provides a relatively grade-free space for class participants to engage in a collective dialogue. I also specifically offer the option of collective work in students' formal essays. Students may submit collectively written essays after having first established (in position papers) a political and theoretical foundation for their collaboration. The discursive subject position, rather than the individual consciousness, is recognized as the source of meaning.

Some may object that the kind of confrontational pedagogy I have described for the introductory course does a disservice to literature. What has happened, some may ask, to the goal of producing students who can appreciate literature? The very fact that such an audience has to be produced—that it will not just be found—begs the question: Why produce it? What interests are served by its production? What does it mean to produce a "fit" audience for a three-hundred-year-old poet such as Milton? As this mission is generally understood, I think, it means producing an audience who will acquiesce in subjection to a conservative historical reverence which supports an oppressive status quo. It is not surprising that students resist this kind of subjection. Producing this sort of faithful "appreciation" of literature is not a proper goal for a college course.[1]

Note

1. The strategies of confrontational pedagogy described in this essay were first formulated in discussions with Rosemary Hennessey, Robert Knowlan, Minette Marcroft, Rajiswari Mohan, and Mark Wood of the Student Marxist Collective at Syracuse University in 1986–87. In addition, I have borrowed the terms "archivist" and "adversary," and I have adapted the "adversarial" relationship between student and teacher from the model of my former professor, Mas'ud Zavarzadeh.

10 The Walls We Don't See: Toward Collectivist Pedagogies as Political Struggle

C. Mark Hurlbert
Indiana University of Pennsylvania

Starting

We can teach for a different America, a radically democratic one. And we can start by designing pedagogies in which students experience alternative ways of reading and writing and knowing; in which students become the makers of their own educational experiences; and in which students may decide, for themselves, to challenge the conditions of capitalist, classed, and privileged knowing on which both American education and society rest.

I am thinking about pedagogies which change classrooms from places of ideological indoctrination into sites of political struggle. According to poststructural-Marxist theoreticians Ernesto Laclau and Chantal Mouffe, political struggle "is a type of action whose objective is the transformation of a social relation which constructs a subject in a relationship of subordination" (1985, 153). Beginning with the idea that the social relations we live shape the people we become, I want to argue for teaching that intervenes in the construction of who and what we and our students are. The objective of this intervention is nothing less than the transforming of competitive, oppressive, and male social relations in our classrooms and in our society into cooperative, collective, and diagendered social relations. I am arguing, in other words, for a new way of being together, for a pedagogy where meaning-making processes produce new social relations, ones in which we and our students think and act differently, ones from which we and our students question what our colleges and our country make of us.

Hope and Fear

It is the last day of classes in the spring semester of 1990. I'm sitting in a circle with forty-seven students, none of whom are English majors.

This is English III, an introduction to literature course at Indiana University of Pennsylvania, a state university near Pittsburgh.

We are talking about the final exam, which, having taken me up on my offer, the students have designed. They plan, first, for each of them to bring to the final a five-page journal response to literature that I select (they don't have time, we decide, to choose it—and they all want to read the same things so that they can share equally in the discussion). Second, at the final they will read and write responses to each other's journals. Third, they will discuss their responses to the literature and each other's journals. Fourth, they will write their concluding remarks in their own journals. They are now deciding if they will all receive the same grade for the final. This makes a half dozen or so of them nervous.

Mike says, "I want to end this class by doing what we've done all semester. Some people might not like it, but personally I don't care. Let's not screw it up."[1]

Marie responds, "I will feel bitter if we all get a C."

I remind the class, "It could happen."

Mike says, "It's not going to happen."

"But more is expected of us now," Teri says. "Mark will expect more of us when he grades this exam."

John adds, "He should."

After a pause, Carol says, "I've got a lot riding on this grade. I want to go to grad school for business. This could screw up my GPA. What if everyone doesn't try to do their best work for the final? What if someone says, 'I'll let the rest of the class do the work for the final?'"

Barb says, "I won't care if other people don't do well if I know I did my best."

Dan adds, "All semester long we have worked collectively. We've got a chance to do something really different here. To do anything else would be hypocritical."

Teri agrees with Dan: "If we lose sight of all that we have done this semester at the end, we won't feel we've accomplished anything. I would feel a lack."

The class is silent for a moment. I ask them to vote on whether they want to all receive the same grade for the exam. I warn them that the grade could be anything from an A to an F. They vote for the collective grade, anyway. And I'm relieved. I see this vote as a statement of support for what we have done all semester. I'm also nervous because I feel as if my students and I are violating the inviolable—the individual grade. What will happen to their averages?

What if they don't get an A? What if their parents or they decide to be angry? What if they complain to my chairperson or the university president? I remind myself that I would welcome a public forum to talk about what I do and why I do it. But I am still uneasy.

Teri raises her hand and says to the class, "We can trust each other."

I then ask the class if I should be the one to grade the final. "Why should I," I ask them, "be the one to grade this exam?" And I'm trying to figure out, as I say this, just how to grade such an exam.

Kelly says, "Why should we grade the final?"

She's right. I'm the one who's "supposed" to judge the quality of their work. At the same time I wonder why they don't want to take the power I am offering? Why, a colleague later asked me, don't they just all say that they are all going to get an A for the class?

I ask them to talk some more about the grade. I say, "Let's discuss the fact that a couple of you spoke against the collective grade. What does it mean? Are you uncertain about this?"

I feel tension in the room. They've worked on this exam for several class periods now.

Chris says, "If we keep talking about this, it's going to get boring."

Todd says, "If we keep talking about the grade we won't be learning anything about literature."

"Yeah," Dan responds, "but we're learning about people."

Teri says to me, "You, Mark, are the only one who is really nervous about the collective grade."

I begin to wonder if I am wrong about there being tension in the room.

And time is up. The university's scheduled-to-be-efficient time has ended our discussion. I tell them that I actually don't see how they would be able, during exam week, to stay after the test and grade it. I add that if anyone has a strong objection to the collective grade they can talk to me after class and work out a compromise. No one does.

This is the way class has gone this semester.

The students read works of contemporary literature.[2] They keep a journal of their responses to and questions about what they are reading. During most classes we spend a portion of our ninety minutes reading each other's entries and writing responses to them (I often vary this activity by randomly putting the students in groups, letting them choose whose journals they want to read, or having them select journals from a "grab bag" pile).

Class discussion then grows directly out of our reading of each other's interpretations. In order to help everyone feel free to talk about and share in someone else's ideas, while also giving credit to that person, I often begin these conversations by asking, "Would someone tell us about something interesting you read in someone else's journal?" Although I make synthesizing remarks during these discussions or pose my own questions about the readings, I try never to call on anyone in class. In fact, one of our class "rules" is that whenever someone talks, they automatically have the right to "invite" someone else to add to the discussion. To regain the floor, I, like the students, have to raise my hand and be invited to speak.

Interpretations are made and changed during journal reading and class discussion. For instance, Robert Coover's "The Babysitter," the first short story we read this semester, confused many of the students. When this happened, other students were sometimes able to write something in a notebook that helped a bewildered reader make peace with the postmodern form of the story. Kim explained in a journal entry how Kathy's comments helped her to do just that:

> When reading this story, I was totally confused. I tried hard to make sense of the story. I wrote in my journal: "The writing moved around and switched between characters too many times for me to keep track." I didn't like this at all.
>
> The responses that Kathy gave me changed my thinking. Kathy liked this style of writing. She was not worried about understanding every paragraph. She wrote, "I didn't try to keep track of the story, but ran with each person's thoughts." This made me feel like I had run into a brick wall. Why didn't I do that? Not worry about every detail, just follow the thoughts. If I had been able to do this when I was reading "The Babysitter," I think I would have enjoyed the story more. Kathy also wrote, "Robert Coover seemed to be writing like a person thinks: in fast, moving, contradictory, crazy patterns." This response made me reread "The Babysitter." The second time I read it I enjoyed it more. I realized that your thoughts were to change with every paragraph.

Kim is learning from Kathy, just as she has learned from and taught other students during the entire semester. Because of Kathy's suggestions in her journal, Kim discovers how to read a postmodern story, how to be more tolerant of texts that make specialized demands on readers. Most significant, she's learned this from another student. Kim and Kathy are not in competition to be the best readers of Coover's story. They are charged with helping each other to become better readers of all texts. Kim learns from reading Kathy's comments, and Kathy learns by formulating ideas about reading Coover's story in Kim's notebook. Taken together, their actions dramatize the social nature of reading and interpreting. Their practice suggests that they may no longer think of reading as a solitary activity in which the process ends when an interpretation created by one reader is established as definitive, as a product to be consumed by others. In pedagogical terms, Kim and Kathy learn from each other in ways they might never experience from a lecture on a teacher's close reading or from a discussion class where the students' task is to discover the teacher's interpretation.

Another story we read this semester was Susan Minot's "Lust," which is made up of narrative fragments in which a young woman tells of her failure to find love after a string of sexual encounters. In her notebook, Barb wrote about how Michael's reading differed from her own, and she connected both interpretations to the class's discussion that day:

> I felt really negative toward the girl in the story. She came across as being weak in that she allowed these men to use her, and she accepted it. There was almost no love involved in her sexual encounters, at least not on the part of the man. She would often tell herself she was falling in love, but then she would get dumped on.
>
> My thoughts were changed first by Michael, and then by the class during our discussion afterward.
>
> Michael's entry spoke more of the man's point of view. He pointed out that it is easy to be a man and sleep around and use women without being ridiculed. Women are often treated badly by men because women have less power than men in this society and usually will not stand up for themselves.
>
> The discussion of "Lust" was one of the most heated ones we've had all semester. The guys in class tended to blame the girl and say she was a slut and that she wanted sex all the time, but now she wants others to take pity on her because she goofed. The girls in the class, on the other hand, did take pity on her and said the guys in the story were pigs. By the end of class, however, we, somewhat, came to the conclusion that she, along with the men she slept with, need to take responsibility for their own actions.

Barb records, in this excerpt from her journal, how readings develop through the class's interaction(s). Barb came to class with one reading of the story. Michael offered another. After a "heated" discussion, the class ended up with yet another, one that, in this case, encompassed and surpassed the vision of the ones offered by individual students.[3]

Because I believed that the class could learn as much, if not more, by thinking about the process of collectively interpreting literature as they could from interpreting literature itself, I often asked them to make their "heated" discussions a topic for further conversation. How, I asked them at several points in the semester, do you arrive at a class interpretation?

They generally agreed that when they read, say, a short story for class, that each of them then comes to class with their own interpretation of the story, about which they aren't very confident. Next, the class discusses the story and, in their terminology, "builds" various, though connected, interpretations: "There is usually one basic interpretation or theme from which the others stem," Ann said. "I think through our discussions we find this basic interpretation. Sometimes it's picked up right in the beginning. Other times it takes until the end of the period, but I feel that it is generally found. Like the story about the girl who lived in the correctional institute, Joyce Carol Oates's 'How I Contemplated the World from the Detroit House of Correction and Began My Life Over Again.' For some time, we went 'round and 'round about that story, but by the end of the period we agreed that this story was trying to say that often in life there is no resolution. Although as a class we said it many different ways—we said just that. I think that's how an effective interpretation is found."

The students mostly agreed that "an effective interpretation" is "one that somehow incorporates all ideas into a collective interpretation." But they were also concerned that the class's actions and decisions should not exclude creative or divergent reading. Kathy pointed out that "No one is forced to accept the conclusion that we collectively arrive at as carved in stone. All opinions are treated equally and respected. I think this strengthens the class interpretation. Everyone understands where the others get their ideas and can accept or disagree with them. It forces you to examine how you really feel about what you read." I have to admit that I admired Kathy's formulation. I, too, realized the class's obligation to honor the attempts of each of its members. Still, I was often concerned that in their desire to avoid hurting anyone's feelings, they would adopt one of two extreme positions: the naive pluralist position that all interpretations of a text are correct or the nihilistic poststructuralist position that all interpretations of a text are equally incomplete and, therefore, incorrect—or correct. When I challenged them to find criteria that would help them to assess the validity of their readings, Karen challenged me by using a word that I often used in class: "I think we should use the term 'meaningful' to describe an interpretation. If we used words like 'good' and 'successful,' it could have a stifling effect on someone's work because they're so closely related to 'bad' and 'failure.' I think that if we had approached our class book with that idea in mind, then writing it wouldn't have been a very pleasant experience. We might have been so worried about writing something that wasn't 'good' or 'successful' that that would have overcome the creativity that went into the book.

Instead, the emphasis was placed on writing 'meaningful' work and 'meaningful' interpretations."

Besides interpreting how the class should think about interpreting, and besides reminding me to trust my students' intellectual integrity, Karen is talking about the first "paper" of the semester. I had asked the students to write a class "book." To do this, I suggested that they form small groups, of their own choosing, with each group collaborating to write one of the chapters. I proposed that these chapters be critical essays about the contemporary literature we read or other examples of contemporary literature chosen by them. But as the students discussed my idea, a counterproposal began to form. As they talked about the class book, the students decided that they would divide themselves into groups called "poets," "fiction writers," "playwrights," and "interpreters." The "creative" writers would produce the subject matter of the book, the interpreters would write responses to this work (with one group writing a critical and historical introduction on contemporary literature), and, finally, the "creative" writers would compose responses to the interpretations of their work, all for inclusion in the book. They also suggested that the interpretations parallel the kind of responding we do for the literature we read. As it turned out, the interpreters also offered the poets, fiction writers, and playwrights suggestions for revising the "creative" sections of the book. Most of this work went on outside of class, but on several days we spent the period reading and writing responses and talking about the poems, the stories, and the play that went into the final 107 typed, single-spaced pages of the book, which, because it deals with pressing social issues, the students named *Emergency Exit*.

I agreed to the students' plan as soon as I heard it. I could see that they were seriously attempting to make this class book assignment something they wanted to do, instead of something they had to do. More important, their idea called for a wider range of literary responses and a wider variety of student interaction than the one I had proposed. The students had provided, in other words, something that I could only set a context for—a way for them to make contemporary literature their own, of their world, a reflection of their culture.

The results were, in many cases, impressive. Stacy, a student committed to feminist issues, wrote a poem, "Excerpts," about being the victim of verbal male violence. In it, a woman's roommate is paid a visit by her "pseudo-intellectual" poet boyfriend. This "poet" boyfriend writes a vulgar limerick at the narrator's expense. Bill, the student who responded to Stacy's poem, wrote that he liked it because "each time I read it I get a different interpretation of where her anger comes from, and each time I get a more intense feeling of anger." I agree with Bill. The speaker in this poem is angry, of course, at the poet boyfriend for his act of cruelty, at the fact that poetry is being used as a weapon against her, at the roommate who brought the boyfriend into the house, and even, as Bill noted, at "her surroundings. The author refers to drugs twice in her poem and each time it gives me a feeling of discomfort."

Another student, Dan, a fan of Bad Brains and Fugazi, wrote a long poem called "Human Assembly Line," about the mechanization of human experience. In it, we enter the "stream of consciousness" of a contemporary human being whose biological and economical existence is patterned and textured by the machines in his or her life. Paul, who responded to this poem, compared the life of the poem's character to the life of a college student whose every waking moment is scheduled by the repetitive actions that he or she lives each day. In his response to his interpreter, Dan wrote, "I would like to create a poetic window to wake people up, a window that acts as a mirror that reflects the horrors that are out there. I like to concentrate on the industrial aspect of society. Poetry, or contemporary poetry in particular, has many mystical properties. It's medicine in many ways, for the self and for others."

From the start of the project, the students knew that each of them would receive the same grade for the class book, as determined through self, peer, and instructor evaluations. To help them with the evaluation process, I designed, after a format suggested by compositionist Mary H. Beaven, a questionnaire for each of the students to fill out as they read the finished book (which I placed in the reserve section of our library). This questionnaire asked the students to write a narrative of their writing process, explain the effort they put into the project, ask questions about the writing of the book, read the book for its strengths and weaknesses (I told them that any weaknesses that they named would not be considered in my grading of the book), and determine a grade based on this writing. I took these questionnaires into account as I assigned the grade. In fact, I agreed with the grade the majority of the students assigned—an A. If I hadn't agreed, we would have had to discuss the reasons for the disparity and come to a resolution of the problem in class. This, however, did not occur. In fact, the book was so powerful that it influenced students outside of our classroom. In her evaluation, Kelly reported: "I was just walking away from the 'Reserve' desk in the library after handing back the class book. There were two girls behind the desk, neither one of whom is in our class. The one girl turned to the other one and said, 'You should read this. This is so good.' Now I'm even more convinced that this book deserves an A."

For the second "paper" of the semester, I asked students to design, with my help, projects for groups of whatever size they preferred. Although the class chose not to do another whole-class book,[4] they decided to work in groups to produce projects ranging from critical essays (critical analyses of characters in August Wilson's *Fences* to the view of culture that Alice Walker presents in interviews) to creative pieces (a postmodern "scrapbook" of documents, including credit cards, medical records, airline tickets, phone bills, personal and business letters, diaries, etc.) that "tell" a story about an incident in the life of a "typical" American family, to video projects on the "rhythm" of contemporary society—all for shared grades. They chose, in other words, their own "collectivist-like groups."

The term "collectivist-like groups" has to rank among the most awkward ever uttered, but I use it on purpose and in light of the fact that I haven't found a better one. I want to call attention to the fact that American educators cannot establish "collectives" in their classrooms—at least not as we traditionally understand the word (so when I use the terms "collective" or "collectivist" to describe my teaching, it is with the understanding that I'm not using them in their conventional sense). Without a direct connection between the economic and political goals of a classroom collective—or any collective—and society as a whole, the groups we establish in our classes are more like examples of what L. P. Bueva calls "illusory collectivism" (1981, 120), groups whose collectivist impulses are contradicted by ideological and economic objectives of society as a whole. But I contend that this reservation doesn't mean that my pedagogy is less politically significant or authentic than if I were teaching in a socialist society. It means, instead, that the political struggle that my teaching shares in is different from one that might occur in a socialist country.

I have much to learn about this political struggle and the ways that students negotiate the experience of this course into their lives. For instance, one student, Meg, spoke of the class in terms that Bueva would call "corporate groupism" (120): "I think the whole class book project was a good experience because it was very similar to working in the real business world in a larger company where everyone has to come together to make decisions for the good of the whole." Clearly, Meg has interpreted my collectivist pedagogy as a collaborative one. Either she has decided, consciously or not, to ignore the potentially volatile politics of communal work, much, it seems to me, as purveyors of collaborative learning such as Kenneth Bruffee do, or else she has decided to interpret communal work as another "skill" which English courses teach so that students such as herself will be "successful" in the academy and in the business world. It is, of course, her right to interpret this course as she chooses. It is my responsibility to learn from her, talk with her, question her interpretation, and not use my power to silence her.

And I have had other disappointments. My students sometimes spoke of new conflicts developing in the classroom. For instance, although I often talked to the groups to see that everyone worked to the best of their ability, my students occasionally spoke of their fear that a few others in the class might be lazy and take advantage of their hard work. Who can blame them for their anxiety? They have been taught throughout their lives that powerful dogs eat less powerful dogs, that getting ahead means "taking advantage of." What's more, who can blame a student who might in fact try to put one over on me and the good will of classmates? True, I would consider any such student ruthless, but this society calls for such "rugged individualism," even demands it. Students need to learn how to act in the best interests of each other and that doing so is acting in the best interest of the self. They need to learn how to be a member of a collective. And any teacher attempting to teach this to students will have to learn to live with the fact that not everyone can learn this lesson in fifteen weeks.

But perhaps most disheartening of all was the fact that the project could lead a student such as Melissa to a new pessimism about American society: "The idea of working collectively for a shared reward will work with students—though maybe not all the time—but I'm not sure it would work with adults in our society. There's too much competition established now to ever move away from it." If Melissa is correct, there is little reason for either of us to hope, and many reasons for all of us to fear.

For Three Days and Three Nights

It is the evening of the final exam. The students come into the room and move the desks into a circle. They seem excited, expecting, it seems to me, to do something important during the next two hours. They also seem anxious to get the exam started, looking forward to reading each other's journals and hearing what they will say during the discussion. They are, perhaps, responding to my anticipation, and even, yes, to the fact that another academic year is drawing to a close.

As a way of exchanging notebooks quickly and orderly, I ask the students to pass their journals to the left three times. They do so and begin reading.

They have written about violence and greed in contemporary society in Lorenzo Thomas's "MMDCCXIII1/2"; the sorrows of contemporary sexuality in Faye Kicknosway's "Rapunzel"; the value of friendship in the face of societal racism and agism in Elaine Jackson's *Paper Dolls;* and the problems of alcohol and suicide in P. J. Gibson's *Brown Silk and Magenta Sunsets.* They have also written about classism and communication failure in August Wilson's *Fences,* as well as the prejudices they themselves exhibited in the interpretations they made for the exam.[5]

During the conversation that follows this reading and responding segment of the exam, they talk about how the woman, Sharon, in Frank Polite's poem "Empty at the Heart of Things" needs contact with her friend Sandy because fulfilling her roles as wife and mother hasn't satisfied her. They discuss racism, oppression, and contradictions in the actions of the main character in Tom Robbins's "The Chink and the Clock People," a story about the travels of a Japanese American character known as the "Chink," who experiences the internment of Japanese Americans in World War II, and the secret life of a mountain tribe of Native Americans, the Clock People. They also talk about contradictions in their own lives and where and how they look for consolation in the face of world problems. They talk about history, hope, and the future.

Nancy says, "I related the story 'The Chink and the Clock People' to one of the poems we read, Judy Grahn's 'The Meanings in the Pattern.' I thought about my history classes. I don't remember ever really learning the history of the Native Americans. In the poem, the Native American woman who is selling the decorated purse is asked where her people are, and she says, 'We have always been here,' which means that nobody has cared about her and her people and all of a sudden a tourist is going to ask her about her history. I just think we're really selective in our history. Americans are always the first people to say something about the Communists, but we and our government never want to admit that we do anything wrong."

"When I first started to read 'The Chink and the Clock People,' " John admits, "I felt guilty. I've never thought about what our government did to Asian Americans in World War II. It has to do with our government not telling us about what it has done to our own people. Unless we go find out for ourselves, we will never know."

Steven offers a summary statement: "Any hope we have, then, is an abstract hope. Everyone needs to know that society is broken if we are going to fix it."

"But we do have to be patient as we try to turn it all around," Bill adds. "I'm thinking about 'The Meanings in the Pattern,' too. The lady tells the tourist that there is a story in the decoration that her son has put on the purse, but it will take three days and three nights to tell it. Change isn't easy to accomplish. It's going to be pretty hard. And it's going to take a long time to make a lot of change—but we'll eventually get there—somehow."

"But we're not all willing to make the kind of commitment it takes," I suggest, "to listen for three days and three nights, are we?"

"No, that's what's taking us so long," Bill responds.

Mary says, "These poems and stories don't come right out and say that there is hope for the future. I think that the only hope we have will have to come from ourselves. These poems have made us think. We only have real hope if we now care enough to hope and work for change."

This discussion goes on for close to an hour. At the end of it, I ask the students to write their concluding remarks and hand in their journals.

As I leave the room, carrying their journals in a large box, I feel exhilarated and exhausted. These students had taken on hard issues. They had challenged themselves to go out and make a better world. All I have to do now, I thought, is go to my office, read the finals, finish their averages, fill out my grade sheets, hand them in, and go home, and think about all that we have accomplished.

I was wrong. The fact of the matter is that I felt bad, really bad, all night and for days later (and it's time we teachers started to talk about how grading makes us feel. We need to talk honestly about teaching if we are going to know what is wrong with educational practice and policy—if we are ever going to fix it). Not all of my students ended up receiving the same grade for the course. Some of the small groups received grades of B or C for their second papers. What's more, some of my students had turned in incomplete notebooks. So I ended up with a grade curve after all, even if it was a top-heavy one.

I began to wonder what I could have done, should have done, didn't do. I felt the hopelessness of teaching in an institution that, at the least, does not allow me to have an attendance policy (so that I use such things as the "completeness" of journals as a way of assuring that those students who would take unfair advantage of the collective by only showing up on days when papers are due or the day when the exam is taken won't be successful) and that, at the most, serves our country's economic and political interests. I asked myself if my teaching can really change anything local, let alone anything national. I had, after all, reached the end of another semester and Indiana University of Pennsylvania, Pittsburgh, and America were all essentially the same. And I had once again filled out computerized grade sheets in which I sorted my students for the purposes of others who will go on sorting my students for the purposes of still others.

I began, in the funk I was in, to question the whole experience of English III. In a letter to a friend I wrote:

> Dear Shannon:
>
> My undergrad intro to lit students designed their own exam for last night—a series of journal writings and discussion that they submitted for a collective grade (an A-). At the end of it I asked them—what now? You've read the racism, sexism, classism, homophobism and agism of the world that contemporary literature reflects—you've tried to do something different here—what now? Their answers ranged from familiar, easy, youthful optimism about changing their lives and the world to utter depression and exhaustion (which made me wonder if I am dragging them down with me) to realistic responses like "I don't know" or "I still need hope" even "I'll do what I can—but I can't do much" to "I'm not sure—but I feel changed." (Is that what I'm really after? For them to feel or be changed? Is that enough? Are my, gulp, educational objectives "sound" and "clear"? Will helping them to feel changed really change anything in America?)
>
> Mark

I had worked myself into a state where I could no longer see a simple fact: that teaching can be—often is—an exploratory activity. It will bring sleepless nights because very little in a classroom is—or should be—certain. Now I know that I'm not the only teacher who has suffered sleepless nights! It's just that in dark times teaching can feel like a useless, if not damaging, activity. What saves me and other teachers I know—maybe all teachers—is the realization that we're not alone.

When I told my English III students that my teaching is based on my reading of Soviet theorists,[6] Michael, an art major, wrote to me: "I kind of had an idea that this theory was related in some way to a bigger political or philosophical idea. I'm not real politically minded, but it's too bad governments and countries can't work as our class did. I wish all my classes were like this. I think we would learn a lot more. I also think I learned that people are inherently good people who want to help others, but our society, because it is a society based on competition, doesn't encourage this way of dealing with others. I think this class is a great example that it could work because we are all so different, yet we work together so well."

In her notebook, Cheryl compared the book project to the smaller group projects, where groups earned individual grades:

> Even though I learned within my group (2nd project) I'm not sure about the competition aspect within the rest of the class.
>
> The book seemed to create a more open, willing to work attitude. Maybe it was for a common goal (the grade). Does that eliminate competition? Maybe I agree with the Soviet educators. I've always felt people attain more when working cooperatively but didn't believe it would work in our society. That's probably cynical of me. But now I see that we all did work well together—there seemed to be more helpful criticism.
>
> What I will take with me from the class book project is the knowledge that group cooperation can work for everyone, and I think it can be carried even further than just education. Maybe these principles can be manifested in economics, politics, etc. on a world wide level—which is where I think we need to be headed anyway (the global community idea).

Cheryl reminds me why teaching for democracy is meaningful. And there are other reasons. We always run the risk of losing students such as Martin, an intelligent student whom I might never have reached had I taught differently. As he wrote in his evaluation of the class book: "In the beginning of the semester, when I was told to read something I would just skim over it, without paying attention to it. I would often find myself in class not knowing where the hell everyone was coming from. To tell the truth, I found myself losing total interest in this course. And then something happened, I started to understand. The group working together brought this about, and I feel that if we never worked as a group I would have never gotten interested in this course whatsoever."

Perhaps another student, however, went through the greatest change of all. He wrote, "I used to be really prejudiced towards some races. Now I feel I'm evolving out of that stereotypical shell, and I'm glad. After this class and our projects we did together, I'm definitely a more open minded person. Not that this class did all of that. But it helped." Having talked to this student in and out of class, having read his work for an entire semester, I can honestly say that he is engaged at the deepest level in what Laclau and Mouffe call "political struggle." The social relations he lives are being transformed. He is learning that he has oppressed others by living in a way that subordinates them, by living a way of life that has also subordinated him to his own prejudices. He is learning, literally, to be someone new.

This Critical Situation

One of my students, Peter, wrote a friendly, though pointed, jibe to me in his evaluation of the class book project: "As for your use of Soviet teaching methods, I hope your future classes will hold together better than East Germany."

If we are to believe the news media, there is only one choice for Eastern Europeans. They can choose capitalist democracy, free-market prosperity, and VCRs, or they can remain oppressed by communist totalitarianism, closed-market austerity, and long bread lines. This simplistic interpretation of a complex social, political and economic situation has caused the American public to see no farther than a very simple and erroneous "truth": the fall of communism means the rise of democracy. This is the line we are exporting to Eastern Europe, and we are led to believe that the Eastern Europeans—even the Soviets—are buying it. We didn't hear much on network news about those at the 1990 Communist Party Congress meetings in Moscow who praised Mikhail Gorbachev's reforms because they are correcting the ills of Stalinism and are leading to democratic socialism. We did hear about it when reformers resigned from the Communist Party, but we didn't hear that most of them are forming new democratic-socialist, not republican-capitalist, parties. Peter's joke, then, is completely understandable, even predictable. I certainly can't criticize him, but I can hope that students like him will begin to wonder why change isn't flowing in both directions through the Berlin Wall. I can hope that something in my teaching and his thinking will lead him to ask, "When is radical reform going to happen here?"

It needs to happen here badly. America's economic and political system is built on the seventeenth-century principle that individuals are truly individual when they are free to possess private property. When people own property, the theory goes, they are free to enter into competitive market relations where they choose. But changes in the nature of how capital is produced in late-capitalist, corporate America have created an economic and political system where market relations are anything but free. Most Americans are controlled by capital relations about which they have no knowledge and in which they have no power. The social contract under which we live and teach and learn is, in a very real sense, null and void.

One response to this situation is to say, "What's the use of teaching students to read if all we are doing is teaching them to be living anachronisms, able to serve ends they don't understand, creating information and capital for a few others and no significant social change for themselves and most others?" Such cynicism may be understandable, but it isn't acceptable. In fact, this country's economic and political system has never supplied us with our uniqueness as individuals or with our personal creativity and integrity. It has merely promised that if we are industrious, we will be free and happy. What we've certainly never been told is that the loss of the possessing selves we've been pledged is a blessing. If we allow the operations of late capitalism and its attendant republicanism to shape the people we are, we miss the opportunity to form social relationships that are something other than self-interested and competitive. We perpetuate an existence where we can't become unique and creative in and through our relations with others—a situation in which we can't become truly free.

We are, then, living in what Soviet psychologist Fyodor Vasilyuk calls a "critical situation." Vasilyuk claims that while we experience everything from a mundane problem to world conflict (and he would say that either is a critical situation), experience is itself "creative" because it restores the "psychological possibility" for action (1988, 195). Living in a critical situation can lead us to the realization that something can be done, that our needs for a better life, society, and world can be met. We can, in other words, decide to initiate creative and practical action. In doing so, Vasilyuk explains, we automatically begin constructing "a new self" to live in the new circumstances we imagine (164). Experience leads us, in other words, to produce a future, rather than to reproduce the past or consume the present. We needn't be who we were and do again what we've already done.

In a country where most of our fellow citizens don't have the same opportunity to be free and possessing as we do, where people of color and women are doubly disenfranchised, English educators can do the important work of teaching students in introductory literature classes to discover how the interpretations they make respond to critical situations. In this way, students can begin to imagine, act for, and even become a more radically democratic America.

True, it is sometimes difficult to imagine the role of collectivism in any America of the future. As the horrors of Stalinism continue to come to light, it is easy to see the collective failures of the Soviet Communist Party. Still, I am always struck by the hope that many Soviet theorists of the last twenty years express when they write about collectivism and personality. They openly admit that their theories are "scientific," that is, are still posing unanswered questions. Yet, in the midst of the political failures their country has endured, they write about the possibility of creating new kinds of collective interaction, new personalities, and a new, more open society (the spirit of perestroika and glasnost are not new)—possibilities that many Americans have forgotten and all Americans need. The Soviet theorists of which I speak also constantly affirm the value and meaning of social activity. Basing their theories on Marx's principle that production is superior—more meaningful as a human activity—to consumption, the Soviet teacher-theorists who have the most to say to their American counterparts stress that choice, self- and social determination, and collectivist social relations and activity are the keystones of creation. As a whole, Americans certainly aren't close to accepting the collectivist impulse, but we are justified in asking why we aren't, especially when so many Americans are oppressed by capitalist ideology and practice.

As I said earlier, I see no reason to give up all hope for a democratic America as long as I'm not alone. For me, experiencing the fact that I'm not alone renews the "psychological possibility" for action. And we aren't alone. We have our students and our colleagues—the ones who think as we do or who are, at least, willing to talk to us if they don't. The tenure-tracked among us often have technologies available to us—the telephone, computer networks, local and national conferences, and, of course, the mail—which allow us to keep in touch with those who share our social and political agendas (we also have the means to assure that the nontenured also have access to the same media). What's more, professional publications such as this book offer us the chance to see how and if our teaching is part of a larger movement toward cultural change.

No, we aren't alone. The experiences that many people are having, both in and out of classrooms, are telling them that they must work to crack the invisible walls separating the economically impoverished people of, say, Pittsburgh's Hill District (pick any city, I choose my own) from the upwardly mobile people of the corporate headquarters of Pittsburgh's "Golden Triangle." Together, we can write on these walls and make them visible. And maybe the collective pressure of what we say will knock them down.

Notes

1. Throughout this article I take quotations from my class notes and audiotapes and from student journals and papers. I do so with my students' permission. I have edited where necessary.

2. I assign readings in contemporary literature—and I'm thinking of works such as Elaine Jackson's *Paper Dolls*—because it powerfully dramatizes for students how cultural conceptions of gender, aging, and race affect contemporary social relations. I have also found that because contemporary writers experiment in representing our world, students feel invited to do the same. And when students discover how to allow the spirit of improvisation to infuse their reading and writing for classroom purposes, they create contexts for imagining a better world, a first step, perhaps, toward making one. A colleague recently suggested that, in keeping with the collective and improvisational nature of my course, I ought to have students select at least some, if not all, of the literature for the class. I agree.

3. When, even after much discussion, the students were unable to make headway with a text, I sometimes had to step in and reframe the discussion by asking a question such as, "Where have your confusions taken us?" or "What can we learn from the various statements we have made?"

4. Paulo Freire explains how time spent in genuine dialogue is never wasted time (1985, 122–23), but the fact remains that dialogue and collectivist activity do take time—lots of time. I fear that the compressed and structured time demanded of students by university requirements and scheduling and, in many cases, by their need to have jobs as they attend college forces them to look for short-cuts. In her evaluation of the class book project, Christy wrote: "I liked doing the book, but there were a few drawbacks. The biggest factor is time. Of course it's going to take a lot of time for 47 students to write a book. The end result was excellent but maybe we could have worked around the time factor." I don't know how to work around the "time factor." I truly wish I did.

5. I particularly remember Kelly's response to Frank Polite's "Empty at the Heart of Things," a poem containing a "letter found Easter Sunday morning, Youngstown, Ohio, 1979": "The poem is written by a man so I naturally thought 'the letter' was written by a man—until I got to the end of it and saw the name 'Sharon.' While reading it (and thinking a man is writing it) I thought the man was gay—then when he talked of children I was confused. (It's very interesting how my perception of men and women—and what the author is—influences how I interpret what I read)."

6. I've built my pedagogy on the work of well-known Soviet theorists, such as M. M. Bakhtin, A. R. Luria, V. N. Vološinov, and L. S. Vygotsky, and on the writing of theorists who are cited less often, but who have also significantly affected my teaching: L. P. Bueva, A. Kuz'min, K. Levitin, L. Novikova and A. Lewin, A. V. Petrovsky, Yu. V. Sychev, and F. Vasilyuk.

11 Feminist Theory, Literary Canons, and the Construction of Textual Meanings

Barbara Frey Waxman
University of North Carolina at Wilmington

I am stirred by educational theorist Henry A. Giroux's notion that American education takes place within a wider social community and that, as a politicizing and socializing process, it should be linked to wider social movements whose aims are to enhance human life. Linked, in particular, to the civil rights movement and the women's movement, American education can prepare students to participate in a democracy and work for "social justice, empowerment and social reform" (1988, 73). I am also inspired by Giroux's idea that teachers are "transformative intellectuals" who name oppression and struggle against it in their society by using a "critical pedagogy." This pedagogy's aim is not merely the reproduction of knowledge and of the dominant culture, but the production of new knowledge, training students through classroom experience to think critically and to learn about our basic social institutions in order to interrogate and transform them (90). As a teacher, I begin with the assumption that I should train students to be discontented with a culture that tolerates and perpetuates oppression.

To implement such training requires that we rethink our traditional conception of authority in the classroom. If we create in our classrooms what Giroux calls an "emancipatory authority," one that is committed to social empowerment and ethics (73–74), then we will see ourselves not just as technocrats who distribute knowledge and values, but also as morally concerned teachers who conceptualize and raise questions about our curricula and the methods that enable students to develop both humanity and sociopolitical savoir faire. Feminist theory and feminist literary criticism can help the English teacher to serve as an emancipatory authority in the introductory literature classroom.

Feminist Theory Meets the Literary Canon

Elizabeth Meese aptly describes the agenda of feminist literary criticism: "The principle task of feminist literary criticism, in providing a necessary re-vision of the politics of 'truth,' is to make its own ideology explicit. If we seek to transform the structures of authority, we must first name them, and in doing so, unmask and expose them for all to see" (1986, 16). Thus, a feminist in the literature classroom must first make her students aware of the academic powers that determine curricula and that choose the texts which are to be taught. Then, explaining her political agenda of empowering women, she should show her students how to interrogate the authority of those who determine curricula, how to redefine the relationship between students and teacher, how to read from a gendered perspective, and how to resist, if appropriate, the authority and embedded values of texts.

As practitioners of critical pedagogy, feminist literature teachers also fight against reproducing the hegemonic values of patriarchal society, a fight which Meese urges: "Phallocentrism [male-centeredness], like any system, is driven by the desire to perpetuate itself . . . The transformation of literature and criticism as cultural institutions demands a language of defiance rather than the silent or unquestioning mimetic complicity. . . If it is any good, feminist criticism . . . is guaranteed to offend the mighty" (17). This defiant stance is similar to one Ronald Strickland argues for: an "oppositional [or confrontational] pedagogy," one which challenges students, views the subject matter with skepticism, exposes canonical knowledge's role in reproducing the dominant ideology, and empowers students to resist an educational system that serves patriarchy and other entrenched powers (1990, 291). A major way to view literary subject matter with skepticism is to read it for the gender issues embedded in it. As Myra Jehlen explains, "Because an ideology of gender is basic to all thought while, by most thinkers, unrecognized as such, gender criticism often has a confrontational edge. One has to read for gender; unless it figures explicitly in story or poem, it will seldom read for itself" (1990a, 273). Reading a "sacred" text for gender means questioning its underlying assumptions about differences between men and women that usually posit women as inferior; the aim is to "offend the mighty" patriarchy whose values inform these texts.

Confronting, resisting, interrogating, re-visioning: this is the vocabulary of the feminist theorist. Jehlen's definition of feminist thinking is apt: "Feminist thinking is really rethinking, an examination of the way certain assumptions about women and the female character enter into fundamental assumptions that organize all our thinking . . . Such radical skepticism is an ideal intellectual stance that can generate genuinely new understandings" (69). Like Meese and Strickland, Jehlen encourages the teacher to examine with her students the structures of academic (literary) authority and the "institutional assumptions and conceptual frames" that underlie knowledge (of literature), so that students can self-consciously make knowledge their own possession (Strickland 1990, 294) without being cowed by the authoritative packaging of most knowledge.

For example, to model a reconsideration of what the subject matter of the literature class should be, a feminist teacher would explain how a syllabus for a survey of British literature or an introduction to literature course is constructed, show the institutional and personal politics behind the literary canon that prompts teachers to select texts in order to propagate "the best that [has been] known and thought" (Arnold 1986 [1865], 1422), and question whose values and politics determine what is "best." Feminists are skeptical of the objectivity and universality of the literary canon, exposing what Judith Fetterley calls its "posture of the apolitical, the pretense that literature speaks universal truths through forms from which all the merely personal, the purely subjective, has been burned away" (1978, xi). As Kenneth Burke reminds us, "whenever you find a doctrine of 'nonpolitical' aesthetics affirmed with fervor, look for its politics" (1969, 28). Feminists sound the clarion of gender politics in canon formation, demonstrating that male norms usually pass for transcendent ones and exposing the "contingencies of gender at the heart of even the most apparently universal writing" (Jehlen 1990a, 265). A student thus learns that the literary canon, for all its claims of being the repository of eternal human verities, is, as Terry Eagleton says, "a construct, fashioned by particular people for particular reasons at a certain time" (1983, 11). This means that individuals who find the means and the power can change the canon.

Reading for Gender and Resisting the Text

In addition to problematizing the construction of a literary canon and a syllabus, the feminist theorist regards texts in new ways. Believing that gender influences and complicates all of our social relationships, the feminist theorist assumes that gender colors all written communication. Reading a text for its sexual politics does not reduce the reading to the particular or oversimplify it—as antagonists of feminist criticism often claim—but rather enriches the reading because we now see in the text the "permanent complexity of engagements and interactions" (Jehlen 1990a, 265).

As Elaine Showalter has remarked, modern criticism, not just feminist criticism, can observe the operation of gender politics in all reading and writing (1987, 42). But a feminist literary critic and teacher can teach a student to read like a woman, that is, "with all the skeptical purity of an outcast from culture" (Auerbach 1987, 156). Because a feminist's ideology "is inseparable from the lived knowledge of subordination" (151), this ideology influences her reading too. A feminist reader might note with anger the relegation of a female character to a domestic role that sacrifices her intellectual and creative abilities; the reader's anger might prompt her to challenge the authority of the text and its underlying assumption that such subordination is acceptable. A feminist teacher/critic would similarly enable the student to become aware of the assumptions embedded in the text and shared by many male critics, and thus to become what Fetterley calls "a resisting rather than an assenting reader and, by refusal to assent, to begin the process of exorcizing the male mind that has been implanted in us" (1978, xxii). Both the authority of the text, the values it advocates, and the (male) critic who constructs one meaning of the text will be questioned by the feminist reader/teacher/student.

In an introductory literature class, then, what is to be learned (the literary canon, syllabus construction, and text selection) and how it is to be learned (the teacher's emancipatory authority in reading a text) can be aided by feminist theory and criticism. Let me first demonstrate how I apply feminist theory to the issues of the literary canon and syllabus construction at the beginning of every semester of my survey course, and then how we read texts in light of this in my introduction to literature course.

Feminist Pedagogy: The Canon and the Syllabus

When I hand out my syllabus in my "Survey of British Literature Since 1800" course, I hold one up along with my copy of *The Norton Anthology of English Literature* and exorcise the sacredness of both, calling them "artificial constructs" and positing that I did not have to select the authors and texts that I did. I ask students to consider why I left out William Blake and D. H. Lawrence but included Christina Rossetti and Virginia Woolf in our curriculum. Acknowledging that my view of British literary history has evolved over fourteen years of teaching the course, I argue that literary history is itself subjectively conceived. We discuss the politics behind my construction of British literary history and my curriculum: my academic politics as a feminist vis-à-vis the literary/academic establishment; the processes and forces by which literary canons are fashioned; the politics of the publishing business and the unavailability of certain texts for the classroom, forcing selection of more traditional texts. I expose the thought process I went through to put one Wordsworth poem in the syllabus but to omit another, giving two or three other examples of decision making. By these means, I demystify the authority of the literary canon and of the curriculum that obeys that canon, as well as the authority of the teacher as all-knowing purveyor of important knowledge.

My feminist British survey curriculum differs both in texts and topics from the standard curriculum by which many of us were educated in the 1960s. It includes more works by women, "noncanonical works" such as Christina Rossetti's "Goblin Market," Mary Shelley's *Frankenstein*, and Virginia Woolf's *A Room of One's Own*. Such works often directly treat gender issues and raise students' consciousness about them, after which students can search out the gender issues embedded in more overtly "universal" texts. Take "Goblin Market," for example. By including it in the course, I can address Rossetti's role as artist and her peripheral position in the Pre-Raphaelite Brotherhood, challenging the phallocentrism of British literary history. I can also discuss the concept of intertextuality, that is, how earlier texts influence the production of later texts, which raises the important issue of the anxiety of (male) influence on a (female) writer. And I can interrogate the notion that literature by Victorian men captures the "universal Victorian experience": the Victorians' double sexual standard ensured major differences between women's and men's sexual experiences and gender roles, yet women are absent from poems like "Ulysses" and "Childe Roland to the Dark Tower Came." "Goblin Market" depicts the young Victorian woman's typical social role and sexual identity, providing an instructive contrast to the depictions of men's roles in traditionally taught poems. Thus Rossetti's presence in a syllabus is an important lesson in reinterpreting and complicating literary history.

In fact, this syllabus "tampering," which can be done in all introductory literature courses as readily as in the survey, extends discussion of the disruptive ideas introduced in the first class: literary history is not cast in stone, so readers must continually reassess and reinterpret it; and curricular designs come and go, subject to the values of the social and political forces in ascendance. But beyond syllabus tampering, when a teacher re-visions the relationship between reader and text and models a feminist reading of even the most conventional or conservative text, she may also begin a cultural revolution. Let us see how small cultural revolutions can take place in an introductory literature class that is reading both "Dreams," by Nikki Giovanni, and "the Cambridge ladies who live in furnished souls," by e. e. cummings.

Feminist Pedagogy: Reading Two Poems

As feminists know, the values of literature depend on which texts are selected and how they are being read. This is why I might begin a discussion of poetry, in our introduction to literature class, with a poem by an African American writer like Giovanni. Giovanni's poem "Revolutionary Dreams" directly addresses gender, race, and socio-political revolution in America:

> i used to dream militant
> dreams of taking
> over america to show
> these white folks how it should be
> done
> i used to dream radical dreams
> of blowing everyone away with my perceptive powers
> of correct analysis
> i even used to think i'd be the one
> to stop the riot and negotiate the peace
> then i awoke and dug
> that if i dreamed natural
> dreams of being a natural
> woman doing what a woman
> does when she's natural
> i would have a revolution†

I begin with the question, "what is a natural woman as opposed to an artificial woman, and what factors do you think can make a woman artificial?" I also ask the students why the speaker needed to have the "artificial" superwoman-fantasy dreams described in the poem, attempting to unpack some cultural assumptions about limits on women's intelligence, perceptivity, and political power. I then discuss the anger of African Americans toward white Americans and the place of militancy and riot in American race relations. The poem needs to be historicized, placed amid the sexual and racial upheaval in the America of the 1960s and 1970s. Jehlen's observation that focusing on gender in any text also uncovers issues of race and class applies to Giovanni's poem: "It is logically impossible to interrogate gender—to transform it from axiom to object of scrutiny and critical term—without also

---

† "Revolutionary Dreams" from *The Women and the Men* copyright © 1970, 1974, 1975, by Nikki Giovanni. Used by permission of William Morrow and Company, Inc.

interrogating race and class . . . to produce a newly encompassing account of cultural consciousness" (1990a, 272).

Then I ask students to explain the revelation of the speaker: What makes dreaming of being a natural woman a truly revolutionary act? If students are floundering, I ask, "What kind of revolution is the speaker envisioning here, an external or internal one?" Students should observe the speaker's growing self-pride and appreciate the necessity of having personal pride in order to foment a sexual revolution after this last question. I might bring in here the feminist shibboleth, "the personal is political," pointing out how the adjectives linked to the dream move from public, political terms like "militant" and "radical" to the more personal word, "natural."

I also ask students to consider how Giovanni's unconventional uses (or "anti-uses") of punctuation and capitalization further her poem's message of revolution. Clearly, when a reader searches out gender issues in a text, many other economic, racial, and aesthetic issues also surface; as Jehlen notes, gendered literary criticism raises not only male-female issues in a text, but also "[other] thematic and formal concerns" (1990a, 270).

Finally, I can be a resisting reader/teacher by questioning even Giovanni's feminist stance, by asking students if any woman could ever really be a natural woman; that is, can any woman move beyond the influences of her culture? This question raises the central feminist issue of nurture/culture versus nature/biology, a good occasion to consider Simone de Beauvoir's famous claim that "one is not born but rather becomes a woman" (quoted in Meese 1986, 75). After this gendered discussion of Giovanni's poem, students have become more aware of the ways in which their culture manipulates their sexual identities, both female and male. Many will begin to criticize the cultural institutions that manipulate them.

After this consciousness-raising experience with Giovanni's poem, students may elicit resistance to cummings's poem, especially after a second reading. When I taught this poem years ago (in my prefeminist days), I was attuned to the speaker's disdain for and satire of the small-mindedness, conventionality, superficiality, and self-complacent charitableness of the ladies he describes:

> the Cambridge ladies who live in furnished souls
> are unbeautiful and have comfortable minds
> (also,with the church's protestant blessings
> daughters,unscented shapeless spirited)
> they believe in Christ and Longfellow,both dead,
> are invariably interested in so many things—

at the present writing one still finds
delighted fingers knitting for the is it Poles?
perhaps. While permanent faces coyly bandy
scandal of Mrs. N and Professor D
. . . . the Cambridge ladies do not care,above
Cambridge if sometimes in its box of
sky lavender and cornerless,the
moon rattles like a fragment of angry candy‡

I began by asking students what it means to have furnished souls, permanent faces, and comfortable minds, usually eliciting comments about the ladies' self-satisfaction, insularity, rigidity, received values, and indifference to probing into the foundations of their religious, political, and aesthetic beliefs. We discussed the speaker's negative attitude toward these ladies, as displayed in the statement that the ladies "are unbeautiful," and in the insults he directs toward their daughters, too, as he predicts their colorless, spiritless imitation of their mothers. We noted the speaker's snide depiction of the ladies' ignorance of the international political crisis they were knitting for by inserting the phrase "is it Poles? perhaps," suggesting that their gossip about the latest local affair preempts their attention to foreign affairs. Finally, we discussed how the speaker, in the unusual imagery of the final lines, captures the ladies' miniaturizing or trivializing of the moon by imaginatively boxing it up like candy. The moon's anger at such trivializing is a projection of the speaker's anger at the ladies' triviality.

But if we read this poem as feminists and as resisting readers, aware through Giovanni's poem of the constraints that our culture imposes on women, we increase the complexity of the poem's imagery and problematize the speaker's attitude of condemnation. We use what Dale Bauer has called a "dialogic" pedagogical strategy, pitting "one kind of mastery, feminist and dialogic in practice, against another, monologic and authoritarian [cummings's speaker]" (1990, 387). Like Nina Auerbach, I enjoy confronting texts by men, and through literary criticism, taking patriarchy's attitudes and values to task. Auerbach asserts that reading and writing about a patriarchal text is her "way of claiming power over it . . . I share the primitive superstition that by writing about the patriarchy, as by eating it, I engorge its power . . . reading is a similar engorgement and appropriation . . . If we make men our property in this way, we can absorb the patriarchy before it embraces and abandons . . . us into invisibility'' (1987, 158). And so, I engorge the power of cummings to condemn these ladies by questioning how it is that they became so narrow, that they gave up the intellectual development, flexibility, and creative energies of ''natural women.'' What doors closed on them in their lives? I now ask students to consider the opportunities that might be open to the Cambridge gentlemen—Harvard? The professions? The corporate club?—and contrast these with the ladies' option: simply to become, at least in 1923 when the poem was written, the marginalized spouses of such gentlemen. Since these ladies' intellectual and creative potential of contributing to society was ignored, their invisibility enforced by patriarchy, it is not surprising that their world became one of gossip over a sex scandal between a professor and a married woman (how else could a professor relate to a woman anyway, except as sex object). I draw out my students' identification with these oppressed women. Moreover, as the speaker suggests, the daughters of these ladies will reproduce their mothers' conformist fates. However, instead of just condemning these ladies' mothering, as cummings's speaker does, I enable students to see this maternal reproduction also as a tragic entrapment, one that stems from the cultural institution of motherhood as negatively conceptualized by patriarchy. I refer here briefly to feminist sociologist Nancy Chodorow's ideas in *The Reproduction of Mothering* (1978).

Thus students move from interpretation of the poem, what Robert Scholes calls the ''positive mode, the mode of listening and obedience,'' into criticism of the text, ''the negative mode of suspicion and rigor'' (1985, 48). This critical mode may elicit some questioning of cummings's speaker and his values, some resistance to reproducing these values in the students' society.

By reading the poem resistingly and by reading it for gender, we develop a more complex view of these ladies' souls, of their relationships with men, and of the society that shaped both their relationships and their sexual identities. By using defiant language in speaking against the poem, as a critic, teacher, and role model, I state and further my aim of transforming ''literature and criticism [and education] as cultural institutions'' (Meese 1986, 17). Since I do not lecture like a patriarchal master to my students about *the* feminist reading of a text, but diminish my authority by collaborating with students, throwing out questions as I puzzle over the text with them, trying out various interpretations, incorporating students' points, in essence thinking out loud and enabling students to do so too as we negotiate meanings together, the students learn to read like feminists. This collaborative and often dialogic pedagogy reinforces my feminist ideology and extends it because, as feminist theorist Paula Treichler argues, "collaboration within the classroom . . . encourages recognition and negotiation of competing vocabularies as well as continued collaborative work" (1986, 97). The political atmosphere of the classroom thus encourages questioning the authority of the teacher and the text, as well as the authority of any one critic's reading, by eliciting a multiplicity of voices and listening to these voices.

Let us take Christina Rossetti's "Goblin Market" as another example. The ways we read Rossetti's poem reflect different political stances. We can read the poem as the original Victorian audience might have done, as an admonitory moral fable for young girls to stay home, away from the dangers of the glen, not acknowledging the sexual behavior that the sisters Laura and Lizzie are being cautioned against since the Victorians would probably have been uncomfortable doing so. Or we can note the forbidden fruit theme of sexual appetite, the association of the demonic with the sexual, and of the sexual with the demonic male goblins. This approach may turn us into resisting readers, repelled by the poem's implication that men are animalistic in their sexuality, that heterosexuality is sinful, and that women should remain asexual. As suspicious readers, moreover, the class may interrogate the firmness of Rossetti's commitment to this moral stance, especially since, as Sandra Gilbert and Susan Gubar have suggested, she presents sexuality as so pleasurable that the only way not to yield is to leap from childhood innocence into mother love and friendships with other women, avoiding the heterosexual urges of adolescence (1979, 567). We can note both the language of desire in Rossetti's speaker—her sensual fruit imagery and erotic verbs for eating the fruit—and displacement of heterosexual feelings onto the physicality of the sisters' love. Then the students and I can extend Rossetti's sexual ambivalence into the realm ("the glen") of the imagination and her role as a woman writing (Gilbert and Gubar 1979, 570–74). Rossetti may have felt guilty for being a writer since the traditional Victorian woman would see it as sinfully self-indulgent and undutiful. Hence, the goblin men would represent the "seductions of the male muse" and Laura, the woman artist tempted by the "self-gratifications of art and sensuality," would have to learn the lesson of renunciation (571).

Feminists, then, can read this text from different perspectives, not necessarily agreeing with the author's point; while her message of sisterhood might please us, Rossetti's religion and her culture's expectations for women turn many students into resisting readers and also into feminist critics who appreciate the multivalence of Rossetti's text.

Conclusion

The feminist's gendered, resistant reading in the classroom thus joins with the feminist teacher's interrogation of literary history and the literary canon through reconceptualized syllabi to expand our students' cultural consciousness. In a feminist's literature classroom, where emancipatory authority prevails, teacher and students share power as they engage in dialogue over meanings and values embedded in texts and in life. This dialogue may even challenge the agenda of the feminist teacher (Bauer 1990, 388). Applying the concept of gender to texts elicits fresh questions about "personal identity and social ideology" that open up new levels of interpretation (Jehlen 1990a, 271).

Feminist pedagogy encourages students to practice new ways of reading and writing about texts, central goals of all education. It also sharpens the skills of questioning and critical thinking. Students learn to analyze the methods by which decisions are made in a democratic society, the "processes by which structures of society are produced and reproduced" (Giroux 1988, 91). These skills are essential for creating what Giroux calls a "critical citizenship," the guardians of our democratic institutions (79, 90).

In addition to honing these skills in students, feminist criticism and pedagogy develop students' moral sensitivity to oppression and their identification with the pain of Otherness. Identification, teaching students "how to identify," is a key concept and primary aim of the feminist teacher, to be placed beside that of resistance (Bauer 1990, 391–93). Kenneth Burke, in *A Rhetoric of Motives*, has explained that in order to persuade an individual to a different point of view, the savvy rhetorician must use the principle of identification; the teacher, in order to introduce ideas and ethics to her students, must do the same: "You persuade a man [or woman] only insofar as you can talk his [or her] language by speech, gesture, tonality, order, image, attitude, idea, identifying your ways with his [or hers]" (1969, 55); and "some of [a person's] opinions are needed to support the fulcrum by which [the teacher/rhetorician] would move other opinions" (56). A feminist teacher encourages identification by connecting texts to experiences of oppression, including those undergone by the teacher herself, and by enabling students to discuss the different varieties of oppression (racial, economic, and sexual) they have felt and witnessed. And identification as a pedagogical strategy in turn informs and strengthens feminist ideology. I rejoice in students' identification with the oppressed as a crucial step leading to resistance of oppressive authority and creation of empowering institutions.

Thus the feminist teacher's engagement with students and texts in the literature classroom becomes an experience of values clarification and the testing of ethical systems. Like Bauer, I take as my premise "the notion that the classroom is a place to explore resistances and identifications, a place also to explore the ambiguous and often ambivalent space of values and ethics" (1990, 387). Education cannot take place in an objective laboratory, a social or moral vacuum. As Burke points out, "any specialized activity participates in a larger unit of action" [is 'identified with' the larger unit] (1969, 27); the agent of this specialized activity—the literature teacher—must be cognizant of the wider sphere of her activity and the nature of her impact, or she may find herself in complicity with an enemy: "The shepherd, qua shepherd, acts for the good of the sheep, to protect them from discomfiture and harm. But he may be 'identified' with a project that is raising the sheep for market" (27).

Today's education should equip students with the knowledge that enhances democracy. Feminism in the introductory literature classroom fosters such an education. Can we afford not to adopt its aims and employ its methods?

12 Coyote Midwife in the Classroom: Introducing Literature with Feminist Dialogics

Patrick D. Murphy
Indiana University of Pennsylvania

Introduction to literature has been defined in catalogues and treated in practice as a course in the appreciation of literature, qua literature, with the implicit notion that literature, like fiber, is good for everyone. And students often conceptualize the course in this way.[1] But in the past two decades practitioners of feminist pedagogy and critical theory have been challenging universalized and aestheticized claims of disinterested judgment and intrinsic worth. Their writings and classroom innovations have placed increasing pressure on the introduction to literature course and its classroom as a site for immediate qualitative transformation. And many faculty with heavy teaching loads and excessive university service responsibilities are responding: "Yes, but I'm not a theorist." My response is twofold: one, that's okay—neither by the implied definition are most of the people teaching theory to graduate students; two, no one can afford not to theorize, because every teacher is already implementing someone's theory in accordance with some ideology. The college professor need not be a theory specialist, but she needs to become self-conscious about what she teaches in the introductory literature course both through her subject matter and her pedagogy. And such self-consciousness, I would wager, will invariably lead to transformations of both form and content in the classroom. There are many ways to go about this, short of taking a three-year sabbatical to catch up on one's reading. Like a basic software package, the method I want to outline here, "coyote midwifery," can be implemented even while being learned and elaborated. And best of all, it is an open-ended, self-correcting program.

Why label a practitioner of a particular pedagogy a "Coyote Midwife"? Since at least part of this project is to decenter traditional Western models of education and critical thinking, the use of such a label draws attention to the ways in which this pedagogy is indebted to non-Western and nonpatriarchal concepts. The "coyote" is a Native

American mythological trickster figure, sometimes identified as a rabbit or other animal by different tribes. He or she, since coyote may be either, is neither a god nor a mortal, but always something in between, something that calls into question both linear and circular constructs of reality and being (see Radin 1972). A "midwife" is, of course, someone who assists a woman giving birth. Traditionally, midwives have been women and have almost always been somewhat suspect within the patriarchal societies in which they have practiced, at times even being considered witches. The term seems to have been first applied to teachers by Mary Field Belenky, Blythe McVicker Clinchy, Nancy Rule Goldberger, and Jill Mattuck Tarule in *Women's Ways of Knowing*:

> Many women expressed—some firmly, some shakily—a belief that they possessed latent knowledge. The kind of teacher they praised and the kind for which they yearned was one who would help them articulate and expand their latent knowledge: a midwife-teacher. Midwife-teachers are the opposite of banker-teachers. While the bankers deposit knowledge in the learner's head, the midwives draw it out. They assist the students in giving birth to their own ideas, in making their own tacit knowledge explicit and elaborating it. (1986, 217)

The coyote midwife, then, serves as a pedagogical model for replacing what Paulo Freire characterized as the banking model of education (Belenky et al. 1986, 216–19; see Maher 1985, 31–33). Coyote teaches by story, paradox, and questioning to help people grow up and individuate without losing their potential for individual vision. Ursula K. Le Guin exemplifies just such an approach in her feminist rendition of coyote in the eminently teachable novella "Buffalo Gals." Coyote, as legend has it, does not chart a path or dispense a treasure map, but highlights the entanglements, whirlpools, and rocks that the ruling ideology utilizes to smash the individual ego and any group solidarity for struggle or change. Such education requires that the student recognize the teacher as guide and aid, but not as monological, monolithic authority (see Bakhtin 1984b, 81; see also Schilb 1985a, 256–57). With a coyote midwife as professor, students learn that they must discover and invent answers, not simply guess what the teacher wants, because, in Gloria Anzaldúa's words, "Voyager, there are no bridges, one builds them as one walks" (1983, v).

In order to conceptualize a coyote midwife pedagogy, we need to take issue with Jean Piaget's belief that the consciousness and relationship to reality of college students have already been established because they have reached the "rational" stage of cognitive development (see Yaeger 1988, 221). Rather than having attained some acme of rationality, college students are far more frequently entering a stage marked by the crystallization of half-understood received values.[2] To unsettle the sediment of an enforced passive receptivity, we must conceive of the teacher as one who can stimulate active and reflective critical thought. The coyote midwife allows for the possibility of engaging in such desedimentation without imposing a new set of received values, hardly better understood than the former ones, which would only replicate the patriarchal monologues of the traditional classroom (see Schilb 1985a, 263). Such a teacher serves as a guide who encourages students toward self-consciousness, self-motivation, and inquiry in search of commitment.

There, I've said it. The introductory literature course is not really "about" literature; it uses literature as a study example. It is about thinking and being in the world. But, really, how could it not be, despite neo-Kantian claims to the contrary? People, many of them well meaning, who teach literature as something utterly self-contained and self-referential—"poems are about other poems"—are also teaching the students about the world by convincing them that literature is irrelevant to the rest of their lives if they do not major in English and become close readers of "The Waste Land." Even other poems are part of the rest of the world. The concern in the coyote midwife classroom focuses on method-as-process rather than interpretive results through a self-conscious, dialogical pedagogy that first of all recognizes and appreciates the difference between "self" and "other." As Carolyn Shrewsbury has noted, "one goal of the liberatory classroom is that members learn to respect each other's differences rather than fear them. Such a perspective is ecological and holistic" (1987, 6). In these terms the discussion of literature serves as vehicle for exploring the dynamics of intellectual and emotional differences among a student's peers—the subject is not the theme.

But some students may learn respect only after having passed through the fear and discomfort that come with one's sense of self being challenged. This challenge arises most directly by assertions of the legitimacy of difference, particularly when these are defined by race, class, gender, and religious beliefs. In the classroom this means the engagement and interaction of other perspectives, attitudes, and beliefs as these are expressed primarily by the students themselves. In Audre Lorde's words, "difference must be not merely tolerated, but seen as a fund of necessary polarities between which our creativity can spark like a dialectic" (1983, 99).[3] Differences need to be addressed through in-class dialogues in plenary and small-group sessions, with dialogue meaning students talking to and with each other rather than just at someone, usually the teacher. There should be no pressure to reach a consensus in such situations—how brief a time to have one's beliefs rethought—but participants might reach an understanding of what other positions exist and why people believe in them.

The term "dialogics" in my title comes from the writings of Mikhail Bakhtin, and "in Bakhtin, the more other, the more self" (Holquist 1986, 148; see Bakhtin 1984b, 64).[4] What this phrase means is that individuals develop and expand their awareness of self through dialogue with others, in a process of mutual cultural constitution—our identities are created in the process of cultural participation. Dialogics as a method of education can serve to empower students in articulating and critiquing their own "latent knowledge" at the same time that they are engaging in the understanding and critiquing of the knowledge of others. But beyond that, students can also come to realize that like themselves, the others they encounter are also mutually speaking "subjects," not merely "objects" of their attention. They need to learn, as Thomas Birch expresses it, that

> An other cannot essentially be what it is objectified, defined, analyzed, legislated, or understood to be if it is to be and remain another. . . . A finalization of the identification of the other is a (self-deceived) absorption or ingestion of the other into the subjectivity of the self, or, on the social level, into the 'system.' . . . Self-becoming in and out of dialectical response to others and to other-becoming is then no longer possible. (1990, 11; see also Benhabib 1986)

A dialogical approach to this self/other dichotomy enables a process of ongoing engagement with mutual respect. It encourages an active exchange in which the ideas and beliefs of others, as well as one's own beliefs, are compared, considered, and scrutinized, rather than merely passively accepted or blindly rejected. Students cannot be simply "taught" such an approach. A changed subject, in both senses of content and student, requires a different pedagogy.

Consider "gender balance." A struggle continues to be waged to gender-balance the curriculum, with the first wave being the balancing of subject matter. But what will it profit women to gain the teaching of their literature, if they fail to gain their voice about that literature? Carole Tarantelli correctly notes that "feminist literary scholarship has rightly emphasized the fact that one of the principal triumphs of the women's literary tradition has been the recovery for visibility of the world *from the female point of view* and of the hidden and unexpressed female part of the world" (1986, 190; my emphasis). Yet many men and not a few women will be more than willing to teach literature by women, if they must, in the same way that they teach works by men, with a male normative audience, androcentric values, patriarchal power structures, and the monological authority of the dominant gender, thereby evading precisely the "female point of view" that such literature represents (see Bezucha 1985, especially 82–83).

Coyote Midwife Practice

As the midwife model for teaching begins to replace the banking model, teachers who would engage in such modeling need not only assist students in giving birth to their own ideas—which may or may not duplicate the ideas of others—within the parameters of complicity and resistance bounded by their ideological construction as subjects within a given culture. They also need to practice self-critical parenting skills while simultaneously undermining the socially defined authoritarianism attendant upon the teacher and parent positions in our contemporary culture. The model of the teacher as a coyote midwife can provide the basis for a transformative pedagogical practice.

In lower-division introductory literature courses dialogics can be introduced in the first week to the students as a theoretical orientation that the professor is adopting, adapting, and applying in that specific classroom. The first practical lessons in dialogics can come with the syllabus itself, through a variety of negotiations. Students will invariably be most interested in negotiating grading, but they frequently need to be presented with a series of options if any fruitful discussion is to develop. Approaches that I have taken involve allowing students to determine the relative percentage value of in-class and take-home assignments, as well as formal and informal writing on an individual basis. In a large class, such as the ones with 45 students at my university, I offer choices among several options that the entire class will adopt, preceded by in-class discussion. In smaller classes, I let each student select the relative weight on an individual basis. Another area of negotiation covers the order and arrangement of readings in terms of whether or not these are to be treated thematically, generically, or in some other fashion; this also includes the pacing of assignments. One component of all such discussions is a presentation of the requirements, deadlines, and workload that I face and with which I have to contend when working out due dates, exams, and grading. It seems to me a foolishly romantic posture for a professor to pretend that all his decisions are made on the basis of the greatest good for the students without recourse to his own needs and his own subject position within the institution.

In relation to the syllabus, these dialogical moves relativize features of their education that students tend to view as authoritatively determined absolutes, neither open to question nor based on any kind of relative knowledge on the part of the professor (see Shuster and Van Dyne 1983, 6–9). Frequently faculty do alter their syllabi or change readings, but without explanation and discussion such maneuvers seem as arbitrary and imperial as the initial establishment of assignments did. It also seems important to me not to create an illusion of unfettered freedom and autonomy; certain university and department requirements have to be met and certain goals are predetermined by the teacher who cannot abrogate responsibility for keeping students from squandering their energy or time. But these limitations can also be explained and, like the students' own opinions, offered to the class as points for discussion and debate, which may lead to some changes even in those aspects of the course that the teacher thought were set.

But in many ways dialogues about the syllabus serve more as warmup exercises than anything else, because it is difficult for students to apprehend the particular implications of such an abstraction in terms of how the organization of material, the connections among texts, and the arrangement of papers, projects, and exams affect both what and how they learn. In my experience the first real dialogical breakthroughs occur in the realm of reconceptualizing "audience," and there are a couple of easy ways to set this up. One is to ask students to consider the past few movies they have seen—or to show one in class—and determine whether or not they thought the film was directed at them, without defining what "them" means. Then use their initial writing as a point of departure for analyzing more specific differences among them, such as class, race, gender, place (urban or rural, domestic or international). Another is to begin with a collection of poems, either book-length or handouts, but not taken from an anthology because that already grants the poems some validity, acceptability, and authority. Last year I used June Jordan's *Living Room* because it is written by a militant black feminist, does not have a single normative audience for every poem, and addresses a series of audience-differentiating features. These differences include race, class, gender, and place but also political and religious beliefs, as well as an attitude toward the future; it also has a book-length structure in addition to the variety of individual poem structures. My students displayed strong resistance to the text and tried to wait me out to discover my reasons for assigning it. But when I indicated that they were not required to "like" or "praise" the poems, but could react negatively, discussion began. The negative responses also gave rise to defenses of Jordan's poetics and ideas and the *reasons* for students' differences. Students then learned more about themselves as an audience constructed by an author, as a socially constructed audience, and as a self-constructing audience. In the end, a number of them did find they "liked" or approved of Jordan's poetry, while many others said that they would still choose not to read her but that they did learn more, particularly about themselves, than they expected from the exercise. Certainly there are many poems in any given anthology that on the surface do not seem controversial but that can generate significant debate when the differences between reader-response interpretations are discussed in class. Such poems can teach students about the experiences of others, not just poets but also other students.

A case in point is Theodore Roethke's almost universally anthologized "My Papa's Waltz." Most students try to read this as a light-hearted poem, but there are always a few, although almost invariably hesitant to speak, who view it as a very grim, dark poem about physical abuse at the hands of an alcoholic father. These students always speak from experience, whether they have so suffered or have witnessed it. This poem strikes me as a case in which the teacher's sharing, or at least explicit validating, of personal experience as a basis for interpretation seems crucial. I am the adult child of an alcoholic, and I reveal that information to my students and explain that, as a result, while I can understand the reasons why some students interpret it lightly, I never can. Such disclosure entails risks in the classroom, just as it does here, but if we do not take any risks in revealing personal experience and its significance for the way we understand literature and the ways in which it helps us understand the world, then what right do we have to expect students to take such a risk among their peers?[5] The crucial thing in such situations (and I think it important not to overdo them just as I think it important not always to present my own interpretations of some works) is to emphasize that I am using my personal experience, with the emphasis clearly on its being *personal* rather than its being *mine,* i.e., an authority's experience.

Roethke provides another convenient avenue into interpretive dialogue if one compares another popular poem of his, "Root Cellar," with the poem "Germinal" in the collection *Savings* by the Native American author Linda Hogan. These two authors have distinctly different reactions to the fecundity, disorder, and nonhuman nature of the root cellar's vitality. Roethke clearly reacts negatively, while Hogan concludes "and all things saved and growing." Students recognize such differences immediately; we can then discuss which attitude they share—not which poem they prefer—and why. And this in turn can be led into discussions of cultural and gender differences (depending on the reactions of the class). It provides an opportunity to discuss another non-white American culture, one about which the students are less likely to have much of an attitude. Students can learn from this comparison how little they know about Native American cultures, and also how culturally and experientially determined their habitual responses tend to be. Since they respond quickly and strongly to the poems rather than having to struggle through them, they reveal a habitual attitude rather than an intellectual response to the poems' differences.

The preceding examples illustrate two types of dialogues that can be engaged using poetry, neither of which is focused on deriving a "correct" or even final interpretation of a particular work, but which do require attention to the responses and differences among the class as audience. Poetry provides a third kind of opportunity in poems that are structured as dialogues or that contain dialogue, even when only one character gets to speak. John Donne's "The Canonization," Percy Shelley's "Ozymandias," and Robert Browning's "My Last Duchess" are three from earlier periods that have worked well for me in emphasizing dialogic engagement of ideas and interpretations, but the two this past year that generated the most discussion were Robert Frost's "Home Burial" and Langston Hughes's "Theme for English B," both frequently anthologized.

I think there are three main reasons for the popularity of "Home Burial." First, as with other Frost poems, it is accessible; students know what is going on and they understand what the characters are saying. Second, the poem ends without closure; the lack of resolution stimulates speculation and withholds authorial validation of either character's position. Third, it addresses familial and relational miscommunication; as relatively new undergraduates, students frequently are experiencing just such failures of communication and misunderstandings in myriad ways. Issues of class, gender, and place quickly come to the fore, with attention generally narrowing down to gender differences and their resulting conflicts. Recognition and ensuing debate over these differences allow me to raise the question of whether the differences are biological or social; this works particularly well since the conflict centers on the husband's and the wife's differing responses to the death of their infant.

In the case of "Theme for English B," students responded well to it in part because it seemed so "reasonable" to them compared with the tones, language, and situations presented in Jordan's *Living Room*. If white students are going to engage issues of racism, not surprisingly they prefer to do so with a poem that is not confrontational or accusatory. They also respond well because they can relate to the position of the poem's speaker: having to write an essay and experiencing the conflict over writing what he wants to say while fearing that this is not what the teacher wants to hear. Many students interpret the "B" in the title as reflecting the best grade the speaker can hope for, since he is the only black in an otherwise white class and because his ideas may irritate the teacher. If encouraged, students address not only issues of racism and segregation, and whether or not significant progress has been made in the U.S. since the penning of Hughes's poem, but also the power dynamics of the college classroom. One of the most valuable results in some cases of such a discussion is that white students find themselves identifying with a black protagonist in such a way that the initial *otherness* that the speaker himself emphasizes is replaced by a recognition of *anotherness* as a result of the affinity felt and verbalized.[6] And this distinction between otherness and anotherness is a crucial one for the coyote midwife to nurture because it enables students to realize that identification and affinities do not need to mean assimilation or denial of differences. It also provides a means of addressing the alteration in perceptions of power and privilege, as well as self-identification, that occur when a person identifies with a character who is "other" in the course of experiencing literature.

As with verse, I like to combine full-length works with short ones in studying prose fiction. To that end I combine the reading of one or two novels with the study of short stories. Since I have habitually taught introduction to literature as a genre course, I have also always included a few plays.[7] Space here precludes discussing every work on my syllabus, so I would like to treat here only one of the novels I have used, Ursula K. Le Guin's *The Dispossessed*, which is widely taught in literature courses around the country, "even though," as many would say, "it is science fiction."[8] Students, it seems, are fairly evenly divided over whether or not they like reading science fiction.

The Dispossessed, subtitled *An Ambiguous Utopia*, combines both structural complexity and thematic sophistication. And, like Frost's "Home Burial," it has the added benefit of a relative closure rather than a monological resolution. I begin by providing background on Le Guin and reviewing some of the conflicting published interpretations with the students. The fact that critics widely diverge makes the students less uncomfortable about their own disparate reactions to the text. I then move to a discussion of its structure, assuming that the students are still working their way through the novel but are at least several chapters into it. Le Guin employs a doubled chronology in which the even-numbered chapters review the life of Shevek, the protagonist, up to the point at which chapter one begins the novel. The odd-numbered chapters then continue this chronology until the end, so that the present of the novel is always being juxtaposed to the past of the protagonist's life. By the time Shevek poses the question of whether or not he will visit the planet Urras, upon which virtually all of the action of the odd-numbered chapters occurs, the reader not only knows that he will go but also what happened as a result of that decision.

Students are quick to generate theories about why the novel might be so structured when it could have been more easily laid out in straight chronological order, particularly given that the chosen reflexive chronology disrupts traditional plot tension. Posing the question of whether or not this is a "novel of ideas" rather than a "novel of action" points the students in one direction, enabling the teacher so inclined an opportunity to discuss the genre of utopian literature and the function of utopian thought in society and in an individual's own daydreaming and planning. The utopian orientation also enables a nice segue into a point students usually raise—that the structure heightens the contrast between the world from which Shevek comes, Anarres, and the world he visits, Urras. And this also generates debate over the degree to which either society can be defined as utopian or dystopian, since Le Guin quickly reveals that the utopian-anarchist Anarres is not so egalitarian and the (from Shevek's viewpoint) dystopian-capitalist country of A-Io on Urras is not so democratic.

Students quickly note as well that Urras contains both a country clearly modeled along the lines of the United States and one modeled along the lines of the Soviet Union, and that these two are engaged in a cold war, including a proxy battle in a Third World country. I find my intervention most important at this point in clarifying the differences between a communist state such as the Soviet Union and the anarchist planet of Anarres that Le Guin creates. Students tend to conflate the two in their own minds, which reveals the trap of dualistic thinking that the superpowers have promoted—a country is either capitalist or communist. And, if the discussion of the utopian genre has not led to it, the foregoing certainly leads to a consideration of the degree to which *The Dispossessed*, as well as other novels like it, is not "about" science fiction or planets in some other solar system, but is about where we are today, or where people were when the novel was written.

Virtually any of these discussions, none of which requires any consensus or resolution except in regard to factual or historical accuracy, can lead to considerations of otherness and anotherness. For readers, to begin with, Shevek and his planet seem initially quite alien. Yet students find themselves almost always identifying to some extent with Shevek and particular events in his life. There is also the interesting reversal in that the country A-Io, which seems the most familiar of any aspect of the novel, seems utterly alien to Shevek, and we learn about it from Shevek's point of view. Then, in a brilliant structural move that heightens this depiction of the relativity of otherness, Le Guin introduces an additional point of view, when Ambassador Keng from our Earth meets Shevek. For Keng, both planets are alien *and* attractive because she finds affinities with her home planet in each of them. Her perspective relativizes Shevek's in a way that no authorial commentary or other character from either of the two main planets could do. Interestingly enough, students' understanding of this relativity of perspective came, in each of two semesters, more from a discussion of a single word than from plot structure or character development. That word was "Earth," and the discussion arose from the fact that it is referred to as "Terra" by the ambassador from our Earth as well as by other characters in the novel. When I asked students why Keng could not call it Earth while talking to Shevek, the silence was profound, but more profound were the expressions when the first student said, "because everybody's planet is Earth to the people who live there, just like everybody's house is home."

At that point, the Odonian slogan repeated in the novel that "true voyage is return" begins to take on more meaning, particularly since all of the people of Anarres, Shevek's planet, originally came from Urras, so that is their "original" home. And this relativity of perspective is further reinforced by the fact that Anarres rotates around Urras, so that each serves as the other's moon when anyone looks into the night sky. This kind of relativity of perspective is reinforced throughout by the multiple dialogic structures of the novel. First, the doubled chronology places the events in Shevek's life on the two different planets and the planets themselves in dialogic relationship. Second, because it is a novel of ideas, much of the text is given over to dialogue between Shevek and others. Third, Shevek engages in a considerable amount of internal dialogue. Fourth, the concept of dialogue is expanded to contain more than two perspectives. And students can engage the dialogic dimensions of the novel in a variety of tangents shooting off from these four major categories. For example, one student developed an essay analyzing how the two chronologies of Shevek's life, on Anarres and on Urras, replicated a structure of naiveté, experience, disillusionment, maturity, and achievement. And this in turn suggested to her that one's life consists of a series of developmental cycles, both influenced by and to some degree transforming beyond previous stages in that life. Other students opted to analyze the differences between the economies and politics of the planets depicted and either the United States or the Superpowers today. Others focused on Le Guin's depiction of the relative degree of gender equality on Anarres and the obvious oppression of women on Urras in terms of the novel as a criticism of American culture.

But limiting oneself to the tasks of generating class discussion and a thoughtful essay on the novel falls far short of the potential for alternative pedagogical practice that this novel encourages. Several options can be practiced in the classroom to nurture the development and exchange of students' ideas about *The Dispossessed*. Students can, of course, break up into small discussion groups and compare group results. Students can be divided up into Urrasti and Anarresti panels and debate some of the crucial differences between the planets that Le Guin depicts. Also, students can be asked first to keep a daybook of their reading and then (after a certain amount of class discussion) to write a critique of their daybook entries. Students can be asked not only to write essays on the novel, but also to break up into teams in which they write brief position papers and then responses to each other's positions in preparation for the writing of their own essay. Alternatively, students can be given the option of doing a group essay in which each of them would assume responsibility for exploring different dimensions of the novel, and then they would write a team conclusion that would in some way integrate these dimensions either through unifying interpretations or identifying unresolvable differences in interpretation among the parts.

Studies in the Dialogical Classroom

The dialogical classroom organized by a coyote midwife should allow students to see that their ideas may be valid and to learn mechanisms by which they not only voice those ideas but also critique them through engaging in an internal dialogue, often put down on paper, and through engaging other students' ideas in an external dialogue. Instead of the presentation of a *correct* view of the world in a monological, authoritative, patriarchal utterance that encourages passive assent rather than active debate, the coyote midwife works with developing "internally persuasive discourse," which "makes a claim on the speaker that may carry authority but is open to questioning and modification" (LaCapra 1983, 314). To help students develop such a discourse, we need to find ways to break down the position of authority awarded us as teachers from the outset, not in some pseudo-egalitarian way limited to just rearranging seats in a circle while simultaneously keeping the grade firmly in our grasp, but in ways that clarify the importance of each student's developing her or his own self-conscious critical posture (see Schilb 1985a, 263–64).

Paula Treichler points out that

> studies of teachers find that, at every educational level, women tend to generate more class discussion, more interaction, more give-and-take between students and teacher and among students. In direct relation to the degree to which this is true, (1) students evaluate these classes as friendlier, livelier, less authoritarian, and more conducive to learning, *AND* (2) students judge the teacher to be less competent in her subject matter. (1986, 86)

If we foreground coyote midwife methods, let the students in on the "secrets" of why the teacher is doing what she or he is doing (thereby performing a metacriticism of the pedagogy in process), and engage in self-critique and group evaluation of the pedagogy and the subject matter, then we can break down the myth of "competence equals patriarchy" that Treichler finds as the only explanation for the contradictory evaluations she has summarized: "Thus behaviors judged as traditionally male—a lecture format, little student give-and-take, the transmission of a given body of content, little attention to process—seem also to signal professional competence" (1986, 86). Treichler's remarks also draw attention to the genderized differences of student expectations that each teacher must confront, and that the male teacher, in particular, must discern and discredit (see Bezucha 1985, 89–92; Friedman 1985). Men need to teach differently from what their training both as teachers and as males in this society has conditioned them to do. Males practicing as coyote midwives, for example, have a specific role to play in altering perceptions about *the* way women and men should and do teach and the social function of teaching in general by challenging patriarchal stereotypes and norms.[9] In addition, through educating their students about and by means of feminism, they can contribute to the development of "a classroom based on the 'authority' radical feminism has granted to women in the process of subverting and transforming patriarchal culture" (Friedman 1985, 207).

Ellen Morgan argues:

> Women's studies classrooms can't tell students how to escape the discomforts of the alienation that comes with role change. . . . But I suggest that as teachers we recognize that our students will very likely need methods to survive and thrive on the feminist madness we may wake in them. . . . I think this means that when we present materials on women to them, we should also prepare them for the possible consequences of their knowing and acting upon it. (6)

Female students who experience such a classroom in or out of women's studies courses should be assisted in realizing the necessity of viewing it not only as an enclave in which to speak "freely" among themselves and to each other, but also as a base camp from which to launch themselves into other ways of thinking and living than the ones into which Madison Avenue continues to encourage them. Similarly, male students who encounter a classroom that is not patriarchally male-normative will be challenged to recognize the relativity of received values and the otherness always coterminous with any conception of self. Both male and female students will be presented with the self-actualizing premise that "alienation and mediation are conditions of agency" (Stewart 1989, 11; see de Lauretis 1987, 17).

But in order to establish a base camp classroom, the coyote midwife needs a theoretical foundation for orientation, tools, and philosophical affirmation. Feminist theory and pedagogy organized by means of a dialogic method, and spiced by a willingness to risk trickster activities, can ground a coyote-midwife-based pedagogical practice that nurtures and empowers as it disrupts and subverts. As Teresa de Lauretis expresses it, "it is power, not resistance or negativity, that is the positive condition of knowledge" (1987, 30; see also Yaeger 1988, 266, 275). While it may be the case that without destruction there can be no construction, the latter produces the necessity for the former. Susan Stewart has claimed that "when we look at the history of 'our discipline' [literary studies] . . . we see that changes in the discipline are not mere changes of topic—they are, rather, changes effecting methodology, hence reorganizing the social network of knowledge and thereby resulting in new objects of knowledge" (10–11). And Barbara Johnson argues that "the profound political intervention of feminism has indeed been not simply to enact a radical politics but to redefine the very nature of what is deemed political" (1987, 31). The politics of education itself remains a focus of intense debate, precisely over what should constitute "the social network of knowledge" and what teachers' "new objects of knowledge" should be. The coyote-midwife-in-training can participate in both of these re-cognitions by rewriting, relearning, and reteaching introductory literary courses.

Notes

1. For example, in response to the request that students "make specific recommendations for improving the course," one of my students wrote: "Stop trying to include social methods in your class. Today you talked about the struggle of the Jews. Some of us could care less. Also it seemed that the sole purpose for you to discuss June Jordan's work was to include social problems. The struggle of the Blacks should be a separate class *not of all things English III*" (my emphasis). Where did the student get the idea that literature and "social problems" are unrelated?

2. The situation is slightly different for older "nontraditional" students in that they have likely crystallized a worldview during the years between their departure from and return to school. But that return quite frequently signals a recognition of the inaccurateness or inadequacy of that worldview. They tend, then, to be either in the process of forming a new one or anticipating that college will provide it for them (see also Bauer 1990, 387).

3. Lorde goes on to say that "only within that interdependency of different strengths, acknowledged and equal, can the power to seek new ways to actively 'be' in the world generate, as well as the courage and sustenance to act where there are no charters. . . . [The] difference is that raw and powerful connection from which our personal power is forged" (1983, 99). And Barbara Smith testifies: "What I really feel is radical is trying to make coalitions with people who are different from you" (Smith and Smith 1983, 126).

4. In addition to the Bakhtin text cited here, *Problems of Dostoevsky's Poetics* (1984b), see also other works by the Bakhtin circle (their exact authorship remains in dispute), such as Bakhtin, *The Dialogic Imagination* (1981a) and *Speech Genres* (1986), and Vološinov, *Freudianism* (1987) and *Marxism and the Philosophy of Language* (1986).

5. I see such an action as part of the effort to break down "the alienated work of the classroom" that, as Dale Bauer points out, students try so hard to maintain (1990, 386–87).

6. In "Appendix II" of Bakhtin's *Problems of Dostoevsky's Poetics* the translator observes a significant distinction that Bakhtin makes in Russian that is lost in English, that between "other" and "another": "Russian distinguishes between *drugoi* (another, other person) and *chuzhoi* (alien, strange; also, the other). . . . The *another* Bakhtin has in mind is not hostile to the *I* but a necessary component of it, a friendly other, a living factor in the attempts of the *I* toward self-definition" (302).

7. Two plays with which I have had the most success are *Trifles* (1916) by Susan Glaspell, probably better known in its short story form, "A Jury of Her Peers," and *"Master Harold" . . . and the Boys* (1982) by Athol Fugard. The former focuses on gender oppression, while the latter takes place in South Africa and focuses on racial oppression. Unfortunately, I have not found an anthology that contains both of them.

8. Actually, Le Guin's novel is probably taught at least as frequently in social science courses, such as political science, economics, sociology, and psychology, as it is in English and philosophy courses. But in those other fields it is usually encountered in an upper-division rather than a general education course.

9. The particular problems and tasks of male professors addressing gender balance and feminist teaching have not yet been adequately addressed. And, while a book such as Jardine and Smith's *Men in Feminism* (1987) proves invaluable for helping to sharpen awareness of the contradictions inherent in such concepts as "feminist men" and "men in feminism," none of the essays in that collection addresses the specific problems of males practicing feminist pedagogy or ways that males can intervene in the classroom to alter student perceptions of feminist pedagogy and feminist teachers. Three essays in Culley and Portuges's *Gendered Subjects* (1985) do address these issues, the two by Bezucha and Schilb cited and one by Diedrick Snoek, but these are clearly just a beginning. If, for example, some of Dale Bauer's contentions are correct (389–92), then a female coyote midwife's assuming of more rhetorical authority in the classroom than male students would tend to give her would be as radically a decentering and disruptive maneuver as the male coyote midwife's refusing to accept the authority that all students tend to invest in him, as long as the gendered construction of authority were being addressed in both cases (see also Shuster and Van Dyne 1983).

IV Curricular Alternatives: Multicultural and Theoretical Transformations of Classroom Practice

13 A Multicultural Introduction to Literature

Phillipa Kafka
Kean College of New Jersey

It is clear that we cannot pretend to live up to course titles such as "Introduction to Literature" or "World Literature" if the list of authors we teach in such courses is limited to or dominated by white, Western males. In 1988, I received a grant from the New Jersey Department of Higher Education to work on integrating perspectives of gender, race, ethnicity, and class into the "Landmarks of World Literature" curriculum at Kean College of New Jersey. Designed for nonmajors and required of all students, in its traditional form this introductory course is typical of many such courses and curricula throughout the country. The course outline stipulated that readings include selections from the Bible, *The Iliad* or *The Odyssey*, a Greek tragedy, a Shakespeare play, a modern work, and a non-Western work. The authors examined were overwhelmingly if not unanimously male, and the emphasis was on the "universality" of theme reputed to transcend different times, places, races, classes, and genders. Students were to be trained to read texts in order to compare and contrast their characterizations, plot structures, and other techniques—and above all else to unearth those great underlying themes, those "universal meanings," that make a work a "landmark" and link it to every other landmark.

Such a traditional course and the set of assumptions underlying it are flawed in several crucial ways. The most blatant inequity is the erasure or marginalization of women and nonwhites. In this context "Literature" means *male* literature just as "woman" was subsumed by the word "man." Dale Spender reminds us that "although there is a widespread belief that the term 'man' has always been used to refer to women," in fact

> it was a rule introduced into (male) scholarly circles in the sixteenth century. In 1553, Thomas Wilson suggested that "man" should precede "woman" because it was more natural. No women were consulted about the "naturalness" of this argument and Wilson's male colleagues apparently agreed on the justice of his case. . . . John

> Kirkby in 1746 helped to set the seal on the case when he insisted that the male gender was the more comprehensive and an all-male parliament found it feasible to pass the 1850 act which decreed that he/man should stand for woman. (1981, 7)

The creation of a male canon was no more natural. Similarly, nonwhite writers were traditionally erased or at best included as token "ethnic writers" in introductory courses. The labeling of such writers, when they have been included at all in white-dominated courses, as "ethnic" reinforces their marginalization. The multi-ethnic scholar R. Radhakrishnan insightfully examines the connotations of the word "ethnic" in terms well worth keeping in mind when thinking about and teaching "ethnic" writers. His analysis of "ethnic foods" is memorable and telling enough to deserve quoting at some length:

> The definitive and taxonomic use of the term "ethnic" suggests that certain foods are so mainstream as to be natural, transparent, and invisible, i.e., these foods are in no need of being "marked," whereas certain other foods are marginal, partial, exotic, and in need of "being marked" as different. These "ethnic items" bear as a mark of their identity the label of difference that is foisted on them by the dominant culture. To state it simply, no Chinese or Mexican-American would describe her food as "ethnic." . . . The term "ethnic" as articulated from the dominant perspective designates an absolute form of racial otherness. In other words, "ethnicity" which is multiple and historically produced is dehistoricized and posited as something alien. . . . In effecting this rhetorical connection, the mainstream ideology conceals the reality that the "mainstream" itself is constituted ethnically, [but] that it has been nationalized and generalized now to the point of absolute ideological dominance. The so-called mainstream thus disallows to other ethnicities the very same political and representational rights and privileges that in the first place made "the mainstream" possible. Also, in its totalized use of the term "ethnic," the dominant point of view lumps together different histories and constituencies, each of which has a history of its own. "Ethnicity" thus operates for the dominant ideology as a way of not dealing with a whole range of "minority" groups and discourses. (1987, 14–15)

We have to be careful not merely to include "ethnic" or "minority" writers, but to avoid tokenizing non-white writers within mostly white courses, leaving them only on the shelf marked "ethnic." Instead, our courses need to take on the qualities of a visit to a mammoth new multicultural supermarket in which a diverse and conflicting array of cultural values is spread out before our students.

Perhaps the most subtle and in some ways most insidious assumption in the traditional introductory course is its central devotion to the "great" unifying theme(s). Barbara Hiura reveals precisely what is subsumed and subsequently erased in the "blending together" of texts in order to unearth "underlying" themes:

> In this neo-conservative political clime . . . such a universal literary approach tends to coincide with an historical ideological base congruent with the immigrant analogy and assimilationist model. World cultures are likened to white ethnic immigrant experiences to the extent that culture and history are devoid of meaning. America has treated its colored ethnic peoples differently from its white ethnics. Such differences are erased when their literature is blended together without thought to cultural, historical, and gender differences. (1988, 75)

To borrow from Sandra Harding's critique of traditional science, what if the very term "unifying themes" and the notion of "coherence among disparate readings" are in fact nothing more than "patriarchal expressive modes [which] reflect an epistemology that perceives the world in terms of categories, dichotomies, roles, stasis, and causation" that are specifically Western (1986, 650)?

We do better to draw from female expressive modes which, as Harding notes, reflect "an epistemology that perceives the world in terms of ambiguities, pluralities, processes, continuities, and complex relationships." What if instead of the traditional devotion to the "unifying theme," we took as our standard fidelity "*parameters* of dissonance," as Harding puts it, "within and between assumptions of partriarchal discourses"? What if we did not "encourage" our students to "fantasize about how we could order reality into the forms we desire" but, instead, located "the ways in which a valuably 'alienated consciousness,' 'bifurcated consciousness,' or 'oppositional consciousness' might function at the level of active theory making—as well as at the level of skepticism and rebellion"? What if instead of looking for coherence in the classroom, we were "able to cherish certain kinds of intellectual, political, and psychic discomforts, to see as inappropriate and even self-defeating certain kinds of clear solutions to the problems we have been posing"? (650)

Students who take the "Landmarks of World Literature" course at Kean College are mostly sophomore nonmajors and, like most such students nationwide, they tend to believe what their professors teach them. Many of the students have never read literary texts at all, except for texts required in previous elementary and secondary school courses. For them, "Landmarks" is one of the most difficult courses in the college curriculum. Whether their professors are traditionalists or transformers, the vast majority of our students accept their teachers' text selections as authoritative, take notes on whatever we talk about, memorize the terms and definitions we give them, and internalize the assumptions underlying our premises. If we teach white Western hegemony, we perpetuate it among our students. On the other hand, if we teach from multicultural perspectives, we can encourage a multicultural awareness among the next generation represented in our classrooms, more and more of whom are female, working-class, and nonwhite. This is, of course, easier said than done, and we are likely to encounter resistance not only among our students but among our own colleagues. Most of us imbibed a Western, patriarchal curriculum in our graduate schools. Western, patriarchal hegemony comes with our territory. It's second nature, a transparency which those of us who remain traditionalists do not (wish to) even notice or think about, like the surrounding water that fish swim in.

In our classrooms we need to begin by actively promoting an attitude of acceptance for a diversity of cultural backgrounds. As David M. Johnson notes:

> The main issue here is to have students feel good about and interested in themselves and their ethnic backgrounds. One way to promote this might be to have students do their own biographies so they can recognize that they have histories and their groups have histories. . . . I think they will become interested in the life stories of their own group and eventually branch out into interests about other groups. (1988, 53–54)

Such an encouragement and celebration of diversity among students can be reinforced by and related to a multicultural diversity of texts in the introductory course. In teaching world literature, I introduce students not only to texts by white males, such as Shakespeare's *Othello,* but also to works by women, such as Jane Austen's *Pride and Prejudice,* and by people of color and from other cultures, such as Alice Walker's *The Color Purple,* Lady Murasaki's *Tale of Genji,* and Buchi Emecheta's *Joys of Motherhood*—thereby incorporating (in the case of these examples) English, African American, Japanese, and Nigerian authors. Keeping the number of "landmark" texts by women approximately equal to the number of works by men, I teach Walker and Emecheta, for example, alongside more traditionally taught texts by Homer (*The Odyssey*), Dante (*The Inferno*), and Ibsen (*A Doll's House*) as well as Shakespeare. The idea is to embrace the cultural diversity found in the syllabus as well as among the students in the classroom, rather than subsume either to any wishful "transcendant theme."

Of course, what matters is not only the authors and texts that we teach, but the kinds of questions that we ask about them and encourage students to ask and try to answer, as in the case of *Othello*. Permeated with sixteenth-century sexism, racism, and class bias, *Othello* is an excellent traditional text to use as a springboard toward transforming a curriculum. Some of my students have been introduced to *Othello* before, usually by a teacher who has stressed Othello's jealousy and Iago's manipulations as the high-tragic cores of the play. I ask my students questions that they are much less likely to have heard even if they have encountered the play previously, questions such as these:

1. What is Othello's status at birth? What is his rank when the tragedy opens? What is his race?
2. What is the basic reason for Iago's vendetta against Othello? Are race and class factors?
3. Why does Emilia obey Iago? How does Emilia's language and attitude toward sex, love, and marriage differ from Desdemona's? What does this show about the two women? Describe their relationship. Do they have similar or different relationships to their husbands?
4. What do the courtship and marriage customs seem to be in the various classes of society found in the play?
5. Are there any stereotypes which bother you in this play?

These kinds of questions move the discussion beyond the traditional classroom focus on Greek tragic notions of *hubris* into an interrogation of the crucial role of race, class, and gender. It can be pointed out that Afrocentric scholars have pinpointed the European beginnings of organized, institutional racism around the time of the sixteenth century. It is significant in this regard that Dale Spender, the Australian feminist critic cited earlier, locates institutionalized sexism as beginning in the same period. Shakespeare's *Othello* reflects this development in its incipient stages. However, note that a prince and a warrior general in command of the Venetian army can at this time in European history still be represented as a black African.

Shakespeare's tragedy also provides an excellent pedagogical opportunity to foreground issues of class as well as race and gender. (Alan Wald's [1987] outline of a "class, gender, and race methodology" provides perhaps the best contextual framework, one I recommend as the basic underpinning for asking such questions about *Othello* or any other text.) Iago is an experienced career officer who has worked his way painstakingly up the ranks. It is his rage against Othello's class bias against him—in favor of the higher born, snobbish candidate, Lieutenant Cassio, who has no experience in the field whatsoever—which first motivates his schemes. Additionally, in scenes between Emilia and Desdemona, Shakespeare creates a counterpoint of ever increasing class differences between mistress and peasant servant in their varying attitudes toward sexual experience, behavior, and language.

As teachers we are free not only to analyze such distinctions of race, class, and gender in literary texts, but also to point out their relevance to our own contemporary world and to encourage our students to join us in critiquing their perpetuation. As one inspiration for my own thinking and teaching, I turned to an African American feminist group, the Combahee River Collective, who "fully integrate the concept of the 'simultaneity of oppression'" as they put it in 1977 when they pledged to struggle simultaneously "against racial, sexual, heterosexual, and class oppression." They saw, as their "particular task, the development of integrated analysis and practice based upon the fact that the major systems of oppression are interlocking" (Jaggar and Rothenberg 1984, 202). In the classroom we can link our analysis of literary texts not only to contemporary political inquiry but also to students' own values. For example, I have asked students to write an essay analyzing the attitude of Shakespeare (or Austen or Dante) toward races and classes other than their own, going on then to examine their own values as compared with the authorial ones. I remind students to keep in mind, before passing unduly harsh judgments, the different cultural contexts in which each author lived and wrote. At the same time, I keep in mind students' own cultural experiences (often different than my own) and do not penalize them for holding different opinions. Such an essay assignment reflects a feminist pedagogical strategy designed to reinforce what students learn in my classroom—that abstractions are grounded in particularities.

Similar questions can be asked about other texts, such as the ones I teach in my introductory course. Useful are fairly basic, revealing questions. When teaching the *Tale of Genji*, for example, I ask how Genji and his male circle of friends spend their days and nights, and what they seem to think are meaningful activities versus frivolous activities. Next, I ask the same questions about the women in Genji's circle. Occasionally in the *Tale of Genji* we catch a glimpse of the lower classes, such as peasants and servants. I encourage students to notice how *they* spend their time, and I ask students to make comparisons and contrasts with themselves. Such a mode of analysis, combined with personal reflection, is enhanced if one teaches a very different text such as *Pride and Prejudice*, asking the same kinds of questions about Austen's characters as we asked about Murasaki's characters as well as about the students' own experiences. It is also important to point to crucial authorial omissions, asking for example about what classes and kinds of people we *don't* find in Austen's novel.

The kinds of questions that I ask my students are part of a challenge to other aspects of the organizing principles of traditional courses. Feminist and multi-ethnic theoreticians dispute traditional definitions for historical periods, as well as definitions of genre and terminology. My questions focus on, for example, the role of gender in typical daily life, while conflict and warfare are considered much more significant by traditionalists. The terms "epic" and "tragedy" tend to be applied by traditionalists to those works which valorize and aggrandize pathetically petty and quibbling male pecking orders. Moreover, such squabbles and murders are traditionally dignified by terms such as "dynastic succession" and "assassination." In contrast, dismissive terms such as "domestic," "comedy of manners," "deviant," and "minority" or "ethnic" literature have been applied to works by women, homosexuals, the working classes, and people of color.

Students will naturally look at Alice Walker's *The Color Purple* from their American perspectives, often colored by the Hollywood version of Walker's novel. I challenge them with Afrocentric and cross-cultural questions, asking them for example to contrast women's relationships and roles in the family structure in Walker's unnamed American southern community versus that of the Olinkas in Africa. How are the experiences of Nettie, Celie's sister, different in Africa than in America? I also ask students to think about why Walker introduces the African segment of the novel, how she utilizes African spiritual beliefs, and what appears to be her view of the causes of the destruction of the Olinka way of life. Such an analysis becomes even more interesting if *The Color Purple* is paired with a text such as the Nigerian Buchi Emecheta's *Joys of Motherhood*, concerning which some of the same kinds of questions can be asked. How are women and children depicted, and how do men and women spend their time in different kinds of ways? Discussion naturally leads into a consideration of how Nigerian training and ways of life as described by Emecheta differ not only from the world depicted by Walker but also from students' own worlds. The truth that one can better understand one's own culture by looking at it from the point of view of a very different culture is brought home by reading and talking about a work such as *Joys of Motherhood*. Such exposure to "cultural relativism," according to Rhadakrishnan, can effectively displace student ethnocentricity. Students begin to realize that the cultural inscriptions embedded in their

American psyches are not unique, are not written in stone, are only one among many variants historically on a global basis.

Focusing on culture in this way naturally leads to an appreciation of the important cultural differences among the diverse authors examined in such an introductory course rather than an illusory insistence on traditional "unifying" themes. Classroom discussion questions, paper topics, and essay exam questions all can provoke a delineation of such cultural differences—a cultural "decentering" rather than a thematic merging or false centering of real cultural differences. At this point the multicultural perspective joins with a poststructuralist one, for Derrida reminds us that the "binary opposition" of traditional "thematic" thinking is "hierarchical thinking," in which one side—inevitably *our* cultural "side"—is seen as superior to another. Feminist and multicultural writers have responded to Derrida's critique. Ludmilla Jordanova, for example, argues that gender is a profoundly unstable, value-laden cultural construct, rather than one ahistoric element in a dialectic of binary oppositions. Like such "destabilizing" feminists who demand particularities, Henry Louis Gates, Jr., of late, has also been looking at Derrida as well as other continental theorists, not to emulate Derrida in his approach to African American literature, but to "change the joke and slip the yoke," as Gates puts it. His purpose is to challenge European critical assumptions about literature by opposing to it a "Black text-specific theory." According to Steven R. Carter, Lorraine Hansberry anticipated Gates and the feminist critics by at least thirty years when she stated to Studs Terkel in an interview about *Raisin in the Sun*: "I believe that one of the most sound ideas in dramatic writing is that, in order to create the universal, you must pay very great attention to the specific" (Carter 1988, 6).

The Anglo American critics who have, on the other hand, adopted Derrida, while leaving out particular cultural concerns, in many ways merely perpetuate the problems of the traditional mode of thought critiqued by Derrida. As Linda Alcoff writes:

> Despite rumblings from the Continent, Anglo-American thought is still wedded to the idea . . . of a universalizable, apolitical methodology and set of transhistorical basic truths unfettered by associations with particular genders, races, classes, or cultures. The [post-structuralist] rejection of subjectivity unintentionally . . . colludes with this [traditionalist] "generic human" thesis of classical liberal thought, that particularities of individuals are irrelevant and improper influences on knowledge. By designating individual particularities such as subjective experience as a social construct, post-structuralism's negation of the authority of the subject coincides nicely with the classical liberal's view that human

> particularities are irrelevant to questions of justice and truth because "underneath we are all the same." (1988, 273)

The antagonism of Radakrishnan to "ahistoricizing ethnics" is shared by most multi-ethnic critics. Cynthia Ward, for example, critiques traditional criticism as "normative criticism" because "it rejects as literarily immature all that does not fit its paradigm of subjectivity." It is therefore part and parcel of "the colonialist enterprise of 'othering': the erasure of individual distinction and historicity within and between groups of people and the subsequent construction of an ahistorical, unified representation to facilitate subjugation and control" (1990, 85).

In the lives of our students, however, what impresses them is not the shortcomings or even the evils of traditional literary criticism, but the messages that they receive in much more visible and popular media. My multi-ethnic (especially African American) students openly express disgust with the continual onslaught in the media of negative or one-sided language about and images of people of color. Bill Cosby notwithstanding, people of color are commonly defined and depicted—in my students' own words analyzing such media portraits—as "depressing," "victim," "loser," "addict," "criminal," "savage," and "deviant." George Bush's TV ads about Willie Horton's furlough from prison swung more votes during the last presidential election than did all the episodes of "The Cosby Show." Recently, an African American student challenged my class and me to come up with the title of "one, even halfway upbeat" book about "unselfconscious, normal" African Americans. Did the publishing industry have anything to do with all the literature being predictably depressing, being always about the same historic subjects and themes from the same point of view? Was there anything from another perspective, unselfconsciously black and American at the same time? If so, what was preventing publication? Ultimately I suggested that the student's best recourse was to take African literature, which fortunately was offered for the first time the following semester at Kean. However, multi-ethnic students with similarly compelling complaints seldom have recourse to a Japanese, Chinese, Native American, Puerto Rican, Mexican, or Cuban literature course, since these topics are rarely offered at many of the schools where we teach. Reforming our curricula is a crucial step that we will have to take and take soon in order to do justice to our students and to the different peoples of our country and the world.

In the meantime, we can take an important first step by incorporating multicultural perspectives into our introductory courses. Through the consideration of questions such as the ones I have been asking my students, inspired by feminist and multi-ethnic critical theory, it is my contention that our classrooms can become explorations of diversity on a global scale. The ingredients for such grounding consist of giving visibility and voice to female authors, to authors of color, and to authors not necessarily heterosexual and/or Anglo European American men from the upper classes. By including such authors, we can more truly represent our student population and our students' needs, as well as our traditional American ideals and values, than do the traditional canon and the customary way of teaching it.

14 "Who Was That Masked Man?": Literary Criticism and the Teaching of African American Literature in Introductory Courses

Pancho Savery
University of Massachusetts at Boston

To signify on Marx, a spectre is haunting African American literature—the spectre of critical theory. On one side of this debate stands the trio of Skip Gates, Robert Stepto, and Houston Baker, arguing for the importance and necessity of theory in order to see and understand and teach African American literature in new ways. On the other side are critics such as Joyce Joyce and Barbara Christian, who seem to suggest that those interested in theory need to go back to *Macbeth*—for their work "is a tale / Told by an idiot, full of sound and fury, / Signifying nothing." Specifically, they charge that contemporary literary theory is filled with vague linguistic jargon which is designed only for a small in-group familiar with the jargon, that specific texts rarely get mentioned, and that by buying into this system, proponents of theory are deemphasizing race and thereby selling out. If such changes are true, then contemporary critical theory is of no use in the teaching of literature, especially at the introductory level.[1]

At the beginning of the second chapter of *Invisible Man*, Ralph Ellison's nameless narrator thinks back to the statue of the college Founder depicting him lifting the veil of ignorance from the eyes of a kneeling slave:

> Then in my mind's eye I see the bronze statue of the college Founder, the cold Father symbol, his hands outstretched in the breathtaking gesture of lifting a veil that flutters in hard, metallic folds above the face of a kneeling slave; and I am standing puzzled, unable to decide whether the veil is really being lifted, or lowered more firmly in place; whether I am witnessing a revelation or a more efficient blinding. (1972 [1952], 36)

Is current literary theory helpful in reading, teaching, and designing courses that involve African American texts? Or is it just pulling the wool over the eyes and making us more blind than before?

At the heart of the work of Baker, Stepto, and Gates is an attempt to right the wrongs of the past—specifically, the notion promulgated by many during the black arts movement of the 1960s and early '70s that the only proper way to view and evaluate African American texts was through the prism of politically correct ideology. Two essays by Amiri Baraka can perhaps serve as paradigmatic. In "The Myth of a 'Negro Literature' " (1962), Baraka states, "From Phyllis Wheatley to Charles Chesnutt . . . the only recognizable accretion of tradition . . . has been of an almost agonizing mediocrity" (105). Later in the same essay, he refers to the "embarrassing and inverted paternalism of Charles Chesnutt" (106). In "The Revolutionary Tradition in Afro-American Literature" (1978), Wheatley and her work are again dismissed, as are James Weldon Johnson's *The Autobiography of an Ex-Colored Man* (246) and Ellison's *Invisible Man* (250). These writers are condemned by Baraka because their content is not "correct." Gates, on the other hand, wants to promulgate "the idea of literature as a system" because "black literature is a verbal art like other verbal arts" (1987b, 40). Thus, "thematic criticism" (41) is out. Instead,

> We urgently need to direct our attention to the nature of black figurative language, to the nature of black forms, to the history and theory of Afro-American literary criticism, to the fundamental relation of form and content, and to the arbitrary relationships between the sign and its referent. Finally, we must begin to understand the nature of intertextuality, that is, the non-thematic manner by which texts—poems and novels—respond to other texts. (41)

Gates's solution is a marriage between "metaphors for black literary relations from within the Afro-American tradition" and "that which is useful in contemporary literary theory" (47). In other words, the black vernacular meets poststructuralism. The resulting product is what Gates calls "signifying":

> Signifyin(g) is a uniquely black rhetorical concept, entirely textual or linguistic, by which a second statement or figure repeats, or tropes, or reverses the first. Its use as a figure for intertextuality allows us to understand literary revision without resource to thematic, biographical, or Oedipal slayings at the crossroads; rather, critical signification is tropic and rhetorical. Indeed, the very concept of Signifyin(g) can exist only in the realm of the intertextual relation. (49)

Throughout *Figures in Black: Words, Signs, and the "Racial" Self*, but particularly in the final essay, "The Blackness of Blackness: A Critique on the Sign and the Signifying Monkey," Gates gives examples of how this process works, both within a text and between texts. He notes for example how in *Their Eyes Were Watching God,* Zora Neale Hurston's main character Janie engages in a signifying ritual with the men on the front porch, with her own husband's impotence as the ultimate butt of the joke: " 'Humph! Talkin' 'bout *me* lookin' old! When you pull down yo' britches, you look lak de change uh life' " (123). Between texts, Hurston revises both specific passages and narrative strategies from Frederick Douglass, W. E. B. Du Bois, and Jean Toomer. Likewise, Ralph Ellison signifies on Richard Wright; Ishmael Reed signifies on Ellison, Wright, and Baldwin; Toni Morrison signifies on Ellison; and Morrison and Alice Walker signify on Hurston.

In *From Behind the Veil: A Study of Afro-American Narrative,* Robert Stepto defines the idea of "pregeneric myths" which "shape the forms that comprise a given culture's literary canon," and argues that for Afro America, the primary pregeneric myth is "the quest for freedom and literacy" (1979, ix). Stepto traces this myth from the early slave narratives through Ellison's *Invisible Man.* Like the work of Gates, Stepto's argument is based on form and assumes a knowledge of the tradition and a conscious use of it on the part of the writers he writes about.

Like Gates and Stepto, Houston Baker attempts to look at African American literature through principles derived from the literature itself rather than principles or theories outside the literature. In *Blues, Ideology, and Afro-American Literature,* Baker argues for a reading of black texts that looks for "the distinctive, the culturally specific aspects of Afro-American literature and culture" (1984, 1). At the center of what is culturally specific is what Baker calls a "blues matrix." This refers not only to blues music as such but to a way of being based in the vernacular that is open to improvisation and "speculative, inventive energies and interests" (10). And in *Modernism and the Harlem Renaissance,* Baker completely discards the traditional (white) definition of Modernism of Pound, Eliot, Yeats, Joyce, Conrad, and the rest and defines a distinctly African American modernism that begins with Booker T. Washington's 1895 Atlanta Exposition speech. For Baker, Washington shows a "mastery of form" that self-consciously dons the minstrel mask and "darky role" (1987b, 28) in order to gain "benefits for the Afro-American masses" (33). The strategy is similarly followed by Charles Chesnutt in *The Conjure Woman* (1899). The next step is "deformation of mastery," realized in W. E. B. Du Bois's *The Souls of Black Folk* (1903), where he openly celebrates African heritage and folk forms. For Baker, these two rhetorical strategies come together in Alain Locke's anthology *The New Negro* (1925), which he calls "the first fully modern figuration of a nation predicated upon mass energies" (91).

With this background in mind, there looms the question of how we move from the theoretical to the practical. How does this theory translate into teaching strategy? The answer to this question is somewhat difficult. On the one hand, I am a strong proponent of the position that to talk about "American literature" and to limit that term to the work of white American males is a mistake. Likewise, to talk about "British literature" and to omit writing produced in British colonies in the Caribbean or Africa is equally a mistake. On the other hand, the critical work of Stepto, Baker, Gates, and others also makes it clear, and no longer a subject of debate, that there is an entity known as African American culture; and that African American literature, as a subset of that culture, has its own rules and organizing principles. I want to make it clear, however, that I am *not* suggesting either that African American literature can only be taught by African Americans, or that it can only be taught in courses exclusively devoted to African American literature. I am suggesting that it is at least somewhat naive to believe that a teacher can just arbitrarily pick one or two African American texts and insert them into an introductory literature course. With most forms of literary criticism—feminist, poststructuralist, Marxist—one can learn the technique and apply it to any number of texts. The kind of literary criticism I am talking about here does not work that way. It assumes knowledge of the entirety of the tradition. Thus, one can't simply insert Ishmael Reed's *Mumbo Jumbo* (1972) into an introduction to literature course. Reed's signifying on Wright, Ellison, and Baldwin means that a teacher must be familiar with these other texts as well.

But this kind of interaction among texts does provide a teaching strategy for introducing African American texts. Once one understands the tradition and the fact that texts are talking back and forth to each other, certain pairs or small groups of texts naturally come to mind for inclusion in "Introduction to Literature." Combining the theories of Gates and Baker, for example, one could teach a unit using Frederick Douglass's *Narrative,* Hurston's *Their Eyes Were Watching God,* and Alice Walker's *The Color Purple.* Hurston signifies on Douglass, Walker signifies on Hurston, and all three texts focus on the gaining of literacy and freedom. Let me give some specific examples here of exactly how this works. Zora Neale Hurston's *Their Eyes Were Watching God* begins,

> Ships at a distance have every man's wish on board. For some they come in with the tide. For others they sail forever on the horizon, never out of sight, never landing until the Watcher turns his eyes away in resignation, his dreams mocked to death by Time. That is the life of men.

> Now, women forget all those things they don't want to remember, and remember everything they don't want to forget. The dream is the truth. Then they act and do things accordingly. (1978 [1937], 9)

This passage can be juxtaposed with the passage from Douglass's 1845 *Narrative* in which he delivers his apostrophe to the ships on the Chesapeake Bay:

> Our house stood within a few rods of the Chesapeake Bay, whose broad bosom was ever white with sails from every quarter of the habitable globe. Those beautiful vessels, robed in purest white, so delightful to the eye of freemen, were to me so many shrouded ghosts, to terrify and torment me with thoughts of my wretched condition. I have often, in the deep stillness of a summer's Sabbath, stood all alone upon the lofty banks of that noble bay, and traced, with saddened heart and tearful eye, the countless number of sails moving off to the mighty ocean. The sight of these always affected me powerfully. My thoughts would compel utterance; and there, with no audience but the Almighty, I would pour out my soul's complaint, in my rude way, with an apostrophe to the moving multitude of ships:
>
> "You are loosed from your moorings, and are free; I am fast in my chains, and am a slave! You move merrily before the gentle gale, and I sadly before the bloody whip! You are freedom's swift-winged angels, that fly around the world; I am confined in bands of iron! O that I were free!" (1968 [1845], 75–76)

In *The Signifying Monkey: A Theory of Afro-American Literary Criticism*, Gates analyzes these two passages and shows how Hurston consciously revises Douglass by using the chiasmus, or inversion of the second of two parallel phrases ("women forget all those things they don't want to remember, and remember everything they don't want to forget"). Gates writes that the chiasmus is Douglass's "major contribution to the slave's narrative," making it "the central trope of slave narration" (1988, 172). Hurston also deliberately reverses Douglass's use of desire and power. Douglass puts his desire for freedom on to the boat and suggests he doesn't have the power to be free. Hurston revises and parodies this notion by suggesting that unlike men, women gain power through "controlling the process of memory" (172). Thus, as Gates concludes, "Hurston, in these enigmatic opening paragraphs, signifies upon Douglass through formal revision" (172).

Later in the same text, Gates advances an extended analysis of Alice Walker's *The Color Purple* in which he makes clear Walker's debt to Hurston in terms of the search for a voice and a listener for that voice, images of self-negation, "double-voiced discourse" (248), and the repetition by Walker of several of Hurston's key metaphors.

Another set of parallels and significations could begin with Du Bois's classic statement from *The Souls of Black Folk:*

> After the Egyptian and Indian, the Greek and Roman, the Teuton and Mongolian, the Negro is a sort of seventh son, born with a veil, and gifted with second-sight in this American world,—a world which yields him no true self-consciousness, but only lets him see himself through the revelation of the other world. It is a peculiar sensation, this double-consciousness, this sense of always looking at one's self through the eyes of others, of measuring one's soul by the tape of a world that looks on in amused contempt and pity. One ever feels his twoness,—an American, a Negro; two souls, two thoughts, two unreconciled strivings; two warring ideals in one dark body, whose dogged strength alone keeps it from being torn asunder. (1965 [1903], 215)

Signifying on this passage, there are quite a few scenes in African American literature of the arrival of the moment of the recognition of racial consciousness and identity, and the irony and pain of the moment. Here is a scene in James Weldon Johnson's *The Autobiography of an Ex-Colored Man*:

> One day near the end of my second term at school the principal came into our room and, after talking to the teacher, for some reason said: "I wish all of the white scholars to stand for a moment." I rose with the others. The teacher looked at me and, calling my name, said: "You sit down for the present, and rise with the others." . . . I sat down dazed, I saw and heard nothing . . . When school was dismissed, I went out in a kind of stupor. (1965 [1912], 400)

Compare this with a similar moment in Hurston's *Their Eyes*:

> "Ah was wid dem white chillun so much till Ah didn't know Ah wuzn't white till Ah was round six years old. Wouldn't have found it out then, but a man come long takin' pictures. . . .
>
> "So when we looked at de picture and everybody got pointed out there wasn't nobody left except a real dark little girl . . . Dat's where Ah wuz s'posed to be, but Ah couldn't recognize dat dark chile as me. So Ah ast, 'where is me? Ah don't see me.'
>
> "Everybody laughed, . . . she pointed to de dark one and said, 'Dat's you, Alphabet, don't you know yo' ownself?'
>
> ". . . Ah looked at de picture a long time and seen it was mah dress and mah hair so Ah said: 'Ah, aw! Ah'm colored!' " (1978 [1937], 21)

And such self-recognition scenes are not limited to "formal literature." This is a passage from *Kareem* by Kareem Abdul-Jabbar:

> The first time I really became aware of myself as a black person

> was when one of the kids at St. Jude's brought a Polaroid camera to school and took a picture of us standing in the back of our third-grade classroom. When I looked at it, I realized how different I was from everybody else; I was darker. Up until then, I hadn't felt that difference, but once I did, it stuck with me. (1990, 153)

I have found in my own teaching that this kind of careful pairing makes a difference. Earlier in my introductory course for nonmajors, I taught James Weldon Johnson's *The Autobiography of an Ex-Colored Man* as a solo text, not paired with anything else. While students found the novel "an easy read," they ended up missing Johnson's point. The primary problem was that they confused the narrator's opinions with those of Johnson. The next time around, I taught the novel as part of a group of three texts, the other two being Chesnutt's *The Conjure Woman* and Du Bois's *The Souls of Black Folk*. When talking about Chesnutt, I introduced Baker's idea about "mastery of form" and Chesnutt's veiled use of language. I also focused on Du Bois's literal use of the image of the veil and Stepto's theories about literacy and authorial control of the text. By the time we got to Johnson, students were ready for veiled uses of language and this time did not miss the point that Johnson's views and those of his narrator are widely divergent. More significantly, having read Du Bois, they immediately noted many passages in Johnson in which it is clear that he is signifying on Du Bois. They didn't use this specific term, but they could see that there were parallel passages in the text and that it was clear that Johnson had read and was responding to Du Bois. Here is one such example (also noted by Stepto), first from Du Bois:

> Out of the North, the train thundered, and we woke to see the crimson soil of Georgia stretching away bare and monotonous right and left. Here and there lay struggling, unlovely villages, and lean men loafed leisurely at the depots; then again came the stretch of pines and clay. Yet we did not nod, nor weary of the scene; for this is historic ground . . . Here sits Atlanta, the city of a hundred hills, with something Western, something Southern, and something quite its own, in its busy life. (1965 [1903], 285)

Johnson signifies on this passage when he writes,

> The farther I got below Washington, the more disappointed I became in the appearance of the country. I peered through the car windows, looking in vain for the luxuriant semi-tropical scenery which I had pictured in my mind. I did not find the grass so green, nor the woods so beautiful, nor the flowers so plentiful, as they were in Connecticut. Instead, the red earth partly covered by tough, scrawny grass, the muddy, straggling roads, the cottages of unpainted pine boards, and the clay-daubed huts imparted a

> "burnt up" impression. Occasionally we ran through a little white and green village that was like an oasis in the desert.
>
> When I reached Atlanta, my steadily increasing disappointment was not lessened. I found it a big, dull, red town. This dull red colour of that part of the South I was then seeing had much, I think, to do with the extreme depression of my spirits—no public squares, no fountains, dingy streetcars, and, with the exception of three or four principal thoroughfares, unpaved streets. It was raining when I arrived and some of these unpaved streets were absolutely impassable. Wheels sank to the hubs in red mire, and I actually stood for an hour and watched four or five men work to save a mule, which had stepped into a deep sink, from drowning, or, rather, suffocating in the mud. The Atlanta of today is a new city. (1965 [1912], 420–21)

At the beginning of this essay, I used the image of the veil of ignorance in Ellison's *Invisible Man* to ask the question of whether or not literary criticism could be of use in the teaching of African American texts in introductory courses. In the title of my essay, I am, of course, appropriating the question asked of the Lone Ranger. By using it, I am asking whether the literary theorist is some masked man or woman who is masking, veiling, or hiding the text from the reader, or whether, like the Lone Ranger, the literary theorist is righting wrongs by helping to make texts more clear. My answer is an unqualified *yes*. Literary criticism is not just jargon-filled prose with no practical purpose. It is useful in choosing texts and thinking about texts. I want to suggest, however, that to stop there is to not go far enough. Literary criticism can help to unmask texts, but to fully empower students, literary criticism itself needs to be unmasked by students. The way to do this, I want to argue, is to actually use literary-critical texts as part of course syllabi,[2] especially literary-critical texts that contradict each other. When literary criticism is used as a text, students are able to see, as they also see when looking at literary texts, that there is more than one way of looking. Too often, students think, or are made to think, that there is only one way of seeing, and that is the teacher/critic's way. The university must function in such a way as to empower students to have trust and confidence in their own abilities, or else we as teachers are, in fact, pulling the veil of ignorance down over their eyes.

Let me suggest a few examples from criticism on Paul Laurence Dunbar and Countee Cullen. In the first significant book of African American literary criticism, Saunders Redding argued in 1939 that Cullen's poetry is "artificial," as well as "effete and bloodless" (108), primarily because of its conventional, nonracial characteristics. On the other hand, Maureen Honey, in her recent anthology of women poets from the Harlem Renaissance, points out that "mastering the poetic forms of a language forbidden their parents or grandparents [is] a political act'' (1989, 6). Similarly, Redding praises Dunbar's poetry, while Houston Baker finds it lacking in sufficient ''mastery of form'' (1987b, 37). There are lots of other examples of this kind of disagreement—for example, the disagreements of Redding and Baker on the value of Booker T. Washington's work. There is also the possibility of deconstructing critical texts and looking at what is missing. To cite only one example, Stepto and Redding (despite the value of their work) have gaps in their books because of a lack of significant treatment of women.

What are the tangible results of this? I have already suggested that students can be empowered by being able to see that literary-critical texts often contradict each other and that no one text or critic can be taken as the final word on any topic. In addition, students, both black and white, are empowered in actual classroom practice. Too often, I have witnessed antagonism in the classroom between white and black students, particularly when an African American text was being discussed. White students speak tentatively; and often, black students don't speak, waiting to pounce on the mistakes of white students. That may be the only time that many black students speak, and white students are afraid to challenge things they disagree with for fear of being called racist. The employment of this critical theory makes clear to everyone, white and black, that they have things to learn about how texts operate.

This also holds true with regard to faculty members. Again, I want to emphasize that African American literature can and must be taught at all levels. In order to teach it, however, it is necessary to learn, know, and fully understand the literary tradition within which it exists. This knowledge is available and readily accessible. One does not have to be African American to teach African American literature. However, just as it is important for students, it is also important that faculty get to the desk, the kitchen table, or the library and do their homework.

In my own department, this has proven true. Last year, I proposed that the department change the major and require one course in African American literature. There was a great deal of opposition, on the supposed grounds that there were only two people in the department of forty-three capable of teaching the material, and that this would ''ghettoize'' the teaching of African American literature. I confronted one member of the department who had an acknowledged interest in the material, was in the process of reading an honors thesis on African American literature, but was initially opposed to the potential new requirement. Interestingly enough, the writer of the thesis was using Gates in her analysis; and after reading her analysis and grasping its applicability, my colleague had a change of opinion.

Not so long ago, Melville and Blake were names not seen on syllabi. More recently, Kate Chopin and Agnes Smedley were unknown. The time has come to fully expand syllabi and give African American writers their full place. And it is literary theory that will help make this change take place.

Notes

1. *New Literary History* featured a debate in 1987 between Joyce Joyce, Skip Gates, and Houston Baker on the uses of literary theory. Also in 1987, in *Cultural Critique*, Barbara Christian joined the debate, and Gates added to what he had said earlier in *New Literary History*. For perspectives on this debate, see the essays by Theodore Mason (1988) and Michael Awkward (1988).

2. For an extended treatment of this topic, see the essay by William Spanos in *Boundary 2*. One of many things to note in Spanos's essay is his disagreement with Gerald Graff, who, one might think, is calling for the same thing Spanos is. But as Spanos points out, theory for Graff ends up being nothing more than "a neutral instrument of humanist pluralism" (1989, 70).

15 Less Is More: Coverage, Critical Diversity, and the Limits of Pluralism

Douglas Lanier
University of New Hampshire

When we teach an introduction to literature, what are we introducing to our students? What was once an obvious answer to that question has been complicated by the present state of literary studies, what Terry Eagleton has described as "at root a crisis in the definition of the subject itself" (1983, 214). Since at least Matthew Arnold, literary study has been defined primarily in terms of conservatorship, the preservation of "the best that has been thought and said." This curatorial mission has taken the form of the detailed exegesis of texts and, just as important, the imparting of a properly appreciative, even reverential attitude toward them. Such a conception of literary study was passed on with minimal revisions to the New Critics, whose distinctive premises and practices—isolating textual meaning from authorial intent and readerly affect, searching for a principle of textual unity (often found in paradox or tension), reading closely, attending to transhistorical "themes"—became the pedagogical norm in the literature classrooms of the postwar period. It is, I dare say, how most readers of this essay were first introduced to literary criticism.

From this curatorial conception of literary study has developed an enormously influential model for introductory literature courses, what we might call the "coverage" model,[1] a model that, consciously or unconsciously, shapes how such courses have long been organized and taught. If we conceive of literary study primarily as the preservation of a body of texts worthy of special attention, it follows that an introductory course should above all introduce students to a representative sampling of those texts. It is for that reason that introductory literature courses typically assign a wide range of texts—one or two per class meeting—to give students a taste of the literary banquet over which English departments preside. This copious smorgasbord of works begs for some principle of unity and organization, and it is typically supplied by one of several models: a "survey" of genres, themes, formal devices, or, less frequently at the introductory level, of geographical regions, ethnic groups, or historical periods. The "coverage" model is supported by a powerful anthology industry as well as a number of institutional factors: professors can teach their favorite texts with a minimum of justification; students can experience "the kaleidoscope of literary expression" (to quote one anthology) without engaging in the difficulties of contextualization or research; both professor and student can fall back on New Critical methods of reading, keeping their preparation times to a minimum; professors can attract potential majors by offering students variety; no interest group within a department need feel that "their" works have been slighted or that their thunder has been stolen for their upper-level courses. The coverage model is designed primarily to "expose" students to a literary canon (however conceived), the value of that exposure being self-evident, never itself a topic for discussion.

Unfortunately, this model—with its stress on a variety and sheer number of texts—can mislead students about the nature of literature and literary interpretation. Since the works studied typically change with each class or two as we strain to "cover" a "representative" sample, an introductory course can rather easily degenerate into the pedagogical version of the two-week package tour of Europe: "If it's Thursday, this must be Eudora Welty." That is, the very form of the course encourages our students—particularly those who have had the least experience with literary works—to see the many and various texts we throw at them as one grand and ill-distinguished intertextual blur, like America seen from an interstate highway. From a speeding tour bus, we provide students with fleeting glimpses of an overly homogenized realm called "literature," whose inhabitants—John Donne, James Joyce, Flannery O'Connor, and Alice Walker—are distinguished by little more than an author's name, a headnote, and stylistic differences, except for the single context provided by the syllabus: Joyce's "Araby" as an example of a short story with an epiphany. Indeed, the coverage model tends to reinforce New Critical assumptions, for when one changes the work with each new class, there is time only to examine those works as "verbal icons," each representative of a single formal characteristic, theme, region, or historical period.[2] What is more, our students are not called upon to examine their own critical presuppositions, to construct multiple contexts for a single text, or to recognize how different strategies of interpretation might reinforce or conflict with one another. They have, in short, little opportunity or incentive to reflect upon the theoretical premises that govern the very activity in which they are engaged.

Recently, the conception of literary studies I have been describing has come under scrutiny as scholars have questioned the political exclusions and ideological assumptions packed into Arnold's phrase "the best." Many have come to argue that literary study is characterized less by its distinctive object "literature" than by its focus upon the process and grounds of interpretation itself (see, for example, Scholes 1985; Graff 1987, 247–62). Armed with a poststructuralist awareness that our knowledge of literary texts is constructed, not merely recovered or preserved, these scholars have stressed that reading is necessarily a transaction between the textual object and reading subject, an encounter or experience profoundly shaped by the interpretive assumptions and procedures readers bring to the text. The questions one asks condition the answers one is likely (though not guaranteed) to "discover." What Patricinio Schweickart has called a "utopian" conception of reading (1989, 121–22)—reading untroubled by differences and inequities among readers—has been replaced by our awareness that we necessarily read from within some intersubjective frame of reference, within the shared premises and procedures of what Stanley Fish has dubbed an "interpretive community" (1980a, 167–73).

This paradigm shift should prompt us to rethink the task of introducing students to literary study. If we conceive of literary study as focused at least as much on interpretive processes as on texts, coverage becomes a much less important goal, particularly in an introductory class. Before students move into studying a body of works in their subsequent English classes, an introductory class can provide them with an opportunity to inquire into their own interpretive premises and moves, to master other ways of construing texts, and, above all, to understand that all literary knowledge is constructed according to principles that are inevitably interested. However, such an inquiry is complicated by our students' epistemological assumptions. Most students claim that they have no literary theories, even though as Frederic Jameson has observed, in reality they enter our classrooms already armed with culturally sanctioned and largely unconscious critical strategies, the contradictions and implications of which they are unaware, but through which they nonetheless read the works we assign (1982, 73–74). Some of those assumptions, gleaned from my students' journals, might be summarized in this way:

- Literature expresses the writer's individuality or unique sensibility; it is best studied in terms of biography and authorial intent.
- Literature is universal, expressive of certain transhistorical and transcultural truths.

- Literature reflects the ideas of the historical period in which it was produced, ideas that are homogeneous and unitary.
- Literature provides a consoling spiritual haven from a heartless world.
- Literature serves to entertain or distract; if a work is designated as entertaining, it is without significant propositional content.
- Literature consists of "hidden meanings"—usually conceived in terms of a moral message or highly wrought symbolic patterns—that a reader must be trained to uncover.

Many of these critical premises accord quite closely with those underlying the "commonsense" aesthetics of expressive realism and New Criticism, an ideological nexus Catherine Belsey has lucidly outlined and critiqued (1980a, 1–20).

It is for that reason that one cannot merely "let the texts speak for themselves." What feels to our students like the bliss of pure unmediated contact with Shakespeare or Brontë is in fact an encounter already fraught with all manner of unexamined theoretical presuppositions and expectations. Thus, perhaps the most crucial aim of an introductory literature class should be to challenge what is the most pervasive of our students' assumptions: that instead of constituting the reading process, literary theories are something added after the fact, abstract "isms" that stand between a reader and some precritical (and hence authentic) experience of a work. One cannot challenge this assumption simply by replacing the standard New Critical approach with another current critical orientation—say, deconstruction or New Historicism. For one thing, such a substitution leaves in place, in the very form of the syllabus, the coverage model with all its essentialist assumptions about the nature of literary study. For another, it potentially plays into the power dynamics of the classroom, replacing one party line with another without ever seriously challenging our students' objectivist or subjectivist notions of interpretation. At worst, students respond by developing strategies of resistance to all theoretical claims, "givin' 'em what they want to hear" without acknowledging their own interpretive assumptions or engaging with the question of how theories shape how we read. Instead the introductory literature class can introduce students to a range of critical strategies in an effort to demonstrate that a single text can be read differently by different interpretive communities. The object is not, really, to introduce students to the current theoretical terrain. As Bruce Henricksen has recently observed, there is good reason to be skeptical about how much an undergraduate is enriched by an introduction to current professional disputes within English departments (1990, 33). But there is value in making our students conscious of their own Platonic conceptions of knowledge, if not to change their minds, at least to make them cognizant that they already hold a theoretical position.[3] The course I am describing seeks to initiate an extended reflection by our students on their own interpretive premises, a reflection that begins by introducing theoretical difference into their first encounter with literary texts at the college level. By doing so, one can be truer to actual critical practice within and without the academy; one can problematize the notion that one interpretive strategy is necessarily more appropriate for a given text than another or that there is a single "correct" approach; one can juxtapose the claims of various interpretive communities so that students can distinguish among them and determine their own commitments. Most important, one can provide students with an extended object lesson in the consequences of theory for their own critical practice.

To these ends, the English department of Allegheny College has designed an introductory literature course that investigates different interpretive models for reading literary texts.[4] The course is divided into four units, each conceived as an introduction to a different interpretive approach: formalist, historical, psychoanalytic, and feminist.[5] At the heart of the class is a single substantial core text chosen by the instructor—a novel, play, or body of poetry or short stories.[6] Class activities are designed to teach the interpretive approaches through supplementary readings and through application, with considerable time devoted to the discussion of critical premises and methodology. With the exception of the formalist unit, in which the core text is treated as a self-sufficient "well-wrought urn," each unit stresses the extent to which criticism is always intertextual, a dialogue in which one text or discourse (and usually more) is used to contextualize or interrogate another. It is for that reason that I assign supplementary texts that might normally be seen as "nonliterary," works of history, psychology, and feminist studies. During the term students write four different essays on the core text, each essay applying a different critical approach. The writing assignments are designed to suggest how a single work can be profitably interpreted using different critical strategies. Each essay requires some research and must move significantly beyond class discussion. Though one might expect students to tire of discussing and writing about the same work, their evaluation forms suggest that most of them enjoy the opportunity to explore a substantial work thoroughly. This approach allows students to focus their energies on honing their interpretive skills and developing a critical self-awareness rather than mastering a kaleidoscope of minimally contextualized anthology selections.

Let me briefly describe how this class operates, using Mary Shelley's *Frankenstein* as a core text.[7] On the first day of class, I pose the question, "How do we know when our reading of a text is correct?" Typically we briefly discuss the problems of making the author's intent, the reader's responses, the historical context, or the "text itself" a final arbiter of interpretive disputes, my goal being to raise the question of validity without resolving it. To make the issue concrete and to extend the discussion, as a class we read several haiku with an eye toward constructing interpretations of them. At the end of the period, I reveal that the haiku are computer-generated, and ask students to write a short essay reflecting, first, upon the assumptions and moves they made in constructing their interpretations, and second, upon the effect my revelation has on what we did in class. This exercise works, admittedly in a dramatic way, toward defamiliarizing my students' own interpretive premises and getting them to ponder how those premises shape how they read.

Formalist Criticism

Formalist criticism is a good place to begin a discussion of interpretive methods, for most students, because of their New Critical training in secondary schools, find its assumptions and procedures familiar. Indeed, so "natural" and "objective" seems this mode of reading that I often find it difficult at first to convince most students that formalism is, in fact, a distinct critical approach. For them, literary criticism could only mean examining a text as a self-explanatory, self-contained artifact composed of formal devices, tropes, and themes. Because formalist criticism entails what is to our students an arcane technical vocabulary, and because we must end up devoting so much time to teaching that vocabulary, students frequently assume that formalist criticism consists primarily of the identification of formal devices—"*Frankenstein* uses the frame tale"—and themes—"*Frankenstein* deals with man versus technology." This assumption is, among other things, a reflex of certain epistemological premises about the relationship of form to content: form is a reified (and ideally transparent) carrier of content. Thus, for example, when discussing point of view in *Frankenstein*, my students are quite capable of identifying the first-person point of view and illustrating it copiously, but they are not nearly as adept at suggesting how that narrative voice creates interpretive possibilities toward which they must adopt a critical stance.

To raise this issue, I ask students to rewrite Victor's terrifying first encounter with the monster from another point of view, either from the monster's or an omniscient perspective. By doing so, students immediately discover that Victor's account is also an interpretation of the events it describes, and perhaps not an altogether reliable one. Is the monster's grin "really" sardonic, or is it joyful? Is his outstretched hand—which Victor interprets as intended "to detain me" (1981 [1818], 43)—threatening or beckoning? Students debate the relative merits of their rewrites, rejecting or accepting each other's accounts on the basis of other passages in the novel and, in the process, creating interpretations of Victor's or the monster's character. This discussion easily broadens into an examination of the Chinese-box structure of the novel as a whole, one function of which is to set up parallels and contrasts between the Romantic perspectives of Walton, Victor, and the monster.[8] We also examine the monster's two other grins, both placed at crucial moments in the narrative, and discuss what sort of pattern those grins form: Progression (ABC)? Sudden change (AAB)? Reversal (ABA)? No pattern at all? The sort of rewriting that opens these discussions teaches two powerful principles of formalist criticism: first, that the interpretive possibilities raised by the rewrite should be settled by referring to the work itself, and second, that formalist criticism depends upon paradigmatic substitution, that is, upon imagining the other possible formal choices an author might have made, but didn't.

After examining several formal elements—imagery, irony, setting, symbolism—in detail, students write drafts of their formalist essay, and as a class we discuss the assumptions and problems in several of the drafts, a procedure we follow at the end of each unit. Two issues invariably arise. We notice that the writers find it difficult to settle some interpretive issues without appealing to extratextual information, such matters as historical background or authorial intent. We also notice that these student writers put much weight on the notion of "themes," a notion we then struggle as a class to define. By so doing, we come to see that this seemingly neutral concept is packed with assumptions about the universality and unity of a work of art, assumptions that, upon examination, some students are less willing to accept. Besides helping students to revise their essays, these discussions highlight the limits and exclusions of the formalist approach and thereby suggest that texts may not, after all, be as autonomous as they seem.

Historical Criticism

This unit is designed to situate the core text within a sociohistorical context. However, as Brook Thomas suggests (1987, 510–11 and passim), merely adding a fifteen-minute lecture on the Romantic Age to the class will not fundamentally change our students' lack of historical consciousness. Because under the "coverage" model we typically treat history as discrete and supplementary "background" and have time to introduce it only through short, necessarily reductive lectures or secondary readings, we unwittingly reinforce our students' supposition that a historical period is demarcated by a single self-consistent set of ideas (a *Zeitgeist*) and that literature *reflects*, rather than enters into dialogue with or changes, that *a priori* "world picture." The student necessarily proceeds passively, "finding" within the literary text those ideas outlined by the professor.

One way of avoiding this approach to historical criticism is to focus, as the New Historicists have, on the textuality of history itself, that is, on the necessity of constructing a historical understanding from texts that must themselves be interpreted. For *Frankenstein* I assemble a small archive of primary texts from the period from science, education, political science, and literature. From this archive we work inductively toward construing the issues of the period, focusing as much on discontinuities and contradictions as on continuities. For example, in her preface Mary Shelley tells us that one germ of *Frankenstein* consisted of discussions between Byron and Percy Shelley about "the nature of the principle of life," in particular "the experiments of Dr. Darwin" (xxv); her reference is almost certainly to Erasmus Darwin's note on spontaneous generation in canto I of his *The Temple of Nature*. After having read passages from Clifford Geertz's *Local Knowledge* (1983) and Stephen Greenblatt's "Culture" (1990), as a class we examine the mechanist-vitalist debate to which Darwin contributed by attempting a "thick description" of several famous biological experiments of the day: Needham, Buffon, Spallanzani, Galvani. We proceed inductively, asking, "what specific questions did each scientist answer and raise with each experiment? How might this experiment have changed the conception of the body? What were the ramifications of this experiment for metaphysics, social policy, revolutionary politics, educational theory, medical practice, scientific ethics, industrial development? How is this experiment described, and what does that description reveal?"[9] We then examine how *Frankenstein* might contribute to our historical construct, noting, for example, that Victor's turn toward a Romantic view of nature in the middle chapters springs from his horror at the mechanistic view of the body his own successful experiment grotesquely confirms. The discussion quickly eddies out into the study of other texts in the archive and basic methodological issues in historicist criticism. For instance, the innocent question "wouldn't Mary Shelley have had to read Buffon's or Galvani's work for it to influence her novel?" might lead to a brief consideration of different models of intertextuality and the circulation of discourse within a culture.

Psychoanalytic Criticism

At the center of Freudian psychoanalytic criticism—my focus for this unit—is Freud's distinction between manifest content (the text) and latent content (the unconscious psychic economy that produces that text). Many of my students are already acquainted with—and skeptical about—the basic psychoanalytic tripartite Id, ego, and superego, and typically they view these as reified sites within the psyche rather than the products of psychic forces.[10] The result can be that students rather mechanically map this psychic topography onto the work, converting every text into a Freudian allegory. To combat this conception of psychoanalytic criticism (and its even more reductive incarnation, the search for "holes and poles"), I stress Freud's account of psychic *processes*: repression, condensation, displacement, negation.

After discussing a passage from *The Interpretation of Dreams* (Freud's analysis of his dream of July 23–24, 1895) and several of Freud's essays ("Formulations on the Two Principles of Mental Functioning," "Repression," "Negation," excerpts from *The Psychopathology of Everyday Life*,[11] we examine Victor's dream:

> I thought I saw Elizabeth, in the bloom of health, walking in the streets of Ingolstadt. Delighted and surprised, I embraced her, but as I imprinted the first kiss on her lips, they became livid with the hue of death; her features appeared to change, and I thought that I held the corpse of my dead mother in my arms; a shroud enveloped her form, and I saw the grave-worms crawling in the folds of the flannel. (43)

On a first reading, most students see this passage as surprising and undermotivated, and that reaction prompts them to ask what unconscious processes are at work here. In his dream Victor substitutes his dead mother for Elizabeth at the very moment he makes a rare show of desire. Does this dream reveal Victor's repression of passion by substituting a doubly blasphemous object for that desire? Does it indicate that Victor regards his passion for Elizabeth as incestuous?

(Elizabeth is, after all, presented as a gift of Victor's mother and has replaced her in the Frankenstein household.) Does it indicate Victor's fear that the possible product of his desire for Elizabeth—a child—might bring death, just as Elizabeth brought death to Caroline? (This dream occurs immediately before the monster, Victor's surrogate child, first gazes at its creator.) By combing the early chapters for evidence and by working out in detail the psychic economy that leads to this dream, students construct a psychoanalysis of Victor's character that, in their third essay, they are invited to extend to other episodes in the novel. We also discuss Shelley's preface, in which she claims that the genesis of the novel is a dream-like vision of the monster's awakening that "arose in [her] mind with a vividness far beyond the usual bounds of reverie" (xxv). A short examination of Shelley's biography, particularly the nexus of births and deaths in the months prior to the novel's genesis, provides plenty of material for discussions of possible psychobiographical readings.

Feminist Criticism

In this section of the course, I assign passages from two ancillary texts, Mary Wollstonecraft's *A Vindication of the Rights of Woman* (1982 [1792]) and Virginia Woolf's *A Room of One's Own* (1929). The first serves as a sketch of culturally determined gender differences during the period and offers a pointed critique of their political and social ramifications in women's lives. To make the link to *Frankenstein,* we examine how Shelley distinguishes the masculine and feminine roles of Felix and Agatha Delacey. From our often lively discussions of Wollstonecraft's polemic, we move to an examination of the women of *Frankenstein,* focusing particularly on Elizabeth, Justine, and Safie. The case of Justine makes a particularly interesting study of patriarchal power at work. Her alleged crime, the murder of William Frankenstein, is all the more horrific because the accused is a woman (and a mother figure at that!); Elizabeth's pleas on her behalf, because they issue from a woman, tragically backfire. My students' irritation at Justine's confession—most are disgusted that she is such a "wimp"—provokes them to consider how the passivity and powerlessness into which women are coaxed can lead to their self-destruction. (Victor's very different fate when he is accused of Clerval's murder makes a telling contrast.) We also discuss the representation of masculinity within the novel, discussing, for example, Victor's tortured inability to resolve the tension between domestic tranquility and Romantic ambition.

A Room of One's Own movingly opens the issue of the difficulties women writers have historically faced in a patriarchal culture, and it leads directly into a discussion of the two prefaces to *Frankenstein*. The 1817 preface, probably the work of Percy Shelley, self-consciously and self-confidently sets the novel within a masculine literary tradition. By contrast, the 1831 preface, by Mary Shelley herself, gives a very different account, playing up her anxieties about publication—"I am very averse to bringing myself forward in print" (xxi)—and about the "blank incapability of invention which is the greatest misery of authorship" (xxiv). Might the novel itself, we ask, exemplify those anxieties, particularly since Shelley speaks of the text as her "hideous progeny" (xxvi)?[12] Why does Shelley say of the scientist she imagines hunched over his creation, "His success would terrify the artist; he would rush away from his odious handiwork, horror-stricken" (xxv)? Is it possible to see in Victor's fears about his terrifying creature the displaced anxieties of a young woman writer addressing herself to a male literary coterie?[13]

The method of teaching an introductory course that I have outlined here is not without its difficulties and risks. Some of the more sophisticated supplementary readings require extended introduction and explication, particularly for less well-prepared students, though by giving up an ideal of coverage one can devote more time to discussions of the mysteries of Freud or Woolf. (The confidence students gain from tackling challenging secondary materials, even at a basic level, is well worth the time spent.) The course can easily degenerate into a class on the core text, or on theory, rather than on the interplay between the two; students will not necessarily emerge from the class with guaranteed "exposure" to the usual battery of formalist concepts. Even more worrisome, this course model might unwittingly encourage precisely the kind of facile critical pluralism—"different but equal" or "the more, the merrier"—that has recently come under attack from a number of quarters. As Eagleton notes in *Literary Theory*, pluralism has its own tacit politics: "seeking to understand everybody's point of view quite often suggests that you yourself are disinterestedly up on high or in the middle, and trying to resolve conflicting viewpoints into a consensus implies a refusal of the truth that some conflicts can be resolved on one side alone" (1983, 199). However, in practice the class need not fall into the pluralist trap. It is true that the success of the class depends in this case upon the faculty bracketing their own cherished critical commitments and teaching approaches they might otherwise find limited or even misleading. But one goal of the class is a certain level of informed critical contention that can flourish only when students become aware of the extent to which different interpretive communities vie with each other over what quickly become theoretical issues, each interpretive approach contradicting or complicating the premises of the one preceding. For example, because psychoanalytic critics insist upon reading texts as symptoms of unconscious psychic forces, they draw into question the empiricist bias of some types of historical criticism; by insisting upon the inequities of gender roles within history and exposing "utopian" modes of reading, feminist critics draw our attention to the elision of gender differences in many accounts of history and subjectivity. By focusing on those and other incompatibilities, by attending to the blindnesses of critical positions even as they master them, students learn to resist the powerful drive toward premature closure upon one theoretical orthodoxy. Students can come to see what is at stake when they adopt an interpretive position and they are better prepared to do so knowingly and responsibly in subsequent classes. What is more, by experiencing critical contention, students can see its value and, if nothing else, sense the difficulty—if not impossibility—of a casual ecumenism.

Perhaps the greatest resistance to posing theoretical questions in an introductory literature class springs from the fear that in the process we sacrifice "the joy of text," that premature forays into Derrida, Gramsci, and Kristeva (to parrot the usual caricature) will rob our students of the pleasure of a "good read." Yet even if we leave aside the questionable assumption that narrative pleasure is itself unshaped by a reader's expectations, expectations that ultimately spring from some theory of reading and ideological positioning within culture, it is on the question of pleasure that, I have found, the rewards of this approach most outweigh its risks. For this class offers my students the pleasure of participating self-consciously in the production of literary meaning. It offers them the pleasure of mastering a repertoire of interpretive approaches from which they can determine their own commitments. It offers the pleasure of posing and refining (if not always answering) those nasty foundational questions our students always ponder but so rarely articulate in literature classes ("How do you know it means that?" "What do you do about the author's intent?" "Why is my interpretation different from yours?"). It offers the pleasure of actively interrogating and challenging, rather than passively accepting, secondary materials and various professorial agendas, and of making links to other disciplines too often walled off from literature by formidable institutional barriers. And most important, if what we finally seek to impart in this class is the pleasure of the literary text, this approach makes available an awareness of the multiple and contestatory pleasures any work of literature makes possible.

Notes

1. I adapt here Gerald Graff's discussion of the "coverage" model of literature departments in the final chapter of his *Professing Literature* (1987).

2. This experience is reinforced by introductory anthologies, for the principles of selection and juxtaposition that govern the anthology tend also to narrow the kinds of interpretive questions students are encouraged to put to a text. Put another way, anthologies, like all organized literary collections, create a certain determinate contextuality for each work within the larger frame of the volume, what Neil Fraistat has called "contexture" (1986, 3). By so doing, they set up a normative "horizon of expectations" without having to defend their critical premises or present alternative critical models. Fraistat's suggestive discussion of "contexture" (3–17) might be fruitfully extended to the ideological critique of literary anthologies, the principal context within which our students read the texts we assign.

3. For an incisive discussion of the relation of epistemological presuppositions of students to the teaching of reading and writing, see Kaufer and Waller (1985, 69–77). Schroeder (1986, 28–30) cannily suggests the link between teaching formats, interpretive premises, and the split between essentialism and radical pluralism within critical theory.

4. A number of recent works, some pedagogical, some theoretical, exemplify a similar critical model. See, as examples, Jeffrey C. Robinson's remarkable *Radical Literary Education* (1987) or the conclusion of William Cain's *The Crisis in Criticism* (1984) for descriptions of similar approaches to introductory literature courses; see also Ross C. Murphin's useful edition of Conrad's *Heart of Darkness* (1989), which includes units on psychoanalytic, reader-response, feminist, deconstructionist, and New Historical criticism, including an introduction, analysis, and a short bibliography keyed to each theoretical approach, as well as his similar edition of Hawthorne's *The Scarlet Letter* (1990). Also forthcoming in this series from St. Martin's are critical editions of *Wuthering Heights*, *Frankenstein*, and *Hamlet*.

5. These units accord with the interests and specializations within the Allegheny department. In other departments, other units might be assigned: structuralism, reader-response, Marxist, deconstruction, etc.

6. Those texts have been both canonical and noncanonical and have included texts by women and persons of color. In the past year, instructors have taught Shakespeare's *Taming of the Shrew* and *Twelfth Night*, the poems of Emily Dickinson, Thomas Hardy's *Tess of the D'Urbervilles*, F. Scott Fitzgerald's *The Great Gatsby*, William Faulkner's *Light in August*, Toni Morrison's *Beloved* and *The Bluest Eye*, Anne Tyler's *The Accidental Tourist*, Nadine Gordimer's *Burger's Daughter*, Margaret Atwood's *The Handmaid's Tale*, and Paule Marshall's *Praisesong for the Widow*.

7. The description that follows, I should stress, sketches out my own adaptation of the basic model outlined above. Although at Allegheny the

general outline of the course—four interpretive approaches, a single core text, all major essay assignments on the same text—is the same for all classes, other instructors have approached the model somewhat differently, including an ancillary literature anthology, for example, and choosing a small number of texts from it to model each critical approach for their students. For the historical unit, for example, one might select from an anthology several American works from a single decade (say, 1860–1870) and use a variety of historical materials to model the process of historical reading for the class. For the psychological unit, one might discuss the notion of displacement and then examine how it operates in several elegies. Still other instructors choose from an anthology a small set of texts they return to in each unit. I am grateful to my colleagues at Allegheny for numerous discussions about issues both theoretical and practical involved in teaching this course; I would also like to thank Glenn Holland and Maureen MacNeil for their helpful comments.

8. One advantage of beginning with point of view is that it dovetails with the opening discussion of critical perspectives. Once students understand, by producing their own texts, that a narrative is inescapably told from some point of view, one that is never neutral or objective, they more easily accept that narrative is also read from a point of view.

9. For an excellent overview of these issues, see MacNeil 1987, passim.

10. See Francoise Meltzer's cogent discussion in "Unconscious" (1990, especially 147–52).

11. With the exception of *Psychopathology*, these passages are available in *The Freud Reader* (1989). Appignanesi's *Freud for Beginners* (1979) provides students a lucid and entertaining introduction to basic Freudian concepts and includes a glossary of terms and a short bibliography.

12. Indeed, the phrase "hideous progeny" seems all the more striking when set next to Percy Shelley's use of the birth *topoi* in his *Defense of Poetry*. There he claims that "a great statue or picture grows under the power of the artist as a child in the mother's womb" (1971, 511), a formulation that calls into question the creator's control over his creation even as it mystifies artifact, artist, and the supposedly ineffable artistic process.

13. On this much explored topic, see Moers (1977, 138–51), Poovey (1980), Sherwin (1981), Gilbert and Gubar (1979, 221–47) and, more generally, studies by Castle (1979) and Friedman (1989). I am also indebted to Marilyn May for her essay "Publish and Perish" on *Frankenstein* and publication anxiety (forthcoming in *Papers on Language and Literature*). As feminist critics have documented, this anxiety has a considerable pedigree; a succinct comparison piece to open discussion on the issue might be Anne Bradstreet's "The Author to Her Book."

V Dialogue and Deconstruction in the Classroom

16 From Discourse in Life to Discourse in Poetry: Teaching Poems as Bakhtinian Speech Genres

Don Bialostosky
University of Toledo

Permit me to open with a hypothetical discourse situation taken from the Bakhtin School text from which I draw my title.[1]

> A couple are sitting in a room. They are silent. One says, "Well!" The other says nothing in reply. For us who were not present in the room at the time of the exchange, this "conversation" is completely inexplicable. Taken in isolation the utterance "well", is void and quite meaningless. Nevertheless the couple's peculiar exchange, consisting of only one word, though one to be sure which is expressively inflected, is full of meaning and significance and quite complete. (Voloshinov 1983, 10)

What do we need to know to make sense of this utterance? It is not enough, the text goes on to say, to "fiddle with the purely verbal part of the utterance" (10). And even if we know the tone in which the word is uttered we will still be at a loss. What we are missing is

> That *"non-verbal context"* in which the word "well" sounded intelligibly for the listener . . . (1) a *spatial purview* common to the speakers . . . (2) the couple's *common knowledge and understanding of the circumstances,* and finally (3) their *common evaluation* of these circumstances.
>
> At the moment of the exchange *both* individuals *glanced* at the window and *saw* that it was snowing. *Both knew* that it was already May and long since time for spring, and finally, that they both were sick of the protracted winter. *Both were waiting* for spring and *were annoyed* by the late snowfall. (11)

Two interlocutors who can take so much in common for granted can say quite a lot with a single adverb, spoken with a tone "indignantly reproachful, but softened with a touch of humor." Jack Benny perhaps showed those of us of a certain age how much could be said by an indignantly intoned "Well!" under well-known circumstances. Clearly, the more knowledge and the more circumstances two or more people share, the more they can say through one or a few words richly intoned. The *"communality of evaluations,"* my text goes on to say, depends upon shared *"real-life conditions"* such as "membership of the speakers to a single family, profession, class, or any other social group, and of course, to the same period for the speakers must be contemporaries" (Voloshinov 1983, 10–12).

I hope my readers will be interested enough by what I am about to say to discover for themselves what use the essay I have been quoting makes of this hypothetical situation. What I want to do here is turn it to a purpose of my own, for it strikes me, as I think about the introductory literature classroom, how little the circumstances of utterance in that classroom resemble those in this Russian room in May. If (a big "if") teachers and students are looking at a poem instead of looking out the window, they cannot be so sure that they are seeing the same thing, for the poem itself is not a visible scene but an utterance from a set of social and spatial circumstances different from that classroom. Teachers and students approach a poem more like those who were not present in the room where the word "well" was uttered than like those looking out the window at the same weather. The "conversation" embodied in the poem may be completely inexplicable to them without some construction of the circumstances it takes for granted.

And the teacher and students cannot take each other for granted any more than they can take the poem for granted, for they cannot presume upon commonalities of family, profession, class, or generation or those, we might add, of race or gender that might have enabled them to share a richly assured tone in which much could be said in few words. The student in an introductory course is by definition and design one who does not share or even necessarily aspire to the teacher's profession. Generational differences, too, are inescapable except for the greenest of new teachers. Family can be shared with none of our students; race, gender, and class only with some, except in women's all-black colleges or other homogeneous teaching situations.

No wonder, then, if teachers and students alike find this situation threatening. If, as the essay I have been quoting remarks, "clarity and conviction" of basic tone depend upon an "atmosphere of shared feeling," the lack of such shared feeling—of the *"supporting chorus"* some teachers take their students to be and few students take their teachers to be—would have affected the intonation differently. It "would have gone in another direction and become more complex: perhaps with tones of challenge or of vexation with the listener, or, in the end, it might simply have contracted, been reduced to a minimum" (Voloshinov 1983, 14). Whereas those who already share experience and knowledge and values can take each other for granted and enjoy allusive, elliptical, ironic utterances, students and teachers in introductory literature classrooms are forced to explain and defend their experiences and knowledge and evaluations, and they may easily feel irritation and distrust for one another that leads them to contract themselves and reduce their tonal risks to a minimum.

The conditions of communication in the introductory literature classroom are treacherous, and the notorious pathologies of that situation, understandable. The teacher who identifies his own voice with the voice of his author, as Geoffrey Durrant does with Wordsworth, may well come to imagine his students as "children of a world so far removed [from that author's], . . . victims of a culture steeped in sensationalism beyond the poet's worst nightmares, many of them barely capable of a literate sentence in English, or of reading aloud a single line of poetry without stammering or blundering . . . [for whom the poem is] nothing more than marks on the page, or at best English words strung unaccountably together" (1985, 352). Students may well see such teachers and their authors as irrelevant or comical or unintelligible, or they may try to mime those teachers' intonations and evaluations without understanding what they understand or seeing what they see.

I have formulated two pedagogical policies in response to this understanding of the situation of introductory instruction in literature. One is to try to imagine and emphasize the knowledge and experience my students might already have that would enable them to read poems with interest and pleasure and enable me to discuss poems with them without despair or condescension. The second is to expect that students will not know much that my authors take for granted and to be prepared to supply them with explicit sources of that knowledge that will help them understand and appreciate their works more fully. In the remainder of this essay I will elaborate on how my attempt to teach according to the first of these policies, like my understanding of the teaching situation itself, is informed by what I have learned from the theories of the Bakhtin School. I will say of the second policy only that it entails introducing students at least to excerpts from theoretical essays like the ones I am drawing upon in this essay, pointing them toward dictionaries, handbooks, and reference works, and confessing my own dependence upon other scholars for my knowledge of essential "background" information. Scholes, Comley, and Ulmer's *Text Book* (1988) to me exemplifies the way in which beginning students can be and should be brought to share in the kinds of texts that inform their teachers' questions and responses.

I have so far emphasized the way in which the Bakhtin School's analysis of discourse highlights the particularities of shared knowledge and evaluation that define and limit communication in situations where "the implied real purview of an utterance is narrow." To pursue my first policy, however, I must also bring out the possibility of "a broader purview" in which "an utterance may be dependent only on constant, stable elements of life and on essential, fundamental social evaluations" (Voloshinov 1983, 13). The difference between these narrow and broad purviews is relative, not absolute, but it is important and warrants inquiry into what students, teachers, and poets can be expected to know despite differences of all the kinds I have already acknowledged.

They will, for one thing, know something about differences of social rank or class, national or racial or religious group, professional expertise, gender, and age, even if they do not always know how to recognize the signs by which a particular group evaluates its relations to another. They may have to infer or inquire into how a Count stacks up against a Duke in the world of "My Last Duchess," but they will be prepared to give weight to differences of this kind and to estimate their role in the relations among speaker, listener, and hero in a given utterance.[2] Though they cannot possibly share all of the social positions of their teachers or of the writers they read, they can recognize and work with signs of social position and their effects in shaping discourse.

They will also know something of what Wordsworth called, in the masculine language of the Enlightenment, "the general passions and thoughts and feelings of men" in their connection, as he put it, with "our moral sentiments and animal sensations, and with the causes which excite these; with the operations of the elements and the appearances of the visible universe; with storm and sun-shine, with the revolutions of the seasons, with cold and heat, with loss of friends and kindred, with injuries and resentments, gratitude and hope, with fear and sorrow" (Owen 1974, 82). Wordsworth, we should remember, also recognized how all these sentiments and passions might be modified by urban as opposed to rural experience, particular losses or injuries suffered or not suffered, and particular climates. He sometimes (though not always) acknowledged differences between masculine and feminine experiencers. Despite these particularities and others that he did not acknowledge, I can say, however, that I have not yet had to explain love to a student who professed not to know what it is, though I must also say that I have learned not to presume that it has been felt only for members of the opposite sex or even for members of the same species. Storm and sunshine have been in everyone's experiential repertoire, but we valued them somewhat differently in Seattle than in Salt Lake City.

Students, too, can be counted on to know many of the basic conceptual metaphors that Lakoff and Turner demonstrate are part of ordinary language as well as poetic diction. Few students have not spoken of dying as "passing away" or death as "rest" or described purposes as "goals" or "targets." Though they may well have not recognized these and many other familiar conceptions as metaphorical and though they may easily confuse what meanings and evaluations are being transferred from one conceptual domain to another when they produce an explicit analysis of such metaphors, they have been speaking metaphors all their lives without knowing it and can be brought to know this.

Explicit grammatical understanding is not widely shared among our undergraduates, but we can count on a remarkable amount of practical grammatical recognition—enough to build on. I have yet to meet a student for whom a poem is "nothing more than marks on a page, or at best English words strung unaccountably together," though I have met some who reassemble the words in their minds to a different pattern than the poet has assembled (I have seen professional critics do this, too). I have, on the other hand, met few students who can diagram a Miltonic sentence without my asking leading questions. Even the study of versification, that most arcane and technical of poetic topics, can find a starting place in the absolutely amazing extent to which native speakers of English can distinguish proper from improper stress on the syllables of words (those who speak English as a second language may have more trouble here). Though the formal rules of prosody must be taught, everyone who has learned those rules can recognize that the first foot in Milton's "Shatter your leaves before the mellowing year" *has to be* a reversed foot, and many can see how that fact might lend special emphasis to the word "shatter."

I have enumerated these several areas of knowledge to which we literature teachers can appeal even where we cannot count on students' knowing something we know or valuing it as we do, because I believe we must trust in this social, cultural, and linguistic knowledge of theirs if we are to lead them to relish and perform more elaborate, self-conscious, and effective verbal performances than they are already accustomed to—the goal, for me, of a literary education. I believe also, and shall now try to demonstrate at some length, that students possess another sort of knowledge, more synthetic and complex than any I have mentioned so far—a kind of knowledge worth making explicit at the outset of their introduction to literature and worth insisting upon throughout it. We professionals share this knowledge with our students, but we are far too likely to take for granted or even to ignore it in pursuit of more exotic game.

I am referring to knowledge of what Bakhtin calls "speech genres," a notion I must pause to explain not because it is hard to grasp overall but because it brings together a lot of aspects that we usually treat separately if we treat them at all.[3] Permit me to open with a definition and some examples. Speech genres are types of utterances (oral or written) with relatively stable thematic content, style, and compositional structure that perform recognizable functions in typical situations of communication. As Bakhtin indicates, there nowhere exists a complete or systematic enumeration of such genres, but our repertoires include lots of them. The apology, the giving of directions, the greeting, the farewell, the invitation, the request, the boast, the taunt, the command, the anecdote are a few of the everyday speech genres we are familiar with. At the more elaborate or complex end—the end Bakhtin calls secondary speech genres—he lists "the elaborate and detailed order, the fairly variegated repertoire of business documents (for the most part standard), and the diverse world of commentary" as well as "the diverse forms of scientific statements and all literary genres (from the proverb to the multivolume novel)" (1986a, 60–61).

What I want to stress about these genres, primary and secondary alike, is that they combine expectations about what will be talked about (thematic content), what sort of language will be appropriate (style), and what parts the utterance must have (compositional structure or what the rhetoricians called "arrangement") with expectations about the situations in which such utterances will be used, the sort of people who will use them, the sort of people they will use them on or with, and the sorts of purposes for which they will be used. At its simplest, knowing about speech genres is a matter of knowing what sort of card to buy with what sort of message to send to what sort of person on what sort of occasion, but it can get pretty elaborate and interesting when the occasion is a commemorative volume for the late Edward King and John Milton writes the message himself and calls it "Lycidas."

Depending on the range of our social relations, all of us have occasion to become able users of some repertoire of speech genres, and as Bakhtin recognizes, and many of us literature teachers know, being good at reading or writing some of the fancy ones doesn't necessarily make us good at some of the others. As he puts it and as I like to tell my students,

> Many people who have an excellent command of a language often feel quite helpless in certain spheres of communication precisely

> because they do not have a practical command of the generic forms used in the given spheres. Frequently a person who has an excellent command of speech in some areas of cultural communication, who is able to read a scholarly paper or engage in scholarly discussion, who speaks very well on social questions, is silent or very awkward in social conversation. Here it is not a matter of an impoverished vocabulary or of style, taken abstractly: this is entirely a matter of the inability to command a repertoire of genres of social conversation. (1986a, 80)

We get good at the speech genres we recognize and practice, and our students are certainly good at speech genres in which we would make fools of ourselves.[4]

We and they and our poets share a considerable repertoire, however, and we can draw on that repertoire to show our students how much they already know about the speech genres many poets are working with, as well as what they can learn from what the poets have done with those speech genres. I have twice now begun an introductory literature class with William Carlos Williams's "This Is Just to Say":

> This Is Just to Say†
>
> I have eaten
> the plums
> that were in
> the icebox
>
> and which
> you were probably
> saving
> for breakfast
>
> Forgive me
> they were delicious
> so sweet
> and so cold.

Students immediately recognize the poem as a representation of an apology, and they can also tell me, when I ask them, that an apology needs a confession of what was done, a declaration of regret or an appeal for forgiveness, and a reason for having done the deed that will somehow extenuate its commission. They recognize that the function of an apology is to restore good relations between its maker and its receiver, relations that have been (or will be in the case of anticipatory apologies) disturbed by the commission of the deed. Further, they also can tell me what is wrong with Williams's apology

† William Carlos Williams: *The Collected Poems of William Carlos Williams, 1909–1939, vol. 1.* Copyright 1938 by New Directions Publishing Corporation. Reprinted by permission of New Directions Publishing Corporation.

according to these criteria for the genre. The last three lines where the extenuating reason belongs don't offer an extenuating reason but an intense declaration of the apology writer's pleasure in doing the deed. Some students take this declaration as a taunt and construct a situation for the utterance in which one roommate has eaten another's plums and wants to rub it in—the two are usually imagined to be of the same sex (usually male) and age. Others imagine a different social relation between writer and addressee in which the writer presumes upon the love of the addressee and imagines that "she"—a lover or wife or mother, but the gender projection remains constant—will be pleased in "his" pleasure—perhaps she was saving them for "his" breakfast anyway. I am struck as I write this that neither my students nor I have noticed until now that the indeterminacy of these alternative accounts of the utterance derives from Williams's choice to omit essential features of the compositional structure of a *written* apology—the salutation to the receiver and the signature of the writer. The opening deictic pronoun requires us to take the apology as a note rather than a spoken apology, but the note does not begin "Darling" and end with "Bill."

The alternative accounts my students invent in the absence of specifying salutations and signatures fill in the kind of situational particulars that the essay I opened with fills in about the adverb "Well!"—thereby determining the tone beyond what is given. I do not see a clear choice between these alternatives, though it pleases me more to imagine the affectionate than the competitive situation. What interests me for present purposes, however, is that students have sufficiently clear and formulable expectations about the speech genre of the apology to recognize the anomaly of Williams's use of it and that they furthermore possess the social sense necessary to construct these alternative readings. They will get the point about salutations and signatures next time I teach the poem as easily as they have seen the problem with the non-extenuating last three lines. With a little pushing, they can also see (though it does not please them at first) that their construals of the situation quickly take them beyond what the poem gives them and lead them to begin elaborating the situation it implies according to their own interests and imaginings, though not without relation to what the poem has provided them. I encourage this elaboration but also encourage them to notice where they leave the evidence of the poem behind and begin to write a text of their own.

Our discussion of "This Is Just to Say" sets the stage for discussion of another poem conveniently included in the third edition of *The*

Norton Anthology of Poetry, Kenneth Koch's "Variations on a Theme by William Carlos Williams":

1‡
I chopped down the house that you had been saving to live in
next summer.
I am sorry, but it was morning, and I had nothing to do
and its wooden beams were so inviting.

2
We laughed at the hollyhocks together
and then I sprayed them with lye.
Forgive me. I simply do not know what I am doing.

3
I gave away the money that you had been saving to live on for
the next ten years.
The man who asked for it was shabby
and the firm March wind on the porch was so juicy and cold.

4
Last evening we went dancing and I broke your leg.
Forgive me. I was clumsy, and
I wanted you here in the wards, where I am the doctor!

Koch's poem, like Williams's, expects us to be able to recognize play with the conventions of the apology, but it also expects us to be able to recognize play with Williams's specific use of those conventions. It provides a concrete opportunity to illustrate Bakhtin's claim that

> Each utterance is filled with echoes and reverberations of other utterances to which it is related by the communality of the sphere of speech communication. Every utterance must be regarded primarily as a *response* to preceding utterances of the given sphere (we understand the word "response" here in the broadest sense). Each utterance refutes, affirms, supplements, and relies on the others, presupposes them to be known, and somehow takes them into account. (1986a, 91)

Koch's "Variations" departs from Williams's utterance in ways that open up a number of interesting lines of reflection. Koch exaggerates the transgressions to which his speaker confesses to the point of serious, though outrageous and unbelievable, harm. He makes the reasons his speaker offers to the offended party extenuating reasons, though not sufficient reasons to extenuate the harm he has done. In the second variation, Koch has the speaker narrate a reason why the speaker's desecration of the hollyhocks is a violation of a special shared trust between speaker and listener, and in the last variation, Koch makes the extenuation confess a motivation that also specifies the speaker's desire for personal and professional power over the listener. Perhaps the most important variation in Koch's poem is the multiplication of variations that leads us to construct from them a pattern or, as some of my students did, a story of the relationship between the speaker and the one he has wronged. Whereas the Williams poem placed all its evaluative emphasis on the qualities of the plums and the speaker's pleasure in them,[5] Koch's variations amplify the seriousness of the transgressions and the speaker's relationship with the listener.

Students who have discussed Williams's poem are ready to explore Koch's "Variations" in considerable detail and to weigh the effects of each changed variable in the speech genre on the variation in which it occurs. They can also debate whether Koch's variations reveal the absurdity of Williams's poem or make new absurd poems that miss the point of Williams's poem. They may also be prepared, however, for a less likely transition to a less user-friendly poem.

I devote several days of class discussion to working through Milton's "Lycidas" because it is a famous poem, because students who have worked through it need not be intimidated by any other poem in English, and because it illustrates wonderfully the usefulness, even the indispensability, of speech-genre analysis. I have worked out a marginal commentary on the poem that leads students through the amazing variety of utterance types (and the amazing variety of speakers, addressees, and heroes of those utterances) that make up the elaborate secondary speech genre Milton is working in, but I will share here only the first of the subordinate speech genres. The poem begins,

> Yet once more, O ye laurels and once more
> Ye myrtles brown, with ivy never sere,
> I come to pluck your Berries harsh and crude,
> And with forc'd fingers rude,
> Shatter your leaves before the mellowing year.
> Bitter constraint, and sad occasion dear,
> Compels me to disturb your season due;
> For *Lycidas* is dead, dead ere his prime,
> Young *Lycidas*, and hath not left his peer:
> Who would not sing for *Lycidas*? He knew
> Himself to sing, and build the lofty rhyme.
> He must not float upon his wat'ry bier
> Unwept, and welter to the parching wind,
> Without the meed of some melodious tear.
>
> (ll. 1–14)

The diction and syntax and allusions to plants which, according to the Norton's editors, "were all traditional materials for poetic garlands" (Alison et al. 1983, 147), and the situation of addressing those plants makes this utterance more difficult to recognize than those we have looked at so far, but when I asked my class what sort of utterance this is and where they have seen one like it before, one student piped up that it is an apology, and that we had seen an apology in Williams's poem. Perhaps I can make this reading clear most economically by quoting the first stanza of my own "Variation on a Theme by John Milton," an exercise which my speech-genre analysis prompted me to write and share with my class.

> Here I am again poetic plants
> To pulverize your leaves before my time.
> I know that it's a crime,
> But you can see that I'm
> Assigned a writing job I wouldn't choose.
> For I've just heard the news.
> A Brother from my poet's frat
> Is dead, drowned in a boating accident;
> Young Edward King has left us just like that.
> Who wouldn't write a poem for Edward King?
> Poems were his thing.
> We can't just let him sink
> Unwept into the drink
> Without some tribute; so I'm forced to sing.

In different styles, but in otherwise identical speech genres, the speakers here and in Milton's poem apologize to the plants—an unusual variation on the recipient of an apology—in anticipation of the harm they will do them by taking them up before they would have chosen to do so, but they extenuate the harm they will do by declaring that they must do it because of the exigency of the poet's death. They don't say "Forgive me" but they name and explain their transgressions as the speech genre of the apology requires. A grasp of that genre is fundamental to a grasp of this part of the poem, as a grasp of invocations, inquisitions, complaints, questions, laments, exhortations, enumerations, commands, and many other speech genres is essential to reading the rest of it. Students know almost all of those speech genres and can learn to recognize others whose formal features, occasions, and functions are made clear to them. Poets depend on that knowledge, and we teachers can draw upon it, make it explicit, and expand it through attention to the variations poets play upon it.

I tell my students that in recognizing the liberties Williams or Koch or Milton takes with the apology, we discover what Bakhtin calls a free and creative reformulation of a standard genre and with it, perhaps, the possibilities and conditions of pursuing what he calls our own "free speech plan" (1986a, 80). I believe with Bakhtin that such freedom as we are capable of in discourse is attainable only through reworking—more or less creatively—the speech genres and specific utterances we have learned from others, and I introduce students to literary elaborations of ordinary speech genres in the expectation that the students will expand, enrich, and reflect upon their discursive repertoires and improve their verbal performances. They will also learn to share in more of the verbal performances that my own literary education has enabled me to produce and enjoy so that, in the end, we will be able to share perhaps a few jokes or allusions (like my "Lycidas" pastiche) I could not have risked at the outset. Some of them may write their own parodies of "Lycidas" and other texts. Though I would resist leading them to share unexplained evaluations based on uncritical participation in my tone, I nevertheless welcome and enjoy our sharing of common critical terms and overlapping repertoires of interesting verbal performances.

Notes

1. See Voloshinov 1983. All parties to the dispute about Bakhtin's possible authorship of works published under Voloshinov's name agree that Bakhtin at the least exercised substantial influence on those works. I choose to treat those works as part of the work of the "Bakhtin School."

2. Relations among speaker, hero, and listener are elaborated in Voloshinov. I develop these relations in *Making Tales: The Poetics of Wordsworth's Narrative Experiments* (1984) and "Teaching Wordsworth's Poetry from the Perspective of a Poetics of Speech" (1986).

3. In a more theoretical paper I would have to distinguish speech genres from what we have been taught to call "speech acts" in one tradition and what have been called "figures of thought" in another. I would also have to explore their relations to specialized literary genres.

4. See, for example, Gates's account in *The Signifying Monkey* (1988) of research into the several speech genres the black verbal tradition cultivates under the general heading of "signifying." Teachers educated outside this tradition would have a hard time keeping up with their students in "the dozens" or "louding." Troyka (1984), however, shows how teachers can mediate between these genres and the classical rhetorical genres they resemble.

5. All three signs of evaluative emphasis that the Voloshinov essay enumerates—the versification, the placement of epithets, and the manner of unfolding—add value to the plums. See Voloshinov 1983, 20.

17 Teaching Deconstruction: Theory and Practice in the Undergraduate Literature Classroom

Lois Tyson
Grand Valley State University

For many of us in America who consider ourselves lovers of literature, phrases such as "post-Saussurean linguistics" and "deconstructing the text" evoke the kind of fear and loathing that the Crusaders must have felt when they learned that the infidels had taken the Holy City. Because deconstruction is frequently misperceived as a superficial analysis of wordplay that dissolves our appreciation of literature and our ability to interpret it in a caustic bath of skepticism, relatively few English teachers use it in their own critical practice, and even fewer use it in their undergraduate classes, where, for the most part, New Criticism—in tandem with a focus on authorial intention—remains the dominant model for the way students are taught to think about literature. The purpose of this essay is to outline an approach to teaching deconstruction in undergraduate literature courses that will put to use the New Critical principles often already operating there. I hope to show that, strange as it may sound, deconstruction is a very effective complement to New Criticism in the undergraduate literature classroom: using the two together can give students a very rich and complex view of literature, of culture, and of human endeavors to make sense of the world.

I have found that using deconstruction in conjunction with New Criticism works especially well if students are able to see critical practice in its relationship to an evolving debate among practitioners, rather than as a mechanical application of fixed principles. For this reason, I preface our first exposure to deconstruction with a discussion of the implicit theoretical principles underlying the ways in which the class has been discussing literature up to this point. A discussion of New Critical assumptions would include, of course, that language is stable, that a good literary text is a unified whole in which all parts support its artistic purpose, and that unproblematical readings, and even a "best" reading, can be determined. The realization that critical theory isn't the property of experts, but the basis for what the class has been doing all along, helps increase students' confidence and receptivity to a new theoretical perspective. The following reading assignment introduces students to that new perspective by clarifying deconstruction's basic premises in the context of what is arguably the most important difference between New Criticism and deconstruction: the problem of reference and its implications for the study of literature.

Language and Literature: Deconstruction versus New Criticism

In our daily lives, most of us use language as if it were a system of signs in which, as semiotics (the study of sign systems) puts it, every sign consists of signifier (sound or image—for example, a word) + signified (concept to which the signifier refers).[1] In its simplest context—picture a person standing in an open field pointing to the only tree in sight—a phrase such as *this tree is big* seems to have a single, clear meaning: there is only one tree in question, and we know that a claim is being made about its size. This is the stable relationship between words and concepts that New Criticism took for granted. However, even in this apparently clear situation, many questions concerning signification, or meaning, arise. When the speaker says "This tree is big," is she comparing the tree to herself? To another tree? What other tree? Is she surprised by the size of the tree? Or is she merely informing us that the tree is big? Is she informing us so that we will know something about the tree or so that we will understand something about the word *big*? What must she think of us if she believes we need such information? Does she think we are just learning to speak English? Or is she being sarcastic? If so, why? This string of questions may seem to push the point a bit far, but it does illustrate that human utterances are rarely, if ever, as clear and simple as the semiotic formula signifier + signified implies. Any given signifier can have any number of signifieds at any given moment. And, although context often helps us to limit the range of possible signifieds for some signifiers, it simultaneously increases the range of possible signifieds for others. This is why communication is such a complicated and uncertain thing.

If we stopped at this point, we could rewrite the semiotic formula as sign = signifier + signified . . . + signified. That is, we could try to explain communication as a sliding accumulation of signifieds. But what does the term *signified* mean? If the signifier is the word *tree*, then the signified must be the tree in our imagination that we can picture. But what do we understand by this imagined tree? Of what does our concept consist? Our concept of the tree consists of every meaning we have come to associate with it over the course of our lives. In my own case it consists of, among other things, the shade my mother always sought on picnics, as I do now; the many varieties of leaves I collected in kindergarten; and the precious resource of beauty and environmental health we are rapidly losing. That is, the word *tree* refers to a chain of signifiers in the mind of the person uttering—or hearing—it. And each signifier in that chain is itself constituted by a chain of signifiers, and so on. What we have been calling the signified is always another chain of signifiers. Texts are thus chains of signifiers that refer to other chains of signifiers, and so is knowledge. In other words, what we really know of the world is our conception and perception of it.

The source of our conceptions and perceptions is ultimately the systems of beliefs and values, called ideologies, of the culture into which we were born because these systems control the way we see and understand our world.[2] For example, I remember a story my high-school biology teacher told us about the attempt to introduce the rhythm method of birth control in an underdeveloped country many years ago. Each woman in the program was given an abacus-like device, consisting of red and white beads arranged to represent her fertility cycle. Each bead represented one day and, if a given day's bead was red, she was not to have sexual intercourse; a white bead meant that sex on that day was safe. After several months passed, statistics showed that the pregnancy rate among women in the program had not changed at all, and social workers were at a loss to understand the problem. They finally discovered that women who wanted to have sex on red-bead days would simply push the beads over until a white one appeared: they assumed the beads were a kind of magic! Thus, the program initially failed because both clients and social workers were able to view the project only in terms of their own cultural, or ideological, perspectives. Because it is through language that we pass on our ideologies, it is not unreasonable to say that it is through language that we come to conceive and perceive our world and ourselves.

The implications of this view for the study of literature are many. Because all writing is viewed in its function as text—as a site of language's ideological productions—literature loses its privileged status over, for example, my last letter to my sister. By the same token, literature is no less real or valuable than history or philosophy.[3] Most important for our purposes, meaning and value are not, as they were for New Criticism, stable elements residing in the text for us to uncover or passively consume; they are created by readers. Great works of art are thus not timeless entities, as the New Critics maintained, but matters of definition: if their appeal lasts over time, it is because different groups of people value them for different reasons. What New Criticism considered the "obvious" or "commonsense" positions from which a text can be interpreted and evaluated are really ideological stances with which we are so familiar that we consider them "natural."[4] For just as a text's composition draws on the author's cultural assumptions, its interpretation and evaluation draw on those of the reader. Because all texts are thus ideological constructs, they can be deconstructed.

Where New Criticism looked for a perfect, seamless art object existing in a timeless space outside the changing course of human events, deconstruction looks for the seams—the ways in which language fails to smooth over contradictions and gaps in logic—in order to understand the ways in which the ideologies from which the text is constructed fall short of their projects. It is not a question of what the author *intends*, which, as even the New Critics agreed, we cannot know with certainty, but of what the text *does* with its ideological content. For deconstruction, a literary text is dynamic: it is a site of cultural production in which multiple unstable meanings vie for dominance. In this way, literature is opened to provide various avenues for understanding history, current social phenomena, the function of language and ideology, and even the nature of literature itself.

The following two classroom exercises are intended to help students experience the unstable, problematic nature of language posited in the introductory reading assignment. While the reading assignment certainly does not answer all the questions students will have, I have found that it enables them to ask more meaningful ones. Students' responses to these classroom exercises have been especially positive, perhaps because, as one student put it, the exercises bring the theory "down to earth" by providing a familiar, nonthreatening, and even playful context in which to approach new theoretical concepts.

Exercise I: Give some examples of the ways in which language operates as if it were stable and reliable—"Mary, please hand John a book"—and point out that, because we are so used to the everyday patterns and rituals in which language seems to work the way we want it to, we assume that it is by nature a stable and reliable means of communicating our thoughts and wishes. Then, with the students' help, find at least three different meanings of the sentence *Time flies like an arrow*.

1. *Time* (noun)	*flies* (verb)	*like an arrow.* (adv. clause)	= Time flies quickly (or straight).
2. *Time* (verb)	*flies* (obj.)	*like an arrow.* (adv. clause)	= Get out your stopwatch and time the speed of flies as you'd time an arrow's flight.
3. *Time flies* (noun)	*like* (verb)	*an arrow.* (obj.)	= Time flies (insects; think of fruit flies) are fond of arrows.

Discuss the implications of this exercise for the nature of language—how meaning is unstable because one word can have multiple referents—and follow with the next exercise.

Exercise II: To show how tone and emphasis further complicate communication, have students imagine that a newscaster is given the following line to read: *President Reagan says the marines do not have to go to El Salvador.* Then, by emphasizing different words each time, have students help you determine at least six different meanings this sentence could have.

1. President Reagan *says* the marines do not have to go to El Salvador (implying that he's lying).
2. President Reagan says the marines do *not* have to go to El Salvador (implying that he's correcting a false rumor).
3. President Reagan says *the marines* do not have to go to El Salvador (implying that some other group has to go).
4. *President Reagan* says the marines do not have to go to El Salvador (implying that another important person had said that the marines have to go to El Salvador).
5. President Reagan says the marines do not *have* to go to El Salvador (implying that they can go if they want to).
6. President Reagan says the marines do not have to go to *El Salvador* (implying that they have to go somewhere else).

Use these two exercises to lead into a discussion of deconstruction's explanation of why language is so uncertain and unreliable, focusing on the multiple meanings created by a lack of one-to-one correspondence between words and their referents. From here, the discussion can be led to the multiple meanings we can find in a literary work, and how deconstruction uses these meanings, by having the class deconstruct a short work together. I have found that students are able to grasp the relationship between New Criticism and deconstruction most readily—and seem to enjoy the exercise most—when our literary examples are fairly concrete and straightforward, both thematically and stylistically. Robert Frost's "Mending Wall" (1914) is a good example.

Mending Wall†

Something there is that doesn't love a wall,
That sends the frozen-ground-swell under it,
And spills the upper boulders in the sun,
And makes gaps even two can pass abreast.
The work of hunters is another thing:
I have come after them and made repair
Where they have left not one stone on a stone,
But they would have the rabbit out of hiding,
To please the yelping dogs. The gaps I mean,
No one has seen them made or heard them made,
But at spring mending-time we find them there.
I let my neighbor know beyond the hill;
And on a day we meet to walk the line
And set the wall between us once again.
We keep the wall between us as we go.
To each the boulders that have fallen to each.
And some are loaves and some so nearly balls
We have to use a spell to make them balance:
"Stay where you are until our backs are turned!"
We wear our fingers rough with handling them.
Oh, just another kind of outdoor game,
One on a side. It comes to little more:
There where it is we do not need the wall:
He is all pine and I am apple orchard.
My apple trees will never get across
And eat the cones under his pines, I tell him.
He only says, "Good fences make good neighbors."
Spring is the mischief in me, and I wonder
If I could put a notion in his head:
"*Why* do they make good neighbors? Isn't it
Where there are cows? But here there are no cows.
Before I built a wall I'd ask to know
What I was walling in or walling out,
And to whom I was like to give offense.
Something there is that doesn't love a wall,
That wants it down." I could say "Elves" to him,
But it's not elves exactly, and I'd rather
He said it for himself. I see him there,
Bringing a stone grasped firmly by the top
In each hand, like an old-stone savage armed.
He moves in darkness as it seems to me,

† From *The Poetry of Robert Frost,* edited by Edward Connery Latham. Copyright 1916, 1923, 1928, 1930, 1934, 1939, 1947, © 1967, 1969, by Holt, Rinehart and Winston; copyright © 1964, 1967, 1970, 1975, by Lesley Frost Ballantine. Used with permission of Henry Holt and Company, Inc.

> Not of woods only and the shade of trees.
> He will not go behind his father's saying,
> And he likes having thought of it so well
> He says again, "Good fences make good neighbors."

A brief New Critical reading of the text—What is the central tension at work in this poem, and how is it resolved in the poem's unified advancement of its main theme?—is a useful first step in deconstructing a literary work because such readings can almost always be found to rest on a binary opposition (a pair of polar opposites presumed to exhaust the field of meaning, such as male/female, good/bad, strong/weak) in which one member is privileged over the other. A few leading questions to open the discussion—What are the opposing viewpoints expressed by the speaker and his neighbor? Which viewpoint are we led to support?—will usually produce the generally accepted main theme: the poem's criticism of mindless adherence to obsolete traditions, for which the wall is a metaphor.

Once this theme is formulated, the board can be used to collect as much evidence as possible in its support. For example, we accept the speaker's view of his neighbor and of obsolete traditions because he clearly shows that the wall has outlived its purpose—"My apple trees will never get across / And eat the cones under his pines" (ll. 25–26)—and because the speaker associates himself with nature ("Spring [a natural event] is the mischief in me," l. 28), which is generally presumed good. Indeed, our faith in nature's wisdom promotes our initial acceptance of the speaker's viewpoint in the poem's opening four lines, which put nature in opposition to the wall: it is nature that "sends the frozen-ground-swell" to spill "the upper boulders in the sun" (ll. 2–3). This theme is reinforced when the men "have to use a spell" to make the unwilling boulders, natural objects, stay in place (ll. 18–19) and when it is implied that the boulders will fall as soon as the men turn their backs (l. 19). Nature's "children"—the hunters in lines 5–7 and the elves in line 36—also support the speaker's attitude toward the wall. In addition, we often associate the word *wall* with barriers to communication or emotional exchange, and this function is insisted upon in lines 13–15, thereby reinforcing our rejection of the wall and of the obsolete tradition that keeps it in place: "And on a day we meet . . . / And set the wall *between us* once again. / We keep the wall *between us* as we go" (my emphasis). Finally, the neighbor is compared to an "old-stone savage" who "moves in darkness . . . / Not of woods only and the shade of trees" (ll. 40–42), that is, who is unenlightened. Thus he contrasts sharply with the enlightened speaker, who knows that obsolete traditions should be abandoned.

Having located the poem's central thematic opposition (nonconformity vs. conformity or progressivism vs. conservatism or nature vs. tradition) and determined which side is privileged (nonconformity/progressivism/nature), the next step is to have students find everything in the poem that conflicts with or undermines this hierarchy. That is, we must find the ways in which the text, as Steven Lynn puts it, "say[s] something other than what it appears to say" (1990, 262) by finding textual evidence that contradicts the evidence we have just gathered in support of our New Critical reading of the poem's main theme. The object now is to show how neither member of the binary opposition(s) supporting the main theme can be privileged over the other. For example, a number of conflicts revolve around the poem's attempt to valorize the speaker's nonconformity—his critical evaluation of tradition and willingness to abandon it if it no longer serves a good purpose—over the unthinking conformity of his neighbor, a difference represented by their attitudes toward the wall that separates their property. Nature—against tradition—wants the wall down, but so do the hunters, who function not only as emblems of nature but of tradition as well: because they use hunting dogs and hunt for sport (they want "the rabbit out of hiding," not necessarily for food, but to "please the yelping dogs": ll. 8–9), the hunters evoke a sporting tradition that has its roots in the traditional "hunt" of the British landed gentry. Analogously, while magic, in the form of elves, wants the wall down (l. 36), magic, in the form of the magic "spell" in lines 18–19, is invoked to keep the wall up. Furthermore, because elves are mischievous creatures who, according to legend, delight in making trouble for human beings, their desire to have the wall down can just as easily undermine our trust in the project rather than promote it. In fact, the speaker's use of such an ambiguous term as *elves* and his difficulty in finding the right word ("it's not elves exactly": l. 37) imply his own unconscious ambivalence toward the wall and toward the tradition it represents. This ambivalence is reinforced by the speaker's having repaired the wall on his own in the past and by his having called on his neighbor to do so now. A similar problem occurs in the poem's association of primitiveness, in the form of the "old-stone savage" in line 40, with the neighbor's mindless adherence to tradition and in the unstable link between the primitive and the traditional that results: modern western culture is informed by the romantic view that the primitive is in harmony with nature, not aligned with tradition against it. Finally, the main idea being criticized in our New Critical reading—good fences make good neighbors—is actually valid within the action of the poem: it is the activity of mending the wall that brings the men together, presumably inspiring the poem's creation, and lets them *be* neighbors through the bonding activity of shared work. Even the poem's title suggests this idea if we read *mending* as an adjective rather than a verb: "Mending Wall" then becomes a wall that mends rather than a wall that is mended.

The final step is to draw out the implications of the collapse of the binary opposition(s) supporting our New Critical reading of the poem's main theme. It would seem, for example, that the meaning, importance, and power of tradition and the meaning, importance, and power of nonconformity are not as easily placed in opposition as "Mending Wall" initially appears to suggest. Against the poem's call for a rational abandonment of a seemingly empty tradition—a project easily associated with the scientific and technological progress that occurred during the five decades preceding the poem's publication in 1914—the value of that tradition, and the dubious nature of the attempt to abandon it, form a powerful counterweight, perhaps suggesting that much of the power of tradition lies in its ability to inform our attitudes without our being aware of its presence. One reason this unresolvable conflict between progressivism and conservativism occurs is that some of the terms used to evoke their difference—especially *nature* and *primitive*—themselves represent ambivalent attitudes in our culture. For example, we associate nature with goodness—innocence, purity, simplicity, health, intuitive wisdom—yet nature usually stands in the way of the scientific and technological progress we value so highly. Similarly, we associate the primitive with the goodness of nature, yet we also associate the primitive with ignorance, the unknown, and the sinister, and this association evokes our fear and contempt. And, as we have seen, ambivalent associations are also evoked by *magic*, *elves*, and *hunters*. Perhaps, then, our deconstruction of "Mending Wall" should make us reconsider other binary oppositions that inform our culture, such as male/female, individual/group, and objective/subjective.

As this reading of "Mending Wall" illustrates, deconstruction sees literary tension not in terms of its New Critical functions in the production of an organic whole, but as a product of ideological conflict and the instability of language. That a literary work has conflicting projects that are not absorbed in some overarching purpose is not considered a flaw, as it was for New Criticism (which is why a New Critical reading, in order to "save" the poem, would have to show either that the power of tradition isn't the disruptive presence I have suggested or that the poem's project is to show the power and value of *both* nonconformity and obsolete tradition). Rather, conflicting meanings are considered an unavoidable product of literature's medium—language—and they are a product that can enrich our experience of the work. This is a vision of art as a seething cauldron of meanings in mutually constitutive flux. As a dynamic entity tied to both the culture that produced it and the culture that interprets it, art becomes, as the following sample writing assignments illustrate, a vehicle for understanding our culture, our history, and ourselves.

Sample Writing Assignments

1. How does our deconstructive reading of Robert Frost's "Mending Wall" suggest that the power of tradition lies in its ability to inform our attitudes without our being aware of its presence? Discuss examples from other areas of American life in which tradition functions similarly.

2. Briefly summarize the New Critical and deconstructive readings of Robert Frost's "Mending Wall" we did in class. What does each reading offer us in terms of our appreciation of the poem and our understanding of American culture? Do you prefer one approach over the other? Why or why not?

3. How does William Blake's "The Little Black Boy" forward the theme of racial equality? How is this theme affected by the use of white as a standard of excellence and by the attitude of the black child toward the white in the final stanza? What does this suggest about the difficulties involved in overcoming bias?

4. How does Judith Minty's "Prowling the Ridge" show the speaker as a liberated or nontraditional woman? How does the final stanza reveal that she is still operating within a value system that depends on male experience instead of female? What does this suggest about the difficulty women (or any devalued group) might have determining their own identity?

I hope it is evident, at this point, that training in deconstruction can be a useful addition to the New Critical approaches that many of us already use in our undergraduate literature classes. By increasing students' responsibility for the production of meaning, deconstruction encourages them to become more engaged in their reading and writing and to reject their uncritical application of the scientific model—one "right" answer for every question—too often imposed on the humanities. In addition, familiarity with deconstruction can help develop critical thinking skills transferable to other domains: it can help students learn to think more critically about issues that arise, for example, in the study of history, politics, science, psychology, and communications. Perhaps the most important insight it can offer our students, however, concerns the nature of knowledge itself.

Catherine Belsey's assertion that the scientific positivism informing modern western culture tends to "push to the margins of experience whatever it cannot explain or understand" (1980b, 117) can be applied to every methodology. In any given object under investigation, we tend to see that which our methodological instrument is tuned to see, not necessarily because there is no objective reality beyond our subjective impressions, but more probably because objective reality is so dense and rich that, like Walt Whitman in "Song of Myself," it "contain[s] multitudes" (l. 1326). The most useful conclusion we can draw from this state of affairs is not that every methodology is, in its own way, correct or that all methodologies are equally useful, but that, no matter how correct or useful any methodology is, it is incomplete. Methodologies can thus be used to interrogate and complement one another within a discipline or among disciplines. Such a dialectical[5] view stresses the interactive and interdependent nature of all ways of approaching reality: changes in one approach imply changes in other approaches, whether or not we are aware of those implications; and concepts usually placed in opposing categories—for example, reason and passion, science and the humanities, psychology and politics—are found to overlap or inhabit each other in new and significant ways. The ability to think dialectically is important for students in every major field of study, both in terms of their own education and in terms of the way their education will impinge globally on political and environmental decisions made over this next crucial decade. If we can give our students some firsthand, positive experience with such an inherently interdisciplinary way of thinking, I believe we will have met a real educational need.

Notes

1. To the instructor: Terence Hawkes's *Structuralism and Semiotics* (1977) provides a thorough explanation of the sign. It is important to note that, while Saussure's original formulation linked sound/image to concept only, deconstruction's claim that the signifier does not refer to a determinate signified often assumes an expanded definition of *signified* as concept or thing. Without this additional connection of *signified* with *thing,* we risk sidestepping one of deconstruction's most important and controversial implications: that we cannot have access to an objective, concrete world unmediated by language.

2. To the instructor: see M. M. Bakhtin's "Discourse in the Novel" (1981b) for a helpful discussion of how language carries ideology through the value-laden discourses that comprise it.

3. To the instructor: borrowing from Derrida, Paul de Man's *Allegories of Reading* (1979) shows how literary texts implicitly acknowledge and exploit their own rhetorical structures, which makes them less deluded than historical and philosophical texts.

4. To the instructor: Catherine Belsey's "Deconstructing the Text" (1980b) provides probably the clearest explanation of the ideological underpinnings of so-called "commonsense" interpretations of literature.

5. Walter Davis illustrates the value of dialectical thinking by using psychoanalysis, existentialism, Hegelian dialectics, and Marxism to constitute for critical theory what he calls "dialectical pluralism." The first four chapters of his remarkable *Inwardness and Existence: Subjectivity in/and Hegel, Heidegger, Marx, and Freud* (1989) enact this method; the fifth chapter articulates its principles.

18 Reading Deconstructively in the Two-Year College Introductory Literature Classroom

Thomas Fink
LaGuardia Community College

There is no single purpose for deconstruction—there are various divergent purposes. In the hands of some practitioners, deconstruction, as a literary critical strategy, primarily promotes an aesthetic appreciation of the irrepressible "play" of words. For others, this critical practice embodies a quest for the "emptying" of all values. In a variety of ways, critics such as Gayatri Spivak, Henry Louis Gates, Jr., Barbara Johnson, and Michael Ryan utilize deconstructive investigations to serve the critique of socially oppressive institutions. In adapting a deconstructive procedure for use in the introductory literature classroom, I have at least partly attempted to follow the lead of Spivak, Gates, Johnson, Ryan, and others who focus on how particular structures of linguistic representation—most notably, binary oppositions—establish, assert, obscure, and alter specific ideological premises that influence the constitution of power relations. Nothing close to the elaborate procedures of deconstructive analysis found in learned journals (not to mention the writings of Jacques Derrida, the method's "originator") can be attempted in an introductory college literature classroom, but I have found that a simplified, yet still valid, version of deconstruction can be taught successfully and fruitfully.[1] Before characterizing that version, I need to state its salient pedagogical advantages:

1. It allows students to come to terms with structural properties in a literary text without falling into a mechanical formalism. The reading process, thus, can include an aesthetic appreciation but does not stop there.
2. A deconstructive approach can use literary texts to open up critical thinking about issues germane to students and thus foster

The chapter appeared in somewhat different form in *Teaching English in the Two-Year College* vol. 12, no. 1 (January 1985): 64–71. Used with permission.

more effective thinking. This strategy serves as a new tool whose fairly rigorous employment can help displace old, sloppy, or simplistic interpretive practices. Also, as some of my students have noted, the approach may help them read nonliterary texts in productive and meaningful ways.

3. If such theorists of psychology as Alfred Adler, Karen Horney, Alfred Korzybski, and Albert Ellis correctly postulate a causal link between overgeneralization and self-sabotaging (and otherwise destructive) behavior and emotion, then the close critical scrutiny involved in deconstruction can help students by providing a way for them to perceive, challenge, and correct the pervasive idealizations and other overgeneralizations which are greatly stimulated by mass culture.

The simplified deconstructive approach that I am advocating—and have employed successfully at LaGuardia Community College—begins with a brief, casual discussion of the class members' sense of the overall theme of the work in question. At a certain point in this discussion, one of three things occurs:

1. Guided by the instructor's comments and questions, the class reaches an awareness that, in characterizing the theme, they are employing a pair of terms that contrast in some way (a "binary opposition").
2. They notice the importance of a particular term (and the instructor can then bring up its opposite).
3. The discussion reaches an impasse, and so the instructor catalogues a few tropes that display binary oppositions in the text (like body/soul, good/evil, serious/humorous), demonstrates connections between them, and comes up with a provisional pair of terms which students can discuss.

Next, through a combination of questioning, information giving, and writing of a double-columned interpretive shorthand on the blackboard, the teacher guides the class in an examination of the interplay of the two terms in the binary opposition. I am not saying that a text "is" or "is about" the interplay of a single binary opposition; rather, I am suggesting that such an examination provides a useful entrance "into" a text. Furthermore, I acknowledge that the play of many different oppositions could be examined fruitfully.

In an interview, Derrida gives a general sense of how binary opposites can be subjected to deconstructive scrutiny. Dividing the process into two phases, he calls the first one

> a phase of *overturning*. To do justice to this necessity is to recognize that in a classical philosophical opposition we are not dealing with the peaceful coexistence of a *vis-à-vis*, but rather with a violent hierarchy. One of the two terms governs the other (axiologically, logically, etc.), or has the upper hand. To deconstruct the opposition, first of all, is to overturn the hierarchy at a given moment. To overlook this phase of overturning is to forget the conflictual and subordinating structure of opposition. (1981, 41)

In philosophical writing, the author normally states intentions about what he or she wishes to prove and thus raises one term in a binary opposition over the other, but the literary author does not necessarily intend any of the seemingly literal assertions in a work, since uses of a persona, various forms of irony, and other disruptive factors can come into play. Thus, in speaking of one binary term "governing" the other, the reader performing a deconstructive reading is not referring to the author's intention, but to one particular reading out of several possible ones. This reading might be termed the "standard" one, because it arises from that cultural tendency to binary thinking that forms the basis of much Western thought, often to the exclusion of other valid intellectual approaches and re-visions.

Once the literature class has performed the reading establishing the superiority of one term in the opposition over the other, it enters the "phase of overturning": it examines how—in tropes, images, narrative structures, characterizations, and abstractions of the work—the "superior" term depends on uses of the "inferior" term for its "superiority." This dependency (for example, the tendency to depict an "exalted" spiritual quality via the physical terms of a metaphor) shows how high and low can trade places. The centrality of one term frequently depends on the arbitrary marginalization of another. Deconstruction seeks whatever latent rhetorical or other power may exist in the marginalized term, and this power almost always subverts the centrality of the previously privileged term.

Derrida goes on to describe a second deconstructive phase, intended to undermine any power structure in binary oppositions uncovered in the first phase:

> [T]o remain in [the first] phase is still to operate on the terrain of and from within the deconstructed system. By means of this double, and precisely stratified, dislodged and dislodging, writing, we must also mark the interval between inversion, which brings low what was high, and the irruptive emergence of a new "concept," a concept that can no longer be, and never could be, included in the previous regime. (42)

One cannot predict the "new 'concept' " that would emerge from the deconstructive reading of a text in a literature class; that would depend heavily on the individual linguistic patterns, experiential associations, habits of observation, and other factors involved in the instructor's and students' acts of interpretation. However, the instructor can prod students to grope towards a conceptual language that acknowledges as much as possible the dynamic, unfixable process by which words in the text acquire significance through their difference from other words, and how situations can be perceived, not as the extension of a static, unchanging "Truth" or certainty, but as the particular intersection of many variable forces.

A consideration of a "specimen text" should clarify how the rather general instructions above can be applied in the introductory literature course. Shakespeare's "Sonnet 116" may be read (with an emphasis on what is conventionally termed "literal statement") as an idealization of love, an idealization that many students share wholeheartedly and unquestioningly—perhaps to their detriment. In pointing out how the "speaker" establishes a definition of "love," this reading asserts the superiority of external fixity to change and of mind to physicality:

> Let me not to the marriage of true minds
> Admit impediments; love is not love
> Which alters when it alteration finds,
> Or bends with the remover to remove.
> O, no! it is an ever-fixèd mark
> That looks on tempests and is never shaken.
> It is the star to every wand'ring bark,
> Whose worth's unknown, although his height be taken.
> Love's not Time's fool, though rosy lips and cheeks
> Within his bending sickle's compass come.
> Love alters not with his brief hours and weeks,
> But bears it out even to the edge of doom.
> If this be error and upon me proved,
> I never writ, nor no man ever loved.

After some help with difficult vocabulary, the students can see what terms are contrasted and how the pairings relate to one another. According to this reading, true "love" is said to transcend and hence negate "impediments," "alteration," and physical removal. Permanence governs time, and fixity governs change. Represented as "an ever-fixèd mark," "love" outlasts the "tempests" of temporality. Viewed as "the star," this fixity stands high above the individual ("wand'ring bark") and offers him an unassailable order to vanquish forces of change and uncertainty that could otherwise divert him from his "true" course. Also, "love" as the immutable expression of "true minds" survives the loss of physical attractiveness, of "rosy lips and cheeks."

In the heroic couplet's syllogism, true "love" and the "ever-fixèd mark" of writing as self-evident presences annihilate the possibility that his thesis "be error and upon [him] proved."

Moving the class toward a deconstructive reading, an instructor now asks how the representation of "fixity" described above depends on the change that it supposedly subdues. At least one student will probably notice that the negation of the opening statement signifies an act of will or intention rather than a perceived truth: "Let me not . . . / Admit impediments," rather than the concept that impediments do not exist. Through enjambment the first two words of the second line "admit" the "impediments" exist; the negation of impediments, used to signal "the marriage of true minds" by contrast, requires the linguistic presence of the term that the speaker wants to banish. Similarly, "love" is defined not as an inherent, isolatable property, but through its difference from "not love." "Not love" itself acquires definition through the proliferation—double use: verb, then noun—of terms of the "prohibited" concept of change, "which alters when it alteration finds, / Or bends with the remover to remove."

If the opening line seems to make love's "true minds" superior to physicality, signs of material presence like "ever-fixèd mark"—itself a reminder of the poem's printed form—and "star" can be brought to the students' attention as the tropes that stand in place of the mental or spiritual "essence," which, apparently, cannot represent itself. The logic of representation subverts the previous reading's drive to associate physically with impermanence and spirituality with permanence, because only a permanent "image" of physicality allows the otherwise absent spirituality to assume its fixed place.

Whereas a traditional reading would probably hold that the "if" and "then" clauses of the closing couplet are arbitrarily thrown together and have no necessary connection, a deconstructive twist would take the relation of the clauses seriously. The instructor might want to inform the class of the etymological joining in the word "error" of the meanings "wandering" and "mistake." If the text's argument is exposed as a "wandering," a process involving change and hence undoing fixity, then the twin ideas of writing and love as "ever-fixèd marks" collapse, and since no other concepts of writing and love are granted credence by the literal reading of the text, any fixed conceptualization of "writing" and "love" is seen to be abolished. Because "wandering" is arbitrarily assigned a wholly negative value and is not permitted the chance to serve as a positive movement, the deconstructive reading focuses on this named but excluded term and shows how its logic undermines the rhetoric authorizing the supremacy of fixity or static definition. From this perspective of reversal, love and writing develop in time—as a process.

In the concluding phase of deconstruction, the students can attempt to characterize what in Shakespeare's text is called "love," not through the hierarchical structure of a binary opposition, but through the articulation of (part of) a chain of differences in which the term can be said to "reside." Neither trying to establish a static definition of "love" nor a phenomenological description of it, the class talks about how "love" as a word is interpreted through the variable interaction of many other words representing many "forces" both "inside" and "outside" the lovers' minds. A typical discussion might surround "love" with such words as "sexuality," "emotional attraction," "appreciation of physical appearance," "common goals," "divergent goals," "shifting goals," "novelty," "continuity," "common ideology," "divergent ideologies," "relations with other people," "socioeconomic status and its changes," and "family history." Thus, students will not fall back on a limp overgeneralization for a thesis statement about "love."

I have been describing a smooth, unproblematic process of deconstructive interpretation, one which would rarely exist in a classroom (in either a two- or four-year college). Given many likely detours, misunderstandings, and other disruptions, one can expect the task of interpretation to take much longer than it appeared to do in my discussion. Some disruptions, though, will provide a chance for crucial illuminations. To cite one example, an instructor may face these questions from students: "This reading is interesting, but what was/is *Shakespeare* trying to say in the poem? What did *he* mean when he wrote it?" One possible answer is to suggest that Shakespeare may have had a particular political, social, economic, aesthetic, religious, or other intention on a highly conscious level, other (perhaps contradictory) intentions on a preconscious or unconscious level, and intentions limited from the outset by such historical factors as conditions set by the availability of literary conventions and the political regulation of discourse. Without arbitrarily foregrounding some of the aspects and excluding others, a reader cannot decide absolutely on the author's overall intention.

A student may then ask, "If it's so hard to understand what someone is saying, why do people communicate so easily a lot of the time?" The instructor does not have to be versed in speech-act theory to help students see that people develop and employ conventions to try to control the creation and reception of discourse for important pragmatic purposes, whereas the many possible conflicting conventions for "reading" of authorial intention in what is called "literature" lacks such clearcut pragmatic purposes or reliable criteria for judging their truth-value. Indeed, even the separation of literal and figurative meaning is often and easily lost in an act of textual scrutiny. Also, one can hardly interpret too gingerly the relation in a text between "speaker" and "author," "persona" and "person."

In responding to the student, the instructor has not denied the existence of authorial intentions but has simply called into question the likelihood of ever discovering them as a unified totality or of being able to know when one had found all of them. Such caution enables the reader to focus instead on a much more modest goal, the articulation of possibilities of reading, which includes the identification of intentions "enclosed" in the fictions (for example, "voices") of the text.[2] As in the work of Barthes and Foucault on the notion of authorship, such a deconstructive position overthrows the idealized view of the writer as a god who *controls* the range of meaning in a text, and it usefully exposes the impossible standard of the "true reading" as a discardable myth.

A few concluding notes of caution seem desirable. First, the deconstructive method should be introduced with extreme care toward the beginning of the course. Using a fairly uncomplicated poem or short story, the instructor can introduce the notion of binary opposites with many examples, lay out the phases of deconstruction on the blackboard in simple terms, perform a skeletal reading and outline it on the board, question the students about their understanding of what one has done until they absorb it, and explain the method's advantages. The instructor can then pass out a "how to deconstruct" chart (see figure 1). In the next session, the students can be led through the process described on the chart. Only after they have had ample practice with the instructor should they use the method in small-group work. Before students use deconstruction in a paper of explication, the instructor should conduct a careful review of the "how to deconstruct" chart. To avoid the analysis of literary works in isolation, the instructor can select several pairs of texts that include the same binary oppositions but deploy them differently, and the class can compare and contrast "deconstructed" passages in each.

In the interest of brevity, I have performed a rather ahistorical reading of Shakespeare's sonnet. Historical detail and analysis can be used in the classroom to help elucidate how models of expression, belief systems, and the representation of specific events impinge upon the establishment and overthrow of hierarchies of binary oppositions in the text. It would surely enhance the students' readings of Shakespeare's love sonnets if they were made aware of the poet's "appro-

1. *Preliminary Phase*
   1.1. What binary oppositions (i.e., good/evil, love/hate, body/soul, light/dark, man/woman, truth/fiction) can you find in the text?
   1.2. How can one term in the opposition be read as truer than, or superior to, the other? List and fully describe four to six examples in the text of this hierarchy (the established superiority of one term over the other).
2. *Deconstruction, Phase One*
   2.1. Find four to six examples in the text which the "lower" term "trades places" with the "higher" one—the "lower" becomes the "higher" and the "higher" becomes the "lower."
   2.2. What makes this "trading of places" happen in each of the four to six examples? Be as specific as possible.
3. *Deconstructing, Phase Two*
   3.1. Take four to six words that relate to the two terms of a binary opposition. In choosing this chain of words, pay close attention to both similarities and differences between words.
   3.2. Choose a particular theme, idea, problem, or question in the text that has something to do with the binary opposition. Discuss this theme, idea, etc., by describing how words in the chain (that you chose in 3.1) relate to and contrast with one another. (For example, if you are discussing the theme of love in a work, you may find that it relates, not only to emotional affection and physical desire, but to money, political power, religious belief, and parental influence. No single word dominates; they all interact.)

Fig. 1. "How to deconstruct" chart.

priation" of Platonic discourse and the "normative" structures of male/female relationships in the Renaissance.

To use a deconstructive approach does not mean shutting the door on fruitful aspects of other modes of inquiry—such as psychological and aesthetic analysis—but rather complementing them by providing a necessary corrective to their sometimes overbearing assumption of completeness.[3]

Notes

1. In "A Short Course in Post-Structuralism," which concentrates heavily on Derrida's deconstructive elucidation of *difference* as a major aspect of poststructuralist theory, Jane Tompkins suggests that an "application" of such theory to the classroom is impossible. According to deconstructive theory, she

observes, neither readers, "objects of investigation," "methods," or interpretations are "free standing." Instead, "language is a system of differences and . . . all articulation proceeds on a model of language" in which "you have effects of language, language which is always in process, always modifying itself" (1990 [1988], 36). Thus, for Tompkins, "'we' are not applying a 'method'; we are acting as an extension of the interpretive code, of those systems of difference that constitute us and the objects of our perceptions simultaneously" (37). Myra Jehlen counters Tompkins's claim in her article "Literature and Authority," which appeared in the same volume, by stating that "it is certainly possible to translate the concepts of deconstruction" and other recent critical strategies "into empowering new ways of reading" (1990b, 9). As the teacher of an introductory literature course at a community college, I am constituted as a "leader" of the process of interpretation whereby a group of individuals act "as an extension of the interpretive code." In accepting this role and in encouraging the class to accept theirs, I do not declare that we are "free-standing" interpreters with an "objective," "neutral" methodology but that we are exploring various possibilities of interpretation without certainty upon which to rely.

2. Sometimes an author states in writing what she/he intends in a literary work. Such an explanation contributes to an authorial reading of the work in question, though one also realizes that authors can consciously or unconsciously lie to themselves and to others.

3. I would like to thank James Cahalan, David Downing, Brian Gallagher, Andrew Pawelczak, Susan Wells, and the members of the New York Circle for Theory of Literature and Criticism for their helpful comments on earlier versions of this essay. I dedicate this text to the memories of Doris Fassler and Alan Berman.

VI Poststructuralism, Postmodernism, and Computer Literacy

19 Practicing Textual Theory and Teaching Formula Fiction

M. H. Dunlop
Iowa State University

Contemporary theories of textuality extend a promise of transforming reading and writing praxis at any educational level. Textual theory defines any written document as a text that is both encoded and decodable, and every text is itself an intertext—a network of codes, fragments, various strands existing in perhaps uneasy relationship to one another. Furthermore, any text is intertextually connected to networks of other texts in webs constituted of cultural codes, common borrowings, repeated narrative lines, and language itself. Texts are not differentiated one from another by either the status of the producer or the essential internal differences; consequently textual theory refuses old hierarchical divisions among literary, nonliterary, and subliterary texts. Since the explanation of a text is not sought in its producer or author, classifications of texts as major and minor are weakened if not erased. The reader, rather than searching for meanings hidden in the depths of a given text, is free to range across the surfaces of a text or to collapse boundaries among texts. A text-based approach to an introductory literature course holds out the promise of producing a classroom of activated readers and critics rather than passive receptors of certified meanings. Instead of awaiting the arrival of meaning, students can mount critiques of the ideologies or beliefs encoded in texts and thereby construct connections between the world and the text. Moreover, students are enabled to enter into the textual process not only as consumers but as producers who may write along with a text, rewrite it, recode it, or add to it.

Before exploring the transit from textual theory to realization of its promises in the classroom, it is perhaps appropriate to consider problems posed by the traditional literature classroom. Students in an introductory literature class, no matter how limited their previous exposure to literary study, may nonetheless be convinced that the behavior required of them in a literature course is to sit passively while the teacher, acting as prime knower, guides them toward the meaning of an anthologized major or minor work, to attempt close readings in an effort to understand great works, to hear the odd biographical fact about the major author, and to write highly tentative interpretive essays aimed at closure on an elevated thought. Robert Scholes points out that in the traditional classroom, "It is usually forbidden to discover truths and beauties not attributable to the author—or to find lies or ugliness in canonical works" (1990, 96). Students who discover correct truths in texts are defined by the course as good students and good readers, though very likely less good writers: students who shine in the classroom activity of reading the text through the teacher's mind often produce, to the teacher's dismay, only timid and confused interpretive essays.

Overcoming the frustrating passivity of the conventional introductory literature classroom is an effort blocked at several points by the very conditions of that classroom. Course readings certified by inclusion in the confines of an anthology seem available to exegesis or admiration but not to manipulation or critique; the teacher as the authority stands with the anthology, certifying it as a repository of meaning; the student reader/writer, without a hope of ever being anthologized, can only retreat into the powerlessness of trying to say the right thing, thereby pleasing the teacher and honoring the anthology's contents. The absence from this classroom of any articulated theory beyond the presumed value of close reading is the final inhibitor in a generally inhibiting classroom construct. Each of the inhibitors—great literature, anthologies, authoritative teacher, close reading, interpretive writing, hidden messages—is tied to the others, making it scarcely possible to extricate just one troublesome element from the situation because the presence of any of the others will not allow it.

A clean sweep can begin by banishing the anthology and its certified contents in favor of cheap and preferably flashy paperbacks so accessible to relatively inexperienced readers as to at once reduce any need for an authoritative teacher to guide the reading. Two such texts serving as examples here are Horatio Alger's *Ragged Dick* (1868) and Raymond Chandler's *Trouble Is My Business* (1939). Students feel "culturally at home" (Scholes 1985, 27) in these texts, and they read them rapidly with considerable interest and pleasure. The presence of such texts significantly alters the teacher's role in the classroom: the teacher is not needed to certify anything about the texts or to guide student readers into or through their mysteries; the teacher is instead required to articulate the textual theory that will allow the students to begin decoding, interrogating, and manipulating the texts. In the text-based classroom, the teacher, like the students, is situated as a reader, and by articulating ways to read becomes a helpful guide on *how* to read instead of a forbidding guardian of meaning, a watchdog over *what* to read.

Nonetheless there is some delicate business here, especially in regard to basic terminology of classifying texts, a matter the teacher must approach with considerable care. For the Alger and Chandler texts, there are old derogatory terms aplenty that need to be avoided, and avoidance may require teachers to consciously retrain themselves. Roland Barthes says that one must be "periodically reborn" as a teacher by a system of "unlearning" (1979, 15). Needing to be unlearned are such terms as "junk fiction," "pop lit," "pop culture," "trash," and any other terms that drop off Alger and Chandler at the bottom of the old literary hierarchy. Textual theory employs no such hierarchies, for the teacher must be able to speak seriously about texts on which the students are going to perform some serious operations. The word "popular" ought never to be abbreviated but even that caution is insufficient, for the label "popular literature" is itself a misnomer based on an unsupportable inference about audience. The accurate term for both the Alger and Chandler texts is "formula fiction," the use of which points directly toward textual theory's revaluation of the repetitious over the original example. The traditional literature classroom's heavy investment in originality has functioned to cut texts loose from culture, stranding them in the unapproachable vacuum of singular genius. The formulaic text, so clearly reproduced and reproducible by one or many, brushes aside by its very conditions of production all questions of originality.

Formula is best defined as consisting of "recognizable conventions which give rise to certain expectations" (D. Dunlop 1975, 377). Identification of those conventions constitutes one of the decoding tasks to be performed by students and can further lead to pleasurable recognition of the sturdiness and durability of the two very different formulas used by Alger and Chandler. The formula Alger used is described by John Cawelti: "By an amazing series of coincidences, and a few acts of personal heroism and generosity, the hero escapes from the plots laid by his enemies . . . and attains the patronage of the benevolent merchant. In generating the action, chance and luck play a dominant role" (1965, 115)—or, in even briefer form, "a street boy's rise to social respectability" (108). Along different formulaic lines, Philip Marlowe, in Chandler's hardboiled formula, is hired to solve or becomes accidentally caught up in a mysterious crime. Marlowe, though threatened by both criminals and police, solves the crime because he is smarter than both; he comes away from the experience with nothing. Although Cawelti suggests that Alger occasionally tried, across the 107 books he wrote, to vary his formula but failed for lack of skill (111), Chandler himself, by contrast, indicated he knew the power of formula:

> As I look back on my own stories it would be absurd if I did not wish they had been better. But if they had been much better they would not have been published. . . . Some of us tried pretty hard to break out of the formula, but we usually got caught and sent back. To exceed the limits of a formula without destroying it is the dream of every magazine writer who is not a hopeless hack. There are things in my stories which I might like to change or leave out altogether. To do this may look simple but if you try, you find you cannot do it at all. You will only destroy what is good without having any noticeable effect on what is bad. (ix)

Fiction built on these two familiar—because culturally embedded—formulas does not invite reverence from students; furthermore, the power of formula disables most reader interest in authorial intention or biographical detail. Even more important, formula fiction short-circuits or averts certain weak but pesky learned responses to literary texts. No pious moralizing over the behavior of fictional characters can compete with the heavily moralizing Alger, and moralizing is irrelevant to Chandler's corrupt and amoral fictional world. Furthermore, student readers seem little tempted to naturalize Alger's or Chandler's characters via personal anecdotes about family or friends: Wax-nose, Anna Halsey, Ybarra, and Lola Barsaly are experienced by students not as personal but as textual, as narrative devices propelling and propelled by formula. Plotting is so heavy in Alger and so obscure in Chandler as to be not worth notice, and meaning is certainly not hidden. In effect, the formula fictions enable readers to perform operations with texts quite different from understanding, interpreting, and revering them. Furthermore, since students do not bother to understand what happens in *Trouble Is My Business*, the reading of formula fiction points ahead to the possibility of working intensely with texts without seeking to understand them.

Decoding formula fiction can begin with Gregory Ulmer's suggestion that one read a text "as a set of instructions for making a text" (1990, 119). Horatio Alger's *Ragged Dick*, obvious even to inexperienced readers, is a made text; it repeats its recipe until each eater can cook the same dish. Into a framework of specific urban detail steps a street boy equipped with certain Virtues but also held back by certain Deficiencies. Chapter by chapter, a Virtue positions Dick for a Stroke of Luck that allows him to overcome a Deficiency and allows Alger to point out a Valuable Lesson. As noted in the preceding discussion of formula, Alger's "recognizable conventions" do indeed "give rise to certain expectations" about the text which the students can decode; but students will also note that Alger works to rein in Dick's expectations by continually representing him as surprised and grateful for small rewards. Inside the formula a most modest version of social respectability is apparently the upper limit that Dick Hunter can reach for: a suit of clothes (secondhand at that), a small savings account, basic literacy, a room in a boardinghouse, and a clerk's job in a mercantile firm.

Both John Cawelti and Richard Weiss point out that American culture has affixed Alger's name to a "rags-to-riches" formula; Alger's name produces that connotation not only in the popular media but also in scholarly treatments. Cawelti and Weiss are at pains to correct the connotation and to demonstrate that Alger's actual formula is closer to "rags-to-respectability." Those few student readers who recognize Alger's name at all may also make the rags-to-riches connection, but to press on them Cawelti's "correct view" is to press also the view that "correct" readings of texts exist, to reinforce lurking beliefs that the teacher is a repository of special information about true meaning, and to halt the students' exploration of the text by, in effect, calling in the text police to break up the reading party. A better alternative would be to transform the "correctness" question about Alger's formula into a cultural question; after the students have themselves located Alger's formula, they may be ready to discuss the cultural resistance to it implied by a century of American insistence on transforming into riches the Algeresque reward of dull respectability.

Ragged Dick's accessibility to manipulative readings is one of its Virtues as a text. Because Alger lays out his own Messages so overtly, they invite subversion through a recasting of his formula: possibly it is a formula of behavior modification designed to transform a free and happy young person into a dull office drudge by encoding such a modification as a rise in life. Possibly the text's overt emphasis on Virtue is an effort at concealing the text's investment in Luck, and if so, Dick Hunter's apparent orderly rise through a world of chance constitutes a notable textual collision. Another decoding asks how it is that Honest Dick Hunter can explicate for his companions and his audience so great a range of street swindles, how they work and how to avoid them, unless Dick Hunter is himself a swindler wearing the mask of an Honest Face and using that mask to swindle his way into the ranks of literate, churchgoing, salary-drawing respectables.

In pushing toward such decodings of *Ragged Dick*—decodings that are by no evidence attributable to authorial meaning—the student reader subverts Alger's heavyhanded moralizing to arrive independently at cultural materials embedded in the text. There is a certain delight in this apparent transfer of power from the encoded text to the decoding reader: *Ragged Dick* is liberated from the grasp of its endlessly preaching author into the arena of manipulable and rearrangeable text. The student, now powerfully resituated in regard to the text, is also in a position to interrogate concepts that drive the text—Honesty, for example, which is encoded in the Alger text as a matter not only of behavior but also of looks. Dick Hunter has a "frank, straight-forward manner" (40) and an "open face" (55) which make benevolent businessmen say to him, "I like your looks" (57). To interrogate the subject of looks, clothes, appearance, and Honesty in *Ragged Dick* is to arrive not only at a cultural understanding of the urban scene but also at an opportunity to read the text's sociocultural ideology—that is, the set of beliefs about individual and group behavior, customs, habits, and attitudes that undergirds the text.

On a certain level of textual irreverence, students can turn *Ragged Dick* upside down, shake out its contents, and rearrange them; on that level they are ready to write not about the text but along with it, by manipulating it, adding to it, or deforming it. Students freed from both the authority of the text and the authority of the teacher over meaning will at this point produce their own plans for transformation at a remarkable rate. One student writer, for example, transported Dick Hunter to the late twentieth century where, finding no boots to black, Dick supports himself by scrounging for returnable cans and bottles; his friend Tommy Noonan is no longer a pluckless charity case but a snappily dressed drug dealer who scorns Dick's grubbing through trash cans. Another student reversed the direction of Dick's Strokes of Luck and thereby managed to also re-gender the text: in this version it is Dick who falls off the ferry boat and is rescued by the athletic—and again scornful—daughter of the prosperous businessman. Dick is left damp, humiliated, and still poor. A good deal of sheer delight in writing emerges from both the transformations themselves and the reactions of students when the transformations are read to them in the classroom.

Raymond Chandler's hard-boiled detective thrillers have, as formula, classroom uses different from those of the Alger text. Chandler's *Trouble Is My Business* is as accessible to students as *Ragged Dick* without, however, being explicable murder by murder. To understand Chandler's plot—the actual whodunit—is not the point of reading

Chandler; no reader cares who killed John D. Arbogast or young Jeeter. Other and more complex matters are encoded by Chandler's formula because that formula, in contrast to the Alger text, is separate from and different from Chandler's plot. A Chandler text must be tugged at more obliquely than an Alger text, and it will be found considerably more resistant. Chandler furnishes an occasion to question the cultural codes a reader uses to process Chandler's text—that is, to locate where Chandler's fictional world is embedded in American culture. Like Dashiell Hammett, who wanted to "get murder out of the Vicar's rose garden and back to the people who are really good at it" (as we learn in Wim Wenders's film about him), Chandler delivers a society run by "the cops, the crooks, and the big rich." In decoding Chandler it should become clear that none of the clichéd binary oppositions familiar to students from television crime shows—good/evil, lawful/unlawful, police/criminals—can be located in *Trouble Is My Business* or *Red Wind*. Cops and criminals unite in their violence, bigotry, and distaste for Marlowe; the nature of most relationships is concealed; everyone breaks and enters; everyone is armed; anyone gets drunk at any time of day. In Chandler texts, the recognizable conventions lie embedded in the undifferentiated behaviors of the entire cast of characters. Consequently students may find themselves working in a distinctly adversarial way toward the text, and interrogating Philip Marlowe as to whether he went into the P.I. trade because it was the handiest way to locate situations in which he might court death. For example, one student writer's shrewd transformation of Chandler placed Philip Marlowe as a contestant on *The Dating Game*; Marlowe's date thinks he has a nice voice but finds him to be too paranoid and self-destructive for her to contemplate a second date with him. He is advised to seek counseling.

Both the Alger and the Chandler texts can begin to suggest to students, first, that a great deal of American literature is about homelessness and that an ideology of homelessness may constitute an intertextual connection between Alger and Chandler; and second, that both formulas not only operate with but also insist upon strict gender distinctions. Both formulas sideline women and when student writers attempt to re-gender the texts—with a young female bootblack on the streets of New York City or a female P.I. in Los Angeles's night world—they take on the challenge of contesting deeply ingrained cultural assumptions. No matter what the quality of their experiments, they nonetheless discover how deeply embedded in formula fiction are the strictest ideologies of gender roles. In a text-based classroom, however, no elements should make students feel that there are limits to their critical activity or that certain texts are excluded or exempt from critique. Gerald Graff says that it is the very ordinary student who has "suffered most from the established curriculum's poverty of theory, for such a student lacks command of the conceptual contexts that make it possible to integrate perceptions and generalize from them. . . . It was the isolation of 'literature itself' in a conceptual vacuum that stranded students without a context for talking about literature" (1986, 41).

Classroom liberation from the weight of passive exegesis into active critique constitutes, however, a mood or an atmosphere that needs to be continually promoted and recreated. If the teacher indicates that after reading formulaic texts the class is going to move on to read something better, or greater, or more serious in order to arrive at understanding, the atmosphere of textual liberation will collapse at that moment, and the students will slide back into passivity. Instead, other possible directions should begin to suggest themselves here: Alger's narrative line can be followed into other texts that rearrange culturally embedded narrative devices. An initial focus on repeated elements in the next texts to be read, postponing discussion of their differences, keeps reader confidence alive and prevents students from dropping back into hesitancy and mind reading. Among the many texts that incorporate the devices of the "rags-to-something-else" story, two interesting possibilities are E.D.E.N. Southworth's *The Hidden Hand* (1859) and Theodore Dreiser's *An American Tragedy* (1925). The first seven chapters of *The Hidden Hand*'s sixty-one chapters accomplish a major and, in American literature, unusual gender shift: the text opens on a homeless girl struggling to survive on the streets of New York City. As noted earlier, strictly gendered cultural controls police the "rags" story and appear in *The Hidden Hand* when Capitola, after disguising herself as a boy in order to get work, is threatened with a trip to Blackwell's Island when her masquerade is uncovered. Early in this long text, however, the "rags" formula asserts its resistance to gender transformation and abruptly shuts down when the stroke of luck functions to transfer the plucky heroine into the more gender-comfortable confines of the gothic romance formula. Student readers usually find *The Hidden Hand* much funnier and more exciting than do their teachers, whose previous training may impede their enjoyment. Regardless of reader pleasure, however, the Southworth text shows how great a resistance to alteration can be mounted by a set of narrative conventions that exist apart from their handling by any individual. The textual path takes another direction with Dreiser's *An American Tragedy*, a relentless retelling of the "rags to" story with a different "to" destination for each figure in the text who collides with the formula. The sheer weight of detail in *An American Tragedy* calls for another resituation of the readers—as, perhaps, mapmakers, accountants of the cost of each "rise," keepers of the formulaic balance sheet, or diagrammers of its disasters. *An American Tragedy* never allows the ease of manipulation afforded by *Ragged Dick;* students may find themselves, robbed of laughter, in a struggle, overmatched against a powerful decoding of themselves and their own desires.

A quite different move away from formula fiction involves reappraising the terms under which it was first assessed in the course. Following Umberto Eco, texts can be reappraised as *closed* or *open.* Formula fiction is, in Eco's view, closed:

> In the process of communication, a text is frequently interpreted against the background of codes different from those intended by the author. Those texts that obsessively aim at arousing a precise response on the part of more or less precise empirical readers . . . are in fact open to any possible "aberrant" decoding. A text so immoderately "open" to every possible interpretation will be called a *closed* one. Every step of the "story" elicits just the expectation that its further course will satisfy. (1979, 8)

An open text, on the other hand, requires a reader "able to master different codes and eager to deal with the text as with a maze of many issues. What matters is not the various issues in themselves but the maze-like structure of the text" (9).

Eco's terms suggest a path from a closed text in which the students have been "culturally at home"—*Trouble Is My Business*—to an open text set in the same California nightworld—Thomas Pynchon's *The Crying of Lot 49* (1966). Because nothing is known of Pynchon the human being, readers cannot backslide into biographical wonderment; on the down side, *The Crying of Lot 49* has been since its publication a field day for exegesis and source hunting. Even a brief foray into Pynchon criticism on the part of the teacher ought to indicate that, if brought into the classroom, the minutiae of Pynchon criticism may stun any group of students into silence. Instead, *The Crying of Lot 49* needs to be given to students as an insoluble puzzle, a maze in which both they and the characters are wandering. Although the text situates its decoders differently from the way they were situated in *Trouble Is My Business,* readers remain aware that they are reading *The Crying of Lot 49* at least partly in dependence on having read *Trouble Is My Business. The Crying of Lot 49* gives readers a choice of what to decode, whether it is the obvious matter of rearranging the call letters of the radio station that employs Wendell "Mucho" Maas or the more demanding search through a book of Remedios Varo paintings for clues to the text. As Umberto Eco says, "The reader finds his freedom (i) in deciding how to activate one or another of the textual levels and (ii) in choosing which codes to apply" (1979, 39).

A reader who has manipulated the closed maze of a Chandler text and who has inserted him- or herself as a decision maker into the open maze of the Pynchon text is also theoretically prepared for the encyclopedic maze, the text in which anyone or no one may be "culturally at home." Such an example is Jorge Luis Borges's "Tlon, Uqbar, Orbis Tertius" from *Labyrinths* (1962), recognizable to student readers first on the level of the maze they have already experienced, second as similar to both Chandler and Pynchon in that "understanding" all its references and events is not only impossible but also unnecessary to reading it, and third as a piece of science fiction. Discussion of "Tlon" should focus on the work as text, on which of its levels the students will choose to activate, and on the codes students apply to their reading of the text.

At this point it will be noted that such old familiar terms for literary exegesis as character and motive, unity, coherence, symbol, and irony have utterly vanished from classroom discourse and have not been replaced. Cary Nelson points out that textual theories "are not constituted as a series of interpretive vocabularies" and that textual theory "resists summary, translation, and codification" (1986, xiii). Nonetheless, students who have read and written their way from Chandler to Pynchon to Borges have engaged in "complex discursive practices" with texts other than the notoriously interpretable types located between the boards of the usual anthology. Textual theory transports into the classroom a set of categories available for open discussion, brings the student into active relation to the text, and sets up texts in the context of their cultural life. At this historical moment, textual theory is liberating for students whose few, previous learned responses to texts can be readily short-circuited and who will thereafter pose little resistance to the power and play that textual theory offers. For the experienced teacher the story is different: a text-based course entails loosened authority over the classroom, the loss of a comfortable old interpretive vocabulary, and the pressure to articulate for students not tricks of exegesis that lead to glossy meanings but concepts, categories, and codes that elicit unpredictable readings and playful pieces of writing.

20 Theory as Equipment for (Postmodern) Living

Thomas McLaughlin
Appalachian State University

Kenneth Burke is often anthologized as an example of a critic who shares the formalists' expertise in close textual analysis but who does not share their aestheticism, their belief that the experience of literature is an end in itself. One of his most widely anthologized essays is "Literature as Equipment for Living" (1941).[1] In this essay, and throughout his career, Burke claims that literature does powerful social and political work. Literary works serve as "complex words" that name and assess "recurrent social situations." They "size things up" and suggest an "attitude," or more actively a "strategy," for dealing with experience. "A work like *Madame Bovary*," he says, "is the strategic naming of a situation. It singles out a pattern of experience that is sufficiently representative of our social structure, that recurs sufficiently often *mutatis mutandis*, for people to 'need a word for it' and to adopt an attitude towards it. Each work of art is the addition of a word to an informal dictionary . . ." (Burke 1941, 515). That dictionary then serves up "equipment for living," allowing us to be canny interpreters and effective participants in social relations.

From Burke's perspective, no course in the university curriculum could do more effective cultural, social, and political work than the introductory literature course. It is in that course that students first encounter an "attitude" toward literature and a "strategy" for reading. They can learn there that literature is a game—a playful manipulation of potential meanings and feelings—and that reading is learning the rules of the game and appreciating exquisite performance. They can learn that literature is a dream, and that reading is its analysis. Or they can learn, as Burke would like, that literature is a "naming" that implies a "strategy," and that in reading we can learn how to make sense of the world. Many other models are of course possible. But it is precisely the goal of the introductory course to provide such a model. In this course, theory is unavoidable. Even those teachers who deny that they teach theory, who claim that they teach literature itself and encourage a spontaneous, feeling response to it, are thereby passing along *a model, a theory,* one among the many possible.

It is not surprising that the model most commonly found in introductory literature courses is a formal approach, often in combination with humanistic or thematic concerns. It is, after all, absolutely necessary for students to learn in this course how a figure of speech works, how narratives can be structured, how characters function. And a formal approach, emphasizing the internal workings of the text, lends itself to the teaching of these techniques. Introduction to literature courses are themselves a creation of New Critics who saw that the contribution that English departments could make to the curriculum was to teach a discipline of textual interpretation (see Graff's *Professing Literature* [1987]). Their project in the creation of these courses was in part driven by the audience of students they worked with. In the fifties and early sixties the universities were filled with students on the GI bill and with other working-class students who came without a high-culture background and in need of a course that would give them the basic critical concepts necessary for serious reading. The formal approach gave—and still gives—them important "equipment for living" in the university and in the professions.

This essay will argue, though, that the students that we serve need a new model, one that will suit them for the cultural situation they—and we—face. For me the model that now provides the most effective "equipment for living" is one that combines the insights into language of structuralism and semiotics with the insights into power of ideology critique.

Students need to see literature in terms of how meaning is produced within language and culture, and in terms of how language encodes the power structures within society. Briefly, the argument of structuralist and semiotic cultural theory is that verbal language should be thought of as a system of meanings and values through which we perceive the world. Language is an embodiment of the values of the culture; it provides the mental framework that makes sense of our experience. From the beginning of structuralist thought, though, this claim has not been limited to verbal language. Even Ferdinand de Saussure, the founder of structural linguistics, saw his work on verbal language as a part of a larger, "semiotic" project which would study all communication systems. The field of semiotics is based on the premise that there are many "languages," that objects and gestures, for example, have a communicative function within a culture. The contribution of more politically oriented thinkers, particularly Marxists, has been to think of these systems of meaning and value as the "ideology" of the society. These frameworks do political work, in the sense that they support the values of the powerful groups within the society that control language and communication systems. Understanding literature, then, is a way of understanding and to some extent resisting the power of language in culture. Those who are aware of the workings of ideology are to some degree able to gain a critical distance from it. For our students, who have grown up in a culture that has raised ideological manipulation to an art and a science, it is essential to learn how such manipulation works.

The argument against using poststructuralist theory in the introductory classroom has been based on the difficulty of these theoretical texts. Certainly few freshmen are ready to read Derrida or Kristeva or their followers. And in terms of ideology critique, Althusser and Jameson are no easier. The difficulty with texts, and with those theorists who argue for or against their ideas, can be explained by the fact that these theoretical works are texts of technical analysis, written for a professional audience. They are also texts which often have as one of their goals the unmasking of the ideological effects of ordinary language, and as a result they seek the difficult and the strange in language as a way of forcing readers out of their usual patterns of thought. Nevertheless, their difficulty has so far limited the extent to which the insights of poststructuralist theory have affected undergraduate and particularly introductory-level instruction. There have been many efforts in the last few years to mainstream poststructuralist theory, to make it available to an undergraduate audience. I want to argue that such projects are crucial in the effort to provide students with "equipment for living" in the postmodern culture they inhabit.

I would claim, further, that today's students are ready to use those strategies. The typical undergraduate, born in the early 1970s, has been brought up in the same culture of the sign that accounts for the very existence of poststructuralist models. Poststructuralist theory makes sense historically as the moment when an economy and society based on information and image becomes aware of itself. And our students have lived that society as if it were natural and inevitable. They are competent in its rules of operation. They have experienced a culture which values image over reality, which has replaced production with information, which has developed a popular culture of intricate semiotic sophistication and technical virtuosity, which deploys spectacular signs, which encourages the creation of personal identity within those sign systems—that is, they have lived in a culture that many critics have come to call postmodern, and they are adept at reading its artifacts. Just ask a freshman class to analyze an advertisement in terms of the messages that are communicated by the clothes, the hair styles, the cars, the interiors of homes, the "signs" in the ad. They can do so with astonishing expertise. They have tremendous "cultural literacy" in the sense of being able to "read" the nonverbal signs of their culture. The field of semiotics, the study of objects as elements in a system of signification, is not a mystery to them.

Nor is the crucial notion of the arbitrary nature of the sign. With just a little prompting, students immediately understand that the meaning of the sign is cultural and historical, not natural or given. Students can easily tell you how the meaning of an object can change over time and in various cultural contexts. Take the current rage for basketball shoes as an example. Every kid knows that some shoes "mean" that you actually play the game, while other brands "mean" a kind of street sensibility, a sense of belonging, even of belonging to a particular group or gang. They also know that these "meanings" shift from neighborhood to neighborhood and from week to week. Reading these signs accurately is, for some students, literally a matter of life and death, since a certain shoe can "mean" membership in a certain gang. Being able to read such signs is a "strategy" for survival in youth culture—definitely "equipment for living."

The power of poststructural thought is not simply in its description of how objects mean; it is in its analysis of how those social and public systems of meaning constitute individual identity. In postmodern culture, identity is to be found inside semiotic systems. We come to know others and even ourselves by the signs we deploy. We *construct* our identities by the signs we choose for ourselves, by the clothes we buy, the cars we drive, the houses we live in. No one understands this better than a kid cruising through the mall, taking in the solicitations of the market, searching for the signs that will say what he needs to say, consuming his way to a personal style. What kind of jeans to buy, what team jacket, what kind of haircut to get, what kind of mall food to eat—all these decisions are supervised by the superego of peer pressure. Each of these decisions at once displays and further defines a personal identity, a set of social affiliations by which students can place themselves.

One key aspect of that self-construction is of course gender. Poststructuralist feminists have theorized gender roles as performances, improvisations within a culturally defined system of gender-specific signs.[2] Those signs change from culture to culture and over time, but their power relies on our forgetting their history, mistaking the contingent for the transcendent. There is, that is to say, an ideology of gender—a cultural formation that offers itself as natural so that current, male-dominated power relations can be maintained. In youth culture today it does appear that this ideological effort in support of traditional gender roles has succeeded. TV images aimed at kids in the 1980s have reversed many of the advances in awareness gained by feminists in the seventies. MTV may seem frightening to many parents in its vivid sexuality, but videos are strikingly conservative in gender presentation. Women are typically sexual decorations or manifestations of male sexual fantasies. There are of course exceptions. Male dancers often play this decorative role in videos featuring female stars, and there are women like Tracy Chapman who have defied the stereotypes. But MTV images of gender are nevertheless very traditional, and they have succeeded in large part in naturalizing themselves.

But MTV itself provides the tools for deconstructing those images, and even the "postfeminist" students of the eighties and nineties can easily become aware that these signs are cultural, not natural. Their insight into signs in general is so keen that it cannot exempt signs of gender. There is the example of Madonna, whose career is a series of improvisations with the signs of male-fantasy femininity. She takes up and discards these signs so quickly, and deploys them with such sly irony, that her identity as a female is clearly a performance, based on a canny recognition of the social and economic rewards of conforming to the stereotype. In general, the sheer repetition of signs and images of gender on MTV at least in part undoes the intended effect. That is, if gender is given and natural, why must it be so frequently and invasively reinforced? Why teach what is natural? Most students, wise to the ways of the market, can see that those images serve an economic and social function, arranging the personal identities of subjects in the market so that their desires can be fulfilled by product consumption.

Our students have been for all their lives the targets of a marketing-advertising system that is hyper-aware of the power of signs. They have been besieged by ads which are based on the premise that products can be sold by associating them with signs of the lifestyle that consumers desire. Connect beer with the outdoor life, wine coolers with urban sophistication, Volvos with family stability, fast food with small-town community, and you are addressing individual consumers on the level of their deepest desires, desires which the advertising itself has participated in creating in its subjects. And if our students have been addressed by signs, even constituted by signs, it is possible for them to know signs as such, to achieve an awareness of their power. Contemporary theory is therefore important "equipment for living" for our students, in that it helps "name" their world and thus makes them less subject to it.

In order for it to be possible to teach an introductory literature course from the perspective of poststructuralist theory, it must be possible for students to transfer their ability to "read" nonverbal languages to the activity of reading written texts. Unfortunately, these two skills have been viewed by many educators to be mutually exclusive. This attitude is understandable, in that the activity of reading does seem to be endangered in children who spend too much time with TV and video games. Nevertheless, there are clearly areas where visual literacy and verbal literacy overlap. TV is a dramatic and narrative medium, after all, and such structuring elements as plot and setting are common to narratives in any medium. More radically, both verbal and visual communication systems rely on *signs*. Our students have learned nonverbal *languages*, and their skills must therefore have some application to the study of verbal language in literature.

One aspect of literature that especially lends itself to this crossover of skills is characterization. The construction of a character in a verbal narrative depends on the same semiotic systems which make possible the construction of an identity in society. And we as readers have to read those signs in fiction (especially in realistic fiction) exactly as we do in the social world. Students' ability to read nonverbal signs can be exercised by looking at an advertisement or a photograph. Take as an example an ad for "Dockers," the Levi's pants for "thirtysomething" guys. The models in the ad show all the signs of casual prosperity—well-groomed hair, expensive but sporty shoes and shirts—with which the advertiser wants to associate the product. And students can "read" the signs these models display right down to their social class, likely professions, marital status, age, and political leanings. A class can move from this kind of pictorial presentation to a verbal description of a character's signs. Let's take as an example Katherine Anne Porter's widely anthologized story "The Grave" (1934).

This brief but powerful story deals with two childhood experiences: the little girl in the story, Miranda, is given a wedding ring in trade by her brother, who has found it in an abandoned family graveyard, and later in the day she sees the fetuses inside a rabbit that her brother has shot. Twenty years later, years that pass in the blink of the narrator's eye, these events are brought back to her by her chancing to see some "dyed sugar sweets" in the shape of baby rabbits. These candies first take her back to the memory of fertility and death, but then to the memory of her brother admiring the silver dove, a decoration from a coffin in the family graveyard, which Miranda had found and traded for the ring. Crucial to the impact of the story is Miranda's stage of development at the time of these experiences. She is nine years old, much more interested in hunting and exploring than in more traditional girlish pursuits. When we first see her, she is "wearing her summer roughing outfit: dark blue overalls, a light blue shirt, a hired-man's straw hat, and thick brown sandals" (73). Miranda knows that her outfit conflicts with decorum; she has a "powerful social sense, which was like a fine set of antennae radiating from every pore of her skin" (74). She has met with social disapproval from the old women in the community who enforce the rules she is breaking.

We can credit our students with Miranda's "powerful social sense," in that they are able to read her signs even better than she reads them herself. They can see her clothes as signs, not only of her defiance of gender roles, but also of the declining social class of her family, a fact that is beyond her understanding. For our students Miranda is an easy character to read. The rules that govern clothing and gender have changed some over time, but Miranda's outfit still "reads" as tomboyish because to a great extent the rules, though amended, are still similar and still remain in force.

After Miranda is given the ring in trade by her brother, her comfortable feeling about her clothing changes:

> Now the ring, shining with the serene purity of fine gold on her rather grubby thumb, turned her feelings against her overalls and sockless feet, toes sticking through the thick brown leather straps. She wanted to go back to the farmhouse, take a good cold bath, dust herself with plenty of Maria's violet talcum powder—provided Maria was not present to object, of course—put on the thinnest, most becoming dress she owned, with a big sash, and sit in a wicker chair under the trees. (74)

Students can easily pick up the change in signs. Miranda now desires the signs of femininity (and luxury or comfort, as the narrator notes). Under the influence of the ring, the traditional sign of marriage, Miranda sees a future for herself that conforms to conventional gender patterns. What students can see in this story is how Miranda defines herself and her future identity in terms of signs. She now rebels against social roles, but she desires and foresees a time when she will adhere faithfully to the rules. A reader who was not competent in these simple social codes would not see this aspect of her character. But our students are not likely to be such naive readers, aware as they are of the nuances of fashion that send messages much more complex than these.

Because of these advanced nonverbal reading skills, our students are capable of more subtle verbal and literary understandings. Take for example the complex notion of the poetic persona, the fictional character created by the poet in order to speak the poem. The concept is of course especially necessary for a successful reading of many important nineteenth- and twentieth-century poets, including Robert Browning, Tennyson, Yeats, and Eliot. In poststructuralist terms, what happens in a poem with a persona is that the poet deploys an array of verbal signs that imply certain mental and emotional habits of mind. The "character" of the poem's persona is a function of its diction, its figurative language, its characteristic sentence structures—in fact, all the verbal strategies of the poem. What distinguishes the poet of such poems is the ability to produce a new and different set of signs in each poem. The poet looms in the deep background, so to speak, as the signs of the poem point to the fictional character of the speaker rather than to the poet. The reader has to learn to distinguish the persona from the poet, a distinction particularly made possible by reading many such poems by the same poet.

Reading William Blake's *Songs of Innocence and Experience* requires just such a reading technique. In each of these poems the verbal texture is quite different. The signs in each poem point to a speaker who is in a state of mind and spirit different from all the others. The speaker of "The Lamb," for example, with his simple diction, sing-song rhymes, and naive personifications, contrasts sharply with the speaker of "The Tyger," with his complex sentence structure, jarring metrical forms, and persistent questionings. Even within the *Songs of Innocence* there are great differences. The speaker of "Holy Thursday" reveals through his verbal signs—including sentence complexity and sophisticated vocabulary—a maturity of thought at odds with his political naiveté, which therefore seems willful and self-serving; the speaker of "Laughing Song," on the other hand, displays in every detail a simplicity that suggests an innocence that has never been tested by experience.

In order to master the reading techniques that these poems require, students need to learn that the words a speaker chooses and the way they are combined serve as signs of their speaker's identity just as nonverbal signs do. If you can "read" a personal identity out of clothing or cars or housing interiors, you can also read a personal identity out of verbal style. In terms of persona, you also have to recognize that such identities can be fabricated by a poet who is knowledgeable in the workings of signs. In terms of students' experience in popular culture, there are models of artists who assume a different persona in each performance. Madonna is again a good example. She creates a new array of signs with every number she performs: she is by turns a street-smart girl, a Marilyn Monroe-style "material girl," an exotic dancer, and a kept woman out of the world of *Metropolis*. What this diversity suggests is that each of these identities, made up of carefully selected signs, is a fabrication, a mask taken up for the occasion of the song, discarded in favor of a new identity in the next. Students can read the signs in her videos very clearly. What is necessary to help them make the move to reading verbal signs is to get them to attend more closely to the lyrics of songs. After all, the lyrics of Madonna's songs are part of the semiotic display. The overheated symbolism of "Like a Prayer" suggests a very different "persona" from that suggested by the dance-floor simplicity of "Vogue." My point is not, of course, that Madonna is as important or as great an artist as William Blake, but rather that kids raised on Madonna have encountered some of the kinds of semiotic play necessary for dealing with Blake.

It is important to note that most students are not aware of the sophisticated skills they possess. That is, they are "competent in" the language of nonverbal signs, but they are often not "aware of" the knowledge that makes their readings possible. They have been the subjects of advertising that assumes semiotic competence, but advertising does not require that its subjects be able to articulate what they know. In fact, the success of advertising depends on denying any such critical self-awareness. The sheer speed of a television ad—a discourse completed in thirty seconds or less—or even of magazine ads, which make a very sophisticated pitch in the time it takes to turn a page, works against analysis. And yet students are capable of such analysis, which suggests that competence in nonverbal semiotic systems can be turned into knowledge. The pattern has been laid down, so to speak, and it is possible for media subjects to bring that pattern to light.

Literature read from the perspective of poststructuralist theory can help that process to occur. Literature does not lend itself to the high-speed, low-awareness reading that pop culture promotes. It is difficult, especially for our students. It slows them down, making every step in the reading process perceptible. The verbal signs it employs are not a "natural" part of the postmodern environment that they have been brought up in. It is the stumbling that they experience, the difficulty of the code of literary language that students can learn from. Thinking through a figure of speech, understanding how the setting of a story affects the plot and characters—these are mental skills that postmodern media culture does not develop, but that are necessary equipment for living within it. Producers of commercials spend a great deal of time and money on the settings for advertisements, for example, because they know that the signs they display in a house, a restaurant, or an office will profoundly affect our processing of the events that take place there. But these advertisers want to keep this knowledge to themselves. They want to subject viewers to their knowledge of signs, and that subjection requires competence but denies and fears analysis. A person who knows how an ad works is less liable to be taken in.

Poststructuralist theory, as I argued earlier, is a product of postmodern culture, but it does at least have the potential to resist some of the dehumanizing elements of that culture. The notion that individual selfhood is to be found only in semiotic systems, only in the social, is on one level a healthy antidote to the atomistic individualism that we Americans are taught so fervently. But it can also lead to a dangerous passivity, a willingness that we have all seen so frequently in our students to take ideological messages as self-evident truths. Poststructuralist theory opposes the ideological tendencies of sign systems. It argues that the "truths" we learn in society are not self-evident. There are other systems of meaning and value, other ways of making sense of experience. Theory is "equipment for living" in postmodern culture in that it provides some measure of critical detachment. It teaches us to read culture more carefully than it desires to be read. It makes us less easily subjected to the marketplace of signs. An introduction to literature course taught from a poststructuralist perspective can make an important contribution to promoting reading strategies that "size things up" for today's students. It "names" the culture they live in, and in so doing gives them some "strategies" for postmodern survival.

Notes

1. Some examples are Richter (1989), Davis and Fink (1989), and Adams's *Critical Theory Since Plato* (1971).
2. See, for example, Myra Jehlen's essay on "Gender" (1990a).

21 Students as Theorists: Collaborative Hypertextbooks

James J. Sosnoski
Miami University

During the 1990s, students will more and more often sit down and boot up on their computers the texts required for their literature classes. Printed anthologies will give way to electronic ones like those developed in the Scholar's Workstation Project at Brown University. Before long, students will read their texts—for instance, Faulkner's "A Rose for Emily"—on hand-held monitors having the feel of books. Unlike printed books, however, these will be linked to other electronic "books," that is, databases containing historical documents, photographs, film clips, music, and commentary. To place Faulkner's story in its historical context, students could explore the post-Civil War period in Mississippi. Hypermedia sources could provide photographs or other graphic material; songs could not only appear as lyrics, but be performed. Film clips of Faulkner could be available on a videodisc. Perhaps dramatizations done by holography would feature Faulkner talking to a group of students simulating the class conferences recorded at the University of Virginia. Not only would the text of "A Rose for Emily" appear on the monitor, but simultaneously available in another "window" of the screen would be the PBS film version and, in a third window, annotations highlighting the differences.

After reading *Intruder in the Dust*, students could watch Clarence Brown's 1949 cinematic version of it on the same screen, and then call up Pauline Kael's note on it from her *Kiss Kiss, Bang Bang*. Study programs would raise questions about the texts assigned. In them, a series of instructions might acquaint students with various genres and subgenres. Passages from *The Sound and the Fury* juxtaposed with passages from Faulkner's film script of Hemingway's *To Have and Have Not* might be used to illustrate the stream-of-consciousness novel. Specific passages from *The Sound and the Fury* might appear in graduated segments designed to show the stylistic differences between conventional realistic prose and Faulkner's style. These might be coordinated with Warren Beck's essay on "William Faulkner's Style." A conventional chronology of events might be used to illustrate the distinction between plot and story. The possibilities are endless.

Students enrolled in English 32 ("English Literature from 1700 to the Present") at Brown University have already studied literature in much the same way I have just described (see Landow 1989; 1990). Their literature texts are "intertextually" linked through computer databases, not only with historical documents and documentaries about the periods studied, but also with materials to aid them in their analyses of the literature they read. Though few universities are currently equipped to house such electronic literature courses, we can expect their rapid expansion in the next decade.

Such electronic "Introduction(s) to Literature" possess a tremendous capacity for developing students' styles of thinking, working, and entertaining themselves.[1] Moreover, our students are primed for using these technological advances. However, as we all instinctively understand, disturbing dangers lie below the surface of these apparently untroubled waters of educational progress. Wondrous short-term improvements may carry with them viruses that can infect us with long-term disabilities.

We are at a historical moment that will determine the future of literary study. We cannot avoid the institutional changes that will take place when schools become electronic educational environments. By and large, the hardware and software for these environments will be modified versions of those made for corporations. Businesses require software that performs logico-mathematical operations because the form of intelligence required in business is logico-mathematical. Educators will continue to adapt software to their situations.[2] In the sciences (where logico-mathematical intelligence is at a premium), logically structured software presents no problem. The humanities, on the other hand, will have much more difficulty in adapting their studies to the available software. At stake is nothing less than control over the modality of literary study, control over the kind of intelligence or style of thinking it will engender in its students.

The electronic revolution is here and will continue to spread into every corner of our lives. This is inevitable. If we do not take care, however, electronification will, as so many of its critics fear, turn the study of literature into a "science." This is not inevitable, but it is possible. It is not difficult to program sequences of searches into a text that identify various formal features. Programs already exist that incorporate formal analyses of word patterns.[3] These sorts of exercises are ideally suited to computer-assisted analyses because they are based upon the binary oppositions that formally structure literary texts.[4] Computer-assisted instruction in literary study is likely to promulgate a more rigidly logical brand of New Criticism than that to which we have become accustomed.[5] An unsanctioned structuralism (a systematic formal analysis) is already surreptitiously infiltrating literary study through its electronification (see below).

Just as humanists at the turn of the century strove to make their methods scientific, so might current "Neo-humanists" (those who promulgate "cultural literacy") strive to make their enterprises computerizable, introducing by default an unwelcome "binarism" into the study of culture. We must keep in mind that "cultural literacy," as delineated by E. D. Hirsch, is fundamentally binary—it reduces the understanding of culture to a classification system. We can expect a CD ROM version of Hirsch's dictionary at any moment. Many teachers, in their efforts to make literature accessible to a generation of students who prefer "the electronic word" (Lanham 1989, 265), may unwittingly foster modes of logical analysis that are as reductive of cultural study as Hirsch's program for cultural literacy.

In the context of cultural literacy, the difference between a printed and an electronically prepackaged anthology is not a trivial matter. Literary study is rooted in the concrete and historically specific understanding of experience.[6] *That understanding cannot be articulated as a set of logical relationships.* At present and for the foreseeable future, literary understanding can be preserved in an electronic educational environment *only through the intervention of a human being.* As a consequence, we must assume responsibility for program design.[7] The reason is straightforward. Software companies design their products for businesses that depend upon logic. We can maintain the analogous character of literary intuitions in electronic environments only through our interventions.

An Instance of the Surreptitious Renaissance of New Criticism

Much has been made recently of the value of hypertext programs in the study of literature. They are remarkably flexible databases. Their users, in principle, can move from any file to any other file with the mere press of a key or click of a mouse. Proponents of the use of hypertexts in literary study often claim that, unlike standard databases, hypertexts more closely match the modality of literary inquiry because the user can move from one text to another intuitively. Hypertext's advocates, however, tend to exaggerate its potential for literary study. Richard Lanham, for instance, writes: "Hypertexts are, in more than a manner of speaking, three-dimensional. Fuguelike, they can carry on an argument at several levels simultaneously. And if we cannot read them exactly simultaneously, we can switch back and forth with great rapidity" (1989, 283). Hypertexts make accessible to the reader an array of textual variations and interpretations as well as historical contexts in which to place them, but they do not carry on arguments "simultaneously." Nor are they "three dimensional." Hypertexts are like variorum editions of texts with heightened speed of use, reliability, and scope. They offer tremendous advantages to the scholar-student.[8] Though the advantages of hypermedia are enormous, we have to remember that (1) hypertexts are highly structured systems and thus likely to inculcate a structuralist or neo-formalist approach to literature, and (2) any interactivity with them depends upon elaborations and applications of their structured forms.[9]

In "Changing Texts, Changing Readers: Hypertext in Literary Education, Criticism, and Scholarship," George Landow, a member of Brown's Scholar's Workshop Project and a teacher of its English 32, claims that historical relationships are not searched in rigidly causal terms (1990, 150) but in a manner closer to the way literary scholars think. For instance, every "event" catalogued in the database is linked to several historical contexts that might be understood as its preconditions.[10] I agree with Landow that it is desirable to encourage students to think about historical events in less simplistic ways, but I disagree with his conclusion that hypertext has this effect. It is not hypertext *as such* that produces this effect but the way in which this particular hypertext application is designed.[11] The students' "realization" that historical events have an elaborate and overdetermined structure of "causes" is an effect of *the structure built into* English 32 of which students are not particularly aware—it is a teacher-oriented "hidden agenda." In English 32, students are given a menu of possible explanations of any given event. As a result, they stop thinking in simplistic cause-and-effect terms and allegedly start thinking of history in terms of Althusser's notion of structural causality. Such hidden agendas are not necessarily desirable. Further, the notion of "causality" built into English 32 is "logical" in character and not, as Landow claims, "decentered" in Derrida's sense of the term. As Landow himself points out, the main advantage of a hypertext environment is "connectivity" (135). The ease of access which is provided by hypertexts is wonderfully helpful. It puts extraordinary quantities of information at one's fingertips. But, in a hypertext environment, the user moves from one file to another *only* as long as links are established. These links are results of *human intervention.*

The remarkable feature that makes a hypertext database suitable to humanistic (or, in my terms, analogical) inquiry is the ease with which the "user" can become a "programmer" and establish "links" for herself. In other words, hypertext becomes an "intuitive" program for the user only at the point where she *theorizes* its design and begins to adapt it to her concerns. Landow appreciates the "freedom" this feature of hypertext environments gives students but sees them as thinkers who *apply* the theory built into the program as a teacher-oriented hidden agenda rather than as thinkers who challenge the program's underlying structure. He does not see students *as theorists.*[12] I will return to this issue in the last section of this essay.

If you do not find it a problem that Brown's English 32 encourages students to apply the theory to which the teacher ascribes, you might find it problematical that the theory purports to be a version of deconstruction. In his description of the program, Landow suggests that the hypertext program upon which it is based is "nonhierarchical" and "decentered" (150). Though I am enthusiastic about Brown's English 32, this is another instance of an exaggerated claim about the educational value of hypertexts. Hypertexts, like the more conventional databases from which they are derived, are highly structured. Students begin with a menu (a table of contents) and work along "linked" pathways that name the data to which the text on screen is connected. The graphs that Landow uses to illustrate the various "pathways" a student in English 32 might follow are quite "hierarchical." His figure 1, for instance, shows a dominating picture of "Alfred Tennyson" [sic] encircled by categories such as "biography," "literary relations," "artistic relations," "cultural context: Victorianism," and so on. All of the contexts are clearly subordinated to Tennyson.

One option on the menu is "how to read a poem." Brown's English 32 hypertext encourages students to read poems "intertextually." Landow quotes Thaïs Morgan's delineation of this pedagogical strategy. It is "a structural analysis of texts in relation to the larger system of signifying practices or uses of signs in culture," which shifts attention from the triad constituted by author/work/tradition to another constituted by text/discourse/culture. In doing so, "intertextuality replaces the evolutionary model of literary history with a structural or synchronic model of literature as a sign system. *The most salient effect* of this strategic change is to free the literary text from psychological, sociological, and historical determinisms, opening it up to an apparently infinite play of relationships" (Landow 1990, 150; see Morgan in

Henricksen and Morgan 1990, 1–2, emphasis mine). From this perspective, Landow finds that hypertext "is related to the ideas of Jacques Derrida and Louis Althusser, both of whom emphasize the need to shift vantage points by decentering discussion" (150).

Landow would have us believe that hypertext is thoroughly compatible with contemporary critical modes like deconstruction. But there is nothing in his description of his students' use of hypertext that suggests they are able to deconstruct the structural categories with which they begin their analysis. The intertextuality they perceive seems entirely dependent upon search routines which identify "matches" in terms of logical attributes. However, that this pedagogy lacks "deconstructive force" is not what worries me.

I am troubled by the way in which an asocial, apolitical, ahistorical[13] neo-formalism dominates the students' activities in English 32. The "innovation" celebrated in Landow's justification of the methods of English 32 is that it "frees" students from "psychological, sociological, and historical determinisms."[14] It leads them, instead, into "the infinite play of relationships" of the triad "text/discourse/culture" as a "signifying *system*" (150, emphasis mine). This "innovation" is reminiscent of the "freedom" New Critics sought to explore the relationships within the text without locating them in historical contexts. Instead of history, we have (in Gregory Ulmer's terms) "mystory." Landow writes that "anyone who uses Intermedia makes his or her own interests the de facto organizing principle (*or center*) for the investigation at the moment" (150, emphasis mine). Landow emphasizes the ways in which hypertexts blur the boundaries between intra- and intertextual forms. English 32, it seems, is also designed to blur the distinction between literary texts and historical contexts. In other words, when history dissolves into mystory, the social component of literary study is diminished. Interpretive communities dissolve into solipsistic or narcissistic "plays" on an infinite variety of intertextual relationships—the study of literature is prone to devolve into a computer game which revolves around a series of formulae (structures) or rules.

This will not trouble everyone. Many will applaud the return of Neo-New Criticism. Not everyone minds that formalisms (of any sort) lack the capacity to critique cultures. In their attention to intertextual relationships, formalisms bracket out of consideration the extratextual links to the culture that must be addressed for a viable cultural criticism to exist. It is not an accident that New Critics eschewed political statements. New Criticism invited political neutrality. So does the Neo-formalism of a database.

We are now faced with the possibility that, despite recent critiques of formalisms, a neo-formalism may sweep away all objections surreptitiously with the advent of computer-assisted literary study. This seems likely for two reasons: (1) literary study will have to adapt to the inevitable institutionalization of electronic educational environments, and (2) literary formalism provides the only viable transformation equations by which literary analysis can be converted into computer-assisted instruction. Hypertexts, while an unquestionably powerful tool for flexible computer-assisted instruction, are not isomorphic to literary inquiry. Moreover, though they solve some problems, they create others.

On the one hand, hypertexts used to introduce students to literary study have the advantage of allowing students to pursue their own interests; on the other hand, this is their most dangerous feature. Students are products of a culture that fosters uncritical attitudes toward it. Students, like their parents, are susceptible to racism, sexism, elitism, and many other social diseases of which they are unaware. Making them aware of the liabilities in their social formations cannot be accomplished by making their interests "the de facto organizing principle (or center) for the investigation at the moment" (Landow 1990, 150). Ironically, students often do not know what their interests are—much less their limitations or their potential. The self-reflexivity required to make them aware is not encouraged by submitting them to a rigidly hierarchical view of canonical literature—the common fault of most printed anthologies. Hypertexts, however, are not inherently self-reflexive; they must be *programmed to invite reprogramming* in order to foster critical reflection on the underlying premises of the database. I advocate the development of such "reflexive instruction." By reflexive instruction I mean an application of a program in which the students are not only presented with a particular subject matter, but also encouraged to call it into question and alter it in the process of negotiating its contested values with collaborators. In short, I believe we should cultivate our students' ability to be theoretical. This would entail some changes in the way we now construct electronic anthologies (or printed ones, for that matter) like English 32. Our students can be of immense help in this respect, if we are willing to take their *spontaneous theorizing* seriously.

Student Librarying

It seems likely that, if asked, students would willingly "library" (anthologize) their culture to conserve artifacts they value.[15] They avidly want to own videotapes and CDs. They assiduously create personal libraries of their most valued cultural items. Therefore, an electronic "Introduction to Literature" anthology could be presented to them as a means of enriching their personal libraries. However, building this library would have to be worth the students' time and effort. But if they felt it would be a valuable resource, they would invest the necessary time and effort.

Reconsider, from the perspective of student librarying, what could be done with a program like Brown's English 32.[16] Interested students could write hypertext applications dovetailed to a particular class project in anthologizing. Instead of searching fields that have predetermined content, students could decide what fields were necessary to store their material and program them into an application specific to their needs.[17] At this point, you might object (as I did with Landow's program) that this tactic places student interests at the center of study. And, I would have to agree, adding that it does so in a much more thoroughgoing manner than Brown's English 32. Before I defend this tactic by arguing that student librarying, as I conceive it, is a publicly negotiated collaboration, let us consider the advantages of having students "edit" and design their own anthologies.[18]

Although anthologies are widely regarded as indispensable pedagogical tools, they have been used in a limited way. Traditionally, anthologies are edited by teachers for other teachers. As a consequence, they invariably present a teacher's view of literature and its interpretation. Since teachers have skills in interpretation that students lack, this perspective has a privileged status. Such is the case with Brown's "Context 32," the program upon which its English 32 is based. But the teacher-oriented anthology has a major drawback—it reflects the teacher's view of student interests. Prior to the 1960s, the teacher's interests governed the compilation of most anthologies. More recently, anthologies have been organized with student interests in mind. Rock lyrics appear in the poetry sections; assignments on films and TV appear alongside more traditional ones; texts are chosen about experiences students are likely to have undergone. Nonetheless, the anthologies still, for the most part, reflect what teachers believe students are or should be interested in. From many students' points of view, this produces a particularly noxious experience of literature. English 32 is not likely to be an exception.[19] I contend that student-authored anthologies are more effective in introducing students to canonical literature than teacher-authored ones.

Having students in introduction to literature courses compose their own anthologies first impressed me in Fall 1989, when I sponsored a student-organized graduate seminar on theory and pedagogy, in which the idea was discussed.[20] I tried it out during the following spring in what I then felt was the most successful introduction to literature class I had ever taught. The course had neither textbooks nor syllabus. On the first day of class I asked the students if they would be willing to compile their own anthologies, indicating that, if not, I would return with a traditional syllabus and textbook. They were willing.[21]

As the first assignment in the course, I asked the students to write a candid essay (which would not be graded)[22] for the other members of the class, describing the difficulties they experienced with previous literature classes. I indicated that the essays would be distributed to everyone in the class and that a meeting would be devoted to discussing the problems they described. Further, they would provide a basis from which we could begin to consider what a student-oriented anthology might accomplish. The essays they wrote ranged over a predictable array of complaints. The meeting, however, revealed a startling unanimity in the students' experience. Many of the writers mentioned that they felt discouraged when they were told by their teachers that their interpretations of a poem or story were "wrong." Once mention had been made of this particular "complaint" in the class discussion, everyone focused in on it, and we spent the entire time talking about the experience of "being told you were wrong."

During the class discussion, one young woman repeated the forceful account that she had given in her essay. She remarked that, time after time, she would read a poem or story at home, find it "tremendously" meaningful, only to be told the next day in class that it did not mean what she had supposed. Her experience of enjoying-the-*wrong*-meaning was for her so frustrating that she simply stopped reading for meaning and began to read for testable information, for "what the teacher wanted." The class discussion came back to this experience again and again.[23]

The use of standard anthologies makes the experience of enjoying-the-*wrong*-meaning inevitable in an introduction to literature class. Unless you think that literature is the more meaningful the further away it is from the reader's experience, then a teacher-oriented anthology, by definition, is a generation removed from student experience. Moreover, most students have had little practice in decoding sophisticated literary techniques. Students in Brown's English 32 do not escape the experience of enjoying-the-*wrong*-meaning. They are subjected to standard questions, for example, on point of view: "Who provides this focus, and who narrates the story and from what angle or consciousness? Is the narrator omniscient? Is this story pitched in terms of the consciousness of one character over another? Are we seemingly 'inside the mind' of one character or two" (Landow 1989, 197). Landow writes:

> My grader for the course, an experienced graduate student teacher who judged the take-home midterm and in-class final examinations the most rigorous she had ever seen, found that answers to both identification and essay questions were in general far more detailed and intellectually sophisticated than any other work by students at this level she had encountered previously. Although after first looking at the examination she warned me that she might have to fail a considerable number of my students, she did not—and in fact discovered that more than 10 percent of the class scored over 100 percent. (1990, 148)

The first assignment for English 32 reads as follows:

1. Open the folder entitled "Swift-G."
2. Open "Waterland OV." (OV = Overview)
3. Follow the link to "History, His Story. . ." Find three explanations or theories of history in the novel. Which do you think the book finally supports?
4. Return to "Waterland OV" and go from there to "Chronology of Events in the Novel"; go to the "Topics" folder and find the four timelines that sit beside the four subfolders. Open one and then place it to the right of "Chronology. . ." (Landow 1989, 196).

English 32 is teacher-oriented. Its approach to literature is neo-formalist.

One of the major advantages of having students make their own anthologies is that the texts they choose are ones they can relate to.[24] This is a significant advantage, indeed. For the most part, students feel that American culture is a "given." It comes from an unknown source.[25] They do not experience themselves as creators of their culture. With respect to culture (as with many other consumer goods), they are passive recipients. At the same time (and somewhat inconsistently), they think of themselves as choosing an individual lifestyle that sets them apart from their peers in at least some respects.[26] Some students, in fact, mark themselves as individuals by choosing *classical* culture. This variety of conflicting student lifestyles and subcultures opens up the possibility of considerable debate among students in any class. Moreover, debates about cultural artifacts of whatever derivation precipitate discussions of meaning and technique. Thus, faced with the task of making their own anthologies, students find that editorial decisions (which texts to include and what instructions to give) reveal to them their reasons for "advocating" these texts to others. Such advocacy and the resulting debates over texts and their interrelationships are lacking in Brown's English 32. Its "anthology," Context 32, differs from traditional printed anthologies only in its speed of retrieval and the scope of its material. It is an encyclopedic anthology that can be searched with tremendous alacrity. From the perspective of student librarying, it is a neo-formalist, teacher-oriented program of instruction upon which the users are rigorously examined. Studying it, students are likely to find themselves uncomfortably enjoying-the-*wrong*-meaning.

By contrast, student librarying places students in the position (not always a comfortable one) of reflecting upon the implications of the culture they have unwittingly absorbed. They find that cultures make up the meanings of symbols, that they ascribe to those made available to them in the media, or, that they are "counter"-cultural. They begin to see themselves as participants in the making of cultural symbols.[27] To make students self-reflexive about their culture and its subcultures is the goal of the hypertext program I am proposing as an alternative to English 32.

Indeed, the study of literature has always been related to the formation and preservation of "culture." Debates over the meaning of cultural symbols are, in large measure, the work of the humanities or, in the designation I prefer, of cultural studies. In the context of this tradition, it may seem unfortunate to some that "classical" or "canonical" texts are not in the forefront of the student-oriented anthology/hypertext I am proposing. Though I no longer subscribe to the view that knowing the classics is an adequate form of education, I would point out to those who do that students leave this program with a less oppressive sense of the "classics" than they obtain from more traditional introduction to literature courses. For example, in my introductory course, my illustrations about editing an anthology usually included canonical material which I presented enthusiastically to students. Since it was the material I planned to include in my anthology, I offered reasons for doing so and some sample analyses. The students in the class were quite receptive to these materials and often extrapolated from my presentations in editing their own anthologies. Our discussions typically revolved around connections between the anthology I was creating (by way of illustration) and their own anthologies.

I do not mean to suggest that the program I have described works to the same ends as traditional introductions to literature—hardly. A substantive difference is marked by the fact that I did not grade students on the basis of their interpretations of texts. Their grade was based on rhetorical criteria, largely having to do with presenting their materials in clear, cogent, and persuasive ways. I did not challenge the interpretive claims they made. Instead, I invited them to challenge my interpretations of their material. Instances in which they did proved the most exhilarating moments during the semester. For example, I badly misconstrued a Pink Floyd lyric during a discussion. They took great delight in pointing out how I was "wrong." In turn, I enjoyed pointing out to them that the reasons they offered for my "error" matched the kind of understanding that typically supported interpretive claims about literature in the traditional sense—information about historical contexts, allusions, techniques (in this case, significantly, point of view), and so on. Such exchanges, together with my stipulation that I would not mark their interpretations wrong, resolved the problem of enjoying-the-*wrong*-meaning. The course became a heuristic experience, leading to more and more complex readings of texts on both sides of the desk. In the process of conducting this student-oriented introduction to literature, I came to realize that my students behaved in highly theoretical ways.

Students as Spontaneous Theorists

The decisions involved in creating and editing an anthology are all warranted by some implicit or explicit literary theory—anthologies are not innocent of theory. Recent discussions of canonization have made us painfully aware of the assumptions that underlie anthologies. To decide which texts should be included in an anthology of literature not only presupposes a theory of literature, but also a set of selection criteria equally theoretical. As I hope to show, raising such theoretical questions is not a matter of applying esoteric credos. Rather, it is the conceptual juncture at which those *interventions* are made which insures that the cultural material to be libraried is not reduced to mere information that can reappear as an answer to an "identification question." The interventions begin with questions of value which lead to questions about preserving them by way of an electronic library.

Students assembling their own anthologies must ask again the most fundamental questions about the study of literature. For example, having "complained" about the frustrations of enjoying-the-*wrong*-meaning, my students had to ask for whom was the meaning valuable that they found in the works they hoped to include. They had to ask, "Why is this and not that work valuable? If it is valuable because of what it means to me, then, are anthologies solely personal possessions? How is meaning negotiated? What is the purpose of this anthology?" In each case, their questions came back at them. Since they were "librarying" their own culture, they had to ask themselves about the value of what they wanted to save.

When my students then turned to address the question of how they would organize their anthologies, they had to engage issues of genre: they had to consider the least reductive way of linking texts to each other. With my encouragement, for instance, one young woman decided to include in her anthology a series of highly literate cartoons. Having made this decision, she had difficulty judging where to locate them in her collection. Since they were too few to merit a section of their own, she had to ask herself if they were, more or less, very-short short stories. Others had to decide whether a film was to be included in the section on dramas or novels, or whether dramatic poems should be mixed in with stories. One young woman wanted to organize her collection around what she called a theme but which she thought of as a topic. This provided me with an occasion to ask if treating a theme as a topic reduces understanding to information.

Fixed categories reduce options and eliminate the kinds of theoretical questions I have mentioned above.[28] Were students to use a preprogrammed database application like Brown's Context 32, they would have no choice in these matters. In English 32, a window featuring the category "Victorian: An Introduction" shows a linked menu—"History," "Queen Victoria," "The Arts," "Medieval Revival," "Victorian Literary Forms"—which is linked to the lists: "Dramatic Monologue," "Perfect Moments," "Epiphanies," "Sage Writing," "Fiction," "Fantasy," "Realist Novel," "Psychological Novel." No questions are raised about the premises upon which these relations are based; no answers are given. Nothing much happens that would not happen in the use of a printed anthology. But if students have to decide on the fields and their criteria, then the question of whether the women's novels of the late 1990s are to be included remains alive and opens up a debate about feminism as a cultural perspective. And when it pertains to saving their own culture, there is no telling how sophisticated students might turn out to be. When what they value is contested, students are spontaneous theorists—they articulate the principles of their conduct.

This may seem to be giving them too much credit. Theory is, after all, supposed to be impenetrably arcane and inaccessibly abstract. And, indeed, in the last two decades, most of what has been called "theory" has this character. But literary theory is arcane and abstract only when it parallels scientific theory. Most of the esoteric literary theory published in recent years is an importation into literary studies of theories from other disciplines, principally philosophy, linguistics, and anthropology.

Theory (any theory!) is the result of the activity of theorizing. That activity is in everyone's repertoire.[29]

Theorizing is a common activity. It is often joyful and exciting. After a long debate with yourself about designing your next introduction to literature class, a scheme comes forcefully to mind. The debate you conducted is very likely to have been an instance of spontaneous theorizing. It is hard to avoid questioning your assumptions about what you are doing when you design a course. Issues of pedagogical strategy are theoretical issues. Theorizing and teaching are inseparable. So, when you get students to begin teaching themselves, they cannot help but theorize spontaneously.

Spontaneous theorizing is the self-reflexive activity during which we raise questions about what we are doing.[30] Theory may be what gets published, but spontaneous theorizing is the condition of its possibility. If students were allowed to theorize their culture spontaneously, many of them would begin to feel more like agents of their own cultural formation rather than victims of it. Most important, their interventions in the process of librarying cultural materials would preserve the analogous character of literary understanding because they would have a stake in preserving and enlarging their own "literary" understanding, which is itself not "binary." As I mentioned above, hypertext becomes an "intuitive" program for the user only at the point when she theorizes its design and begins to adapt it to her concerns.[31] Many of these interventions may seem bizarre to other users of the resulting library and will have to be negotiated as a matter of cultural politics. Libraries create cultures. Student librarying involves students' involvement in their cultural formation. Elsewhere they are already thus involved. Our task is to draw out their theoretical potential by helping them address the value of what they are already doing.

Conclusion

Few activities carry the intellectual passion characteristic of spontaneous theorizing. This is probably because all theorizing is derived from the question, "Who am I?" To want to understand what you are doing is to want to understand who you are. No matter how far from this question our theorizing may seem to take us, we can always return to it. To ask, "What is the value of the works I wish to include in my library?" is to ask "Who am I?" This question precipitates humanistic study. It is as important to students as it is to us. Like us, they are theorists.

Notes

1. Within the next decade introduction to literature classrooms will be electronic educational environments. By this I mean a learning situation in which computers, VCRs, modems, CDs, and other electronic devices are programmatically interfaced to provide a course of study.

2. It is not likely that humanists will develop hardware that matches literary or analogical intelligence rather than a logico-mathematical one. Ironically, analogical intelligence has been a subject of study in Artificial Intelligence research conducted by "scientists."

Nor is it immediately likely that humanists will develop basic software for their electronic educational environments. MLA has taken a major step forward in inaugurating a program to develop software designed for humanistic use. Nonetheless, the software presently being developed is not capable of stemming the tide of digitalization. Last year, for instance, MLA awarded a contract to Elaine C. Thiesmeyer and John E. Thiesmeyer, the creators of a text-checking program, Editor, which functions in ways much like programs marketed by software firms. It gives its users much more flexibility than, say, RightWriter or Grammatik IV, but marks only the beginning of what has to be done.

3. One, for example, takes Wolfgang Iser's conception of "consistency building" and identifies various "consistencies" for students in particular poems by asking them to answer a series of questions designed to mark formal patterns in the poem. (Although Wolfgang Iser's work is usually associated with reader-oriented approaches to literature, as many of its critics have noted, it is basically a method of formal analysis.) The program was developed by Patricia Harkin and Susan McFarland at Denison University, with funds provided by a Carnahan-Jackson Grant. It was used by students in an introduction to literature course.

4. The historical perspective through which we should view the computerization of literature is that of the valorization of logico-mathematical intelligence. From this perspective, we can trace the logification of literature study. It begins with a pattern of institutionalization developed in the late nineteenth century, which turned the study of literature into a departmental discipline requiring models and methods parallel to those which the modern American university was designed to foster. This inaugurated the scientizing of literary study. First, philology took a foothold as a scientific method of literary analysis. It gave way to literary history based on rigorous methods of inference. Literary history gave way to "New Criticism" hailed as a "science" by critics like John Crowe Ransom, but more modestly believed by others to be a way of establishing "valid" interpretations. Northrop Frye, as you may recall, proposed a different "science" of criticism, foreshadowing the brief heyday of structuralism (purposefully based on the secure science of linguistics). The 1980s have seen a variety of critiques of this historical tendency, the most notorious being deconstruction. I give an account of this pattern of institutionalization in a forthcoming book entitled *The Magister Implicatus and the Call to Orthodoxy*.

Like many traditionalists who oppose turning the study of literature into a form of logical analysis, many postmodern critics are critical of structuralism.

Deconstruction is notorious in this regard. But a critic does not have to be committed to deconstruction to realize the limitations of structural analysis. Since formalism is based on the view that language is logical in its structure, the formal approaches to literature this perspective induces are amenable to computerization. The likelihood of a match between a rigorous formalism and electronic introductions to literature is increased by the fact that most printed introductions to literature still presuppose New Critical (formalist) approaches to the study of literature.

Just as persons entering literary studies a decade or so ago were generally unaware of the history of their profession and thus uncritical of the *new* criticism in which they were being schooled, so too will future students of literature working in their electronic educational environments be unaware of the *new* structuralism or "neo-formalism" that pervades their practice. The scientification of literary study will therefore continue unabated. It is now well known that, during the last two decades of the nineteenth century, the study of literature modeled itself on successful patterns of institutionalization inaugurated by the sciences. This historical tendency, propelled by socio-economic developments like the electronic revolution, is about to reform literary study once again. Just as the wake of the industrial revolution forced educational institutions to adapt to the changing socio-economic conditions of the time, so too will the electronic revolution force us to adapt to it.

5. In principle, considering how critical interpretations must be transferred to database archives, it is likely that the more "binary" the formalization of literary study, the easier it will be to translate it into electronic programs, even flexible hypertext ones like those used in English 32 at Brown.

6. Such understanding germinates largely through analogies. Since I cannot argue the case for this premise in detail here, I will merely point to the role that metaphors play in reading poetry as a cardinal instance of a mode of thought that cannot be captured by logical syntax. The understanding of genres, crucial to a reader's ability to frame the text in an appropriate context of conventions, is also fundamentally analogical. Our understanding of characterization, even of stereotypes, is also an analogical matter. A computer, unless programmed to do otherwise, will convert the analogical character of cultural study into a binary form, turning understanding into information. Storing the imaginative experiences that literature depicts in a database reduces them to bits of information whose interrelationships are logical. If computers are not programmed to ask students to draw analogies, no available search or selection routine can produce an analogical relationship.

7. This means resisting the tendency of software companies to reduce the number of choices a user has. Ironically, the more "friendly" the program, the less freedom a user has.

Advocates of hypertext argue that these revolutionary databases increase the students' choices. However, it must be understood that this pertains only to choices of information. It does not pertain to the strategies of selection. Reading a database, like reading a book, involves selection strategies. In literary matters such strategies are often analogical rather than logical. In a database, including a hypertext database, they are invariantly logical.

8. Further, hypertexts can easily be made interactive. Lanham asks us to

> Imagine a major "textbook," continuing over a generation, continually in

> touch with all the teachers who use it, continually updated and rewritten by them as well as by the "authors," with the twenty-four-hour-electronic bulletin boards and the other one-to-one devices of communication such a network inevitably stimulates. (1989, 272)

9. Hypertexts do not solve the problems entailed when analogical understanding is reduced to logically related categories which I described above. Like other databases, they are dependent upon search operations which are logical in character.

10. Given his invocation of Althusser, it would seem that the hypertext model is developed in ways that reflect Althusser's notion of "structural causality" rather than a simple one-to-one cause/effect "determinism" (137, 150).

11. After all, Althusser's printed work makes us aware of the overdetermination of historical conditions without the aid of hypertext.

12. In an earlier version of his essay published in *Computers and the Humanities* (1989), Landow articulates the rules he developed for designing intertextual links. Rule #1 states that "Hypertext links condition the user to expect purposeful, important relationships between linked materials"; rule #2: "The emphasis upon linking materials in hypertext stimulates and encourages habits of relational thinking in the users"; and rule #3 that "Since hypertext systems predispose users to expect such significant relationships among files, those files that disappoint such expectations appear particularly incoherent and nonsignificant." These remarks illustrate the manner in which Landow perceives his students. They are being "conditioned" to apply the principles (theories) upon which the "system" is designed by its "authors" (teachers). He wishes to take every advantage of their "predisposition" to follow a predetermined structure. This is a teacher-oriented system in which students learn to apply the theories of their teachers. They are encouraged in particular "habits" of thought.

13. Even though English 32 provides many "historical" contexts in its various files, Landow points out that the distinction between these historical texts and the literary texts which are the subject of analysis "blurs." The historiography underlying English 32 is highly debatable.

14. It is one thing to be freed from a deterministic view of historical relationships that attributes a cause to a historical event and quite another to be "freed" from its "psychological, sociological, and historical" contexts.

15. To succeed in maintaining a mode of intellection appropriate to the humanities, we will have to rely upon our students, who, if we trust them rather than bind them, will no doubt wish to help us for the simple reason that their cultures are not binary either. Therefore, if culture was construed as inclusive rather than as exclusive of their experiences, it would be in their interests to save it from logification.

16. Patricia Harkin, the Director of Freshman Composition at the University of Akron, and I are presently involved in designing a program on the rationale that follows.

17. Such tasks may seem too much to ask of students. But, with the advent of hypertexts, this pedagogical tactic presents little more difficulty than teaching students how to use a particular word-processing program in order to teach them how to write.

18. The anthology is the principal means through which students are introduced to literature. Its history is coextensive with the modern study of literature. In many respects, the production and publication of anthologies dominates the study of literature. Recent discussions of the canonization of texts have brought to light the importance of anthologies in the schooling of literary critics. Without a doubt, the most influential anthology ever marketed was *Approaches to Literature,* edited by Cleanth Brooks and Robert Penn Warren ([1938] 1960). It introduced at least two generations of students to New Critical analysis. From its pages students learned how to read texts closely. It provided a clear and cogent critical apparatus by means of which students learned a set of procedures that rendered otherwise obscure texts meaningful. Since its publication in 1938, it has been a model for similar "Introduction to Literature" anthologies.

19. Brown's teacher-oriented English 32 works well in competition with more traditional lecture courses. In addition, students at Ivy League schools are more receptive to survey courses in canonical literature. After the novelty of an electronic environment wears off, it is doubtful that English 32 would work much better than traditional survey courses at state universities.

20. I am much indebted to several of the students who participated in that seminar, in particular Marian Sciachitano, Holly Dawson, Cher Uhl, Rory Ong, Dan Dawson, and Don Armstrong, but especially in this case, to Bob Broad who introduced me to the idea which he and Julie Hile jointly employed in their practice as high school teachers in Baltimore. They were also influenced by Anne McCrary Sullivan's practices as she details them in her "The Personal Anthology: A Stimulus for Exploratory Readings" (1988).

21. After discussing what I meant by the idea, 95 percent of the class indicated that they wanted to test "my" notion. I met after class with the students who had voted against the idea. Given the option to follow a more conventional track "on their own," all of the students wanted to stay in the course.

22. I also used this essay as a "diagnostic" device to obtain a general sense of their writing abilities.

23. It is easy to understand why this experience would be so discouraging. On the one hand, the student believed herself to be doing exactly what her teacher had asked her to do, since she followed his instructions about how to read as faithfully as she could. On the other hand, she felt that she had not, since she had enjoyed-the-*wrong*-meaning. This is the "no-win" situation we typically call a double bind. No matter what the student did, she was going to feel wrong. If she accepted the teacher's reading, she was wrong from her point of view. If she stayed with her reading, she was wrong from her teacher's point of view. Like most students, she accepted the teacher's reading as the "right" one, but found herself uninterested in the reading.

Most students in introduction to literature classes experience enjoying-the-*wrong*-meaning. It presents them with an inordinate difficulty—how to believe in themselves and still make their way in the academy. The experience damages students' self-esteem. But when students work hard following instructions, especially when they are encouraged to rely on their own instincts in doing so, and are nonetheless told that they have arrived at the wrong interpretation, it becomes difficult for them to continue believing in themselves as readers. Having enjoyed making sense on their own of the complex texts that are designated as "literature," they are made to feel that this enjoyment is wrong.

24. This is a major disadvantage for those inclined to think that students will only choose the texts with which they are already acquainted. That problem (not a common one in my experience) is easily solved by asking students to search for texts appropriate to their conception of an anthology.

25. They experience the various subcultures in which they participate as "given" but by identifiable sources.

26. Individuality is a problematic concept in postmodern thought. In general, students are not aware of the problems presented by a valorization of the individual. When they assemble their own anthologies, they have to confront some of these problems by addressing the "inconsistency" I just alluded to.

27. The question of a subject's agency in the formation of a culture that is, by definition, the formation of them as subjects is quite problematic. For the most part, I agree with Paul Smith's analysis in his *Discerning the Subject* (1988). The debates among students over their subculture reveal to them gaps and fissures, contradictions and inconsistencies in their subject positions, which can open up the possibility of their agency in the matter of their own cultural formation.

28. This problem exists in a printed anthology but is more threatening in an electronic one. In "Circuitous Subjects in the Timemaps," an MLA presentation in 1990, I responded to the objection that problems in an electronic educational environment also occur in a book-oriented learning environment and are not different in kind but only in degree. I answer this objection by arguing that, in some matters, scope and speed change the relationship between kind and degree. The reduction of choices (possible questions having already been "answered") in a print environment is usually understood to be censorship. In an electronic environment, the "censorship" of analogical thinking could render it extinct, creating an entirely different state of affairs.

29. Sociologists have recognized this for some time. Part Two of Roy Turner's influential collection of essays on how people construct their worlds, *Ethnomethodology* (1974), is entitled, "Theorizing as Practical Reasoning." More recently, Stephen North (1988) has brought a similar recognition to workers in composition studies. In "The Post-disciplinary Politics of Lore," Patricia Harkin writes that

> North delineates a notion he names "lore": "the accumulated body of traditions, practices, and beliefs in terms of which Practitioners [of composition study and teaching] understand how writing is done, learned and taught" [22]. Lore is North's name for those rituals of our profession like teaching the modes, sitting in a circle, assigning double-entry notebooks, using a red pen, forming peer-group workshops, commenting on students' papers according to the codes in *The Harbrace Handbook*, establishing a list of "fatal errors," valuing "voice," encouraging revision, and so on. "Literally anything," North writes, "can become a part of lore" and "nothing can ever be dropped from it either" [24]. (Harkin, 125)

Harkin calls attention to the fact that lore about writing acquired in the practice of teaching has a potent theoretical dimension. It is not usually counted as theory because it lacks the formalities (logical consistency, systematicity, and explanatory force) required of those studies that merit the designation "disciplines." She writes,

> Lore is "non-disciplinary": it is actually defined by its inattention to disciplinary procedures. Lore cannot provide abstract accounts of the writing act; it tells us what practitioners *do*. And practitioners rarely attend to the theoretical implications of their practice, even if they do adopt, adapt, and apply theoretical articulations. (125)

Lore is not a theory; it is a spontaneous theorizing.

30. A question like "What am I doing when I dream?" is reflexive. A person perceives herself doing something—in this case dreaming. If she asks "Why am I dreaming?" or "What am I doing when I dream?" or "How do I dream?" she theorizes. Freud asked such questions and answered them in *The Interpretation of Dreams*, a highly respected theoretical work.

31. The links students create will not be the product of a single-minded neo-formalism because they do not approach their culture in this way. They are more likely to resist the neo-formalism into which databases tend to force their users, much as they resist the formal approaches to literature their teachers often take.

VII Bibliographic Essay and Comprehensive Works Cited

22 Selected Further Resources for Theory and Pedagogy: A Bibliographic Essay

James M. Cahalan and David B. Downing
Indiana University of Pennsylvania

That we have only loosely attempted, here, to reproduce the general organization of our book, beginning with reader response and ending with poststructuralism, indicates the provisional nature of any attempt to outline what few would even call an academic "field" in the ordinary sense of a disciplined "body" of knowledge. The thorniest problems of implementing such bibliographic categories for narrative convenience arise when, for example, some feminist theorists are as readily identified with reader-response theories, or when deconstructionists draw equally on Lacan and psychoanalysis. We want neither to reduce significant differences within the categories we have constructed nor to deny the multiple discursive intersections in what Joseph Natoli terms the polymorphous "theory body." Since our concerns lie less with lines of influence than might be the case in a bibliographic study of theory alone, we wish to disclaim at once any notion that one can compile a definitive or comprehensive set of enumerative categories. Rather, the narrative structure of this essay suggests that, in contrast, the very terrain we have attempted to map is part of a history which continues to produce new kinds of knowledge, new kinds of teaching modes and resources. The complexity of the terrain, however, should not serve as failure to provide any map at all.

Anyone seeking a more extended bibliography of literary theory per se might consult Joseph Natoli's *Tracing Literary Theory* (1987). An excellent scholarly resource is the now annually produced *New Literary History International Bibliography of Literary Theory and Interpretation* (beginning with 1984–85, under the general editorship of Ralph Cohen). Together, these sources provide very concrete evidence of the remarkable production and proliferation of theoretical texts worldwide. The simple conclusion would be that no one could ever read, let alone "master," so much material. And indeed, contemporary theories critique the very notion of mastery.

Our main guiding assumption has been that most theoretical discourse has consequences for teaching which have not often been realized. With this in mind, we begin each section that follows with a view of those resources that we felt would be most helpful to teachers entering this discourse with an interest in changing their own teaching. In some cases this has seemed to lead to the practice of separating theory from practice by first articulating the theories under consideration before moving more directly to the pedagogical consequences. But most of the theories we discuss here critique any such separation of theory and practice. Our belief is that, as we discusssed in our introduction, we are encountering in this case a historically produced social and institutional gap. Historically speaking, then, it is true that, for instance, Derrida wrote *De la Grammatologie* (1967), or *Of Grammatology* (1976), prior to any impact that deconstruction could have had on the classroom. Moreover, it hardly needs to be pointed out that Derrida's texts found their initial reception in the research institutions, not in the teaching institutions and community colleges. To proceed with the historical model—first comes the theory and then comes the pedagogical deployment of the theory—reproduces the "research before teaching" hierarchy, but it is also a frustrating course of reading for the nontheoretical specialist since the earlier historical texts often tend to be the least self-explanatory within the contemporary context. Moreover, in some particular areas, such as reader response, more recent articles and collections successfully serve as introductions linking the theory to pedagogy, whereas, for example, deconstruction (with some notable exceptions) has tended to remain in the province of the critics despite its perpetual claims to transform the conditions of knowledge and pedagogy altogether. Our aim, in other words, has been to meet the needs of the teacher beginning a study of theoretically informed pedagogy while also serving the theorist who may be already well-versed in the discourse of a given theory/practice but in search of further pedagogical resources. In any case, we would not expect this essay to be "read" in any ordinary way from beginning to end, but to be examined piecemeal—"intertextually"—in sections, or parts of sections with the hope that in those instances it may help orient one's reading in a given area.

Finally, what we do not treat in the body of this essay are those anthologies and collections that are aimed toward teaching theory in more specialized courses such as "Contemporary Literary Theory" or "Introduction to Theory." Such collections as Hazard Adams and Leroy Searle's *Critical Theory Since 1965* (1986) or Richter's *The Critical Tradition* (1989) may be very useful in graduate courses, and they may also serve as very useful resources for a wide range of theoretical texts. Nor have we attempted to address the much more pedagogically oriented work in composition theory and rhetoric, much of which is immensely useful in literary and cultural studies courses. (For example, the essays collected in Patricia Donahue and Ellen Quandahl's *Reclaiming Pedagogy* [1989] address the potential contributions to composition pedagogy of theorists including Bakhtin, Barthes, Burke, Derrida, and Fish. In more general terms, Peter Elbow's recent *What Is English?* [1991] is worth reading to help make sense of the interrelations and tensions between people in literature and composition.) Again, our primary concern has been the impact we believe such resources should begin to have with respect to the wide-ranging social and political transformations that affect teachers of introductory undergraduate courses in literature and in cultural studies.

General

For teachers seeking a general introduction to recent theory, Terry Eagleton's *Literary Theory: An Introduction* (1983) is quite helpful. Ironically, while Eagleton set out to popularize his subject with students who had "little or no previous knowledge of the topic," the main audience has been graduate students and other faculty. Since we envision this as our audience, it is in this context that Eagleton provides an engaging overview of the field from Matthew Arnold to Jacques Derrida and after, managing the added redoubtable feat of being frequently entertaining and amusing about what many nonspecialists often assume must be a dry and arcane subject. He rejects the notion that literary theory can be introduced impartially or objectively, since his persuasive thesis is that all theories and indeed all discourses are already implicated in the cultural ideologies within which they operate, so instead he advances a Marxist critique of the other major theoretical approaches. In his final chapter on "Political Criticism," Eagleton deliberately disappoints the reader who was expecting a review of Marxist theory, repeating instead his thesis that *all* theories are political and that all his preceding chapters exemplify his Marxist position; this allows him to avoid a critique of his own theoretical stance, but the absence of such a critique and the necessarily somewhat dated nature of this book are its chief shortcomings. Nonetheless, it is still probably the best place to start. Eagleton's point about how literary criticism has gradually shifted its focus from the author (in Romanticism and old historicism) to the text (in Russian formalism and New Criticism) and more recently to the reader (not only in reader response but contemporary theory in general) is useful (74).

Readers seeking an overall introduction to the field can then proceed to other, more recent books such as Raman Selden's *A Reader's Guide to Contemporary Literary Theory* (1985), G. Douglas Atkins and Laura Morrow's anthology *Contemporary Literary Theory* (1989), and Joseph Natoli's collections *Tracing Literary Theory* (1987) and *Literary Theory's Future* (1989). These books also provide intelligent overviews of the major theories, including Marxism. *Contemporary Literary Theory*, a very useful and current book, includes a chapter entitled "Political Criticism," in which Michael Ryan *does* examine Marxism, as well as chapters assessing New Criticism, archetypal criticism, structuralism and semiotics, reader-response ("audience-oriented") criticism, phenomenological criticism, hermeneutics, deconstruction, psychoanalysis, feminism, dialogic criticism, and the "genealogical critique" of Michel Foucault (with a helpful annotated bibliography at the end of each chapter). However, like Eagleton's book and most other general introductions to the field, these ones neglect African American and other varieties of multicultural criticism and aesthetics. A very useful and current source that does not neglect these areas is Frank Lentricchia and Thomas McLaughlin's *Critical Terms for Literary Study* (1990), a collection of twenty-three essays by well-known theorists on particular critical terms (including "canon," "gender," "race," "ethnicity," and "ideology"). One also does well to follow up Eagleton (who understandably tends to direct his gaze toward the British and European scenes) with Gerald Graff's *Professing Literature: An Institutional History* (1987), in which Graff examines the rise of American New Criticism in the specific institutional setting of the U.S. university, shows just how persistent and adaptable the "coverage model" has been, and argues that we ought to be teaching our theoretical conflicts in the classroom rather than pretending there that they do not exist.[1] *Professing Literature* can be read in conjunction with the collection Graff published with Reginald Gibbons, *Criticism in the University* (1985), which focuses not on pedagogy but on the move of criticism from the public realm into the academic world in the postwar era. Robert Scholes has consistently worked to bring structural and poststructural concerns to teachers, and his *Textual Power* (1985) can be profitably read with his more recent essay "Toward a Curriculum in Textual Studies" (1989) in *Reorientations: Critical Theories and Pedagogies* (1990). Scholes offers a liberal view of "textual studies" according to which "the exclusivity of literature as a category must be discarded" (16). William E. Cain's *The Crisis in Criticism* (1984) begins with a more specialized consideration of the problems of interpretation in E. D. Hirsch and J. Hillis Miller, but he makes a plea for the attention of theory to the institutional needs of teachers. Those interested in more politically radical critiques of the profession can look to work by the GRIP Project (the successive volumes of *The GRIP Report*) and to several books published by Routledge (and one by Hodder and Stoughton): Peter Brooker and Peter Humm's *Dialogue and Difference: English into the Nineties* (1989), which first examines the institutions of English in England, then "Theories, Pedagogies, Initiatives," and finally a series of case studies; Peter Widdowson's *Re-reading English* (1982), which contains a group of fine poststructural and Marxist critiques of the profession; *Rewriting English: The Politics of Gender and Class* (Janet Batsleer et al., eds., 1986); Marjorie Boulton's *The Anatomy of Literary Studies* (1980); Peter Abbs's *English within the Arts: A Radical Alternative for English and the Arts in the Curriculum* (1982); and Jane Miller's *Eccentric Propositions: Essays on Literature and the Curriculum* (1991). These last six books from England derive from the considerable work in cultural studies in that country, which has been generally more widespread and successful than in America.

The reader anxious to see contemporary theory at work on specific literary texts can turn to Selden's more recent *Practicing Theory and Reading Literature* (1989), in which he reads particular (though mostly male and all white) texts in light of major contemporary theories (though again not African American or multicultural ones).[2] Following this vein, one may wish to follow more specific literary interests by seeking out the MLA "Approaches to Teaching" series, especially such recent volumes as the ones on (for example) Willa Cather's *My Antonia* (Susan J. Rosowski, ed.), Scott Momaday's *The Way to Rainy Mountain* (Kenneth Roemer, ed.), and Kate Chopin's *The Awakening* (Bernard Koloski, ed.); and the St. Martin's/Bedford critical editions (consisting thus far of Conrad's *Heart of Darkness* and Hawthorne's *The Scarlet Letter*) incorporating primary texts and a variety of current critical essays.

Useful short supplements to such book-length studies can be found in several recent articles. James C. Raymond's "What Good Is All This Heady, Esoteric Theory?" is aimed at teachers at two-year schools and argues that poststructuralist theory facilitates a liberatory posture on the part of teachers, who can now abandon the teacher-centered, know-it-all approach so pervasively and persistently encouraged by the old New Criticism. Steven Lynn's "A Passage into Critical Theory" is an exemplary, concise exercise in practical criticism in which he reads and rereads a short passage from Brendan Gill's book *Here at the New Yorker* from New Critical, structuralist, deconstructive, psychoanalytic, and feminist perspectives. Lynn's essay can be read profitably in conjunction with Douglas Lanier's essay in our own book, as well as Selden's 1989 book, and Jeffrey C. Robinson's *Radical Literary Education: A Classroom Experiment with Wordsworth's "Ode"*, in which Robinson focuses on rereading Wordsworth's poem from a variety of critical perspectives, as does Lynn with Gill's excerpt and Lanier with *Frankenstein*. One can then imbibe Jasper Neel's wonderfully entertaining and pragmatically intelligent "Writing about Literature (or Country Ham)," in which he provides good advice about writing (and selecting the right journals for such writing) from particular contemporary theoretical points of view; this advice comes after Neel examines the shifting managerial interpretations of the listing "Country Ham .30 Extra" on the menu at the Venus Pancake House in Florence, South Carolina, as the arena in which he most memorably learned the shifting, deconstructive nature of language.

Looking for sources on the subject of literary pedagogy, one finds that anything like a comprehensive consideration of the specific classroom applications—especially at the introductory level—of contemporary literary theory has been slow in coming. This has been the case even though one finds many scattered pleas over the past twenty-five years for such study as well as a number of examinations of the pedagogical applications of particular theories (mostly reader-response and feminism, as detailed below). Practically speaking, this has meant that there are very few textbooks available for introductory courses which take a theoretically informed perspective. The noticeable exceptions are Kathleen McCormick, Gary Waller, and Linda Flower's *Reading Texts: Reading, Responding, Writing* (1987), and Robert Scholes, Gregory Ulmer, and Nancy Comley's *Text Book* (1988). The new Routledge Interface series now includes a practically oriented series of activities for students in *Literary Studies in Action* (1990) by Alan Durant and Nigel Fabb. With respect to introductory anthologies, one can adopt, for example, Waller and McCormick's *The Lexington Introduction to Literature* (1987) or Thomas McLaughlin's *Literature: The Power of Language* (1989).

Looking for a historical perspective, we find that one of the first sustained attempts in America to explore the links between theory and pedagogy occurred in 1982, when Barbara Johnson edited the special issue of *Yale French Studies* called "The Pedagogical Imperative: Teaching as a Literary Genre" (1982), which contains several important essays including Paul de Man's well-known "The Resistance to Theory," Shoshana Felman's "Psychoanalysis and Education: Teaching Terminable and Interminable," and Michael Ryan's deconstructive analysis of the politics of the university in his "Deconstruction and Radical Teaching." But in general, these essays still work at a highly sophisticated theoretical level since the direction they take is to raise pedagogy to the level of a literary genre rather than to enter specific and concrete classroom situations. Whether or not one agrees with de Man,[3] we have certainly had to overcome considerable resistance, not only from old New Critical teachers who do not read contemporary theory, but even from such well-known humanist critics as Wayne Booth, who argued in 1964 in "Criticism in Teaching Literature" that students should be taught to "read for themselves" (13) and not be exposed to any literary theorists until the senior year (*College English* did publish a dissenting reply by Frederick Hoffman), and repeated this thesis as recently as 1986: "To me, the worst disaster that could befall any student . . . would be the conviction that what I or any other critic has to say about it is as important as the encounter with, the experience of, the possession by, the work itself" (1986, 474). We may want our students to "read for themselves," but the notion that they should do so devoid of critical self-consciousness or that anyone (students or teachers) can "read for themselves" free of the ideologies in which we are all implicated seems illusory at best. Dwight Eddins undoubtedly speaks for many teachers when he cavils similarly and more recently,

> Are we really to spend the time that might have been spent discussing the intricate internal dialectics of Wordsworth's "Tintern Abbey," and their relevance to the stages of all human lives, discussing the difference between Marxist, feminist, deconstructivist, and Lacanian approaches to the poem? . . . Might it not be better to "smuggle in" . . . a frazzled, moth-eaten amalgam of New Criticism and the old historicism and enjoy the countryside in terms that the countryside itself seems to dictate? (1989, 573–74)

This begs the question of why we are, in the first place, reading "Tintern Abbey" (instead of, say, *The Color Purple*) and focusing on its "intricate internal dialectics" (instead of its external cultural contexts), which human lives it is relevant to (is it not arrogant to assume that it is equally relevant to "all human lives"?), and how the "countryside itself" can ever really "dictate" the "terms" as if we readers operate free of any theoretical assumptions and ideological constraints. As Eagleton trenchantly observes, "Hostility to theory usually means an opposition to other people's theories and an oblivion of one's own" (1983, viii).

As one reviews over the years *College English, Teaching English in the Two-Year College,* and other professional journals in which the teaching of literature has been an ongoing concern, much more commonly found than such statements of resistance to theory in introductory courses are fairly frequent—but scattered and apparently largely ineffectual—appeals for the necessity and inevitability of theory in teaching, like voices in the wilderness. F. Parvin Sharpless's lamentation in 1967 of the chaotic, theoretically uninformed state of the teaching of literature has lost none of its relevance. In 1970 Bruce Franklin assailed the white male elitism of literary teaching, and in 1973 two graduate students indicted the failure to expose undergraduate students to criticism in any organized way (Marian Reed) or to alternative literatures on an equal footing (Nancy Burr Evans). In 1974 Elizabeth Wooten made the important point that the traditional graduate English education does not adequately prepare the community college teacher, and Francis Connolly advocated the inclusion of literary theory in teaching (though in terms now outdated). Mary Wilkinson (1981) found in a survey at Penn State that freshman nonmajors were frequently interested in taking literature courses and would do so if offered appealing courses with the right kind of teaching approaches. Brian Gallagher introduced a February 1985 special issue of *Teaching English in the Two-Year College* on the teaching of literature with the observation that "rather than stressing the privileged status of literature, it is necessary to stress instead the connections of literary works with students' own attempts at communication, with their writing, indeed with events in their lives" (3). In that same issue of *TETYC*, Marie Jean Lederman argued that literature should reenter the composition classroom and become a vital part of a course teaching language skills as a continuum.

In sharp contradiction to Wayne Booth, Gerald Prince asserts that literary theory should be placed at the forefront of the undergraduate curriculum, with a theory course required as a prerequisite to all other literature courses. Prince is one of the theorists and teachers in the numerous foreign language and literature departments where a new theoretical self-consciousness about pedagogy runs parallel to and supportive of developments in English.[4] Jonathan Arac, Christian Messenger, and Gerald Sorensen describe a year-long, NEH-funded English curriculum at the University of Illinois at Chicago informed by theory, though rather conservative in its selection of literary texts. They note that "the idea . . . is not to have freshmen reading Derrida and Gadamer," whereas Prince's enthusiasm is such that he advocates the teaching of theory beginning in high school and insists that "theory can even help improve writing skills: Jonathan Culler, Stanley Fish, and Barbara Herrnstein Smith afford excellent models" (1984, 39).

Similarly, Alan Durant (1985) argues that we need to reform our curricula to reflect the new diversity of theoretical approaches, and also points out that these approaches are hospitable and adaptable to progressive developments in secondary education. Writing out of a situation in which a theoretical component to the introductory course was voted down by the English department at SUNY–Binghamton, William Spanos makes a strong case that theory is crucial—rather than obfuscating as its opponents claim—because it is itself a form of praxis that seeks to make "a critical difference in the world" (1989, 65).

In addition to the February 1985 issue of *TETYC* mentioned above, there have been a few other special issues of journals devoted to theory and pedagogy, such as the Winter 1981 issue of *Focus: Teaching English Language Arts*, edited by Raymond E. Fitch, on "Literary Theory in the English Classroom" and the almost identically titled 1989 issue of the *Iowa English Bulletin* on "Literary Theory in the Classroom," edited by Scott Cawelti and Nancy Williams (recently available from NCTE). Though rather dated in its dominance by structuralism, the *Focus* collection includes useful articles such as James J. Sosnoski's "Can We Teach the Latest Literary Theories to College Freshmen?" The Spring 1991 issue of *Works and Days: Essays in the Socio-Historical Dimensions of Literature and the Arts* is a special issue on "The Role of Theory in the Undergraduate Literature Classroom: Curriculum, Pedagogy, Politics," selected proceedings from the September 1990 conference at Indiana University of Pennsylvania. *Works and Days 16* (1990) is a special issue on "Theory and Pedagogy," guest-edited by C. Mark Hurlbert and with articles by Paul Bové, James Sosnoski, and the Miami University Theory/Pedagogy Group. Earlier, *Works and Days 7* (1986) was a special issue on "The Social Function of the Teaching of Literature in a Time of Cultural Flux."

Book collections on the subject, including the most cohesive general sources on theory and pedagogy, have appeared only very recently.[5] Cary Nelson's *Theory in the Classroom* (1986) is a forward-thinking collection in which contributors consider the classroom ramifications of deconstruction, feminism, psychoanalysis, "radical theory," popular culture, and technical discourse. It is severely limited, however, in its lack of specificity about actual classroom practices, creating the impression (despite its title) that the essays in it are mostly *theory* with very little *classroom*. (A notable exception is Paula Treichler's essay on "Teaching Feminist Theory," discussed below.) A more sharply ironic title is James Engell and David Perkins's *Teaching Literature: What Is Needed Now* (1988), which one takes from the library shelf with great anticipation that fairly quickly vanishes as soon as one realizes that it is a book of essays by people at or attached to Harvard, who seek to tell us all how to teach from their most privileged (and therefore atypical) situation, and who are even more reluctant or unable to get specific about what they actually do in their classrooms (with the single exception of the sole composition specialist, Richard Marius).[6]

Much more specifically applied and useful books are Ben F. Nelms's *Literature in the Classroom: Readers, Texts, and Contexts* (1988), Bruce Henricksen and Thaïs E. Morgan's *Reorientations: Critical Theories and Pedagogies* (1990), and Charles Moran and Elizabeth F. Penfield's *Conversations: Contemporary Critical Theory and the Teaching of Literature* (1990). One might well think from scanning these three book titles that our own book duplicates them and that each of them covers the same material. This is not the case. At the same time, these books are quite complementary, and their appearance indicates that earlier pleas that literary theory and pedagogy be joined and addressed are finally being heard, just as we have sought to respond to that need. The Nelms collection is focused on secondary education and brings to it an eclectic variety of approaches like we have sought to bring to introductory college courses.[7] The preponderance of more traditional reader-response essays in it reflects both the popularity of that approach at the secondary level and the shift of reader-response theory into more cultural directions just within the last couple of years (imagine talking about "traditional reader response" a few years ago!). *Reorientations* considers the impact on the college curriculum in general (rather than on the individual introductory course and classroom in particular) of progressive developments in theory. Some of its essays do take up specific classroom applications, and those are mentioned below. With their attention respectively to secondary education and curricular issues, these two books are very useful companion collections to ours.

Under our initial "general" rubric here, we have saved nearly for the last the book most useful for teachers, which can be read in conjunction with ours. Published like the Nelms collection and ours by NCTE, *Conversations* (as we highlighted in our introduction) grew out of NCTE's first two Summer Institutes on the Teaching of Literature to Undergraduates, held in Myrtle Beach in 1987 and 1988. These institutes themselves are evidence of the growing attention to this subject, and those of us who attended them (like the editors and organizers themselves) remember "the setting and hear the voices of the seminar leaders and the participants" (1). *Conversations* is a very useful product of these institutes, which have been continued annually with new subjects such as teaching literature cross-culturally. It makes no attempt to comprehensively "cover" all the major current theories, but its first section does include essays by Jane Tompkins on post-structuralism, Steven Mailloux on reader-response criticism, Henry Louis Gates, Jr., on African American canon formation, Janet Emig on learning theory, James C. Raymond on cultural literacy, and Myra Jehlen on literature and authority. The second section includes eleven diverse and different essays by other institute participants and interested parties, some more concerned with readings of individual texts and some more focused on teaching. On the one hand, the separation of the mostly lesser-known writers (with the exception of Walker Gibson) at teaching institutions in the second section from the nationally known presenters from prestigious research universities in the first section perpetuates the gap that was apparent at the institutes themselves between theory and prestige at the research universities and heavy introductory teaching loads at the typical two- and four-year schools. On the other hand, within that second section there is a commendable inclusion of voices from the ranks of the profession, including six essayists who teach at two-year or other small colleges. In "Local Canons: Professing Literature at the Small Liberal Arts College," Bobby Fong reminds us that doctoral departments represent only six percent of English departments in the country and considers how the canon (though addressed mostly by writers at large research universities) is an issue with different kinds of ramifications within the curriculum of a small college where the "coverage model" was never even a pretense in a department of only a few members. Fong adds that most versions of the American canon, whether conservative or progressive, have sought to be national in scope, whereas teachers at small schools often do best to attend to the local canons to which students can be most responsive—emphasizing Appalachian writers in Kentucky and Hispanic writers in California, for example.

Further research on literary theory and pedagogy will have to continue to attend more closely to what specific teachers do in specific classrooms within particular institutional settings. In her essay in *Conversations,* Janet Emig exhorts people in literature to become aware of the major learning theorists such as Luria and Vygotsky and to apply their work in research on literary pedagogy. An exemplary text in another context is Dixie Goswami and Peter R. Stillman's *Reclaiming the Classroom: Teacher Research as an Agency for Change* (1987). We need a bridge between literary theory and pedagogy and composition studies, which have been much more pedagogically focused. Such a subdisciplinary juncture has been advocated for years in trenchant articles by people such as W. Ross Winterowd, James Berlin, Patricia Bizzell, Jim W. Corder, Patricia Harkin, Joseph Harris, C. Mark Hurlbert and Michael Blitz, C. H. Knoblauch, Susan Miller, Stephen M. North, Bruce T. Peterson, and Edward Rocklin, as well as in several of the essays in Winifred Bryan Horner's collection, significantly entitled *Composition and Literature: Bridging the Gap* (1985). Literary theory and composition theory have been examined together in articles by Joseph Comprone (1987) and John Clifford and John Schilb (1985), and in an MLA book, *Contending with Words,* edited by Patricia Harkin and John Schilb (1991).

Among the many recent contributions to the history and theory of rhetoric, C. H. Knoblauch and Lil Brannon's *Rhetorical Traditions and the Teaching of Writing* (1984) spawned an ongoing debate in composition and rhetorical studies that provides arguments relevant to literary and cultural studies. They argue for a critical, epistemic rhetoric in contrast to classical, formalist rhetorical models. Teachers "must become philosophers in order to carry out the work of improving instruction by first improving the theoretical underpinnings of instruction" (18). Stephen M. North's *The Making of Knowledge in Composition* (1987) has been influential for his notion of theoretical "lore" as resource for "practitioners" of writing and teaching. James Berlin argues strongly for a "social-epistemic rhetoric" that foregrounds the need for "an explicit critique of economic, political, and social arrangements" at the core of our teaching practices ("Rhetoric and Ideology" [1988]). In *The Methodical Memory* (1990), Sharon Crowley offers a critique of formalist models of rhetorical invention. Such other recent books as Susan Miller's *Rescuing the Subject: A Critical Introduction to Rhetoric and the Writer* (1989) and Susan C. Jarratt's *Rereading the Sophists: Classical Rhetoric Refigured* (1991) provide important reconsiderations of the importance of the Sophists and their pedagogical models as they pertain to contemporary rhetorical and cultural studies classrooms. Jarratt's final chapter, "Sophistic Pedagogy, Then and Now," articulates a "progressive political" pedagogy joining feminist and other oppositional theoretical perspectives. One of the most innovative books to emerge from such a perspective is C. Mark Hurlbert and Michael Blitz's *Composition and Resistance* (1991), which contains a collection of essays, dialogues, and exchanges by educators exploring what we as teachers can do to resist repressive educational practices in America. Many of these issues have been explored prominently and early in the important journal *Pre/Text: A Journal of Rhetorical Theory,* edited by Victor Vitanza.

More connections will also have to be forged with teacher education programs, where recent work indicates a growing awareness that the more strictly empirical studies have been reaching towards more sophisticated sociocultural theories that have an impact on pedagogy. Thus, work by Jerry Gebhard (such as "Beyond Prescription: The Student Teacher as Investigator") and others on the theory and practice of the observation and transformation of teaching practices offers important connections for teachers concerned with theory and pedagogy. As a resource for specific instances of how classroom transformations must be linked to broader institutional and curricular changes, one can look to David Downing's forthcoming *Changing Classroom Practices: Resources for Literary and Cultural Study* (1992). In general, we still need work that is able to address, on the one hand, the larger, institutional, curricular, and sociocultural situation without losing focus on specific classrooms where teachers' daily needs may differ widely, depending on the many diverse circumstances in which "introductory" literature and cultural studies classes carry a significant role in undergraduate education.

Reader-Response Theory and Pedagogy

The close relationship between early reader-response criticism and psychoanalytic theory (our next section below) is suggested by the fact that the chief advocate, beginning in the 1960s, of what came to be called "reader-response criticism" was Norman Holland, who is also typically included in most surveys of psychoanalytic criticism and theory. Richard Wheeler, for example, notes that after Ernest Jones's *Hamlet and Oedipus* (1949), "the most notable post-Freudian psychoanalytic landmark of Shakespeare criticism is Norman N. Holland's *Psychoanalysis and Shakespeare* [1966]" (20). Holland had thus established himself as a leading psychoanalytic critic before he became the champion of "reader response," and his early reader-response works, such as *The Dynamics of Literary Response*, are based on psychoanalytic models.

The most current, concise, and accessible introduction is Steven Mailloux's "The Turns of Reader-Response Criticism" in *Conversations* (1990), a reworking of his 1987 NCTE seminar session for college teachers. Mailloux points out that (as is also true of most other critical approaches) "reader response" was a label somewhat belatedly applied to the work of such theorists as Holland, Wolfgang Iser, David Bleich, and Stanley Fish rather than one adopted by the theorists themselves, and that this term disguises considerable differences and inconsistencies among the many writers to whom it has been attached. He also critiques the willful forgetting of the pioneering work of Louise

Rosenblatt, *Literature as Exploration* (1938), during the most active period of reader-response criticism in the 1970s and until the early 1980s. This first reader-response book appeared in the same year as the single most influential work of New Critical theory and pedagogy, Cleanth Brooks and Robert Penn Warren's *Understanding Poetry* (1938). Mailloux hypothesizes that "Rosenblatt's work and its implicit neo-pragmatism had to be 'forgotten' in order for the new reader-response criticism to establish its theoretical ethos and carry out a decade of intense theoretical debate over the question of its 'epistemological skepticism'" (40). But the recent NCTE collection *Transactions with Literature: A Fifty-Year Perspective* (1990) attempts to redress this neglect by bringing together a group of essays documenting the remarkable influence that Rosenblatt's book continues to exert in such diverse areas as children's and young adult literature, college literature classrooms, and literary research. The book also contains a "Retrospect" chapter by Rosenblatt herself and a very useful two-part bibliographic section drawing first on the Center for the Learning and Teaching of Literature at SUNY–Albany and a second section with annotated entries on "Research on Response to Literature." As the editors of this book, Edmund J. Farrell and James R. Squire, remark in their preface, "No one who has really read *Literature as Exploration* has ever been able to think about literature and its teaching in quite the same way as before" (viii).

Nevertheless, no selection from Rosenblatt—who also published a revised edition of *Literature as Exploration* in 1968 (3rd edition, 1976; 4th edition, 1983) and the recently very influential *The Reader, The Text, The Poem: The Transactional Theory of the Literary Work* (1978)—is included, for example, in Jane Tompkins's collection *Reader-Response Criticism: From Formalism to Post-Structuralism* (1980). Tompkins's book is otherwise an extremely useful selection of the work of theorists ranging from Walker Gibson and Gerald Prince to Iser, Fish, Jonathan Culler, Holland, and Bleich. Mailloux sees this collection and his own *Interpretive Conventions: The Reader in the Study of American Fiction* (1982) as "retrospective" books marking the end of reader response as a theory, with the various writers subsumed under that label since moving in even more divergent directions (though with a common and commendable tendency to consider how individual readers fit into broader cultural contexts). Like feminism, then, reader-response criticism reflects wider theoretical developments. Mailloux's most recent book, *Rhetorical Power* (1989), extends his historical overview and critique of reader-response criticism to his advocation of "rhetorical hermeneutics," a politically engaged interpretive and pedagogical practice that draws on neo-pragmatist, rhetorical, and Marxist critiques of many "foundationalist" theories.

The more ambitious reader can move beyond Mailloux's survey and Tompkins's collection into individual books by the major theorists. The early formalist phase outlined by Tompkins is exemplified in such works as Holland's *The Dynamics of Literary Response*, Iser's *The Implied Reader* (1974) and *The Act of Reading* (1978), and Rosenblatt's *The Reader, The Text, The Poem*. Each of them emphasizes the interactions between the reader and the text, with Holland focusing on how the reader is governed by the terms of individual identity formation and Iser and Rosenblatt examining how readers' responses are conditioned by texts as much as they are generated by readers; Iser's notion of how readers fill "gaps" deliberately left by texts has been influential. Holland and Rosenblatt were especially aware early in their careers of how their work was specifically aimed at examining and confounding the "affective fallacy"—the "confusion between the poem and its results . . . the psychological effects of the poem," ending in "impressionism and relativism" attacked by the New Critics Monroe C. Beardsley and W. K. Wimsatt in their famous 1949 essay—which was later critiqued by Fish as "the affective fallacy fallacy." Fish's own early book *Surprised by Sin: The Reader in Paradise Lost* (1967) reflects the shadow of formalism. Perhaps more than any other reader-response critic, Fish's career evidences wider critical trends, as he abandoned early belief in a "competent reader" who has the right kind of textual responses in favor of a theory of how "interpretive communities" determine such competence; the increasingly poststructuralist direction of his thinking is best encapsulated in his collection of essays *Is There a Text in This Class?* (1980). His more recent *Doing What Comes Naturally: Change, Rhetoric, and the Practice of Theory in Literary and Legal Studies* (1989) brings together a collection of his more recent essays and begins with an introduction where he clearly articulates his antifoundationalist perspective on interpetation, literature, rhetoric, language, and the profession.

Like Holland, Bleich began by working within a psychoanalytic model, with articles in 1971 ("Psychological Bases of Learning from Literature") and 1975 ("The Subjective Character of Critical Interpretation") in *College English*, largely echoing Freud and Holland. Unlike Holland, however, who attended to the identity themes of individual readers (as in *Five Readers Reading* [1975]), and somewhat more like Fish, Bleich increasingly focused not on a reductively stable identity theme but on the intersubjective transactions between readers and texts that could be negotiated between one subjective reader and others, as in his very influential books *Readings and Feelings* (1975) and *Subjective Criticism* (1978) and in later articles in *College English* ("Pedagogical Directions in Subjective Criticism" and "The Identity of Pedagogy and Research in the Study of Response to Literature"). Mailloux argues that Bleich's attempt to reconcile radically subjective individual responses and social, group negotiations was fraught with contradiction, but adds, "I am now less concerned with these theoretical contradictions than with the pedagogical consequences of Bleich's theory. Throughout the 1970s and 1980s his work was adapted and used to empower many teachers in their revisions of traditional classroom practices" (1990, 45). Anyone who has ever used journals and small groups in literature classes is reflecting the influence of Bleich and Rosenblatt, whether or not they are aware of it or have instead picked up these practices from others who have read them.

More recently, Bleich has been concerned with examining the cultural contexts of readers' responses, as developed in *The Double Perspective: Language, Literacy, and Social Relations* (1988) and in his essay at the beginning of the present book. Earlier Kathleen McCormick, author of articles examining the phases of student responses (such as " 'First Steps' in 'Wandering Rocks' ") and coauthor, with Gary Waller and Linda Flower, of the introductory textbook *Reading Texts*, had criticized Holland and Bleich for not taking sufficient account of cultural factors (1985, 836); John Schilb pointed out how traditionally canonical all the early reader-response critics tended to be, in his introduction to the special issue of the journal *Reader: Essays in Reader-Oriented Theory, Criticism, and Pedagogy* on "Teaching Noncanonical Literature" (1986, 7); in *College English* back in 1973, John Franzosa had chided Holland for appearing to forget that literature, "more like jokes than dreams, is a social process" (930), and Marjorie Roemer argued in 1987 that reader-response criticism begs larger political questions. Like the writings of Fish and Bleich, the successive issues of *Reader*, a very valuable journal edited in recent years by Elizabeth A. Flynn, evidence the impact of wider trends; early issues focus on Bleich and Rosenblatt, whereas more recent ones include special issues on feminism and noncanonical literatures. Flynn is herself an important reader-response theorist (see for example "Composing Responses" [1983] and "The Classroom as Interpretive Community" [1990a]) whose work has increasingly focused on gender (as highlighted later).

Like feminists, reader-response people have written much more about the classroom than other kinds of theorists have, perhaps because reader-response and feminist approaches are by definition concerned with the empowerment of students. A good place to begin with reader-response pedagogy is Charles R. Cooper's anthology *Researching Response to Literature and the Teaching of Literature: Points of Departure* (1985), a result of a conference at SUNY–Buffalo (which has been a center of reader-response and psychoanalytic work, with Holland as the best-known figure teaching there) including essays by Holland, Bleich, and several others focused specifically on the classroom. A useful though necessarily dated source is Alan C. Purves and Richard Beach's *Literature and the Reader: Research in Response to Literature, Reading Interests, and the Teaching of Literature* (1972), which includes a bibliographical essay on the teaching of literature (145–76); more recent are Beach's *Research on the Learning and Teaching of Literature: Selected Bibliography* (1989) and Purves, Rogers, and Soter's *Teaching a Response-Centered Literature Curriculum* (1990). A very pedagogically specific and detailed book, inspired by Bleich and Rosenblatt, is Marian Price's *Reader-Response Criticism: A Test of Its Usefulness in a First-Year College Course in Writing about Literature* (1989). Reader-response approaches have been perhaps even more popular at the secondary than at the college level, as exemplified by numerous articles in the *English Journal* and elsewhere and the anthology *Readers, Texts, and Teachers* (1987) by Bill Corcoran and Emrys Evans.

The February 1985 issue of *TETYC* included useful essays on reader-response teaching methods by Patricia Prandini Buckler and Dan C. Jones, and *TETYC* has in general been an active forum for such articles.[8] *College English* has published articles not only by Bleich, Holland, and McCormick but also other reader-responders such as John J. Ruszkiewicz and Alan Purves. Not only has Bleich moved on to cultural criticism; even Holland, when writing in *College English* about an actual classroom ("The Delphi Seminar"), was much more interested in the collaborative, group model of his seminar than on individual student responses. Especially as influenced by Bleich and his emphasis on group interaction, at this point reader-response pedagogy becomes collaborative pedagogy (a topic considered later herein).

Psychoanalytic Theory and Pedagogy

Richard P. Wheeler points out that "psychoanalytic literary criticism . . . did not simply appear early in the development of psychoanalysis, but participated in the origins of the movement" (20), since Freud's thinking about *Oedipus Rex* and *Hamlet* was a crucial part of the development of his theory of the Oedipal complex. Robert N. Mollinger provides a very useful, brief "Review of Psychoanalytic

Literary Criticism" (1–29) in his *Psychoanalysis and Literature: An Introduction* (1981). His survey is divided into psychoanalytic approaches respectively to the text (character), the author, and the reader (audience). Eagleton's chapter "Psychoanalysis" (1983, 151–93) is very helpful for understanding the work of post-Freudians such as Jacques Lacan and Julia Kristeva in light of Freud. Like deconstruction, psychoanalysis is a powerful critical strategy that feminists, Marxists, and other kinds of theoreticians have also found useful. A challenging but often-cited essay by Shoshana Felman, "Psychoanalysis and Education: Teaching Terminable and Interminable" (1982b), draws on Lacan to articulate an alternative to the dominant teaching models of transmitting an objective body of knowledge. As Felman argues, an alternative "pedagogical approach, which makes no claim to total knowledge, which does not even claim to be in possession of its own knowledge, is, of course, quite different from the usual pedagogical pose of mastery, different from the image of the self-sufficient, self-possessed proprietor of knowledge, in which pedagogy has traditionally featured the authoritative figure of the teacher" (34).

At the point where psychoanalysis enters the classroom, it very often becomes reader-response pedagogy, as sketched above. Yet there are some useful sources devoted to teaching in light of psychoanalysis per se. Wheeler, for example, emphasizes that only psychoanalysis can tap into the parental conflicts in *Hamlet* "for students who are themselves perplexed at deep levels about whose agenda they are pursuing in their lives, their parents' or their own, and where one leaves off and the other begins" (22). H. R. Wolf found that his students' initial resistance at SUNY–Buffalo to his course on the "Literature of Mental Crisis and Madness" led him to ask them about it, and to the class as a whole deciding to "*take the group itself as subject*," writing their own narratives and seeking to analyze themselves in a liberatory way. On the other hand, in "An Erotics of Teaching," John Rouse criticizes Holland and Bleich for pretending that they can observe and explain individual and group student responses as if their privileged positions as teachers did not exist. Recalling an anecdote about Freud shouting at a young female patient, "The trouble is . . . I am an old man—*You do not think it is worth your while to love me*" (1983, 535), Rouse argues that teaching "requires an erotic element for its success" that we all, of course, sublimate. On one level or another we all want to be loved by our students—we want them to love our courses—but we know that it is necessary to remain within our formal position of reserve and power. Albert Hutter found that students at UCLA learned a lot by analyzing patients' narratives as literary texts, just as psychoanalysts gained much by working on their writing.

The most accessible and current collection of essays on psychoanalysis and pedagogy can be found in a special double issue of *College English* (49/6 [October 1987] and 49/7 [November 1987]) edited by Robert Con Davis. As Davis writes in his introduction ("Freud's Resistance to Reading and Teaching"), "The essays of both issues argue that the resistance to reading is also the force that makes them possible—particularly that reading and teaching must in an important sense 'fail' before they succeed. . . . The problematics of psychoanalytic therapy (defined by 'resistance,' 'transference,' and 'repression') are the same as 'the problematics of teaching'" (622). To counter those who think that psychoanalysis is too difficult and mechanical for students, Patricia Donahue and Ellen Quandahl explain how they taught Freud's *Dora: An Analysis of a Case of Hysteria* very successfully to basic writers at UCLA. Patrick McGee argues that psychoanalysis allows the teacher to abandon the posture of "master" in favor of one who comes before students as a learner and hands "their questions back to them in a way that reveals a rhetorical function" (676). Elsewhere, Shoshana Felman has similarly asserted that "the position of the teacher is itself the position of *the one who learns*, of the one who *teaches* nothing other than *the way he learns*" (quoted in Atkins 1989, 16).

For the teacher looking for specific pedagogical examples, Gregory S. Jay's article on "The Subject of Pedagogy" in the special *College English* double issue is the most useful. He writes:

> The value of an introduction to literature is not to make a "civilized man" in the Arnoldian view, but to question authority, the authority found in so many other university courses, in a poststructuralist way—a good way to begin an introductory literature course . . . We empower students by showing them the different critical approaches and how interpretations are implicated in (and by) them. . . . Psychoanalysis, by helping to separate the person from the subjective position, helps separate interpretations from interpreters, and so at once demystifies the hermeneutic process and puts the *student* into the position of the subject who is supposed to know. (1987, 798–99)

Best of all, Jay's essay is filled with examples of differing interpretations of *Heart of Darkness*, "Young Goodman Brown," *Othello*, and other texts.

Further reading in the connections between psychoanalysis and poststructuralism can be found in the earlier collections *Psychoanalysis and the Question of the Text* (1978), edited by Geoffrey Hartman and *Literature and Psychoanalysis* (1982), edited by Shoshana Felman. An overview of the relations between psychoanalysis and feminism up to the early 1970s can be found in Juliet Mitchell's *Psychoanalysis and Feminism* (1974), and Jane Gallop offers a Lacanian exploration of psychoanalysis and feminism in *Feminism and Psychoanalysis: The Daughter's Seduction* (1982). A more recent collection by Shirley Nelson Garner et al., *The (M)other Tongue: Essays in Feminist Psychoanalytic Interpretation* (1987), provides a fine spectrum of strong readings in this area. The implications of all these works bear on pedagogy, but much work remains to directly adapt these interpretive issues to the classroom.

Cultural Theory and Pedagogy: Reception Theory, New Historicism, and Marxism

In their insightful and helpful surveys, both Terry Eagleton (1983, 55–89) and Peter J. Rabinowitz (1989) group the leading reception theorist Hans-Robert Jauss together with reader-response critics such as Iser and Fish (at the same time that they make careful distinctions among them). On the one hand, this is a natural connection to make: like reader response, reception theory is part of the shift toward a new emphasis on the reader (away from New Criticism's and structuralism's obsession with the text), and Jauss and Iser formulated their theories while teaching at the same university. On the other hand, Jauss and reception theory are as determinedly historical and cultural in focus as Iser and other reader-response critics tend to be ahistorical and individual, and this attention suggests a closer linking of Jauss and reception theory to the New Historicist and Marxist thinkers and teachers grouped together with them here (admittedly with perhaps no more consistency than found in the configuration preferred by Eagleton and Rabinowitz).

The most accessible book about Jauss is Robert C. Holub's *Reception Theory: a Critical Introduction* (1984). Holub adds the distinction that while reader-response criticism was not an organized movement, reception theory is, and that "there has been practically no contact between the two groups" beyond the presence of Jauss and Iser at the same school. Like deconstruction, reception theory is a European construct that critics in the United States have recently found useful to put to work in pragmatic ways, as Louise Smith does in her essay (which opens with an insightful, lively *précis* of Jauss) in the present book. Holub writes: "The 'aesthetics of reception,' as Jauss called his theory in the late 1960s and early 1970s, maintains that the historical essence of an artwork cannot be elucidated by examining its production or by simply describing it. Rather, literature should be treated as a dialectical process of production *and reception*" (57). When students open a canonical text in a classroom, they are conditioned not only by the text itself and by their own individual experiences, but also by the history of the reception of the text—by what has been said about it and how it has been judged and canonized from its earliest reviews until the present moment (as mediated by teachers like us whose readings tend to be thoroughly marked by these forces). Jauss's most accessible book is *Toward an Aesthetic of Reception* (1982).

New Historicists find reception theory very useful, because they too are determined, as Marilyn Butler puts it, to "localize" a text in terms of all of the available cultural codes of its time (1985, 43–44). However, in "Against Tradition: The Case for a Particularized Historical Method" (1985), Butler criticizes Jauss for sticking too closely, like the formalists, to literary texts and their literary reviews as if they were isolated from the rest of history. New Historicists include in their examination not only literary texts and reviews, but also political editorials, nonfictional books, and the materials of history in general. Butler, like Jauss, faults the old historicist critics of the late nineteenth and early twentieth centuries for assuming that history was a linear progression (involving authors influenced only by previous literary masters) toward their own bourgeois present (33–35). New Historicists are convinced that a literary text is part of its own historical moment, as reflected in its author's life, the history of the period, and its critical as well as popular reception—but also that we read texts in light of our own historical moment and our own individual experiences. New Historicists not only openly read and write about texts with their own present, progressive political self-interests in mind, but, following Gadamer's hermeneutics, they argue that the only way *anyone* can read texts is with their historicized self-interests in mind.

In addition to Butler's essay, the two best essays introducing New Historical criticism are Herbert Lindenberger's "Toward a New History in Literary Study" (1984) and Jerome J. McGann's introduction to *Historical Studies and Literary Criticism* (1985), in which Butler's essay also appears.[9] McGann assails New Critics and deconstructionists alike for their rejection of the referentiality of texts. He points out that the best of the "old" historical scholars, such as the great Homeric scholar Millman Parry, avoided a reductive view of history and insisted that when examining literature as part of history, "I make for myself a picture of great detail" (quoted in McGann 1985b, 11). We read literature and history in light of our own particular, contemporary history, resulting in an understanding that is as true as we can be both to history and to our own concerns about the present and the future. When we write about literature, McGann notes, we enter into a rhetorical collaboration among the historical text, our present critical concerns, and our future audience.

By definition, New Historicists are applied critics who work on specific writers and particular eras. In addition to American and Victorian literature, thus far they have focused especially on the Romantics (as in the case of McGann, Butler, and others) and the Renaissance (with Stephen Greenblatt and others), perhaps because they find that those eras speak strongly to our own; this is certainly not a new notion, but the New Historicists' documentary detail and the progressive and openly political nature of their pursuit of it are new. Important representative studies are McGann's *The Beauty of Inflections: Literary Investigations in Historical Method and Theory* (1985) and *Social Values and Poetic Acts: The Historical Judgment of Literary Work* (1988),[10] and Greenblatt's *Renaissance Self-Fashioning: From More to Shakespeare* (1980) and *Shakespearean Negotiations: The Circulation of Social Energy in Renaissance England* (1988). Primarily an intellectual historian, Dominick La Capra has also been influential in the New Historicist movement, and a book that formulates the historical arguments with respect to language, history, and culture is his *Rethinking Intellectual History* (1983). Equally if not more influential has been the work of the anthropologist Clifford Geertz and his insistence on the need for interdisciplinary, "thick description"; useful sources are his collection of essays *The Interpretation of Culture* (1973) and his more recent *Local Knowledge: Further Essays in Interpretive Anthropology* (1983). A convenient and representative anthology is H. Aram Veeser's *The New Historicism* (1989), and a useful brief example of applied New Historicist criticism, on *Measure for Measure*, can be found in Selden's *Practicing Theory and Reading Literature* (1989, 94–99).

As Robert Scholes writes in *Textual Power*, "One does not have to be a Marxist to endorse Fredric Jameson's battle cry, 'Always historicize!' (the first words of *The Political Unconscious* [1981])" (1985, 16). Lindenberger notes:

> That the Marxist model happens to play a considerable role in the new history is a sign less of its adherents' political commitments than of their recognition that Marxism has provided tools to analyze a number of matters with which they are concerned. . . . The new history does not even recognize a single form of Marxism but uses a number of contemporary Marxist variants, as well as the alternatives to the Marxist view of historical change proposed by Michel Foucault. (1984, 19)

In works such as *The Order of Things, The Archaeology of Knowledge,* and *Discipline and Punish,* Foucault developed a cultural "archaeology" that has challenged and influenced New Historicist, Marxist, and poststructuralist perspectives. Although Foucault might usually be placed in a poststructuralist category, he may be more profitably seen as a cultural critic who assimilated many poststructuralist principles regarding language to the study and critique of cultural and disciplinary practices. He advanced his version of history as a series of endlessly warring, unresolved *epistemes*—distinct both from the old historicist, bourgeois version of history as liberal progress or Marx's examination of historical class conflict as destined toward the liberation and victory of the proletariat. Foucault's disciplinary critique has had a tremendous impact on many radical poststructuralist critics. A useful introduction to his work is David Shumway's *Michel Foucault* (1987), and among the important work's adapting Foucault to a critique of the literary disciplines are Paul Bové's *Intellectuals at War* (1986), Karlis Racevskis's *Michel Foucault and the Subversion of Intellect* (1983), and Edward Said's *The World, The Text, The Critic* (1983). These works, however, do not easily lend themselves to the classroom, as they are aimed primarily at critical debates over theory and politics.

Recent Marxist work in the academy has tended to assimilate many poststructuralist beliefs as it moves toward what many have called "post-Marxism" or "postmodern Marxism." The recently inaugurated journal *Rethinking Marxism* has rapidly become a forum for such discussions, but it tends not to be an easy place to begin a study of recent Marxist theory. A more useful starting place is Philip Goldstein's *The Politics of Literary Criticism: An Introduction to Marxist Criticism* (1989), where he provides a clear exposition of the various radical Marxist critiques of humanist literary critical movements. Helpful brief overviews of Marxist theory can also be found in Selden's *Reader's Guide to Contemporary Literary Theory* (1985, 23–51) and Atkins and Morrow's *Contemporary Literary Theory* (1989; see Ryan, "Political Criticism," 200–13). Raymond Williams's *Marxism and Literature* (1976) and his complementary *Keywords* (1976) remain very useful introductions to the link between Marxist cultural theory and literary discourse.

Earlier, the pioneering work of George Lukács in *The Theory of the Novel* (1920), *History and Class Consciousness* (1923), and *The Historical Novel* (1938) provided the first sophisticated Marxist models of literary production, emphasizing the impact of class structure on realistic nineteenth-century literature. Lukács continues to stir heated debate among Marxist critics. In the 1950s, Lucien Goldmann, much influenced by Lukács, wrote *The Hidden God* (1956), which Eva Corredor claims "was one of the first detailed Marxist analyses of literature available to the Western world" (119). By the 1960s, Pierre Macheray, in *A Theory of Literary Production* (1966), offered an even more detailed study of the materialist mode of the production of literary discourse. Eagleton's *Criticism and Ideology* (1978) remains a useful, if technical, overview of the Marxist view of literature. Many recent Marxists have been greatly influenced by the French theorist Louis Althusser, whose *Reading Capital* (1968) offered a structuralist revision of Marxism whereby the ideological positioning of individual subjects within the social structure occurs when one is identified, "hailed," or "interpellated" within a given social discourse.

The most influential Marxist critic in America, Fredric Jameson, has had a tremendous impact on theoretical debates but, again, much of his work is not easily assimilable in the classroom. Anyone interested in pursuing his work might consult William Dowling's *Jameson, Althusser, Marx* (1984). Jameson has written several important interpretations of postmodernism from a Marxist perspective such as "Postmodernism, or the Cultural Logic of Late Capitalism" (1984). These essays and Douglas Kellner's collection *Postmodernism—Jameson— Critique* (1989) suggest directions for many changes in pedagogy, but much work still needs to be done to bring these discussions out of the scholarly debate and into the classroom.

One of the important Marxist studies of the political conditions of academic English is Richard Ohmann's *English in America* (1976). This book offered one of the first polemical accounts of the relations of literary and composition studies to the power structure of American society. During the 1980s it was sometimes critiqued by the poststructuralists such as Stanley Fish for its "essentialized" view of literature that was "polluted" by the politics of the university. But Ohmann's recent work continues to develop important links between social criticism and radical pedagody. As founding editor of the journal *Radical Teacher*, he has fostered attention to the concerns of teachers at all academic levels. His *The Politics of Letters* (1989) continues this concern, and his *College English* article "Graduate Students, Professionals, Intellectuals" (1990) points out the difficulties of radical work in the university while sympathetically arguing for an oppositional pedagogy and criticism. Jim Merod's *The Political Responsibility of the Critic* (1987) presents a forceful argument for an oppositional criticism and for teaching sensitive to the Foucauldian perspective, but drawing more heavily on a Marxist sense of social activism. For a review of the work of the "oppositional critics" see Robert Con Davis's "A

Manifesto for Oppositional Pedagogy: Freire, Bourdieu, Merod, and Graff" in *Reorientations* (Henricksen and Morgan 1990).

The entire *Boundary 2* project initiated by William Spanos at SUNY–Binghamton and now edited by Paul Bové at the University of Pittsburgh has played an important role in bringing the work of Heidegger, Lukács, Adorno, Benjamin, Marcuse, Foucault, Gramsci, Althusser, and other oppositional critics to bear on issues of interpretation and pedagogy. Also significant in this connection, Mas'ud Zavarzadeh and Donald Morton at Syracuse University have produced an important body of oppositional pedagogical theories. Their students formed the Syracuse Marxist Collective, and Zavarzadeh's and Morton's work has now appeared in many places besides *Boundary 2*. Their essay "Theory-Pedagogy-Politics" (1986/1987) outlines their critique of traditional disciplinary and pedagogical practices. By assimilating poststructuralist principles of discourse analysis with an Althusserian Marxist perspective, they argue for a confrontational, transdisciplinary pedagogy and cultural critique which is relentless in its pursuit of the forms of complicity with the dominant culture in even the most ostensibly radical positions. The recent book they have edited, *Theory/Pedagogy/Politics: Texts for Change* (1991), now makes some of this important work readily available. In our own book, Ronald Strickland, who was a student of Zavarzadeh, draws on their work in his article on "Confrontational Pedagogy," another version of which first appeared in *College English* (1989). Evan Watkins's *Work Time* (1990) provides a detailed Marxist study of the hierarchical distribution and social circulation of work in English studies. Another book that further develops the political dimensions of teaching is Maria-Regina Kecht's *Pedagogy Is Politics: Literary Theory and Critical Teaching* (1991), which also contains essays by Zavarzadeh, Ohmann, Merod, Shumway, and others.

Several works have now appeared that try either to critique or to assimilate Marxist with deconstructive positions, most notable among which are Michael Ryan's *Marxism and Deconstruction* (1982) and more recently Paul Smith's *Discerning the Subject* (1988), where Smith offers a challenging but powerful argument to the effect that the reification of a fragmented, decentered "subject" has depleted the oppositional force of individual "agents" as effective sites of political struggle, a struggle which Smith sees as engaging the connections between classroom politics and global politics.

A very important early work that continues to influence those engaged in radical teaching is Paulo Freire's *Pedagogy of the Oppressed* (1970). Freire developed his radical pedagogy through the practical experience of teaching literacy to Brazilian peasants. His critique of the "banking" method of traditional educational practices derives from the passive, authoritarian, and alienated method of "depositing" bits of knowledge in passive students. Freire advocates instead a collectivist, student-centered pedagogy where learning emerges out of the communal negotiation of needs. His notion of "*conscientizaçaõ*," or critical consciousness, has two basic tenets: (1) learning to perceive social, economic, and political contradictions, and (2) learning to take action against the oppressive and dominant elements within the contradictory situations. See also his more recent *The Politics of Education* (1985). In America, Henry Giroux's books, such as *Theory and Resistance in Education: A Pedagogy for the Opposition* (1983), have developed Freirean pedagogy in a Marxist perspective as he argues for an education aimed at a kind of democratic socialism and activism. Also useful in this connection is Stanley Aronowitz and Giroux's *Education Under Siege* (1985), in which their notion of "critical literacy" works to expose the connection between knowledge and power. More recently, Jane Tompkins has, in "Pedagogy of the Distressed" (1990), suggested that literary pedagogy has shifted from the banking model to what she calls the "performative model" of teaching, but the consequences of this shift remain quite similar to Freire's critique of the traditional hierarchies of the knowing teacher and the passive student.

Further resources specifically addressing the pedagogical applications of reception theory, New Historicism, and Marxism—especially at the introductory level—are scattered and surprisingly slim. We are aware of no pedagogical books or anthologies of essays in these areas to which the reader can be steered as in the case of the other theories outlined here. The Soviet theorists that Mark Hurlbert draws on in his essay in this book are very important, but many of their books are not readily available and there has been no effort to present their work in accessible collections and anthologies. The closest thing to a Marxist literary pedagogy may be Ira Shor's *Critical Teaching and Everyday Life* (1980), which addresses the expository writing rather than the introductory literature classroom but which, as Carl Freedman notes, "examines the foremost theoretical problems for radical pedagogy in American education, and posits hundreds of concrete ideas for overcoming them" (1987, 568). Shor also edited *Freire for the Classroom* (1987), which provides concrete examples of Freirean pedagogy across a wide range of educational contexts from high school reading classes to a college mathematics course. The essays by Louise Smith and Brook Thomas in our book (the latter having originally appeared in *College English* in 1987) represent just about the first thoroughgoing efforts to apply, respectively, reception theory and New Historicism to the introductory literature classroom in a specific way.[11] Freedman critiques how Marxist academics in U.S. English departments ironically play out the more general institutional gap between theorists and teachers, as reflected in two rather different allied organizations of the MLA, "the (mainly theoretical) Marxist Literary Group and the (mainly pedagogic) Radical Caucus" (70), and also in the difference between a theoretical study such as Jameson's *Marxism and Form* (1971) (lacking applied praxis) and a pragmatic book such as Ohmann's *English in America* (short on theoretical depth), which are otherwise excellent and certainly very important and influential books (71–82).

As a bridge between reader-response and radical pedagogy, it is useful to look at early advocates of collaborative learning in *College English*, such as Peter Elbow in 1971 ("Exploring My Teaching") and the several articles by Kenneth A. Bruffee.[12] As Hurlbert points out, Bruffee neglects the political implications of a collaborative pedagogy, but such pedagogical developments in the 1970s and 1980s did help to create an institutional atmosphere in which Ronald Strickland can now practice confrontational pedagogy and Hurlbert can pursue collectivist-like teaching.[13] Even back in 1972 in *College English*, though, Brent Harold criticized most "student-centered" teaching of the time as too vague and still caught in the inadequate idealism of the traditional lecture course—the notion that there remains an Everystudent who can discover transcendent truths in texts. Harold emphasized the process of getting students to recognize their dialectically materialist position in reading texts, beginning with a short course in Marxism, setting up the class as a collective, and admitting that the avoidance of letter grades at Brown allowed him to avoid the usual "conflict of motives between individual advancement and participation in group problem-solving" (211). In a reply, however, (the apparently perfectly named respondent) Harold Brent argued that a teacher cannot successfully mandate a collective consciousness: "Collective consciousness cannot be imposed by fiat—it comes only after much struggle and arises as a social phenomenon only *after* a socialist revolution" (214).

Feminist Theory and Pedagogy

This has been an extremely rich area of publication in both theory and pedagogy in recent years, and the reader can find many valuable resources in both books and journals. An excellent first article to read is Paula A. Treichler's "Teaching Feminist Theory" (1986). Treichler provides a very clear historical overview, beginning with the assumption that "feminist theory is not recent," and offering "Seven Basic Plots" which characterize contemporary feminist criticism and teaching. She provides clear pedagogical examples from her own teaching, and her essay also includes one of the most complete bibliographies of feminist theory now available (see also Treichler, Cheris Kramarae, and Beth Stafford's *For Alma Mater: Theory and Practice in Feminist Scholarship* [1985]). An important feature of Treichler's bibliography is that it is so clearly transdisciplinary: it includes work by feminist psychologists, sociologists, and political theorists such as Jean Baker Miller's *Toward a New Psychology of Women* (1976), Nancy Chodorow's *The Reproduction of Mothering* (1978), and Carol Gilligan's *In a Different Voice: Psychological Theory and Women's Development* (1982), all of which have been very influential for feminists in many fields and have significant consequences for teaching. Also, an excellent resource that can be used in the classroom is Kramarae and Treichler's *A Feminist Dictionary* (1985). See also Myra Jehlen's essay "Gender" (1990).

When looking for the specific influence of feminist theories on the literary curriculum, canon, and pedagogy, one can begin with Annette Kolodny's "Dancing through the Minefield: Some Observations on the Theory, Practice, and Politics of a Feminist Literary Criticism" (1980). Kolodny advocates "a playful pluralism, responsive to the possibilities of multiple critical schools and methods, but captive of none, recognizing that the many tools needed for our analysis will necessarily be largely inherited and only partly of our own making" (511). Hence we find a historical approach in an already classic study such as Elaine Showalter's *A Literature of Their Own: British Women Novelists from Brontë to Lessing* (1977), a Harold Bloomian psychoanalytic model at work in Sandra Gilbert and Susan Gubar's equally classic *The Madwoman in the Attic: The Woman Writer and the Nineteenth-Century Literary Imagination* (1979), and a poststructuralist critique influenced by Jacques Lacan in Julia Kristeva and other French feminists—all illuminating gender in literature in original and exciting ways. One might begin with such useful anthologies as Showalter's *The New Feminist Criticism: Essays on Women, Literature, and Theory* (1985), Gayle Greene and Coppelia Kahn's *Making a Difference: Feminist Literary Criticism* (1985), or Shari Benstock's *Feminist Issues in Literary Scholarship* (1987), and then proceed to more specialized sources such as Judith Fetterly's *The Resisting Reader* (1978), Barbara Christian's anthology *Black Feminist Criticism: Perspectives on Black Women Writers* (1985), or Elissa D. Gelfand and Virginia Thorndike Hules's *French Feminist Criticism: Women, Language, and Literature: An Annotated Bib-*

liography (1985). The debates between American and French feminists led to a number of important contributions, and Toril Moi, in *Sexual/Textual Politics* (1985), provides a good overview of these differing yet overlapping perspectives. Alice Jardine's *Gynesis: Configurations of Woman and Modernity* (1985) attempts an assimilation of radical French feminism with more pragmatic American feminism. See the recent articles by Chris Weedon ("Post-Structuralist Feminist Practice") and Juliet MacCannell ("Resistance to Sexual Theory") for political critiques of the intersection of French and American feminist theory. Catharine Stimpson's *Where the Meanings Are* (1989) is a fine collection of essays that covers a twenty-year period; founding editor of the important feminist journal *Signs*, Stimpson covers a wide range of subjects. The relation of men to the feminist movement has been explored in Jardine and Smith's *Men in Feminism* (1987). In general, feminists have written just about every variety of literature, so the examples of applied feminist criticism are legion.[14]

Feminism is the most active arena of recent pedagogical study. This is reflected by the fact that the only essay in Cary Nelson's anthology *Theory in the Classroom* (1986) that gets specific about classroom practices is Treichler's "Teaching Feminist Theory" (see especially 80–86), which is in turn representative of the personal and collaborative nature of feminist pedagogy and writing in general. Several valuable anthologies are available: Elizabeth Flynn and Patricino Schweichart's *Gender and Reading* (1986), Leonore Hoffman and Deborah Rosenfelt's *Teaching Women's Literature from a Regional Perspective* (1982), Leonore Hoffman and Margo Culley's *Women's Personal Narratives: Essays in Criticism and Pedagogy* (1985), Margo Culley and Catherine Portuges's *Gendered Subjects: The Dynamics of Feminist Teaching* (1985), and Susan L. Gabriel and Isaiah Smithson's *Gender in the Classroom: Power and Pedagogy* (1990). Each of these collections contains essays refreshingly packed with personal experiences and specific classroom practices. Flynn and Schweichart's collection includes Flynn's earlier essay "Gender and Reading," first published in *College English* (1983), and several theoretical as well as empirically based studies of gender differences in the classroom. The two volumes coedited by Hoffman (both the results of projects published by the MLA) contain several essays devoted to strategies for empowering students to work with archival materials and their own local and familial resources; an appendix to *Teaching Women's Literature from a Regional Perspective* includes sample syllabi and exercises.[15] *Gendered Subjects*, a cross-disciplinary anthology, contains essays of interest to people in English, including a pair of memorable essays by Mary Helen Washington and Erlene Stetson about the experience of teaching as the only black woman in an English department (Stetson's is entitled "Pink Elephants: Confessions of a Black Feminist in an All-White, Mostly Male English Department of a White University Somewhere in God's Country"). *Gender in the Classroom* is particularly current and valuable. It includes, for example, admirably concentrated feminist reader-response studies by Cheris Kramarae and Paula Treichler, Elizabeth A. Flynn ("Composing as a Woman"), and Susan L. Gabriel; and essays about the need for teachers to overcome gender bias in marking papers (Barnes) and to create specific training and faculty development mechanisms to ensure gender equity in the classroom (Sadker).

A number of valuable individual essays and articles are also available in other anthologies and in journals. In one of them, in *Reorientations,* Barbara C. Ewell writes:

> Florence Howe . . . singles out three . . . strategies that have characterized feminist teaching: small group collaboration, including discussion, group projects, and group grades (which deprivilege the single viewpoint and validate other perspectives); the action project, internship or research directly related to women's issues (which demonstrate the interaction of intellectual concepts and experience); and journal writing (which both legitimizes experience as a subject of analysis and encourages the personalizing of theory through the act of writing). (1990, 161–62)

Reflected here are the fruitful interactions of feminist pedagogy with reader-response and collaborative models. Also included in *Reorientations* is Nancy Comley's examination ("Reading and Writing Genders") of male and female student responses to and parodies of Hemingway's story "Hills Like White Elephants." *Conversations* includes Nancy Vogel's essay on gender-balancing an American literature survey, and in *TETYC,* Barbara Frey Waxman has advanced a similar argument and parallel strategies for the British literature survey.[16] *College English* volume 40, number 8 (April 1979), devoted to "Women and Writing: Writers, Critics, Teachers, Students," included an essay by Elly Bulkin on teaching lesbian poetry; another special issue in 1974 (volume 36, number 3), focused on gay and lesbian concerns and contained an article by Ron Schreiber on "Giving a Gay Course." The most important recent article is Dale Bauer's "The Other 'F' Word: The Feminist in the Classroom." Bauer counters the resistance of students conditioned by the "banking" model of education (as identified by Freire) and expecting a "value-free" class that is free of feminist "bias" by foregrounding "dialogics in the classroom." She explains how she pursued such strategies while teaching Pat Barker's *Blow Your*

House Down, a novel about working-class British women, as a way to challenge patriarchal (and student) values.[17]

The emphasis in most recent feminism has been on the intersections of multiple differences of race, class, ethnicity, and nationality that intersect with gender differences. Lillian Robinson's *Sex, Class, and Culture* (1978) was one of the important earlier works that emphasized these interrelations. More recently the work of many feminist-Marxists, including Gayatri Spivak, Catharine MacKinnon, the contributors to Judith Newton and Deborah Rosenfelt's *Feminist Criticism and Social Change* (1985), and others continue to produce important critiques in this area. Most recently, Chandra Talpade Mohanty's "On Race and Voice: Challenges for Liberal Education in the 1990s" (1989–90) brings together the issues of gender, race, and class in liberal education curricula and pedagogies. She builds on the important work of feminist education theorists such as Charlotte Bunch, Sandra Pollack, Elizabeth Minnich, Marilyn Schuster, and Susan Van Dyne. These contributions complicate the pedagogical issues, especially since most academics are still straight, white, and middle class, which points to, as Jardine and Smith suggest, "a serious institutional problem." In any case, the intersections of feminist and multicultural perspectives will play a large part in the pedagogical transformations we might see in the next decade.

African American and Multicultural Theory and Pedagogy

African American literature is a field that has generated as much scholarship as criticism on other major, burgeoning U. S. "minority" literatures—Asian American, Hispanic American, Native American—combined. We put "minority" in quotation marks because as far back as 1974, Leslie Fielder (anticipating Radhakrishnan's critique of the word "ethnic" as cited in Phillipa Kafka's essay in the present collection) pointed out in "Is There a Majority Literature?" that in an important sense, "there is not nor has there ever been a 'majority literature.' There are only competing 'minority literatures,' one or another of which becomes from time to time established" (3). It is difficult to point to a single brief overview of African American and multicultural theory, partly because most of the aforementioned convenient surveys of literary theory as a whole neglect these fields. One can read Kwame Anthony Appiah's essay on "Race" and Werner Sollors's on "Ethnicity" in Lentricchia and McLaughlin's *Critical Terms for Literary Study* (1990).

Another good place to start is Henry Louis Gates, Jr.'s, essay "The Master's Pieces: On Canon Formation and the Afro-American Tradition" in *Conversations* (one other book on theory and pedagogy that does not neglect African American literature and theory). To the persistent question of whether African American literature should be studied and taught within the contours of U. S. literature at large or rather treated within its own distinctive contexts, Gates gives an answer that has been equally persistent among many scholars in the field—that it should be studied and taught in both ways. There is a vital, crucial relationship between African American and other U. S. literatures, but at the same time we find "by the repetition and revisions of shared themes, topoi, and tropes, a process that binds the signal texts of the black tradition into a canon just as surely as separate links bind together into a chain" (72).

Gates is one of several very sophisticated and productive African American scholars who reflect changes in theory in general in their development from fairly structuralist to much more cultural approaches. Instructive in this regard is Gates's anthology *Black Literature and Literary Theory* (1984), and important individual works include Robert Stepto's *From Behind the Veil: A Study of Afro-American Narrative* (1979), Houston Baker's *The Journey Back: Issues in Black Literature and Criticism* (1980) and *Blues, Ideology, and Afro-American Literature: A Vernacular Theory* (1984), and Gates's *Figures in Black: Words, Signs, and the "Racial" Self* (1987) and *The Signifying Monkey: A Theory of Afro-American Literary Criticism* (1988). The Summer 1984 issue of the *ADE Bulletin* included Richard Yarborough's essay on African American literature and the American canon as well as Jerry Ward's "Selected Bibliography of Afro-American Literature." An excellent, more textually focused study is Abdul JanMohamed's *Manichean Aesthetics: The Politics of Literature in Colonial Africa* (1983), which deploys Fredric Jameson's Marxist hermeneutics in the comparative study of three black African writers and three white colonialist writers. One of the most recent compendiums of African American criticism—especially interesting due to its guest-editor Reginald Martin's avowed interest in linking African American criticism to other literary theories—is the November 1990 special issue of *College English*.

The most wide-ranging and accessible single introduction to Chicano, Native American, Chinese American, and Japanese American literatures—one compiled specifically for the teacher—is the collection *Three American Literatures* (1982), edited by Houston Baker. The *ADE Bulletin* published a series of issues on "Multicultural Literature," including Native American (75 [December 1983]), African American (78 [Summer

1984]), Asian American (80 [Spring 1985]), and Chicano and Puerto Rican (91 [Winter 1988]) literatures. A great many other sources are listed in the voluminous *Comprehensive Bibliography for the Study of American Minorities* (1976), edited by Wayne C. Miller et al.[18] A useful recent critique is Gregory Jay's "The End of American Literature: Toward a Multicultural Practice" (1991).

Turning to pedagogy, one finds that Darwin T. Turner and Barbara Dodds Stanford's *Theory and Practice in the Teaching of Literature by Afro-Americans* (1971) is aimed at secondary teachers and necessarily somewhat dated theoretically but still a very useful source for someone interested in working up a unit on African American writers for an introductory college course, as it includes Turner's brief overview of the periods and the major writers (20–34) and Stanford's compilation of classroom discussion questions and working syllabi. In an essay published in *College English* in 1970, at which time African American literature had "become visible in colleges only within the past two years," Turner anticipated Gates (and Pancho Savery in our book) in arguing that African American writers should be taught within general survey courses as well as in separate courses. For the general introductory course he suggested some Black-White pairings: David Walker and Tom Paine, slave narratives and white autobiographies, Paul Laurence Dunbar and James Whitcomb Riley, Charles Chestnutt and Joel Chandler Harris, James Weldon Johnson and William Dean Howells, Claude McKay and Hemingway or Fitzgerald, and Jean Toomer and Sherwood Anderson or Gertrude Stein.[19] He encouraged whites to teach African American literature while cautioning against unprepared, subconsciously racist, or sentimental white teachers.[20] Others have argued, like Turner and Pancho Savery, against teaching the occasional African American writer isolated as a token within a mostly white introductory course, and in favor of building African American units within general introductory courses. Glenda Gill, for example, outlines a unit on the black woman while pointing out that similar units could be done on the black male, the black middle class, the black slave, or the Harlem Renaissance. In *Conversations*, Warren Rosenberg instructively recounts his experience of first running into trouble teaching Harriet Jacobs's *Incidents in the Life of a Slave Girl* in between Melville and Whitman, and then doing much better pairing it with the *Narrative of the Life of Frederick Douglass* while having students read excerpts from Gates. Valerie Lee explains how she helped her white students get over their initial resistance to non-white literature. R. Radhakrishan's "Canonicity and Theory" offers one of the most theoretically sophisticated critiques of the link between canons, ethnicity, authority, and privilege.

Also accessible is Dexter Fisher and Robert Stepto's *Afro-American Literature: The Reconstruction of Instruction* (1979). A useful general source is Dolores E. Cross, Gwendolyn C. Baker, and Lindley J. Stiles's anthology *Teaching in a Multicultural Society: Perspectives and Professional Strategies* (1977). Specific articles on teaching Native American literature, by A. LaVonne Browne Ruofs and Franchot Ballinger, and on teaching Asian American literature, by Linda Ching Sledge, are available.[21]

Dialogic, Deconstructionist, and Poststructuralist Theory and Pedagogy

One may object that Bakhtinian dialogics could be as appropriately categorized under Marxist criticism, and in general we would not disagree. However, following the structure of our book, we consider dialogics together with deconstruction, here—not because they represent versions of the same project, which indeed they do not. Rather, they do share at least a theme of the critique of any "monologic" authority that attempts to provide an ahistorical foundation to resist the play of multiple meanings and deny the social basis of communication and language. The most concise and accessible overview of dialogic theory and criticism is Don Bialostosky's chapter on "Dialogic Criticism" in *Contemporary Literary Theory*. Studies of Bakhtin have proliferated at an amazing rate since the 1976 publication of *The Dialogic Imagination* (translated by Michael Holquist). A good introduction to Bakhtin is Clark and Holquist's *Mikhail Bakhtin* (1984), which provides an excellent intersection of biographical, social, and theoretical material on Bakhtin. Natoli's "Tracing a Beginning through Past Voices" in *Tracing Literary Theory* provides a good example of how one might view the entire "carnival" of theory through a Bakhtinian lens. A good place to begin reading Bakhtin may be *Problems of Dostoevsky's Poetics* (trans. 1984) where Bakhtin offers, as Bialostosky explains, "a full-scale rearrangement of Aristotle's hierarchy of plot, character, thought, and diction" (217). This can be followed by *The Dialogic Imagination* (trans. 1981), *Rabelais and His World* (trans. 1984), and *Speech Genres and Other Late Essays* (trans. 1986).

The most lively survey and critique of structuralism and poststructuralism are provided by Terry Eagleton's two chapters in *Literary Theory: An Introduction* (1983, 91–150). As Eagleton points out, the assimilation of deconstruction in America mainly took the form of an interpretive activity of seeking out the instability of meanings that could be applied to canonical texts, so that the pedagogical consequences were slight indeed. On the other hand, deconstruction and poststructural perspectives offer potential challenges to all traditional pedagogical practices, and it is the more politically engaged version of deconstruction that we find most important to engage in the classroom. The work of the "uncanny" American (mostly Yale) deconstructors—Paul de Man, J. Hillis Miller, Geoffrey Hartman, Barbara Johnson—represents the less politically motivated form of deconstruction (although Johnson's recent work has moved more in this direction). The writings of Michael Ryan and Gayatri Spivak have been most important in politicizing deconstructive activity. For a useful bibliographic overview of this work, most of which does not directly address pedagogy, see Richard A. Barney's "Uncanny Criticism in the United States" in *Tracing Literary Theory*. Barney's starting point is that "writing an account of deconstruction in the United States is difficult if only because two main methods for approaching it—either as a coherent body of work or as a historical development—have been severely criticized by deconstructors themselves" (177). For example, in her shorter and insightful overview of deconstruction in the classroom, "A Short Course in Post-Structuralism" (1990 [1988]), Jane Tompkins concludes with the remark that an "application" of poststructuralism is impossible primarily because there is no "free-standing" theory that can be applied to a body of texts.

These inauspicious signs at the beginning of our section on deconstruction and pedagogy suggest the self-defeating nature of the deconstructive claims for dramatic pedagogical transformations on the one hand and the impossibility of adapting deconstruction to pedagogy on the other. But, as G. Douglas Atkins and Michael Johnson propose in their collection *Writing and Reading Differently: Deconstruction and the Teaching of Composition and Literature* (1985), "deconstruction has immense practical value for teachers of English as well as of other languages" (10) because "deconstruction is principally characterized by its orientation toward pedagogical use, practice, praxis" (11). Most of the contributors to their book, such as Gayatri Spivak, J. Hillis Miller, Barbara Johnson, and Geoffrey Hartman, are the main deconstructive critics, so there is still a focus more on problems of reading and interpretation than pedagogy. Gregory Ulmer's "Textshop for Post(e)pedagogy," however, focuses directly on altering the shape and content of student tasks so as to emphasize the creative, open-ended, playful dimensions of textual production.

For those coming to deconstruction for the first time, Sharon Crowley's *A Teacher's Introduction to Deconstruction* (1989) is perhaps the best place to start. One might follow this with G. Douglas Atkins's *Reading Deconstruction: Deconstructive Reading* (1983), which provides a brief and easily readable introduction to the Yale critics and their version of "deconstructive reading." Crowley remarks that "I am not sure that a deconstructive pedagogy can be realized—the term is itself an oxymoron" (45). This sentence begins her final section on "Deconstructive Pedagogy," but Crowley offers a strong rationale that "deconstructive insights about teaching, language, and writing offer up a critique on which we can hang much of the pedagogical practice that has been adopted by writing teachers in recent years" (31). In this sense a deconstructive pedagogy "would reject the traditional model of authority. . . would adopt the position that knowledge is a highly contextualized activity. . . that knowledge itself is a volatile construct" (46). In other words, deconstruction focuses on the problematic nature of language by upending any unquestioned reliance on the correspondence theory of reference whereby words "mean" what they signify and texts "represent" the objective world. Since conventional pedagogical models depend on a sense of objective knowledge that teachers can communicate through the medium of their own language and authority, one can readily see Crowley's and others' insistence that any rigorous attention to deconstruction in the classroom will challenge most of our usual ways of lecturing, grading, assessing students, leading discussions, and devising assignments and syllabi. We believe, however, that following the lead of Thomas Fink's argument in his essay in our book, to deny deconstruction as a pedagogical practice is only to reinforce an essentialized version of deconstruction that cannot be "contaminated" by its contact with the compromises of power relations and meaning production in the classroom. Derrida himself advocates such activism, particularly in relation to his work with GREPH, the Group for Research on Philosophic Teaching, founded in 1974. As Vincent Leitch explains in "Deconstruction and Pedagogy" (in Nelson's *Theory in the Classroom*), "Derrida states that 'deconstruction . . . has, then, always borne in principle on the apparatus and the function of teaching in general'" (46). The practical application with respect to the institutionalized teaching of literature is that, as Leitch explains, "the focus on pedagogy in Derrida's work has the broadening effect of bringing into the foreground the potential of deconstruction to become activist *cultural* criticism" (48). The boundaries of the "literary" and the "English" no longer contain an "object" or "field" in any traditional sense.

Turning to a historical perspective, we find that it was in the early 1980s that several critics attempted to overcome the theoretical disavowal of the possibility of comprehensive introductory overviews of deconstruction: Christopher Norris's *Deconstruction: Theory and Practice* (1982), Vincent Leitch's *Deconstructive Criticism: An Advanced Introduction* (1983), and Jonathan Culler's *On Deconstruction* (1982). Norris's book succeeds in its brevity and its emphasis on the relations between Derrida and Nietzsche. Leitch emphasizes deconstruction's ties to the earlier structuralist work of Levi-Strauss and the Heideggerian "destructive" poetics developed by William Spanos and Paul Bové. Culler's book may be read as a sequel to his earlier *Structuralist Poetics* (1975), the latter taking a more moderate position regarding the "competent reader." *On Deconstruction* begins with a controversial chapter, "Reading as a Woman," which Culler probably should have called "Reading as a Feminist," as a number of critics have pointed out. But again, all of these books focus on problems of interpretation rather than on pedagogical practices.

For pedagogical purposes, the best of the many collections oriented around deconstruction is, again, Atkins and Michael Johnson's *Writing and Reading Differently*. A good complement to this book is Catherine Belsey's *Critical Practice* (1980) since she offers a more politically activist form of critical/pedagogical practice incorporating many Marxist perspectives on the subject, ideology, and language. Following this, there have appeared a number of collections engaging various dimensions of deconstructive activity, ranging from the earlier focus on the 1966 Johns Hopkins symposium in Richard Macksey and Eugenio Donato's *The Structuralist Controversy* (1972) and Geoffrey Hartman's collection *Deconstruction and Criticism* (1979) to the more broadly poststructuralist collection of Josue Harrari, *Textual Strategies* (1979), to a focus on the Yale critics in Jonathan Arac et al.'s *The Yale Critics* (1983), to Mark Krupnick's *Displacement: Derrida and After* (1983), which focuses on the social and political dimensions of the linguistic displacements of deconstruction. But again, little of this work will have immediate practical effects on classroom practice for most undergraduate teachers despite its potential call for such transformations.

One disciple of deconstruction who has made the greatest effort to pursue its consequences for pedagogy is Gregory Ulmer. In *Applied Grammatology* (1985) Ulmer asks, "Does Derrida have a pedagogical theory? Edward Said suggests that perhaps he has nothing else but a pedagogy" (157). Ulmer's thesis in his chapter on "The Scene of Teaching" (157–88) is that "grammatology is committed to a pedagogy that . . . will collapse discipline into invention" (188). Ulmer's version of a poststructuralist pedagogy is the "textshop," in which (as he explains in *Reorientations*) he creates a laboratory in which students can create their own texts ("Textshop"). A Marxist view, sharply critical of Ulmer, can be found in Mas'ud Zavarzadeh's "Theory as Resistance" (1989). Zavarzadeh's critique provides a lucid presentation of the charges that deconstruction is "complicitous" with the dominant educational structures, an issue that will continue to foster heated debate with respect to the radical challenges of deconstructive theory. In short, Zavarzadeh argues that Ulmer's version of pedagogical "laughter/parody/pastiche" merely "conserves the system in which it operates" because "the pedagogy of 'lec(ri)ture' becomes the pedagogy of evasion . . . rather than a pedagogy of 'practice': praxis means forming, grasping, and changing oneself and a historical world through collective productive work that mediates between the object and the subject" (63). Nevertheless, Ulmer's efforts to incorporate the work of the "modern experimental arts" in the literature and the language classroom continue to challenge our usual disciplinary protocols, and his recent essay in *Reorientations* includes a section on "Assignments: Ideology and Resistance" that leads students to question their own assumptions about artistic and cultural values. His work in multimedia and electronic environments underlies his more recent *Teletheory: Grammatology in the Age of Video* (1989).

Besides the direct influence of Derrida, Leitch points out in *Theory in the Classroom* that Roland Barthes contributes a focus on the deconstructive classroom as subversive of a neurotic society, whereas an increasingly active Derrida has sought to critique society at large, and Leitch notes that U. S. academics began to talk about deconstruction and pedagogy only in the early 1980s, one of the principle examples being *The Pedagogical Imperative* mentioned in the first section of this essay.[22] Also of strong interest as we look to the technological future, as James Sosnoski notes in the closing essay of our book, are some of the versions of computer hypertext that have been created, most notably by George P. Landow at Brown University. In *Reorientations* Landow explains how students in his introductory courses use his program Context 32 to direct the computer intertextually, accessing many kinds of historical and literary sources related to the primary text and in the process reading and learning more and discussing and writing better. Of special interest is *Hypermedia and Literary Studies* (1991), a recent collection of essays by Paul Delany and Landow. Sosnoski is strongly cautious, however, about the hidden agendas in hypertext computer environments that will play a much greater role in literary and cultural education in the coming decade.

Other sources on deconstruction and pedagogy are few and far between; the original version of Thomas Fink's essay in our book that appeared in the February 1985 *TETYC* is one of the few. Pam Gilbert's *Writing, Schooling, and Deconstruction: From Voice to Text in the Classroom* (1989), which draws also on reader-response approaches, is a book focused on secondary teaching in Australia. A useful (though fairly jaded) college classroom example is Lawrence I. Lipking's deconstructive approach to Yeats's "Sailing to Byzantium." But the more positively useful examples of deconstruction in the classroom can be found in the Gibson, Goldman, and Dupras essays in *Conversations*. Walker Gibson suggests in a playfully serious tone that linguistic play and ambiguity are not so new: close rhetorical readings of texts suggest the difficulties and subtleties of language in social use, as in his example from *Pride and Prejudice*. Irene C. Goldman draws out the connections between feminism, deconstruction, and a reader-response approach to Thoreau's *Walden*. Joseph Dupras recounts in a lively way his experience of bringing poststructuralist principles of uncertainty and inconclusiveness to the classroom "to bring students to the pleasures of literature" rather than perpetuating his formalist techniques, which had led to a pedagogical "texticide" on the part of his students rather than the "textasy" he had experienced by way of his own intellectual mastery (179).

Janet Emig's essay in *Conversations*, "Our Missing Theory," offers an important note of caution for all textual theories: the difference in the theoretical backgrounds of college teachers versus public school teachers is typically a difference between those trained in sophisticated text-based theories of interpretation and those trained in the "developmental dimension of learning and teaching" (88). If students are to become theorists, then theorists at the college level need to become aware of developmental and learning theorists who have much to say about how not to alienate students even further from the otherwise difficult "expertise" of the professional literary theorists. As Emig reminds us, "we were not born Marxists or feminists; . . . we evolved, often tortuously, to whatever current sets of beliefs and theories we now hold" (94). Nor were we born teachers; we all have to keep striving to become theoretically informed as well as practically effective if we are to make a difference *as* teachers.

Notes

1. For an extended discussion and critique of Graff's book, see the special issue of *Critical Exchange* (23 [Summer 1987]) devoted to Graff's work.

Downing's "The Cultural Politics of Graff's History of Literary Studies" (45–63) specifically addresses Graff's ambivalence about the separation of theory and politics. See also Bruce Henricksen's "Teaching Against the Grain," in which he arrives at a similar conclusion—that Graff "does not . . . contextualize his model within the problematic of education as a class- and power-allocating activity" (31). For a more detailed historical account of contemporary American critical theory, see Vincent Leitch's *American Literary Criticism from the Thirties to the Eighties* (1989). Frank Lentricchia's controversial account in *After the New Criticism* poses problems because of its dense prose and the fact that it is addressed to those already familiar with the theorists whom he addresses.

2. For a recent overview of contemporary anthologies of theory, see Brian Caraher's review article in *Yearbook of Comparative and General Literature*. Recent criticism on the works of James Joyce provides a focused and extensive case study in applied criticism; for an overview and critique, see Cahalan, "James Joyce and Joycean Scholarship: A Historical View" (1988), 156–78.

3. See Sosnoski's "Why Theory? Rethinking Pedagogy" for a critique of de Man's notion of theory and resistance.

4. Mary Lee Bretz and Margaret Persin, for example, organized a graduate course at Rutgers on "Approaches to the Teaching of Hispanic Literature," and Yolanda Stern Broad edited a special issue of the *ADFL Bulletin* on using literary theory in the classroom. See Gary Waller on "'Theory' in the English Major" at Carnegie Mellon University.

5. Bruce Miller's *Teaching the Art of Literature* (1980) contains some helpful suggestions but seems largely uninformed by contemporary theory. Susanne Kappeler and Norman Bryson's collection *Teaching the Text* (1983) usefully advances British theorists' responses to contemporary theory but focuses on individual readings rather than specific classroom practices.

6. The editors of *Teaching Literature: What Is Needed Now* note that Harvard University Press required the strong university affiliation and disclaim agreement among their contributors, but as Nancy Comley notes in a review of the book, "some readers will say that drawing on so narrow a segment of the profession to deal with so large an issue is a bit presumptuous. The appeal of this text is certainly restricted by the predominantly privileged status of Harvard students and by the contributors' concluding about half the time that 'what is needed now' is 'what we had (or thought we had) then'" (45).

7. Another collection of essays focused on theory and pedagogy at the secondary level is Charles Chew, Rosanne DeFabio, and Patricia Honsbury's *Reader Response in the Classroom* (1986), which despite its title considers the applications of not only reader-response but also formalist, historical/cultural, psychological, mythological, archetypal, and feminist approaches.

8. See, for example, the articles by Robert M. Holland, Nancy MacKenzie, Christine McMahon, Sylvia Spann, Stan Sulkes, and Gloria Young.

9. See also the conclusion to William Cain's *The Crisis in Criticism* (1984).

10. For a critical review of McGann's recent work see David Gorman.

11. Peggy Ann Knapp ("'Stay, Illusion,' or How to Teach *Hamlet*") and Kathleen McCormick ("Theory in the Reader," 840–42) have described something like a reception-theory approach to teaching *Hamlet* in introductory courses at Carnegie Mellon University. William C. Dowling addresses the

particular relevance of New Historicism to teaching eighteenth-century literature, reflecting on the earlier seductive escapism of New Criticism for the teacher challenged to make such historically particularized writings at all appealing to introductory students, but not giving many specific examples of his own current New Historicist teaching strategies.

12. In "The Way Out" in 1972, Bruffee criticized Elbow for the "rampant individualism" (463–64) of his student-run introductory class, arguing instead for collaborative models (see also "Collaborative Learning: Some Practical Models") and later picking up the notion of "interpretive communities" (in "Collaborative Learning and the 'Conversation of Mankind,'" which includes a quick history of collaborative learning [636–38]). John Trimbur argues that Bruffee assumes too much by facilely linking collaborative learning and "interpretive communities," and that "we need to begin collaborative classes by asking why interpretation has become the unquestioned goal of literary studies and what other kinds of readings thereby have been excluded and developed" (613).

13. The way in which collaborative learning could be applied to very different political ends earlier is exemplified by Joseph Kau's 1976 article advocating a "Corporate Approach to Introductory Literature Courses." At the opposite end of the spectrum, a supplement to Strickland's approach (but unfortunately a much more abstract and less useful essay than Strickland's) is Robert Con Davis's "A Manifesto for Oppositional Pedagogy" (in *Reorientations*).

14. Cahalan found it interesting and instructive to teach selections from Suzanne Juhasz's collection *Feminist Critics Read Emily Dickinson* (1983) in pointed contrast to selections from Richard B. Sewall's New Critical anthology *Emily Dickinson: A Collection of Critical Essays* (1963), along with several poems treated by both the New Critics (frequently misogynist in this case) and the feminists.

15. See also Hoffman's article on "Student Readers and the Civil War Letters of an Ohio Woman" in *Reader*.

16. See also Brenda Sluder's "The Voice of the Other" in *TETYC*.

17. See also Carol Thomas Neely's "Feminist Criticism and Teaching Shakespeare."

18. See also the periodical *Minorities in America* (annual since 1976).

19. Similarly, see Linda Wagner's article on pairing Toni Morrison's *The Bluest Eye* with (among others) Faulkner's *The Sound and the Fury*, Twain's *Huckleberry Finn*, Hemingway's *In Our Time*, or Rudolfo Anaya's *Bless Me, Ultima*.

20. See also Frederick C. Stern's 1974 article.

21. See also Kenneth M. Roemer's collection *Approaches to Teaching Momaday's "The Way to Rainy Mountain"* (1988).

22. The Winter 1981 issue of *Focus*, edited by Raymond E. Fitch, on "Literary Theory in the Classroom," mentioned earlier, contains several articles on teaching informed by structuralism.

Works Cited

Literary Texts

Abdul-Jabbar, Kareem, with Mignon McCarthy. 1990. *Kareem*. New York: Random House.

Alger, Horatio. 1962 [1868]. *Ragged Dick and Mark, the Match Boy*. New York: Macmillan.

Alighieri, Dante. 1954. *The Inferno*. Translated by John Ciardi. New York: Penguin/Mentor.

Alison, W. Alexander, et al., eds. 1983. *The Norton Anthology of Poetry*. 3rd, shorter ed. New York: Norton.

Angelou, Maya. 1969. *I Know Why the Caged Bird Sings*. New York: Random House.

Austen, Jane. 1962 [1814]. *Mansfield Park*. New York: Washington Square Press.

———. 1972 [1813]. *Pride and Prejudice*. New York: Penguin.

Barker, Pat. 1984. *Blow Your House Down*. New York: Putnam.

Beowulf. 1986. New York: Random House.

Blake, William. [1789]. "The Lamb." In *The Poetry and Prose of William Blake*, edited by David V. Erdman and Harold Bloom. New York: Doubleday, 1965. Rpt. in *The Norton Anthology of English Literature*, edited by M. H. Abrams. 3rd ed. 2 vols. New York: Norton, 1974, 1: 32.

———. [1789]. "Laughing Song." In Abrams et al., 1: 34.

———. [1789]. "The Little Black Boy." In Abrams et al., 1: 51–52.

———. [1789]. "The Tyger." In Abrams et al., 1: 39.

Borges, Jorge Luis. 1962. *Labyrinths*. New York: New Directions.

Bradstreet, Anne. 1967 [1650]. "The Author to Her Book." In *The Works of Anne Bradstreet*, edited by Jeannie Hensley, 221. Cambridge: Belknap Press.

Brontë, Charlotte. 1966 [1847]. *Jane Eyre*. In *The Penguin Brontë Sisters*. Harmondsworth, England: Penguin.

Browning, Robert. 1988 [1842]. "My Last Duchess." In *The Riverside Anthology of Literature*, edited by Douglas Hunt, 819–21. Boston: Houghton-Mifflin.

Cassill, R. V., ed. 1988. *The Norton Anthology of Contemporary Fiction*. New York: Norton.

Cather, Willa. 1954 [1918]. *My Antonia*. Boston: Houghton-Mifflin.

Chandler, Raymond. 1972 [1939]. *Trouble Is My Business*. New York: Ballantine.

Chestnutt, Charles. 1969 [1899]. *The Conjure Woman*. Ann Arbor: University of Michigan Press.

Chopin, Kate. 1976 [1899]. *The Awakening*. New York: Norton.

Conrad, Joseph. 1989 [1899; 1921]. *Heart of Darkness: A Case Study in Contemporary Criticism*. Edited by Ross C. Murfin. New York: St. Martin's.

Coover, Robert. 1988. "The Babysitter." In Cassill, 78–99.

Crane, Stephen. 1989 [1898]. "The Blue Hotel." In *The Norton Anthology of American Literature*, 3rd ed., edited by Nina Baym, Ronald Gottesman, et al., vol. 2, 805–25. New York: W. W. Norton.

Cullen, Countee. 1947. *On These I Stand*. New York: Harper & Row.

cummings, e. e. 1982. "The Cambridge Ladies Who Live in Furnished Souls." In *Literature: The Human Experience*, edited by Richard Abcarian and Marvin Klotz, 399–400. New York: St. Martin's.

Darwin, Erasmus. 1803. *The Temple of Nature, or the Origin of Society*. London.

Dead Poets Society. 1984. Directed by Peter Weir. Touchstone Home Video.

Dickens, Charles. 1961 [1854]. *Hard Times*. New York: New American Library.

Donne, John. 1988 [1633]. "The Canonization." In *The Riverside Anthology of Literature* (see Browning), 693–94.

Douglass, Frederick. 1968 [1845]. *Narrative of the Life of Frederick Douglass, an American Slave, Written by Himself*. New York: Signet-NAL.

Dreiser, Theodore. 1964 [1925]. *An American Tragedy*. New York: Signet

———. *Sister Carrie*. 1970 [1900]. New York: Norton.

Du Bois, W. E. B. 1965 [1903]. *The Souls of Black Folk*. In Franklin, 207–390.

Dunbar, Paul Laurence. 1913. *The Complete Poems of Paul Laurence Dunbar*. New York: Dodd, Mead.

Ellison, Ralph. 1972 [1952]. *Invisible Man*. New York: Vintage.

Emecheta, Buchi. 1979. *Joys of Motherhood*. New York: George Braziller.

Erdrich, Louise. 1989. "Lulu's Boys." In *The Norton Anthology of American Literature* (see Crane), 2364–72.

Faulkner, William. 1948. *Intruder in the Dust*. New York: Random House.

———. 1987 [1930]. "A Rose for Emily." *Literature: An Introduction to Fiction, Poetry, and Drama*, edited by X. J. Kennedy, 24–31. Boston: Little, Brown.

———. 1987 [1929]. *The Sound and the Fury*. Edited by Noel Polk. New York: Random House.

Fitzgerald, F. Scott. 1961 [1925]. *The Great Gatsby*. New York: Scribner's.

Flaubert, Gustave. 1982 [1857]. *Madame Bovary*. Translated by Francis Steegmuller. New York: Random House.

Franklin, Benjamin. 1986 [1791; 1868]. *Autobiography and Other Writings*. Edited by Kenneth Silverman. New York: Penguin.

Franklin, John Hope, ed. 1965. *Three Negro Classics*. New York: Avon.

Freeman, Mary Wilkins. 1985 [1909]. "Old Woman Magoun." In *The Norton Anthology of Literature by Women*, edited by Sandra Gilbert and Susan Gubar, 1104–19. New York: Norton.

Frost, Robert. 1988 [1918]. "Home Burial." In *The Riverside Anthology of Literature* (see Browning), 909–12.

———. 1963 [1914]. "Mending Wall." In *Selected Poems of Robert Frost*, 23–24. New York: Holt, Rinehart and Winston.

Fugard, Athol. 1988. "'Master Harold'... and the Boys." In *The Riverside Anthology of Literature* (see Browning), 1821–57.

Gibson, P. J. 1986. "*Brown Silk and Magenta Sunsets*." In *Nine Plays by Black Women*, edited by Margaret B. Wilkerson, 427–505. New York: New American Library.

Gilman, Charlotte Perkins. 1973 [1892]. *The Yellow Wallpaper*. New York: The Feminist Press.

Ginsberg, Allen. 1985 [1956]. "Howl." In *The Concise Anthology of American Literature*, 2nd ed., edited by George McMichael, 1946–54. New York: Macmillan.

Giovanni, Nikki. 1982. "Revolutionary Dreams." In *Literature: the Human Experience* (see cummings), 429.

Glaspell, Susan. 1987. "Trifles." In *Literature: An Introduction to Fiction, Poetry, and Drama*, edited by X. J. Kennedy, 4th ed., 839–50. Boston: Little, Brown.

Grahn, Judy. 1987. "The Meanings in the Pattern." *American Poetry since 1970: Up Late*, edited by Andrei Codrescu, 282. New York: Four Walls Eight Window.

Gramsci, Antonio. 1971. *Selections from the Prison Notebooks*. New York: International Publishers.

Hansberry, Lorraine. 1966. *A Raisin in the Sun*. New York: New American Library.

Hawthorne, Nathaniel. 1990 [1850]. *The Scarlet Letter: A Case Study in Contemporary Criticism*. Edited by Ross C. Murfin. New York: St. Martin's.

Hemingway, Ernest. 1987 [1929]. *A Farewell to Arms*. New York: Scribner's.

———. 1985 [1938]. "The Short Happy Life of Francis Macomber." In *Fictions*, edited by Joseph F. Trimmer and C. Wade Jennings, 503–25. Chicago: Harcourt.

———. 1988 [1937]. *To Have and Have Not*. New York: Macmillan.

Hogan, Linda. 1988. "Germinal." In *Savings*, 3. Minneapolis: Coffee House Press.

Homer. 1946. *The Odyssey*. Translated by E. V. Riew. New York: Penguin.

Hughes, Langston. 1988. "Theme for English B." In *The Riverside Anthology of Literature* (see Browning), 1022–23.

Hurston, Zora Neale. 1978 [1937]. *Their Eyes Were Watching God*. Urbana: University of Illinois Press.

Ibsen, Henrik. 1965 [1879]. *The Doll's House and Other Plays*. New York: Penguin.

Jackson, Elaine. 1986. "Paper Dolls." In *Nine Plays by Black Women* (see Gibson), 347–423.

Johnson, James Weldon. 1965 [1912]. *The Autobiography of an Ex-Colored Man*. Rpt. in *Three Negro Classics*, edited by John Hope Franklin, 391–511. New York: Avon.

Jordan, June. 1985. *Living Room*. Chicago: Thunder's Mouth Press.

Kafka, Franz. 1963. "The Vulture." In *Parables and Paradoxes*, translated by Tania and James Stern, 149. New York: Schocken.

Keats, John. 1978 [1820]. "Ode on a Grecian Urn." In *The Poems of John Keats,* edited by Jack Stillinger, 372–73. Cambridge, MA: Belknap.

Kicknosway. 1987. "Rapunzel." In *American Poetry since 1970: Up Late* (see Grahn), 272.

Kingston, Maxine Hong. 1975. "No Name Woman." In *The Woman Warrior: Memoirs of a Girlhood Among Ghosts,* 3–16. New York: Knopf.

Koch, Kenneth. 1983. "Variations on a Theme by William Carlos Williams." In Alison et al., 763.

Lawrence, D. H. 1984 [1920]. *Women in Love.* New York: Penguin.

Le Guin, Ursula K. 1987. *Buffalo Gals and Other Animal Presences.* Santa Barbara: Capra.

———. 1975 [1974]. *The Dispossessed.* New York: Avon.

Lorde, Audre. 1978. *The Black Unicorn.* New York: Norton.

Melville, Herman. 1985 [1855]. "Benito Cereno." In *The Norton Anthology of American Literature,* 2nd ed., edited by Nina Baym et al., 2272–2338. New York: Norton.

Miller, Arthur. 1976 [1949]. *Death of a Salesman.* New York: Penguin.

Miller, Jordan Y., ed. 1976. Sophocles's *Oedipus Rex.* In *The Heath Introduction to Drama,* 31–76. Lexington, MA: D.C. Heath.

Milton, John. 1957. *Complete Poems and Major Prose.* Edited by Merritt Y. Hughes. New York: Macmillan.

———. 1983 [1637]. "Lycidas." In *The Norton Anthology of Poetry* (see Koch), 147–51.

Minot, Susan. 1988. "Lust." In *The Norton Anthology of Contemporary Fiction* (see Coover), 308–16.

Minty, Judith. 1984 [1981]. "Prowling the Ridge." *In the Presence of Mothers.* Pittsburgh: University of Pittsburgh Press. Rpt. in *The Generation of 2000,* edited by William Heyen, 184. Princeton: Ontario Review Press.

Momaday, N. Scott. 1969. *The Way to Rainy Mountain.* Albuquerque: University of New Mexico Press.

Morrison, Toni. 1988. *Beloved.* New York: New American Library.

———. 1973. *Sula.* New York: Knopf.

Needham, John Turberville. 1749. *Observations upon the Generation, Composition, and Decomposition of Animal and Vegetable Substances.* London.

Oates, Joyce Carol. 1988. "How I Contemplated the World from the Detroit House of Correction and Began My Life Over Again." In *The Norton Anthology of Contemporary Fiction* (see Coover), 355–67.

Owen, W. J. B., ed. 1974. *Wordsworth's Literary Criticism.* London: Routledge and Kegan Paul.

Polite, Frank. 1987. "Empty at the Heart of Things." In *American Poetry Since 1970: Up Late* (see Grahn), 446–47.

Porter, Katherine Anne. 1934. "The Grave." In *The Leaning Tower and Other Stories,* 69–78. New York: Harcourt.

Pynchon, Thomas. 1966. *The Crying of Lot 49.* New York: Bantam.

Reed, Ishmael. 1972. *Mumbo Jumbo.* New York: Doubleday.

Rhys, Jean. 1982. *Wide Sargasso Sea*. New York: Norton.

Robbins, Tom. 1988. "The Chink and the Clock People." In *The Norton Anthology of Contemporary Fiction* (see Coover), 410–23.

Roethke, Theodore. 1988a [1948]. "My Papa's Waltz." In *The Riverside Anthology of Literature* (see Browning), 1059.

———. 1988b. "Root Cellar." In *The Riverside Anthology of Literature* (see Browning), 1060.

Rossetti, Christina. 1979 [1859]. "Goblin Market." In Abrams et al., 2: 1523–35.

Salinger, J. D. 1984 [1951]. *The Catcher in the Rye*. New York: Bantam.

Shakespeare, William. 1988 [1604]. *Hamlet*. New York: Bantam.

———. 1980a [1600]. *The Merchant of Venice*. BBC production on PBS, 23 February.

———. 1968 [1604]. *Othello*. New York: Penguin. BBC production on PBS, 12 October 1981.

———. 1948 [1609]. "Sonnet 87." In *Shakespeare: The Complete Works*, edited by G. B. Harrison, 1611. New York: Harcourt.

———. 1972 [1609]. "Sonnet 116." In *The Complete Signet Classic Shakespeare*, 1750. New York: Harcourt.

———. 1980b [1596]. *The Taming of the Shrew*. BBC production on PBS, 16 January.

Shelley, Mary. 1981 [1818]. *Frankenstein*. New York: Bantam.

Shelley, Percy Bysshe. 1971 [1820, 1841]. "A Defense of Poetry." In *Critical Theory Since Plato*, edited by Hazard Adams, 498–513. New York: Harcourt Brace Jovanovich.

———. 1988 [1818]. "Ozymandias." In *The Riverside Anthology of Literature* (see Browning), 1031.

Shikbu, Lady Murasaki. 1985. *The Tale of Genji*. Translated by Edward Seidensticker. New York: Random.

Southworth, E.D.E.N. 1988. *The Hidden Hand*. New Brunswick: Rutgers University Press.

Steinbeck, John. 1937. *Of Mice and Men*. New York: Triangle.

Stoker, Bram. 1988 [1897]. *Dracula*. New York: Penguin.

Thomas, Lorenzo. 1987. "MMDCCXIIII/2." In *American Poetry Since 1970: Up Late* (see Grahn), 446–47.

Twain, Mark. 1985 [1884]. *The Adventures of Huckleberry Finn*. Edited by Walter Blair and Victor Fischer. Berkeley: University of California Press.

Walker, Alice. 1982. *The Color Purple*. New York: Harcourt.

———. [1973]. "Everyday Use." In *The Norton Anthology of Short Fiction*, edited by R. V. Cassill, 1631–39. New York: Norton.

———. 1974. "In Search of Our Mothers' Gardens." In Mitchell 25–32. Rev. and rpt. *Ms.* 2 (January 1974): 70ff. Rpt. *Radcliffe Quarterly* 60 (June 1974): 2–6.

———. 1983. *In Search of Our Mothers' Gardens: Womanist Prose*. New York: Harcourt.

———. 1979. "Other Voices, Other Moods." *Ms.* 7 (February). Rpt. as "Looking to the Side, and Back." *In Search of Our Mothers' Gardens,* 313–19.

Washington, Booker T. 1901. *Up from Slavery.* Rpt. in *Three Negro Classics* (see Johnson), 23–206.

Wenders, Wim, dir. 1983. *Hammett.* With Frederic Forrest, Peter Boyle, Marilu Henner and Elisha Cook, Jr. Zoetrope.

White, E. B. 1969 [1941]. "Once More to the Lake." In *Essays of E. B. White,* 197–202. Rpt. New York: Harper and Row.

Whitman, Walt. 1989 [1855]. "Song of Myself." In *Anthology of American Literature,* volume 2, edited by George McMichael, 34–78. New York: Macmillan.

Williams, William Carlos. 1983. "This Is Just to Say." In *The Norton Anthology of Poetry* (see Koch), 562.

Wilson, August. 1986. *Fences.* New York: New American Library.

Wollstonecraft, Mary. 1982 [1792]. *A Vindication of the Rights of Woman.* Edited by Miriam Brody. New York: Penguin.

Woolf, Virginia. 1974. "Death of a Moth." *The Death of the Moth and Other Essays.* New York: Harcourt.

———. 1929. *A Room of One's Own.* New York: Harcourt Brace Jovanovich.

Yeats, W. B. 1966. *Selected Poems and Two Plays.* Edited by M. L. Rosenthal. New York: Collier.

Theory, Pedagogy, and Other Research Sources

Adams, Hazard, ed. 1971. *Critical Theory Since Plato.* New York: Harcourt.

———, and Leroy Searle, eds. 1986. *Critical Theory Since 1965.* Tallahassee: Florida State University Press.

Alcoff, Linda. 1988. "Cultural Feminism versus Post-Structuralism: The Identity Crisis in Feminist Theory." In *Reconstructing the Academy: Women's Education and Women's Studies,* edited by Elizabeth Minnich, Jean O'Barr, and Rachel Rosenfeld, 257–88. Chicago: University of Chicago Press.

Althusser, Louis. 1971a. *Reading Capital.* Translated by Ben Brewster. New York: Pantheon.

———. 1971b. "Ideology and Ideological State Apparatuses." In *Lenin and Philosophy and Other Essays,* translated by Ben Brewster, 127–86. London: Monthly Review Press.

Anzaldúa, Gloria. 1983. "Foreword to the Second Edition." In Moraga and Anzaldúa, iv–v.

Appiah, Kwame Anthony. 1990. "Race." In Lentricchia and McLaughlin, 274–87.

Appignanesi, Richard, and Oscar Zarate. 1979. *Freud for Beginners.* New York: Pantheon.

Arac, Jonathan, Christian Messenger, and Gerald Sorenson. 1985. "The Place of Literary Theory in the Freshman Literature Class." *ADE Bulletin* 82 (Winter): 22–26.

Arac, Jonathan, et al., eds. 1983. *The Yale Critics: Deconstruction in America.* Minneapolis: University of Minnesota Press.

Arnold, Matthew. 1986 [1864; 1865]. "The Function of Criticism at the Present Time." In *The Norton Anthology of English Literature,* 5th ed., vol. 2, edited by M. H. Abrams et al., 1408–24. New York: Norton.

Aronowitz, Stanley, and Henry A. Giroux. 1985. *Education Under Siege.* South Hadley, MA: Bergin and Garvey.

Astin, Alexander W. 1985. "Involvement: The Cornerstone of Excellence." *Change* 17(4): 35–39.

Atkins, G. Douglas. 1989. "Introduction: Literary Theory, Critical Practice, and the Classroom." In Atkins and Morrow, 1–23.

———. 1983. *Reading Deconstruction: Deconstructive Reading.* Lexington: University of Kentucky Press.

———, and Michael L. Johnson, eds. 1985. *Writing and Reading Differently: Deconstruction and the Teaching of Composition and Literature.* Lawrence: University of Kansas Press.

———, and Laura Morrow, eds. 1989. *Contemporary Literary Theory.* Amherst: University of Massachusetts Press.

Auerbach, Nina. 1987. "Engorging the Patriarchy." In *Feminist Issues in Literary Scholarship,* edited by Shari Benstock, 150–60. Bloomington and Indianapolis: Indiana University Press.

Awkward, Michael. 1988. "Race, Gender, and the Politics of Reading." *Black American Literature Forum* 22: 5–27.

Baker, Houston A., Jr. 1984. *Blues, Ideology, and Afro-American Literature: A Vernacular Theory.* Chicago: University of Chicago Press.

———. 1987a. "In Dubious Battle." *New Literary History* 18: 363–69.

———. 1980. *The Journey Back: Issues in Black Literature and Criticism.* Chicago: University of Chicago Press.

———. 1987b. *Modernism and the Harlem Renaissance.* Chicago: University of Chicago Press.

———, ed. 1982. *Three American Literatures: Essays in Chicano, Native American, and Asian-American Literature for Teachers of American Literature.* Introduced by Walter J. Ong. New York: MLA.

Bakhtin, Mikhail. 1981a. *The Dialogic Imagination: Four Essays by M. M. Bakhtin.* Translated by Michael Holquist and Caryl Emerson. Edited by Holquist. Austin: University of Texas Press.

———. 1981b. "Discourse in the Novel." In *The Dialogic Imagination: Four Essays by M. M. Bakhtin,* edited by Michael Holquist, translated by Caryl Emerson and Michael Holquist, 259–422. Austin: University of Texas Press.

———. 1986a. "The Problem of Speech Genres." *Speech Genres and Other Late Essays.* 60–102.

———. 1984a. *Problems of Dostoevsky's Poetics.* Translated and edited by Caryl Emerson. Minneapolis: University of Minnesota Press.

———. 1984b. *Rabelais and His World.* Translated by Helene Iswolsky. Bloomington: Indiana University Press.

———. 1986b. *Speech Genres and Other Late Essays.* Translated by Vern W.

McGee. Edited by Caryl Emerson and Michael Holquist. Austin: University of Texas Press.

Ballinger, Franchot. 1984. "A Matter of Emphasis: Teaching the 'Literature' in Native American Literature Courses." *American Indian Culture and Research Journal* 8(2): 1–12.

Baraka, Amiri. 1966. "The Myth of a 'Negro Literature.'" In *Home: Social Essays,* 105–15. New York: Morrow.

———. 1979. "The Revolutionary Tradition in Afro-American Literature." In *Selected Plays and Prose of Amiri Baraka/LeRoi Jones,* 242–51. New York: Morrow.

Barnes, Linda Laube. 1990. "Gender Bias in Teachers' Written Comments." In Gabriel and Smithson, 140–54.

Barney, Richard A. 1987. "Uncanny Criticism in the United States." In Natoli 1987, 177–212.

Barthes, Roland. 1977. "The Death of the Author." In *Image—Music—Text,* translated by Stephen Heath, 142–48. New York: Hill and Wang.

———. 1979. "Lecture in Inauguration of the Chair of Semiology, College de France." Translated by Richard Howard. *October* 8: 3–16.

Batsleer, Janet, et al., eds. 1986. *Rewriting English: The Politics of Gender and Class.* New York: Routledge.

Bauer, Dale M. 1990. "The Other 'F' Word: The Feminist in the Classroom." *College English* 52: 385–96.

Beach, Richard. 1989. *Research on the Learning and Teaching of Literature: Selected Bibliography.* Albany, NY: SUNY–Albany Center for the Learning and Teaching of Literature.

Beaven, Mary H. 1977. "Individualized Goal Setting, Self-Evaluation, and Peer Evaluation." In *Evaluating Writing: Describing, Measuring, Judging,* edited by Charles R. Cooper and Lee Odell, 135–56. Urbana: NCTE.

Belenky, Mary Field, Blythe McVicker Clinchy, Nancy Rule Goldberger, and Jill Mattuck Tarule. 1986. *Women's Ways of Knowing: The Development of Self, Voice, and Mind.* New York: Basic Books.

Belsey, Catherine. 1980a. *Critical Practice.* London and New York: Methuen.

———. 1980b. "Deconstructing the Text." In *Critical Practice,* 103–24.

Benhabib, Seyla. 1986. "Autonomy as Mimetic Reconciliation." In *Critique, Norm, and Utopia: A Study of the Foundations of Critical Theory,* 186–233. New York: Columbia University Press.

Benjamin, Walter. 1969. "Theses on the Philosophy of History." In *Illuminations,* translated by Harry Zohn, 253–64. New York: Schocken.

Benstock, Shari, ed. 1987. *Feminist Issues in Literary Scholarship.* Bloomington: Indiana University Press.

Bentley, C. F. 1972. "The Monster in the Bedroom: Sexual Symbolism in Bram Stoker's *Dracula.*" *Literature and Psychology* 22(1): 27–34.

Berlin, James. 1988. "Rhetoric and Ideology in the Writing Class." College English 50(5): 477–95.

———. 1987. *Rhetoric and Reality: Writing Instruction in American Colleges, 1900–1985.* Carbondale: Southern Illinois University Press.

Berthoff, Ann E. 1982. *Forming/Thinking/Writing*. Portsmouth, NH: Boynton/Cook.

Bezucha, Robert J. 1985. "Feminist Pedagogy as a Subversive Activity." In Culley and Portuges, 81–95.

Bialostosky, Don. 1989. "Dialogic Criticism." In Atkins and Morrow, 214–28.

———. 1984. *Making Tales: The Poetics of Wordsworth's Narrative Experiments*. Chicago: University of Chicago Press.

———. 1986. "Teaching Wordsworth's Poetry from the Perspective of a Poetics of Speech." In *Approaches to Teaching Wordsworth's Poetry*, edited by Spencer Hall and Jonathan Ramsey, 153–56. New York: MLA.

Birch, Thomas H. 1990. "The Incarceration of Wildness: Wilderness Areas as Prisons." *Environmental Ethics* 12: 3–26.

Bizzell, Patricia. 1986. "On the Possibility of a Unified Theory of Composition and Literature." *Rhetoric Review* 4(2): 174–80.

Bleich, David. 1988. *The Double Perspective: Language, Literacy, and Social Relations*. New York: Oxford University Press.

———. 1980. "The Identity of Pedagogy and Research in the Study of Response to Literature." *College English* 42: 350–66.

———. 1976. "Pedagogical Directions in Subjective Criticism." *College English* 37: 454–67.

———. 1971. "Psychological Bases of Learning from Literature." *College English* 33: 32–45.

———. 1975a. *Readings and Feelings: An Introduction to Subjective Criticism*. Urbana: NCTE.

———. 1975b. "The Subjective Character of Critical Interpretation." *College English* 36: 739–55.

———. 1978. *Subjective Criticism*. Baltimore: Johns Hopkins University Press.

Bloom, Harold. 1973. *The Anxiety of Influence: A Theory of Poetry*. New York: Oxford University Press.

Booth, Wayne. 1964. "Criticism in Teaching Literature." *College English* 27: 1–13.

———. 1986. "Pluralism in the Classroom." *Critical Inquiry* 12: 468–79.

Bourdieu, Pierre, and J. C. Passeron. 1977. *Reproduction in Education, Society, and Culture*. Translated by Richard Nice. Beverly Hills, CA: Sage Publications.

Bové, Paul. 1986. *Intellectuals in Power: A Genealogy of Critical Humanism*. New York: Columbia University Press.

Brand, Stewart. 1987. *The Media Lab: Inventing the Future at MIT*. New York.

Brent, Harold. 1972. "Comment." *College English* 34: 212–14.

Bretz, Mary Lee, and Margaret Persin. 1987. "The Application of Critical Theory to Literature at the Introductory Level." *Modern Language Journal* 71(2): 165–70.

Broad, Yolanda Stern. 1988. "Introduction. Constructing Critical Readers—Pedagogical Approaches to Literature That Make Use of Literary Theory." *ADFL Bulletin* 19(2): 4–6.

Brooker, Peter, and Peter Humm. 1989. *Dialogue and Difference: English into the Nineties*. London and New York: Routledge.

Brooks, Cleanth. 1947. "Criticism, History, and Critical Relativism." In *The Well Wrought Urn*, 215–47. New York: Harcourt.

———, and Robert Penn Warren. 1960 [1938]. *Understanding Poetry*. 3rd ed. New York: Holt, Rinehart and Winston.

Brooks, Peter. 1987. "The Idea of a Psychoanalytic Literary Criticism." In Rimmon-Kenan, 1–18.

Bruffee, Kenneth A. 1984. "Collaborative Learning and the 'Conversation of Mankind.' " *College English* 46: 635–52.

———. 1973. "Collaborative Learning: Some Practical Models." *College English* 34: 634–43.

———. 1985. "Liberal Education, Scholarly Community, and the Authority of Knowledge." *Liberal Education* 71: 231–39.

———. 1972. "The Way Out: A Critical Survey of Innovations in College Teaching, with Special Reference to the December 1971 Issue of *CE*." *College English* 33: 457–70.

Buckler, Patricia Prandini. 1985. "Reading, Writing, and Psycholinguistics: An Integrated Approach Using Joyce's 'Counterparts.' " *Teaching English in the Two-Year College* 12: 22–31.

Bueva, L. P. 1981. *Man: His Behavior and Social Relations*. Edited by Yu. Davydov. Moscow: Progress.

Buffon, Count de [George-Louis Leclerc]. 1791. *Natural History*. 9 vols. 3rd ed. Translated by William Smellie. London: R. Strahan and T. Cadell.

Bulkin, Elly. 1979. " 'A Whole New Poetry Beginning Here': Teaching Lesbian Poetry." *College English* 40: 874–88.

Bunch, Charlotte, and Sandra Pollack, eds. 1983. *Learning Our Way: Essays in Feminist Education*. Trumansburg, NY: Crossing Press.

Burke, Kenneth. 1989. "Literature as Equipment for Living." In *The Critical Tradition: Classic Texts and Contemporary Trends*, edited by David H. Richter, 512–17. New York: St. Martin's.

———. 1969. *A Rhetoric of Motives*. Berkeley and Los Angeles: University of California Press.

Butler, Marilyn. 1985. "Against Tradition: The Case for a Particularized Historical Method." In McGann 1985b, 25–47.

Cahalan, James M. 1988. "James Joyce and Joycean Scholarship: A Historical View." In *The Irish Novel: A Critical History*, 127–78. Boston: Twayne.

Cain, William E. 1984. *The Crisis in Criticism: Theory, Literature, and Reform in English Studies*. Baltimore: Johns Hopkins University Press.

Caraher, Brian. [1989] in press. "Theory as Pedagogy: Four New Anthologies of Literary Criticism and Theory." In *Yearbook of Comparative and General Literature*, vol. 38. Bloomington: Indiana University Press.

Carter, Margaret L., ed. 1988. *"Dracula," the Vampire and the Critics*. Ann Arbor: UMI Research Press.

Carter, Steven R. 1988. "Inter-ethnic Issues in Lorraine Hansberry's *The Sign in Sidney Brustein's Window*." *Explorations in Ethnic Studies* 11(2): 1–12.

Castle, Terry J. 1979. "Lab'ring Bards: Birth *Topoi* and English Poetics." *JEGP* 78: 193–208.

Cawelti, John G. 1965. *Apostles of the Self-made Man: Changing Concepts of Success in America.* Chicago: University of Chicago Press.

———, and Nancy Williams. 1990. *Literary Theory in the Classroom.* Special issue of *Iowa English Bulletin.* Rpt. Urbana: NCTE.

Chew, Charles, Rosanne DeFabio, and Patricia Honsbury. 1986. *Reader Response in the Classroom.* Albany: New York State English Council.

Chodorow, Nancy. 1978. *The Reproduction of Mothering: Psychoanalysis and the Sociology of Gender.* Berkeley: University of California Press.

Christian, Barbara. 1984. "Alice Walker: The Black Woman Artist as Wayward." In *Black Women Writers (1950–1980): A Critical Evaluation,* edited by Mari Evans, 457–77. Garden City, NY: Doubleday.

———. 1985. *Black Feminist Criticism: Perspectives on Black Women Writers.* New York: Pergamon Press.

———. 1987. "The Race for Theory." *Cultural Critique* 6: 51–63.

———. 1986. "We Are the Ones That We Have Been Waiting For: Political Content in Alice Walker's Novels." *Women's Studies International Forum* 9: 421–26.

Clark, Katerina, and Michael Holquist. 1984. *Mikhail Bakhtin.* Cambridge, MA: Harvard University Press.

Clifford, John. 1980a. "Beyond Subjectivity: Transactional Reading and Writing." *Teaching English in the Two-Year College* 7: 95–100.

———. 1990. "Enacting a Critical Literacy." In *The Right to Literacy,* edited by James Slevin, 255–61. New York: MLA.

———. 1989. "The Reader's Text: Responding to Loren Eiseley's 'The Running Man.' " In *Literary Nonfiction,* edited by Chris Anderson, 247–61. Carbondale: Southern Illinois University Press.

———. 1986. "A Response Pedagogy for Noncanonical Literature." *Reader: Essays in Reader-Oriented Theory, Criticism, and Pedagogy* 15: 48–61.

———. 1980b. "Using Intuition in the Composing Process." *English Record* 31: 6–9.

———, and John Schilb. 1985. "Composition Theory and Literary Theory." In *Scholarship in Composition,* edited by Ben W. McClelland and Timothy R. Donovan, 45–67. New York: MLA.

Cohen, Ralph, et al., eds. 1988. *New Literary History International Bibliography of Literary Theory and Criticism.* Baltimore: Johns Hopkins University Press.

Coles, William E., Jr. 1978. *The Plural I.* New York: Holt.

———. 1974. *Teaching Composing.* Rochelle Park, NJ: Hayden.

Combahee River Collective. "A Black Feminist Statement, April 1977." Rpt. in Jagger and Rothenberg, 202.

Comley, Nancy. 1990. "Reading and Writing Genders." In Henricksen and Morgan, 179–92.

———. 1990. Review of Engell and Perkins. *ADE Bulletin* 95: 45–48.

Comprone, Joseph J. 1987. "Literary Theory and Composition." In *Teaching*

Composition: Twelve Bibliographical Essays, edited by Gary Tate, 291–330. Fort Worth: Texas Christian University Press.

Connolly, Francis X. 1974. "Literary Theory and the Teaching of Literature." *English Record* 25(4): 65–70.

Cooper, Charles R., ed. 1985. *Researching Response to Literature and the Teaching of Literature: Points of Departure*. Norwood, NY: Ablex.

Corcoran, Bill, and Emrys Evans, eds. 1987. *Readers, Texts, and Teachers*. Upper Montclair, NJ: Boynton/Cook.

Corder, Jim W. 1981. "Rhetoric and Literary Study: Some Lines of Inquiry." *College Composition and Communication* 32: 13–20.

Coughlin, Ellen K. 1989. "Scholars in the Humanities Are Disheartened by the Course of Debate over Their Disciplines." *The Chronicle of Higher Education* 36(2): A1, A14–15.

Cross, Dolores E., Gwendolyn C. Baker, Lindley J. Stiles, eds. 1977. *Teaching in a Multicultural Society: Perspectives and Professional Strategies*. New York: Free Press.

Crowley, Sharon. 1990. *The Methodical Memory: Invention in Current-Traditional Rhetoric*. Carbondale: Southern Illinois University Press

———. 1989. *A Teacher's Introduction to Deconstruction*. Urbana: NCTE.

Culler, Jonathan. 1982. *On Deconstruction: Theory and Criticism after Structuralism*. Ithaca, NY: Cornell University Press.

———. 1981. *The Pursuit of Signs*. Ithaca, NY: Cornell University Press.

———. 1975. *Structuralist Poetics: Structuralism, Linguistics, and the Study of Literature*. Ithaca, NY: Cornell University Press.

Culley, Margo, and Catherine Portuges, eds. 1985. *Gendered Subjects: The Dynamics of Feminist Teaching*. Boston: Routledge.

Davis, Robert Con. 1987. "Freud's Resistance to Reading and Teaching." *College English* 49: 621–27.

———. 1990. "A Manifesto for Oppositional Pedagogy: Freire, Bourdieu, Merod, and Graff." In Henricksen and Morgan, 248–67.

———, and Laurie Fink, eds. 1989. *Literary Criticism and Theory: The Greeks to the Present*. New York: Longman.

Davis, Walter. 1989. *Inwardness and Existence: Subjectivity in/and Hegel, Heidegger, Marx, and Freud*. Madison: University of Wisconsin Press.

de Lauretis, Teresa. 1987. *Technologies of Gender: Essays on Theory, Film, and Fiction*. Bloomington: Indiana University Press.

Delaney, Paul, and George P. Landow, eds. 1991. *Hypermedia and Literary Studies*. Cambridge, MA: MIT Press.

Deleuze, Gilles and Felix Guatteri. 1977. *Anti-Oedipus: Capitalism and Schizophrenia*. Translated by Robert Hurley, Mark Seem, and Helen R. Lane. New York: Viking.

de Man, Paul. 1979. *Allegories of Reading*. New Haven: Yale University Press.

Derrida, Jacques. 1982. *Margins of Philosophy*. Translated by Alan Bass. Chicago: University of Chicago Press.

———. 1976. *Of Grammatology*. Translated by Gayatri Spivak. Baltimore: Johns Hopkins University Press.

———. 1981. *Positions*. Translated by Alan Bass. Chicago: University of Chicago Press.

Donahue, Patricia and Ellen Quandahl. 1987. "Freud and the Teaching of Interpretation." *College English* 49: 641–49.

———, eds. 1989. *Reclaiming Pedagogy: The Rhetoric of the Classroom*. Carbondale: Southern Illinois University Press.

Dowling, William C. 1984. *Jameson, Althusser, Marx: An Introduction to the Political Unconscious*. Ithaca, NY: Cornell University Press.

———. 1987. "Teaching Eighteenth-Century Literature in the Pocockian Moment (Or, Flimnap on the Tightrope, Kramnick to the Rescue)." *College English* 49(5): 523–32.

Downing, David B., ed. 1992 (forthcoming). *Changing Classroom Practices: Resources for Literary and Cultural Studies*. Urbana: University of Illinois Press.

———. 1987. "The Cultural Politics of Graff's History of Literary Studies." *Critical Exchange* 23: 45–63.

———. 1987. "Deconstruction's Scruples: The Politics of Enlightened Critique." *Diacritics* 17(3): 66–81.

Dunlop, Donald. 1975. "Popular Culture and Methodology." *Journal of Popular Culture* 9: 375–83.

Durant, Alan. 1985. "Modern Literary Theory in the Teaching of Literature." *Prose Studies* 8(1): 58–78.

———, and Nigel Fabb. 1990. *Literary Studies in Action*. London and New York: Routledge.

Durrant, Geoffrey. 1978. "An Elementary Strategy for Teaching Wordsworth's Poetry." *Wordsworth Circle* 9: 352–53.

Dworkin, Susan. 1985. "The Strange and Wonderful Story of the Making of 'The Color Purple.' " *Ms.* 13: 65–70, 95.

Eagleton, Terry. 1978a. *Criticism and Ideology: A Study in Marxist Literary Theory*. Minneapolis: University of Minnesota Press.

———. 1983. *Literary Theory: An Introduction*. Minneapolis: University of Minnesota Press.

———. 1985/86. "The Subject of Literature." *Cultural Critique* 2: 95–104.

Eastman, Arthur M., et al., eds. 1984. *The Norton Reader*. 6th ed. New York: Norton.

Eco, Umberto. 1979. *The Role of the Reader: Explorations in the Semiotics of Texts*. Bloomington: Indiana University Press.

Eddins, Dwight. 1989. "Yellow Wood, Diverging Pedagogies; Or, The Joy of Text." *College English* 51: 571–76.

Elbow, Peter. 1991. *What Is English?* Urbana and New York: NCTE and MLA.

Emig, Janet. 1990. "Our Missing Theory." In Moran and Penfield, 87–96.

Engell, James, and David Perkins, eds. 1988. *Teaching Literature: What Is Needed Now*. Cambridge, MA: Harvard University Press.

Evans, Nancy Burr. 1973. "Looking Back Over Four Years: A Student's Approach to Literature." *College English* 35: 240–55.

Ewell, Barbara C. 1990. "Empowering Otherness: Feminist Criticism and the Academy." In Henricksen and Morgan, 43–62.

Farrell, Edmund J., and James R. Squire, eds. 1990. *Transactions with Literature: A Fifty-Year Perspective*. Urbana: NCTE.

Farson, Daniel. 1976. *The Man Who Wrote "Dracula": A Biography of Bram Stoker*. New York: St. Martin's.

Felman, Shoshana. 1987. *Jacques Lacan and the Adventure of Insight: Psychoanalysis in Contemporary Culture*. Cambridge: Harvard University Press.

———, ed. 1982a. *Literature and Psychoanalysis: The Question of Reading Otherwise*. Baltimore: Johns Hopkins University Press.

———. 1982b. "Psychoanalysis and Education: Teaching Terminable and Interminable." *Yale French Studies* 63: 21–44.

Ferry, Anne. 1983. *The "Inward" Language: Sonnets of Wyatt, Sidney, Shakespeare, Donne*. Chicago: University of Chicago Press.

Fetterley, Judith. 1978. *The Resisting Reader: A Feminist Approach to American Fiction*. Bloomington: Indiana University Press.

Fiedler, Leslie A. 1974. "Is There A Majority Literature?" *CEA Critic* 36(4): 3–8.

Fink, Thomas A. 1985. "Reading Deconstructively in the Two-Year College Literature Class." *Teaching English in the Two-Year College* 12: 64–71.

Fish, Stanley. 1989. *Doing What Comes Naturally: Change, Rhetoric, and the Practice of Literary and Legal Studies*. Durham: Duke University Press.

———. 1980a. "Interpreting the Variorum." In *Is There a Text in This Class?: The Authority of Interpretive Communities*, 147–73. Cambridge, MA: Harvard University Press.

———. 1980b. *Is There a Text in This Class? The Authority of Interpretive Communities*. Cambridge, MA: Harvard University Press.

———. 1980c [1970]. "Literature in the Reader: Affective Stylistics." *New Literary History* 2: 123–62. Rpt. in *Is There a Text in This Class? The Authority of Interpretive Communities*, 21–67. Cambridge, MA: Harvard University Press.

———. 1971. *Surprised by Sin: The Reader in "Paradise Lost."* Berkeley: University of California Press.

Fisher, Dexter, and Robert B. Stepto, eds. 1979. *Afro-American Literature: The Reconstruction of Instruction*. New York: MLA.

Fitch, Raymond E. 1981. "Literary Theory in the English Classroom." (Special issue.) *Focus: Teaching English Arts* 7(2): 1–96.

Flynn, Elizabeth A. 1990a. "The Classroom as Interpretive Community: Teaching Reader-Response Theory and Composition Theory to Preprofessional Undergraduates." In Henricksen and Morgan, 193–215.

———. 1990b. "Composing as a Woman." In Gabriel and Smithson, 112–26.

———. 1983. "Composing Responses to Literary Texts: A Process Approach." *College Composition and Communication* 34: 342–48.

———, and Patrocino P. Schweichart, eds. 1986. *Gender and Reading: Essays on Readers, Texts, Contexts*. Baltimore: Johns Hopkins University Press.

Fong, Bobby. 1990. "Local Canons: Professing Literature at the Small Liberal Arts College." In Moran and Penfield, 200–10.

Ford, George H. 1965. *Dickens and His Readers: Aspects of Novel-Criticism Since 1836*. New York: Norton.

———, and Sylvère Monod, eds. 1966. *Charles Dickens'* Hard Times. New York: Norton.

Foucault, Michel. 1972. *The Archaeology of Knowledge*. Translated by A. M. Sheridan Smith. New York, Pantheon.

———. 1979 [1978]. *Discipline and Punish: The Birth of the Prison*. Translated by Alan Sheridan. New York: Pantheon. Rpt. New York: Random House.

———. 1971. *The Order of Things: An Archaeology of the Human Sciences*. New York: Pantheon.

———. 1977. "What Is an Author?" In *Language, Counter-Memory, Practice*, edited by Donald F. Bouchard, translated by Bouchard and Sherry Simon, 113–38. Ithaca: Cornell University Press.

Fraistat, Neil. 1986. "Introduction: The Place of the Book and the Book as Place." In *Poems in Their Place: The Intertextuality and Order of Poetic Collections*, edited by Neil Fraistat, 3–17. Chapel Hill: University of North Carolina Press.

Franklin, Bruce. 1970. "The Teaching of Literature in the Highest Academies of the Land." *College English* 31: 548–57.

Franzosa, John C., Jr. 1973. "Criticism and the Uses of Psychoanalysis." *College English* 34: 927–33.

Freedman, Carl. 1987. "Marxist Theory, Radical Pedagogy, and the Reification of Thought." *College English* 49: 70–82.

Freire, Paulo. 1973. "Extension or Communication." In *Education for Critical Consciousness*, translated by Louise Bigwood and Margaret Marshall, 91–164. New York: Continuum.

———. 1970. *Pedagogy of the Oppressed*. Translated by Myra Ramos. New York: Continuum.

———. 1985. *The Politics of Education: Culture, Power, and Liberation*. Translated by Donaldo Macedo. Introduction by Henry Giroux. South Hadley, MA: Bergin and Garvey.

Freud, Sigmund. 1925 [1911]. "Formulations Regarding the Two Principles in Mental Functioning." In *Collected Papers*, vol. 4, edited by Ernest Jones, translated by Joan Riviere. London: Hogarth.

———. 1960. *The Psychopathology of Everyday Life*. Edited by James Strachey. New York: Norton.

Friedman, Susan Stanford. 1985. "Authority in the Feminist Classroom: A Contradiction in Terms?" In Culley and Portuges, 203–8.

———. 1989. "Creativity and the Childbirth Metaphor: Gender Difference in Literary Discourse." In *Speaking of Gender*, edited by Elaine Showalter, 73–100. New York: Routledge.

Froula, Christine. 1983. "When Eve Reads Milton: Undoing the Canonical Economy." *Critical Inquiry* 10: 321–47.

Frye, Northrop. 1973. "The Critical Path: An Essay on the Social Context of

Literary Criticism." In *Issues in Contemporary Criticism*, edited by Gregory T. Polletta, 50–57. Boston: Little.

Gabriel, Susan. 1990. "Gender, Reading, and Writing: Assignments, Expectations, and Responses." In Gabriel and Smithson, 127–39.

———, and Isaiah Smithson. 1990. *Gender in the Classroom: Power and Pedagogy*. Urbana: University of Illinois Press.

Gadamer, Hans Georg. 1986. *Truth and Method*. 1960. Translated by Garrett Barden and John Cumming. New York: Crossroad.

Gallagher, Brian. 1985. "Guest Editorial: On the Utility of Literature." *Teaching English in the Two-Year College* 12(1): 3–4.

Gallop, Jane. 1982. *The Daughter's Seduction: Feminism and Psychoanalysis*. Ithaca, NY: Cornell University Press.

Galvani, Luigi. 1935. "The Electric Current." In *A Source Book in Physics*, edited by William Francis Magie, 420–27. New York: McGraw-Hill.

Garner, Shirley Nelson, Claire Kahane, and Madelon Sprengnether, eds. 1985. *The (M)other Tongue: Essays in Feminist Psychoanalytic Interpretation*. Ithaca, NY: Cornell University Press.

Gates, Henry Louis, Jr. 1987a. "Authority, (White) Power and the (Black) Critic: Or, It's All Greek to Me." *Cultural Critique* 7: 19–46.

———, ed. 1984. *Black Literature and Literary Theory*. New York: Methuen.

———. 1987b. *Figures in Black: Words, Signs, and the "Racial" Self*. New York: Oxford University Press.

———. 1990. "The Master's Pieces: On Canon Formation and the Afro-American Tradition." In Moran and Penfield, 55–75.

———. 1988. *The Signifying Monkey: A Theory of Afro-American Literary Criticism*. New York: Oxford University Press.

———. 1987c. " 'What's Love Got To Do With It?': Critical Theory, Integrity, and the Black Idiom." *New Literary History* 18: 345–62.

Gay, Peter, ed. 1989. *The Freud Reader*. New York: Norton.

Gebhard, Jerry G., Sergio Caitan, and Robert Oprandy. 1990. "Beyond Prescription: The Student Teacher as Investigator." In *Second Language Teacher Education*, edited by Jack C. Richards and David Nunan, 16–25. Cambridge, MA: Cambridge University Press.

Geertz, Clifford. 1973. *The Interpretation of Cultures: Selected Essays*. New York: Basic Books.

———. 1983. *Local Knowledge: Further Essays in Interpretive Anthropology*. New York: Basic Books.

Gelfand, Elissa D. 1985. *French Feminist Criticism: Women, Language, and Literature: An Annotated Bibliography*. New York: Garland.

Gilbert, Pam. 1989. *Writing, Schooling, and Deconstruction: From Voice to Text in the Classroom*. New York: Routledge.

Gilbert, Sandra, and Susan Gubar. 1979. *The Madwoman in the Attic: The Woman Writer and the Nineteenth-Century Literary Imagination*. New Haven: Yale University Press.

Gill, Glenda. 1974. "Teaching Black Literature on the College Campus." *College Composition and Communication* 25: 264–68.

Gilligan, Carol. 1982. *In a Different Voice: Psychological Theory and Women's Development*. Cambridge, MA: Harvard University Press.

Giroux, Henry A. 1988. *Schooling and the Struggle for Public Life: Critical Pedagogy in the Modern Age*. Minneapolis: University of Minnesota Press.

———. 1983. *Theory and Resistance in Education: A Pedagogy for the Opposition*. South Hadley, MA: Bergin and Garvey.

Goldmann, Lucien. 1956. *Le Dieu Cache*. Paris: Gallimard.

Goldstein, Phillip. 1990. *The Politics of Literary Theory: An Introduction to Marxist Criticism*. Gainesville: Florida State University Press.

Goswami, Dixie, and Peter R. Stillman. 1987. *Reclaiming the Classroom: Teacher Research as an Agency for Change*. Portsmouth, NH: Boynton/Cook, Heinemann.

Graff, Gerald. 1989. "The Future of Theory in the Teaching of Literature." In *The Future of Literary Theory*, edited by Ralph Cohen, 250–67. New York: Routledge.

———. 1987. *Professing Literature: An Institutional History*. Chicago: University of Chicago Press.

———. 1986. "Taking Cover in Coverage." *Profession 86*: 41–45.

———, and Reginald Gibbons. 1985. *Criticism in the University*. Evanston, IL: Northwestern University Press.

Greenblatt, Stephen. 1982. "Introduction." In "The Forms of Power and the Power of Forms in the Renaissance." (Special issue.) *Genre* 15: 1–4.

———. 1980. *Renaissance Self-Fashioning*. Chicago: University of Chicago Press.

———. 1988. *Shakespearean Negotiations: The Circulation of Social Energy in Renaissance England*. Berkeley: University of California Press.

Greene, Gayle, and Coppelia Kahn, eds. 1985. *Making a Difference: Feminist Literary Criticism*. New York: Methuen.

GRIP Report. 1982. Vols. 1–7: 1982– . Miami, OH: The Society for Critical Exchange.

Harari, Josué V., ed. and trans. 1979. *Textual Strategies: Perspectives in Post-structuralist Criticism*. Ithaca, NY: Cornell University Press.

Harding, Sandra. 1986. "The Instability of the Analytical Categories in Feminist Theory." *Signs* 1: 645–64.

Harkin, Patricia. 1991. "The Post-disciplinary Politics of Lore." In Harkin and Schilb, 124–38.

———, and John Schilb, eds. 1991. *Contending with Words: Composition and Rhetoric in the Postmodern Age*. New York: MLA.

Harold, Brent. 1972. "Beyond Student-Centered Teaching: The Dialectical Materialist Form of a Literature Course." *College English* 34: 200–14.

Harris, Joseph. 1987. "The Plural Text/The Plural Self: Roland Barthes and William Coles." *College English* 49: 58–70.

Hartman, Geoffrey, ed. 1979. *Deconstruction and Criticism*. London: Seabury Press.

———, ed. 1985. *Psychoanalysis and the Question of the Text*. Baltimore: Johns Hopkins University Press.

Hatlen, Burton. 1980. "On the Return of the Oppressed/Repressed in Bram Stoker's *Dracula*." In Carter, 117–35.

Hawkes, Terence. 1977. *Structuralism and Semiotics*. Berkeley: University of California Press.

Henricksen, Bruce. 1990. "Teaching against the Grain." In Henricksen and Morgan, 28–39.

———, and Thaïs E. Morgan, eds. 1990. *Reorientations: Critical Theories and Pedagogies*. Urbana: University of Illinois Press.

Hernton, Calvin. 1984. "The Sexual Mountain and Black Women Writers." *Black American Literature Forum* 18: 139–45.

Higham, John. 1970. "The Schism in American Scholarship." In *Writing American History: Essays on Modern Scholarship*, 3–24. Bloomington: Indiana University Press.

Hillocks, George, Jr. 1989. "Literary Texts in Classrooms." In *From Socrates to Software: The Teacher as Text and the Text as Teacher*, edited by Philip W. Jackson and Sophie Haroutunian-Gordon, 135–58. Eighty-eighth yearbook. Chicago: National Society for the Study of Education.

Hirsch, E. D., Jr. 1976. *The Aims of Interpretation*. Chicago: University of Chicago Press.

———. 1987. *Cultural Literacy: What Every American Needs to Know*. Boston: Houghton Mifflin.

Hiura, Barbara. 1988. Review of Werner Sollors, *Beyond Ethnicity: Consent and Descent in American Culture*. *Explorations in Sights and Sounds* 8: 74–75.

Hoffman, Frederick. 1965. "The Use of Criticism in the Teaching of Literature: A Reply." *College English* 27: 13–17.

Hoffmann, Leonore Noll. 1986. "Student Readers and the Civil War Letters of an Ohio Woman." *Reader* 15: 34–47.

———, and Margo Culley. 1985. *Women's Personal Narratives: Essays in Criticism and Pedagogy*. New York: MLA.

———, and Deborah Rosenfelt. 1982. *Teaching Women's Literature from a Regional Perspective*. New York: MLA.

Holland, Norman N. 1968. *The Dynamics of Literary Response*. New York: Oxford University Press.

———. 1975a. *5 Readers Reading*. New Haven: Yale University Press.

———. 1966. *Psychoanalysis and Shakespeare*. New York: McGraw.

———, and Murray Schwartz. 1975b. "The Delphi Seminar." *College English* 36: 789–800.

Holland, Robert M., Jr. 1989. "Anonymous Journals in Literature Survey Courses." *Teaching English in the Two-Year College* 16: 236–40.

Holquist, Michael. 1986. "The Surd Heard: Bakhtin and Derrida." In *Literature and History: Theoretical Problems and Russian Case Studies*, edited by Gary Saul Morson, 137–56. Stanford: Stanford University Press.

Holub, Robert C. 1984. *Reception Theory: A Critical Introduction*. New York: Methuen.

Honey, Maureen, ed. 1989. *Shadowed Dreams: Women's Poetry of the Harlem Renaissance*. New Brunswick: Rutgers University Press.

Hooks, Bell. 1985. "Black Women Writing: Creating More Space." *SAGE* 2: 44–46.

Horner, Winifred Bryan, ed. 1983. *Composition and Literature: Bridging the Gap*. Chicago: University of Chicago Press.

Howard, Jean E. 1986. "The New Historicism in Renaissance Studies." *English Literary Renaissance* 16: 13–43.

Hull, Gloria T., Patricia Bell Scott, and Barbara Smith, eds. 1982. *All the Women Are White, All the Blacks Are Men, but Some of Us Are Brave*. Old Westbury, NY: The Feminist Press.

Hurlbert, C. Mark, and Michael Blitz. 1991. *Composition and Resistance*. Portsmouth, NH: Boynton/Cook, Heinemann.

Hutter, Albert D. 1986. "Literature, Writing, and Psychoanalysis: A Reciprocity of Influence." In Nelson, 201–44.

Iggers, Georg C. 1968. *The German Conception of History*. Middletown: Wesleyan University Press.

Iser, Wolfgang. 1978. *The Act of Reading: A Theory of Aesthetic Response*. Baltimore: Johns Hopkins University Press.

———. 1974. *The Implied Reader: Patterns of Communication in Prose from Bunyan to Beckett*. Baltimore: Johns Hopkins University Press.

Jagger, Alison M., and Paula S. Rothenberg, eds. 1984. *Feminist Frameworks: Alternative Accounts of the Relations between Women and Men*. New York: McGraw-Hill.

Jameson, Fredric. 1976. "Criticism in History." In *The Weapons of Criticism*, edited by Norman Rudich, 31–50. Palo Alto: Ramparts.

———. 1982. "Interview." *Diacritics* 12: 72–91.

———. 1971. *Marxism and Form: Twentieth-Century Dialectical Theories of Literature*. Princeton: Princeton University Press.

———. 1979. "Marxism and Historicism." *New Literary History* 11: 41–73.

———. 1981. *The Political Unconscious: Narrative as a Socially Symbolic Act*. Ithaca: Cornell University Press.

———. 1984. "Postmodernism, or the Cultural Logic of Late Capitalism." *New Left Review* 146: 53–92.

JanMohamed, Abdul. 1983. *Manichean Aesthetics: The Politics of Literature in Colonial Africa*. Amherst: University of Massachusetts Press.

Jardine, Alice. 1985. *Gynesis: Configurations of Woman and Modernity*. Ithaca, NY: Cornell University Press.

———, and Paul Smith, eds. 1987. *Men in Feminism*. New York and London: Methuen.

Jarratt, Susan C. 1990. *Rereading the Sophists: Classical Rhetoric Refigured*. Carbondale: Southern Illinois University Press.

Jauss, Hans Robert. 1989 [1983]. "Historia Calamitatum et Fortunarum Mearum or: A Paradigm Shift in Literary Study." In *The Future of Literary Theory*, edited by Ralph Cohen, 112–28. New York: Routledge.

———. 1970. "History of Art and Pragmatic History." In Jauss 1982, 56–75.

———. 1967. "Literary History as a Challenge to Literary Theory." In Jauss 1982, 3–45.

———. 1982. *Toward an Aesthetic of Reception*. Translated by Timothy Bahti. Minneapolis: University of Minnesota Press.

Jay, Gregory S. 1991. "The End of American Literature: Toward a Multicultural Practice." *College English* 53: 264–81.

———. 1987. "The Subject of Pedagogy: Lessons in Psychoanalysis and Politics." *College English* 49: 785–800.

Jehlen, Myra. 1983. "Archimedes and the Paradox of Feminist Criticism." In *The "Signs" Reader: Women, Gender, and Scholarship*, edited by Elizabeth Abel and Emily K. Abel, 69–96. Chicago and London: University of Chicago Press.

———. 1990a. "Gender." In Lentricchia and McLaughlin, 263–73.

———. 1990b. "Literature and Authority." In Moran and Penfield, 7–18.

Johnson, Barbara. 1980. *The Critical Difference: Essays in the Contemporary Rhetoric of Reading*. Baltimore: Johns Hopkins University Press.

———, ed. 1982. *The Pedagogical Imperative: Teaching as a Literary Genre. Yale French Studies* 63.

———. 1987. *A World of Difference*. Baltimore: Johns Hopkins University Press.

Johnson, David M. 1988. "Comments on Controversy and Change." *Explorations in Ethnic Studies* 2(2): 53–54.

Jones, Dan C. 1980. "Affective Response: A Plea for a Balanced View." *Teaching English in the Two-Year College* 6: 129–31.

Jones, Ernest. 1949. *Hamlet and Oedipus*. New York: Norton.

Jordanova, Judmilla. 1989. *Sexual Violence: Images of Gender in Science and Medicine Between the Eighteenth and Twentieth Centuries*. Madison: University of Wisconsin Press.

Joyce, Joyce A. 1987a. "The Black Canon: Reconstructing Black American Literary Criticism." *New Literary History* 18: 335–44.

———. 1987b. " 'Who the Cap Fit': Unconsciousness and Unconscionableness in the Criticism of Houston A. Baker, Jr., and Henry Louis Gates, Jr." *New Literary History* 18: 371–84.

Juhasz, Suzanne, ed. 1983. *Feminist Critics Read Emily Dickinson*. Bloomington: Indiana University Press.

Kael, Pauline. 1968. *Kiss Kiss, Bang Bang*. Boston: Little.

Kaplan, Carey and Ellen Cronan Rose, eds. 1989. *Approaches to Teaching Lessing's "The Golden Notebook."* New York: MLA.

Kappeler, Susanne and Norman Bryson, eds. 1983. *Teaching the Text*. London: Routledge. Kau, Joseph. 1976. "The Corporate Approach to Introductory Literature Courses." *College English* 38: 50–61.

Kaufer, David, and Gary Waller. 1985. "To Write Is to Read Is to Write, Right?" In *Writing and Reading Differently: Deconstruction and the Teaching of Composition and Literature*, edited by G. Douglas Atkins and Michael L. Johnson, 66–92. Lawrence: University Press of Kansas.

Kecht, Maria-Regina, ed. 1991. *Pedagogy Is Politics: Literary Theory and Critical Teaching*. Urbana: University of Illinois Press.

Keller, Evelyn Fox. 1984. *Reflections on Gender and Science*. New Haven: Yale University Press.

Kellner, Douglas, ed. 1989. *Postmodernism/Jameson/Critique*. Washington, DC: Maisonneuve Press.

Knapp, Peggy Ann. 1974. " 'Stay, Illusion,' or 'How to Teach *Hamlet*'." *College English* 36: 75–85.

Knapp, Steven, and Walter Benn Michaels. 1982. "Against Theory." *Critical Inquiry* 8: 723–42.

Knoblauch, C. H., and Lil Brannon. 1984. *Rhetorical Traditions and the Teaching of Writing*. Upper Montclair, NJ: Boynton/Cook.

Kolodny, Annette. 1980. "Dancing Through the Minefield: Some Observations on the Theory, Practice, and Politics of a Feminist Literary Criticism." *Feminist Studies* 6(1): 1–25.

Koloski, Bernard, ed. 1988. *Approaches to Teaching Chopin's "The Awakening."* New York: MLA.

Kramarae, Cheris, and Paula A. Treichler. 1985. *A Feminist Dictionary*. London and Boston: Routledge and Kegan Paul.

———. 1990. "Power Relationships in the Classroom." In Gabriel and Smithson, 41–59.

Kristeva, Julia. 1987. "On the Melancholic Imaginary." In Rimmon-Kenan, 104–23.

———. 1984. *Revolution in Poetic Language*. Translated by Margaret Waller. New York: Columbia University Press.

Krupnick, Mark, ed. 1983. *Displacement: Derrida and After*. Bloomington: Indiana University Press.

Kuz'min, A. 1976. "Ideological Work and the Communist Upbringing of the Individual." *Soviet Education* 13(6): 19–38.

Lacan, Jacques. 1977. *Ecrits: A Selection*. New York: Norton.

———. 1978. *The Four Fundamental Concepts of Psychoanalysis*. New York: Norton.

LaCapra, Dominick. 1983. *Rethinking Intellectual History: Texts, Contexts, Language*. Ithaca: Cornell University Press.

Laclau, Ernesto, and Chantal Mouffe. 1985. *Hegemony and Socialist Strategy: Towards a Radical Democratic Politics*. London: Verso.

Lakoff, George, and Mark Turner. 1989. *More Than Cool Reason: A Field Guide to Poetic Metaphor*. Chicago: University of Chicago Press.

Landow, George P. 1990. "Changing Texts, Changing Readers: Hypertext in Literary Education, Criticism and Scholarship." In Henricksen and Morgan, 133–61. (A revised version of "Hypertext in Literary Education, Criticism and Scholarship.")

———. 1989. "Hypertext in Literary Education, Criticism and Scholarship." *Computers and the Humanities* 23: 173–98.

Lanham, Richard A. 1989. "The Electronic Word: Literary Study and the Digital Revolution." *New Literary History* 20: 265–90.

Lasch, Christopher. 1978. *The Culture of Narcissism: American Life in an Age of Diminishing Expectations*. New York: Norton.

Lederman, Marie Jean. 1985. "Literature and Composition in the Two-Year

College: Love Affair or One-Night Stand?" *Teaching English in the Two-Year College* 12: 9–13.

Lee, Valerie. 1986. "Responses of White Students to Ethnic Literature: One Teacher's Experience." *Reader* 15: 24–33.

Leitch, Vincent B. 1989. *American Literary Criticism from the Thirties to the Eighties*. New York: Columbia University Press.

———. 1986. "Deconstruction and Pedagogy." In Nelson, 45–56.

———. 1983. *Deconstructive Criticism: An Advanced Introduction*. Ithaca, NY: Cornell University Press.

Lentricchia, Frank. 1983. *Criticism and Social Change*. Chicago: University of Chicago Press.

———, and Thomas McLaughlin, eds. 1990. *Critical Terms for Literary Study*. Chicago: University of Chicago Press.

Levitin, K. 1982. *One Is Not Born a Personality: Profiles of Soviet Education Psychologists*. Moscow: Progress.

Lindenberger, Herbert. 1984. "Toward a New History in Literary Study." *Profession 1984*, 16–23.

Lipking, Lawrence L. 1983. "The Practice of Theory." *ADE Bulletin* 76: 22–29.

Lipsitz, George. 1990. *Time Passages: Collective Memory and Popular Culture*. Minneapolis: University of Minnesota Press.

Locke, Alain, ed. 1970 [1925]. *The New Negro*. New York: Atheneum.

Lorde, Audre. 1983. "The Master's Tools Will Never Dismantle the Master's House." In Moraga and Anzaldúa, 98–101.

Lukács, Georg. 1962 [1938]. *The Historical Novel*. Translated by Hannah and Stanley Mitchell. London: Merlin.

———. 1971a. *History and Class Consciousness: Studies in Marxist Dialectics*. Translated by Rodney Livingston. Cambridge, MA: MIT Press.

———. 1971b. *The Theory of the Novel*. Translated by Ann Bostock. Cambridge, MA: MIT Press.

Lynn, Steven. 1990. "A Passage into Critical Theory." *College English* 52: 258–71. Rpt. in Moran and Penfield, 99–113.

MacCannell, Juliet Flower. 1991. "Resistance to Sexual Theory." In Morton and Zavarzadeh, 64–89.

Macherey, Pierre. 1978. *A Theory of Literary Production*. London: Routledge and Kegan Paul.

MacKenzie, Nancy. 1985. "Subjective Criticism in Literature Courses: Learning through Writing." *Teaching English in the Two-Year College* 12: 228–33.

Macksey, Richard, and Eugenio Donato, eds. 1970. *The Structuralist Controversy: The Languages of Criticism and the Sciences of Man*. Baltimore: Johns Hopkins University Press.

MacNeil, Maureen. 1987. *Under the Banner of Science: Erasmus Darwin and His Age*. Manchester: Manchester University Press.

Maher, Frances. 1985. "Classroom Pedagogy and the New Scholarship on Women." In Culley and Portuges, 29–48.

Mailloux, Steven. 1982. *Interpretive Conventions: The Reader in the Study of American Fiction*. Ithaca, NY: Cornell University Press.

———. 1989. *Rhetorical Power*. Ithaca, NY: Cornell University Press.

———. 1990. "The Turns of Reader-Response Criticism." In Moran and Penfield, 38–54.

Marcus, Jane. 1989. "Alibis and Legends: The Ethics of Elsewhereness, Gender, and Estrangement." In *Women's Writing in Exile*, edited by Mary Lynn Broe and Angela Ingram, 269–94. Chapel Hill: University of North Carolina Press.

Martin, Reginald, ed. 1990. *College English* 52: 727–822. (Special issue on African American Literary Criticism.)

Mason, Theodore O., Jr. 1988. "Between the Populist and the Scientist: Ideology and Power in Recent Afro-American Literary Criticism or, 'The Dozens' as Scholarship." *Callaloo* 11: 606–15.

McCormick, Kathleen. 1988. " 'First Steps' in 'Wandering Rocks': Students' Differences, Literary Transactions, and Pleasures." *Reader* 20: 48–67.

———. 1985. "Theory in the Reader: Bleich, Holland, and Beyond." *College English* 47: 836–50.

———, Gary Waller, and Linda Flower. 1987. *Reading Texts: Reading, Responding, Writing*. Lexington, MA: Heath.

McGann, Jerome J. 1985a. *The Beauty of Inflections: Literary Investigations in Historical Method and Theory*. New York: Oxford University Press.

———, ed. 1985b. *Historical Studies and Literary Criticism*. Madison: University of Wisconsin Press.

———. 1988. *Social Values and Poetic Acts: The Historical Judgment of Literary Work*. Cambridge, MA: Harvard University Press.

———. 1981. "The Text, the Poem, and the Problem of Historical Method." *New Literary History* 12: 269–88.

McGee, Patrick. 1987. "Truth and Resistance: Teaching as a Form of Analysis." *College English* 49: 667–78.

McLaughlin, Thomas, ed. 1989. *Literature: The Power of Language*. New York: Harcourt Brace Jovanovich.

McMahon, Christine. 1985. "Writing across the English Curriculum: Using Journals in Literature Classes." *Teaching English in the Two-Year College* 12: 269–71.

Meese, Elizabeth A. 1986. *Crossing the Double-Cross: The Practice of Feminist Criticism*. Chapel Hill and London: University of North Carolina Press.

Meltzer, Francoise. 1990. "Unconscious." In Lentricchia and McLaughlin, 147–62.

Merod, Jim. 1987. *The Political Responsibility of the Critic*. Ithaca, NY: Cornell University Press.

Miller, Bruce E. 1980. *Teaching the Art of Literature*. Urbana: NCTE.

Miller, Jane. 1991. *Eccentric Propositions: Essays on Literature and the Curriculum*. London: Routledge, Chapman, and Hall.

Miller, Jean Baker. 1976. *Toward a New Psychology of Women*. Boston: Beacon Press.

Miller, Jonathan. 1981. "Introduction." *Othello* (BBC), PBS, 12 October.

———. 1980a. "Introduction and Interview with Warren Mitchell." *The Merchant of Venice* (BBC), PBS, 23 February.

———. 1980b. "Introduction and Interview with John Cleese." *The Taming of the Shrew* (BBC), PBS, 16 January.

Miller, Jordan Y., ed. 1976. Preface to *The Heath Introduction to Drama*. Lexington, MA: D. C. Heath, 1–29.

Miller, Susan. 1989. *Rescuing the Subject: A Critical Introduction to Rhetoric and the Writer*. Carbondale: Southern Illinois University Press.

Miller, Wayne C., Faye Nell Vowell, et al., eds. 1976. *A Comprehensive Bibliography for the Study of American Minorities*. 2 vols. New York: New York University Press.

Millett, Kate. 1970. *Sexual Politics*. New York: Doubleday.

Minnich, Elizabeth, et al., eds. 1988. *Reconstructing the Academy: Women's Education and Women's Studies*. Chicago: University of Chicago Press.

Mitchell, Doris J. and Jewel H. Bell, eds. 1975. *The Black Woman: Myths and Realities*. Selected papers from the Radcliffe Symposium "The Black Woman: Myths and Realities" 4–5 May, 1973. Cambridge, MA: Radcliffe College.

Moers, Ellen. 1977. *Literary Women: The Great Writers*. New York: Anchor.

Moffett, James. 1981. *Active Voice: A Writing Program across the Curriculum*. Montclair, NJ: Boynton/Cook.

Moglen, Helen. 1976. *Charlotte Brontë: The Self Conceived*. New York: Norton.

Mohanty, Chandra Talpade. 1989–90. "On Race and Voice: Challenges for Liberal Education in the 1990s." *Cultural Critique* 14: 179–208.

Moi, Toril. 1985. *Sexual/Textual Politics: Feminist Literary Theory*. New York: Methuen.

Mollinger, Robert M. 1981. *Psychoanalysis and Literature: An Introduction*. Chicago: Nelson-Hall.

Montrose, Louis. 1981. "A Poetics of Renaissance Culture." *Criticism* 23: 349–59.

———. 1986. "Renaissance Literary Studies and the Subject of History." *English Literary Renaissance* 16: 5–12.

Moraga, Cherrie, and Gloria Anzaldúa, eds. 1983. *This Bridge Called My Back: Writings by Radical Women of Color*. 2nd ed. New York: Kitchen Table/Women of Color Press.

Moran, Charles and Elizabeth F. Penfield, eds. 1990. *Conversations: Contemporary Critical Theory and the Teaching of Literature*. Urbana: NCTE.

Morgan, Ellen. 1978. "The One-Eyed Doe." *Radical Teacher* 10: 2–6.

Morris, Wesley. 1972. *Toward a New Historicism*. Princeton, NJ: Princeton University Press.

Morton, Donald, and Mas'ud Zavarzadeh, eds. 1991. *Theory, Pedagogy, Politics: Texts for Change*. Urbana: University of Illinois Press.

Moynihan, Daniel Patrick. 1965. *The Negro Family: A Case for National Action*. Washington, D.C.: Government Printing Office.

Murray, Heather. 1991. "Charisma and Authority in Literary Study and Theory Study." In Morton and Zavarzadeh, 187–200.

Natoli, Joseph, ed. 1989. *Literary Theory's Future.* Urbana: University of Illinois Press.

———, ed. 1987. *Tracing Literary Theory.* Urbana: University of Illinois Press.

Neel, Jasper P. 1982. "Writing about Literature (or Country Ham)." In *Publishing in English Education,* edited by Stephen N. Judy, 53–72. Montclair, NJ: Boynton/Cook.

Neely, Carol Thomas. 1987. "Feminist Criticism and Teaching Shakespeare." *ADE Bulletin* 87: 15–18.

Nelms, Ben F., ed. 1988. *Literature in the Classroom: Readers, Texts, and Contexts.* Urbana: NCTE.

Nelson, Cary, ed. 1986. *Theory in the Classroom.* Urbana: University of Illinois Press.

Newkirk, Thomas. 1984. "Looking for Trouble: A Way to Unmask Our Readings." *College English* 46: 756–66.

Newton, Judith, and Deborah Rosenfelt, eds. 1985. *Feminist Criticism and Social Change.* New York: Methuen.

Norris, Christopher. 1982. *Deconstruction: Theory and Practice.* London and New York: Methuen.

North, Stephen M. 1987. *The Making of Knowledge in Composition: Portrait of an Emerging Field.* Boston: Boynton/Cook.

Novikova, Ludmila I., and Aleksander Lewin. 1970. "The Collective and the Personality of the Child." *International Review of Education* 16(3): 323–41.

Ogunyemi, Chikwenye Okonjo. 1985. "Womanism: The Dynamics of the Contemporary Black Female Novel in English." *Signs: The Journal of Women in Culture and Society* 11(11): 63–80.

Ohmann, Richard. 1976. *English in America: A Radical View of the Profession.* New York: Oxford University Press.

———. 1990. "Graduate Students, Professionals, Intellectuals." *College English* 52: 247–57.

———. 1987. *Politics of Letters.* Middletown, CT: Wesleyan University Press.

Olsen, Solveig, ed. 1985. *Computer-Aided Instruction in the Humanities.* Technology and the Humanities. New York: MLA.

Penley, Constance. 1986. "Teaching in Your Sleep: Feminism and Psychoanalysis." In Nelson 129–48.

Perrin, Noel. 1988. "Another Sojourner." Review of Alice Walker's *Living By the Word. New York Times Book Review,* 5 June: 42–43.

Peterson, Bruce T. 1982. "Writing about Responses: A Unified Model of Reading, Interpretation, and Composition." *College English* 44: 459–68.

Petrovsky, A., ed. 1973. *Age-Group and Pedagogical Psychology.* Moscow: Progress.

———. 1985. *Studies in Psychology: The Collective and the Individual.* Moscow: Progress.

Poovey, Mary. 1980. " 'My Hideous Progeny': Mary Shelley and the Feminization of Romanticism." *PMLA* 95: 332–47.

Porter, Carolyn. 1988. "Are We Being Historical Yet?" *South Atlantic Quarterly* 87: 743–86.

Price, Marian. 1989. *Reader-Response Criticism: A Test of Its Usefulness in a First-Year College Course in Writing about Literature*. New York: Peter Lang.

Prince, Gerald. 1984. "Literary Theory and the Undergraduate Curriculum." *Profession 84*: 37–40.

Pryse, Marjorie. 1985. "Zora Neale Hurston, Alice Walker, and the 'Ancient Power' of Black Women." In *Conjuring: Black Women, Fiction and Literary Tradition*, edited by Marjorie Pryse and Hortense J. Spillers, 1–24. Bloomington: Indiana University Press.

Purves, Alan C., and Richard Beach. 1972. *Literature and the Reader: Research in Response to Literature, Reading Interests, and the Teaching of Literature*. Urbana: NCTE.

———, Theresa Rogers, and Anna O. Soter. 1990. *How Porcupines Make Love: Teaching a Response-Centered Literature Curriculum*. New York: Longman. (Rev. ed. of *How Porcupines Make Love* [1972].)

Rabinowitz, Peter J. 1989. "Whirl without End: Audience-Oriented Criticism." In Atkins and Morrow, 81–100.

Racevskis, Karlis. 1983. *Michel Foucault and the Subversion of Intellect*. Ithaca, NY: Cornell University Press.

Radhakrishnan, R. 1991. "Canonicity and Theory. Toward a Poststructural Pedagogy." In Morton and Zavarzadeh, 112–35.

———. 1987. "Culture as Common Ground: Ethnicity and Beyond." *MELUS* 14(2): 5–18.

Radin, Paul. 1972 [1956]. *The Trickster: A Study in Indian Mythology*. New York: Schocken Books.

Raymond, James C. 1990a. "Authority, Desire, and Canons: Tendentious Meditations on Cultural Literacy." In Moran and Penfield, 76–86.

———. 1990b. "What Good Is All This Heady, Esoteric Theory?" *Teaching English in the Two-Year College* 17: 11–17.

Redding, J. Saunders. 1988 [1939]. *To Make A Poet Black*. Ithaca: Cornell University Press.

Reed, Marian V. 1973. "Serendipity Versus Training in Literary Criticism." *College English* 35: 270–75.

Rich, Adrienne. 1979. *On Lies, Secrets, and Silence*. New York: W. W. Norton.

Richards, I. A. 1968. *Design for Escape: World Education through Modern Media*. New York: Harcourt.

———. 1955. *Speculative Instruments*. Chicago: University of Chicago Press.

Richter, David H., ed. 1989. *The Critical Tradition: Classic Texts and Contemporary Trends*. New York: St. Martin's.

Riffaterre, Michael. 1966. "Describing Poetic Structures: Two Approaches to Baudelaire's 'Les Chats.' " In *Structuralism*, edited by Jacques Ehrmann, 200–42. *Yale French Studies* 36/37.

Rimmon-Kenan, Sholomith, ed. 1987. *Discourse in Psychoanalysis and Literature*. New York: Methuen.

Robinson, James Harvey. 1912. *The New History: Essays Illustrating the Modern Historical Outlook*. New York: Macmillan.

Robinson, Jeffrey C. 1987. *Radical Literary Education: A Classroom Experiment with Wordsworth's "Ode."* Madison: University of Wisconsin Press.

Robinson, Lillian. 1978. *Sex, Class, and Culture*. New York: Routledge.

Rocklin, Edward. 1991. "Converging Transformations in Teaching Composition, Literature, and Drama." *College English* 53: 177–94.

Rodriguez, Richard. 1981. *Hunger of Memory: The Education of Richard Rogriguez*. Boston: David R. Godine.

Roemer, Kenneth, ed. 1988. *Approaches to Teaching Momaday's "The Way to Rainy Mountain."* New York: MLA.

Roemer, Marjorie Godlin. 1987. "Which Reader's Response?" *College English* 49: 911–21.

Rosenberg, Warren. 1990. " 'Professor, Why Are You Wasting Our Time?': Teaching Jacobs's *Incidents in the Life of a Slave Girl*." In Moran and Penfield, 132–48.

Rosenblatt, Louise. 1983 [1938]. *Literature as Exploration*. 4th ed. New York: MLA.

———. 1978. *The Reader, The Text, The Poem: The Transactional Theory of the Literary Work*. Carbondale: Southern Illinois University Press.

Rosowski, Susan J., ed. 1989. *Approaches to Teaching Cather's "My Antonia."* New York: MLA.

Rouse, John. 1983. "An Erotics of Teaching." *College English* 45: 535–48.

Rudall, B. H., and T. N. Corns. 1987. *Computers and Literature: A Practical Guide*. Cambridge, MA: Abacus.

Ruofs, A. LaVonne Browne. 1983. "Teaching American Indian Authors, 1772–1968." *ADE Bulletin* 75: 39–42.

Ruszkiewicz, John J. 1979. "Parody and Pedagogy: Explorations in Imitative Literature." *College English* 40: 693–701.

Ryan, Michael. 1982a. "Deconstruction and Radical Teaching." *Yale French Studies* 63: 45–58.

———. 1982b. *Marxism and Deconstruction: A Critical Articulation*. Baltimore: Johns Hopkins University Press.

———. 1989. "Political Criticism." In Atkins and Morrow, 200–13.

Sadker, Myra, and David Sadker. 1990. "Confronting Sexism in the College Classroom." In Gabriel and Smithson, 176–87.

Said, Edward. 1983. *The World, The Text, and The Critic*. Cambridge, MA: Harvard University Press.

Schilb, John. 1986. "Canonical Theories and Noncanonical Literature: Steps toward a Pedagogy." *Reader* 15: 3–23.

———. 1985a. "Pedagogy of the Oppressors?" In Culley and Portuges, 253–64.

———. 1985b. "Transforming a Course in American Literary Realism." In *Women's Place in the Academy: Transforming the Liberal Arts Curriculum*, 201–20, edited by Marilyn R. Schuster and Susan R. Van Dyne. Totowa, NJ: Rowman and Allenheld.

Scholes, Robert. 1985. *Textual Power: Literary Theory and the Teaching of English*. New Haven: Yale University Press.

———. 1990. "Toward a Curriculum in Textual Studies." In Henricksen and Morgan, 95–112.

———, Nancy R. Comley, and Gregory Ulmer. 1988. *Text Book: An Introduction to Literary Language*. Inst. ed. New York: St. Martin's.

Schreiber, Ron. 1974. "Giving a Gay Course." *College English* 36: 316–23.

Schuster, Marilyn, and Susan Van Dyne. 1985. *Women's Place in the Academy: Transforming the Liberal Arts Curriculum*. Totowa, NJ: Rowan and Allenheld.

Sharpless, F. Parvin. 1967. "Reflections on The College Teaching of English." *College English* 29: 32–39.

Schroeder, William R. 1986. "A Teachable Theory of Interpretation." In Nelson, 9–44.

Schweickart, Patricinio. 1989. "Reading Ourselves: Toward a Feminist Theory of Reading." In *Contemporary Literary Criticism: Literary and Cultural Studies*, 2nd ed., edited by Robert Con Davis and Ronald Schleifer, 118–41. New York: Longman.

Scott, Patricia Bell. 1982. "Debunking Sapphire: Toward a Non-Racist and Non-Sexist Social Science." In Hull et al., 85–92.

Selden, Raman. 1989. *Practicing Theory and Reading Literature*. Lexington: University of Kentucky Press.

———. 1985. *A Reader's Guide to Contemporary Literary Theory*. Lexington: University of Kentucky Press.

Sewall, Richard B., ed. 1963. *Emily Dickinson: A Collection of Critical Essays*. Englewood Cliffs, NJ: Prentice-Hall.

Sherwin, Paul. 1981. "*Frankenstein*: Creation of Catastrophe." *PMLA* 96: 883–903.

Shor, Ira. 1987a [1980]. *Critical Teaching and Everyday Life*. Chicago: University of Chicago Press.

———. 1987b. *Freire for the Classroom: A Sourcebook for Liberatory Teaching*. Portsmouth, NH: Heinemann/Boynton-Cook.

Showalter, Elaine. 1977. *A Literature of Their Own: British Women Novelists from Brontë to Lessing*. Princeton, NJ: Princeton University Press.

———, ed. 1985. *The New Feminist Criticism: Essays on Women, Literature, and Theory*. New York: Pantheon.

———. 1987. "Women's Time, Women's Space: Writing the History of Feminist Criticism." In *Feminist Issues in Literary Scholarship*, edited by Shari Benstock, 30–44. Bloomington: Indiana University Press.

Shrewsbury, Carolyn M. 1987. "What Is Feminist Pedagogy?" *Women's Studies Quarterly* 15: 6–14.

Shumway, David. 1987. *Michel Foucault*. Boston: Twayne.

Shuster, Marilyn R., and Susan R. Van Dyne. 1983. "Transforming the Curriculum: The Changing Classroom, Changing the Institution." Working Paper No. 125. Wellesley College Center for Research on Women.

Silverman, Kaja. 1983. *The Subject of Semiotics*. Oxford: Oxford University Press.

Sledge, Linda Ching. 1985. "Teaching Asian-American Literature." *ADE Bulletin* 80: 42–45.

Sluder, Brenda. 1989. "The Voice of the Other: Effecting Change Through Feminist Criticism." *Teaching English in the Two-Year College* 16: 206–9.

Smith, Barbara, and Beverly Smith. 1983. "Across the Kitchen Table: A Sister-to-Sister Dialogue." In Moraga and Anzaldúa, 113–27.

Smith, Paul. 1988. *Discerning the Subject*. Minneapolis: University of Minnesota Press.

Sollors, Werner. 1990. "Ethnicity." In Lentricchia and McLaughlin, 288–305.

Sosnoski, James J. 1981. "Can We Teach the Latest Literary Theories to College Freshmen?" *Focus: Teaching English Language Arts* 7(2): 32–38.

———. 1990. "Why Theory? Rethinking Pedagogy." *Works and Days 16* 8(2): 29–40.

Spallanzani, Lazaro. 1964. "Whether, According to a New Theory of Generation, Animalcula Are Produced by a Vegetative Power in Matter." In *The Origins and Growth of Biology*, edited by Arthur Rook, 86–95. Baltimore: Penguin.

Spanos, William V. 1989. "Theory in the Undergraduate English Curriculum: Towards an Interested Pedagogy." *Boundary 2* 16(2/3): 41–70.

Spender, Dale. 1981. Introduction to *Men's Studies Modified: The Impact of Feminism on the Academic Disciplines*. Oxford: Pergamon Press, 1–8.

Spiller, Robert. 1963. "Is Literary History Obsolete?" *College English* 24: 345–51.

Spivak, Gayatri Chakravorty. 1981. "Reading the World: Literary Studies in the 1980s." *College English* 43(7): 671–79. Rpt. in Atkins and Johnson, 27–37.

Stepto, Robert B. 1979. *From Behind the Veil: A Study of Afro-American Narrative*. Urbana: University of Illinois Press.

Stern, Frederick C. 1974. "Black Lit, White Crit?" *College English* 35: 637–58.

Stetson, Erlene. 1985. "Pink Elephants: Confessions of a Black Feminist in an All-White, Mostly Male English Department of a White University Somewhere in God's Country." In Culley and Portuges, 127–30.

Stewart, Susan. 1989. "The Interdiction." *Profession 89*: 10–14.

Stimpson, Catharine R. 1988. *Where the Meanings Are: Feminism and Cultural Spaces*. New York: Methuen.

Strickland, Ronald. 1990. "Confrontational Pedagogy and Traditional Literary Studies." *College English* 52: 291–300.

Sulkes, Stan. 1985. "Two Strategies for Teaching Literature to Two-Year College Students." *Teaching English in the Two-Year College* 12: 105–7.

Sullivan, Anne McCrary. 1988. "The Personal Anthology: A Stimulus for Exploratory Readings." *English Journal* 77: 27–30.

Sychev, Yu. V. 1978. *The Individual and the Microenvironment*. Moscow: Progress.

Tarantelli, Carole B. 1986. "And the Last Walls Dissolved: On Imagining a Story of the Survival of Difference." In *Women in Culture and Politics: A Century of Change*, edited by Judith Friedlander, et al., 177–93. Bloomington: Indiana University Press.

Tate, Claudia. 1983. "Alice Walker" (Interview). In *Black Women Writers at Work*, edited by Claudia Tate, 175–87. New York: Continuum.

Thomas, Brook. 1987. "The Historical Necessity for—and Difficulties with—New Historical Analysis in Introductory Literature Courses." *College English* 49: 509–22.

Tompkins, Jane. 1990. "Pedagogy of the Distressed." *College English* 52: 653–60.

———, ed. 1980. *Reader-Response Criticism: From Formalism to Post-Structuralism*. Baltimore: Johns Hopkins University Press.

———. 1990. "A Short Course in Post-Structuralism." *College English* 50 (1988): 733–47. Rpt. in Moran and Penfield, 19–37.

Treichler, Paula A. 1986. "Teaching Feminist Theory." In Nelson, 57–128.

———, and Cheris Kramarae. 1981. "Women's Talk in the Ivory Tower." *Communication Quarterly* 32(2): 118–32.

Trimbur, John. 1989. "Consensus and Difference in Collaborative Learning." *College English* 51: 602–16.

Troyka, Lynn Quitman. 1984. "Classical Rhetoric and the Basic Writer." In *Essays on Classical Rhetoric and Modern Discourse*, edited by Robert J. Connors, Lisa S. Ede, and Andrea A. Lunsford, 193–202. Carbondale: Southern Illinois University Press.

Turner, Darwin T. 1970. "The Teaching of Afro-American Literature." *College English* 31: 666–70.

———, and Barbara Dodds Stanford. 1972. *Theory and Practice in the Teaching of Literature by Afro-Americans*. Urbana: NCTE.

Turner, Roy. 1974. *Ethnomethodology: Selected Readings*. Baltimore: Penguin.

Ulmer, Gregory L. 1985a. *Applied Grammatology: Post(e)-Pedagogy from Jacques Derrida to Joseph Beuys*. Baltimore: Johns Hopkins University Press.

———. 1989. *Teletheory: Grammatology in the Age of Video*. New York: Routledge.

———. 1990. "Textshop for an Experimental Humanities." In Henricksen and Morgan, 113–32.

———. 1985b. "Textshop for Post(e)pedagogy." In Atkins and Johnson, 38–64.

Vasilyuk, Fyodor. 1988. *The Psychology of Experience*. Moscow: Progress.

Veeser, H. Aram, ed. 1989. *The New Historicism*. New York: Routledge.

Vogel, Nancy. 1990. "Gender Differences: Both/And, Not Either/Or." In Moran and Penfield, 223–32.

Voloshinov, V. [Vološinov, V. N.]. 1983. "Discourse in Life and Discourse in Poetry: Questions of Sociological Poetics." In *Bakhtin School Papers*, edited by Ann Shukman, translated by John Richmond, 5–30. Russian Poetics in Translation No. 10. Oxford: RPT Publications.

———. 1987 [1976]. *Freudianism: A Critical Sketch*. Translated by I. R. Titunik. Edited by Titunik and Neal H. Bruss. Bloomington: Indiana University Press.

———. 1986. *Marxism and the Philosophy of Language*. Translated by Ladislav Matejka and I. R. Titunik. Cambridge, MA: Harvard University Press.

Wagner, Linda W. 1986. "Teaching *The Bluest Eye*." *ADE Bulletin* 83: 28–31.

Wald, Alan. 1987. "Theorizing Cultural Difference: A Critique of the 'Ethnicity School'." *MELUS* 14(2): 19–33.

Waller, Gary F. 1986. "A Powerful Silence: 'Theory' in the English Major." *ADE Bulletin* 85: 31–35.

———, Kathleen McCormick, and Linda Flower, eds. 1987. *The Lexington Introduction to Literature: Reading and Responding to Texts*. New York: Heath.

Walter, William. 1963. *Monarch Notes: The Plays of Sophocles*. New York: Monarch Press.

Ward, Cynthia. 1990. "What They Told Buchi Emecheta: Oral Subjectivity and the Joys of 'Otherhood'." *PMLA* 105: 83–97.

Ward, Jerry. 1984. "Selected Bibliography of Afro-American Literature." *ADE Bulletin* 78: 40–42.

Washington, Mary Helen. 1985. "How Racial Differences Helped Us Discover Our Common Ground." In Culley and Portuges, 221–30.

———. 1982. "Teaching Black-Eyed Susans: An Approach to the Study of Black Women Writers." In Hull et al., 208–17.

Watkins, Evan. 1991. "Intellectual Work and Pedagogical Circulation in English." In Morton and Zavarzadeh, 201–21.

———. 1990. *Work Time*. Palo Alto: Stanford University Press.

Waxman, Barbara Frey. 1989. "Politics of the Survey Course: Feminist Challenges." *Teaching English in the Two-Year College* 16: 17–22.

Weedon, Chris. 1991. "Post-Structuralist Feminist Practice." In Morton and Zavarzadeh, 47–63.

Weiss, Richard. 1969. *The American Myth of Success*. Urbana: University of Illinois Press.

Wheeler, Richard P. 1987. "Psychoanalytic Criticism and Teaching Shakespeare." *ADE Bulletin* 87: 19–23.

White, Hayden. 1973. *Metahistory: The Historical Imagination in Nineteenth-Century Europe*. Baltimore: Johns Hopkins University Press.

Wilkinson, Mary A. 1981. "Introductory Literature: Survey of Freshman Attitudes." *College English* 43: 516–22.

Williams, Raymond. 1976. *Keywords: A Vocabulary of Culture and Society*. New York: Oxford University Press.

———. 1977. *Marxism and Literature*. New York: Oxford University Press.

Wimsatt, W. K., Jr., and Monroe Beardsley. 1954. "The Affective Fallacy." In *The Verbal Icon: Studies in the Meaning of Poetry*, edited by W. K. Wimsatt, Jr., 21–39. New York: Noonday.

———. 1958. "The Intentional Fallacy." In *The Verbal Icon*, 2–18.

Winterowd, W. Ross. 1987. "The Purification of Literature and Rhetoric." *College English* 49: 257–73.

Wolf, H. R. 1971. "The Classroom as Microcosm." *College English* 33: 259–67.

Wooten, Elizabeth. 1974. "Graduate Departments and Community College English Teachers." *College English* 35: 997–1000.

Yaeger, Patricia. 1988. *Honey-Mad Women: Emancipatory Strategies in Women's Writing*. New York: Columbia University Press.

Yarborough, Richard. 1984. " 'In the Realm of the Imagination': Afro-American Literature and the American Canon." *ADE Bulletin* 78: 35–39.

Young, Gloria L. 1987. "Teaching Poetry: Another Method." *Teaching English in the Two-Year College* 14: 52–56.

Zavarzadeh, Mas'ud. 1989. "Theory as Resistance." *Rethinking Marxism* 2(1): 50–70.

———, and Donald Morton. 1986/1987. "Theory Pedagogy Politics: The Crisis of 'The Subject' in the Humanities." *Boundary 2* 15: 1–21.

Index

Absolute knowledge, 117
Academic background, 61
The Act of Reading (Iser), 307, 353
The Adventures of Huckleberry Finn (Twain), 67, 58, 333, 339
Advertising, 125, 126, 127, 128, 264, 265, 269–270
Aesthetic approach to reading, 38
Aesthetic distance, 75
Aesthetics, literature as, 60, 202
"The Affective Fallacy" (Wimsatt and Beardsley), 307, 365
African American perspectives, 8, 13, 16, 63, 154, 184, 187
  critical theory, need for, 189–190
  integration of into introductory courses, 192, 197–198
  pairing of texts, 195–196
  resources for information on, 323–326
  signifying, 13, 78, 84, 190–191, 226
Age, 3, 61, 109, 148, 218
Ahistorical approach, 87
The Aims of Interpretation (Hirsch), 352
Alger, Horatio, 14, 252, 253, 254–256, 257, 335
Althusser, Louis, 104–105, 109, 117, 118, 123, 263, 276, 287, 316, 317, 340
An American Tragedy (Dreiser), 258–259, 336
Angelou, Maya, 65, 335
Anotherness, 169, 175
Anthologies
  banishing, 252–253
  and coverage model of education, 200
  electronic, 271, 277, 286, 289
  student-generated, 278–282, 288–289
  weaknesses of, 61, 65, 211, 252, 288
The Anxiety of Influence: A Theory of Poetry (Bloom), 343
Archetypal criticism, 296
Aristotle, 87, 128, 326
Arnold, Matthew, 199, 201, 295, 340
Aronowitz, Stanley, 318, 340
Artificial intelligence, 285
Arts and Humanities Citation Index, 83
Atkins, G. Douglas, 296, 311, 315, 327, 328, 329, 341
Auden, W. H., 47
Audience analysis, 73
Austen, Jane, 72, 82, 182, 184–185, 335
Author-function, 63
Authorial intention, 62–63, 254
Authoritarian teaching, 6, 9, 76, 116–117, 120, 149
"The Author to Her Book" (Bradstreet), 212, 335
Autobiography (Franklin), 65, 336
The Autobiography of an Ex-Colored Man (Johnson), 190, 194, 195–196, 337
Autonomy, 54, 55, 85, 118, 120, 205
The Awakening (Chopin), 67, 297, 335

"The Babysitter" (Coover), 134, 335
Baker, Houston A., Jr., 189, 191, 195, 197, 198, 324, 341
Bakhtin, Mikhail, 5, 12, 13–14, 64, 148, 162, 164, 175, 215, 220, 237, 295, 326, 341
Bakhtin School, 217–218, 226. *See also* Speech genres
Baldwin, James, 191, 192
Bambara, Toni Cade, 79
Banking model of education, 6, 162
Baraka, Amiri, 190, 341
Barthes, Roland, 38, 245, 253, 295, 330, 342
Bauer, Dale M., 156, 159, 160, 175, 176, 322, 342
Beardsley, Monroe, 307, 365
Beloved (Morrison), 25–33 , 211, 338
Belsey, Catherine, 202, 237, 238, 329, 342
"Benito Cereno" (Melville), 29, 338
Benjamin, Walter, 96, 317, 342
Bennett, William, 2
Beowolf, 51, 335
Berthoff, Ann E., 69, 71, 342
Bialostosky, Don, 14, 215, 326, 342, 387
Bibliographies, 120, 293
Binary opposition, 186, 239, 240–241, 245

Bizzell, Patricia, 303, 343
Black English, 66
Black literature, 90
The Black Unicorn (Lorde), 65
Blake, William, 14, 152, 198, 236, 268, 269, 335, 338
Bleich, David, 9, 11, 19, 74, 121, 305, 306, 307–308, 309, 343, 387
Bloom, Alan, 2
Bloom, Harold, 63, 320, 343
"The Blue Hotel" (Crane), 37, 38, 40, 41, 42, 44, 336
Blues matrix, 191
Book Review Digest, 82–83
Booth, Wayne, 299, 300, 343
Borges, Jorge Luis, 260, 335
Bove, Paul, 301, 315, 317, 329, 343
Bradstreet, Anne, 212, 225
Brontë, Charlotte, 53, 78, 202, 335
Brooks, Cleanth, 288, 306, 343
Browning, Robert, 168, 268, 335
Brown Silk and Magenta Sunsets (Gibson), 141
Bruffee, Kenneth A., 139, 319, 333, 343
Buffalo Gals and Other Animal Presences (Le Guin), 162, 338
Burke, Kenneth, 2, 151, 159, 160, 261, 295, 344
Bush, George, 187

Cain, William E., 7, 211, 296, 332, 344
"The Cambridge ladies who live in furnished souls" (cummings), 154, 155–156, 157, 336
Canon, 67, 151, 152–154, 188, 296
"The Canonization" (Donne), 168, 336
Capitalism, 94, 146
Career aspirations (student), 61
Censorship, 83–84
Centrifugal tendency, 98
Chandler, Raymond, 14, 252, 253–254, 256–257, 260, 335
Chapman, Tracy, 265
Characterization, 266
Cheney, Lynne, 2
Chesnutt, Charles, 190, 191, 195, 325, 335
"The Chink and the Clock People" (Robbins), 141, 338
Chodorow, Nancy, 157, 320, 344
Chopin, Kate, 67, 198, 298, 335
Christian, Barbara, 189, 198, 320, 345
Chronological ordering, 89, 92, 170
Civil rights, 64, 102, 149
Class (social), 3, 10, 20, 61, 64, 88, 106, 109, 111, 166, 168, 179, 183–184, 218
Class discussion, 69, 106, 133–135, 165, 172, 186
Classic(s), 76, 78, 80, 82, 84
Classroom
  as community, 9
  as an electronic environment, 285
  as a place of exploration, 160
Classroom-as-clinic approach, 54, 55
Clifford, John, 9, 11, 78, 84, 101, 345, 387–388
Cliffs Notes, 123
Closed texts, 259
Close reading, 38, 62, 102, 122
Collaboration, 21, 129, 139–140, 158
Collective grading, 132–133, 140, 141, 142–143
Collective interpretation, 136
Collectivist-like group, 139
Collectivist pedagogies, 131
  assignments, 137–140
  class book project, 137–139, 145
  class interpretation in, 135–136
  classroom conflicts, 140
  collective grading, 132–133, 140, 141, 142–143
  final exam, 132–133, 140–142
  outlook for, 146–147
  students learning from each other, 134–135
  time factor, 148
The Color Purple (Spielberg film), 76, 81, 185
The Color Purple (Walker), 65, 66, 81–82, 84, 182, 185, 192, 193, 299, 339
Communality of evaluations, 216
Community(ies)
  blurring of boundaries, 33
  classroom as, 9
  interpretive, 63, 67, 68, 201, 307, 333
  introductory classes as threat to, 19
  literature as emerging from, 22
  membership in, 21, 22–23, 33–34
Complete Poems of Paul Laurence Dunbar (Dunbar), 336
Computer-assisted instruction for literature
  cultural literacy and, 273
  historical perspective on, 285–286
  hypertext programs, 273–277, 286–287
  limitations of software for, 272–273, 285
Computer-cybernetic theory, 9
Computer literacy, 14, 15, 123–124
Confrontational pedagogy
  arguments against, 129
  confronting students, 119–122
  resisting cultural hegemony, 122–129

resisting individualism, 129
underlying premise of, 115
The Conjure Woman (Chesnutt), 191, 195, 335
Connectivity, 274
Conrad, Joseph, 191, 211, 298, 335
Consistency building, 285
Contextual texts, 123–129
Coover, Robert, 134, 335
Corporate groupism, 139
Coverage model of education, 13, 199, 200–201, 202, 303
Coyote midwife, 12, 161
defined, 161–162
and the distinction between otherness and anotherness, 169
grading, 165–166
men as, 173, 176
as a model for teaching, 165–172
studies in the dialogical classroom, 172–175
syllabus, 166–167
Crane, Stephen, 37, 39–40, 41, 336
Critical pedagogy, 149
Critical thinking, 14, 124, 128
Criticism and Ideology (Eagleton), 347
"The Crying of Lot 49" (Pynchon), 259, 338
Cullen, Countee, 196, 336
Culler, Jonathan, 85, 300, 306, 329, 346
Cultural amnesia, 11, 85–86
Cultural decentering, 286, 274
Cultural differences, 168
Cultural hegemony, 122–129, 182
Cultural influences, 21–22, 24–25
Cultural literacy, 264, 273
Cultural Literacy: What Every American Needs to Know (Hirsch), 352
Cultural relativism, 185
Cultural studies, ix, 1
Cultural theory, 16
cummings, e. e., 12, 154–156, 336

"Dancing Through the Minefield" (Kolodny), 320, 354
Dante, 182, 184, 335
Davis, Robert Con, 311, 316, 333, 346
Dead Poet's Society, 127, 336
"Death of a Moth" (Woolf), 45, 340
Death of a Salesman (Miller), 65, 91, 338
"The Death of the Author" (Barthes), 342
Deconstruction, 9, 14, 16, 62, 63, 64, 128, 202, 211, 286, 296
advantages of, 239–240
in combination with New Criticism, 227–228
exercises to teach, 230–231
multiple meanings, use of, 231–235
and New Criticism compared, 14, 228–237
phases of, 240–242
purposes of, 239
resistance to, 227
resources for information on, 327–331
sample writing assignments, 236
specimentexts for teaching, 242–245
"A Defense of Poetry" (Shelley), 212, 339
de Lauretis, Teresa, 174, 346
Delphi Seminar, 309
de Man, Paul, 238, 298, 299, 327, 346
Derrida, Jacques, 14, 60, 63, 128, 186, 238, 239, 240–241, 263, 274, 276, 294, 295, 328, 330, 346
Determinism, 287
Dewey, John, 101
Dialectical notebook, 69
Dialectical pluralism, 238
Dialogical classroom, 172–175
Dialogics, 5, 9, 16, 64, 154, 164, 165, 175, 296
resources for information on, 326
Dialogues/monologues, 39, 164
Dickens, Charles, 83, 84, 336
Dickinson, Emily, 211, 333
Disciplinary specialization, 87, 88
Discussion groups, 107, 172
The Dispossessed (Le Guin), 169–172, 338
Diversity, 182, 188, 269
Doctoral departments, 3
A Doll's House (Ibsen), 182, 337
Donne, John, 168, 336
Dostoyevsky, Fyodor, 47, 175, 326
Douglass, Frederick, 13, 191, 192, 193, 336
Dracula (Stoker), 10, 50–53, 54, 339
"Dreams" (Giovanni), 154–155, 337
Dreiser, Theodore, 67–68, 258, 336
DuBois, W. E. B., 191, 194, 195, 336
Dunbar, Paul Laurence, 196, 197, 325, 336
The Dynamics of Literary Response (Holland), 305, 307, 352

Eagleton, Terry, 2, 6, 73, 118, 123, 151, 199, 209, 295, 299, 310, 312, 316, 326–327, 347
Eco, Umberto, 259, 260, 347
Efferent approach to reading, 38
Eiseley, Loren, 103
Eliot, T. S., 21, 34, 191, 268

Ellison, Ralph, 189, 190, 191, 192, 196, 336
Emancipatory authority, 12, 149, 152, 159
Emecheta, Buchi, 13, 182, 185, 336
Empowerment, 10, 45, 54, 116, 149
"Empty at the Heart of Things" (Polite), 141, 148, 338
English in America (Ohmann), 103, 316, 319, 359
Erdrich, Louise, 37, 41, 336
Ethnicity, 3, 10, 61, 64, 66, 109, 179, 180, 296
Ethnic writers, 13, 180
Evaluations, 121–122, 173
Experience *vs.* explanation, 73
Explication de texte, 69

A Farewell to Arms (Hemingway), 62, 337
Faulkner, William, 211, 271–272, 333, 336
Felman, Shoshana, 10, 47, 48–49, 55, 116, 298, 310, 311, 347
Feminism, 8, 10, 12, 13, 16, 47, 63, 64, 116, 296
Feminist literary criticism, 150–151, 159, 208–211, 211
Feminist men, 176
Feminist pedagogy, 4, 150, 152
  advantages of, 159
  applied to canon and syllabus, 152–154
  and dialogics, 174
  identification as a strategy for, 159–160
  as a means to emancipatory authority, 149, 152, 159
  reading two poems, examples of, 154–159
  resources for information on, 308–309, 319–323
  student perception of, 176
Feminist readers, 151–152
Feminist thinking, 150–151
Fences (Wilson), 139, 141, 340
Fetterly, Judith, 62, 151, 152, 320, 348
Feudalism, 94
Figures of thought, 226
Final exam, 132–133, 140–141
Fish, Stanley, 63, 74, 99, 201, 295, 300, 305, 306, 308, 312, 316, 348
Fisher, Dexter, 326, 348
Fitzgerald, F. Scott, 65, 211, 325, 336
5 Readers Reading (Holland), 307, 352
Flaubert, Gustave, 76, 78, 336
Flynn, Elizabeth A., 308, 321, 322, 348
Formalism, 6, 10, 13, 47, 203, 286, 295
Formalist criticism, 204–205
Formula fiction, 14
  closed *vs.* open text, 259
  defined, 253
  gender roles in, 257–258
  use of in the classroom, 254–258
Foucault, Michel, 63, 71, 245, 296, 315, 317, 348
Fragmentation, 88, 89–91
Frankenstein (Shelley), 13, 153, 204–211, 298, 339
Franklin, Benjamin, 65, 336
Freeman, Mary Wilkins, 30, 336
Free speech plan, 226
Freire, Paulo, 6, 148, 162, 317–318, 349
Freud, Sigmund, 47, 50, 207, 209, 290, 309, 311, 349
Frost, Robert, 14, 168, 169, 232, 336
Frye, Northrop, 98, 285, 349
Fugard, Athol, 175, 336
"The Function of Criticism at the Present Time" (Arnold), 340

Gadamer, Hans Georg, 74–75, 313, 349
Gates, Henry Louis, Jr., 13, 63, 71, 72, 186, 189, 190–191, 193–194, 198, 226, 239, 303, 324, 350
Gay liberation, 64
Geertz, Clifford, 206, 314, 350
Gender
  in formula fiction, 257–258
  influence of on student thinking, 10, 20, 61, 64, 66, 88, 106, 109, 120, 148, 166, 168, 218
  integrating perspectives on into classroom, 179, 183–184
  male literature, 179–180
  reading for, 111, 151–152, 157
  resources for information on, 296
  reversal, 126
  roles as performances, 164–165
  socialization, 54
Gender balance, 164, 176
Genealogical critique, 296
Generational differences, 216
Genre, 61, 169, 185
"Germinal" (Hogan), 167, 337
Gibson, P. J., 141
Gilbert, Sandra, 56, 158, 212, 320, 350
Gilligan, Carol, 320, 350
Gilman, Charlotte Perkins, 53, 337
Ginsberg, Allen, 51, 337
Giovanni, Nikki, 12, 154–155, 156, 337
Giroux, Henry A., 12, 149, 318, 340, 350
Glasnost, 147
Glaspell, Susan, 175, 337
Gorbachev, Mikhail, 145

Grading, 121–122, 129, 132–133, 138, 140, 141, 142–143, 165
Graff, Gerald, 4, 59, 89, 119, 198, 201, 211, 258, 262, 296, 317, 331–332, 350
Grahn, Judy, 141, 337
Grammatical understanding, 219
Gramsci, Antonio, 104, 115, 210, 317, 337
"The Grave" (Porter), 15, 266–267, 338
The Great Gatsby (Fitzgerald), 65, 211, 336
Greenblatt, Stephen, 100, 206, 314, 351
GRIP Project, 297
Gubar, Susan, 56, 158, 212, 320, 350

Haiku, 204
Hamlet (Shakespeare), 49–50, 211, 309, 310, 339
Hammett (Wenders), 339
Hansberry, Lorraine, 65, 186, 337
Hard Times (Dickens), 83, 336
Hartman, Geoffrey, 327, 329, 351
Hawthorne, Nathaniel, 211, 297, 337
Heart of Darkness (Conrad), 211, 297, 311, 335
Hemingway, Ernest, 111, 271, 322, 325, 333, 337
Henricksen, Bruce, 2, 202, 302, 332, 351
Hermeneutics, 296, 313
Hicks, Granville, 103, 352
The Hidden Hand (Southworth), 258, 339
Hierarchical thinking, 20
Hillocks, George, Jr., 60–61, 352
Hirsch, E. D., Jr., 63, 273, 297, 352
Historical criticism, 206–207
Historical Studies and Literary Criticism (McGann), 357
Historicism, 6, 13, 64
History, as text, 64–65
Hogan, Linda, 167, 337
Holland, Norman N., 74, 305, 306, 307, 308, 309, 352
"Home Burial" (Frost), 168, 169, 336
Homer, 13, 182, 337
Hooks, Bell, 81, 352
Horton, Willie, 187
"How I Contemplated the World from the Detroit House of Correction and Began My Life Over Again" (Oates), 136, 338
"Howl" (Ginsberg), 51, 337
Hughes, Langston, 168, 337
Humanities Index, 83
Hurston, Zora Neale, 13, 65, 66, 71, 78, 191, 192, 193–194, 337
Hypertexts, 15, 273–277, 286–287

Ibsen, Henrick, 13, 182, 337
Ideological manipulation, 15
Ideology(ies), 190, 296
  in the classroom, 104–105
  critique, 123
  knowledge and, 116, 117–118
  an an outgrowth of historical, cultural, and economic forces, 107–108
  as the source of individual perception, 229
  verbal language, effects of on, 263
"Ideology and Ideological State Apparatuses" (Althusser), 123, 127, 340
Ignorance, 116–117
I Know Why the Caged Bird Sings (Angelou), 65, 335
Illusory collectivism, 139
Implied reader, 74
The Implied Reader (Iser), 307, 353
Individualism, 12, 34, 118–119, 129
The Inferno (Dante), 182, 335
Informed reader, 74
Inquiry, 65–68
"In Search of Our Mothers' Gardens" (Walker), 11, 72, 76–77, 80, 84, 339
In Search of Our Mothers' Gardens: Womanist Prose (Walker), 82, 339
Integrated studies, 7
"The Intentional Fallacy" (Wimsatt and Beardsley), 365
Intergenerational chain, 75–76, 78–80
Internally persuasive discourse, 173
Interpretive communities, 63, 67, 68, 201
Interpretive methods
  feminist criticism, 208–211
  formalist criticism, 204–205
  historical criticism, 206–207
  psychoanalytic criticism, 207–208
Intersubjectivity, 20–21
Intertextuality, 64, 153, 203, 272, 276
In the Presence of Mothers (Minty), 338
Intratextuality, 276
Introductions (to literary texts), 125, 127
Introductory teaching, 3–4, 34–35
  coverage model of, 13, 199, 200–201, 202, 303
  formal approach to, 262
  goals of, 261–262
  literary theory in, x, 59–61, 161, 210–211
  problems posed by, 251–252
  selecting works to stimulate inquiry, 65–68
  text-based approach to, 251
  traditional courses, 118–119, 161, 179, 199–200
  unifying themes, 181

writing, uses of, 69–70
Intruder in the Dust (Faulkner), 271, 336
Invisible Man (Ellison), 189, 190, 191, 196, 336
Iser, Wolfgang, 74, 285, 305, 306, 353

Jackson, Elaine, , 141, 148, 337
Jameson, Fredric, 64, 100, 201, 263, 314, 316, 319, 353
Jane Eyre (Brontë), 53–54, 335
Jardine, Alice, 321, 353
Jargon, 189, 196
Jauss, Hans Robert, 74, 75, 76, 80, 312, 313, 353
Jehlen, Myra, 150–151, 152, 155, 159, 247, 270, 303, 320, 353
Johnson, Barbara, 2, 174, 239, 298, 327, 354
Johnson, James Weldon, 13, 190, 194, 195–196, 337
Jordan, June, 166, 167, 169, 175, 337
Journals, 69, 106, 110, 120–121, 132, 142, 201
Joyce, James, 21, 191, 200, 332
Joys of Motherhood (Emecheta), 182, 185, 336
Jung, Carl, 47

Kafka, Franz, 9, 21, 22–23, 24, 25, 27–28, 30, 35, 337
Kazin, Alfred, 47
Keats, John, 11, 95–97, 337
Kicknosway, Faye, 141, 337
Kingston, Maxine Hong, 11, 103, 105–109, 110, 338
Knowledge, 117, 149
Koch, Kenneth, 223–224, 338
Kolodny, Annette, 354
Kramarae, Cheris, 354
Kristeva, Julia, 49, 50, 64, 210, 263, 310, 320, 354

Labyrinths (Borges), 260, 335
Lacan, Jacques, 47–48, 49, 117, 127, 310, 320, 354
Lanham, Richard A., 273, 274, 286, 354
Lawrence, D. H., 65, 152, 338
Learning styles, 20
Le Guin, Ursula K., 162, 169–172, 176, 338
Lentricchia, Frank, 103–104, 296, 323, 332, 354
Literary criticism, 6, 192, 196
Literary-historical process, 75
Literary history, 153
Literary period, 61
Literary response, 22
Literary theory
  resources for general introduction to, 295–305
Literary Theory: An Introduction (Eagleton), 209, 295, 347
Literature-across-the-curriculum programs, 91
Literature
  as a means of reform, 101–102
  student assumptions about, 201–202
  as a vehicle for exploration, 163
"Literature as Equipment for Living" (Burke), 261, 344
Literature as Exploration (Rosenblatt), 102, 306, 361
"The Little Black Boy" (Blake), 236, 335
Living Room (Jordan), 166, 169, 337
Lorde, Audre, 65, 163, 175, 338
Lore, 289–290
Lukács, Georg, 315, 317, 355
"Lulu's Boys" (Erdrich), 37, 40, 41, 43, 44, 336
"Lust" (Minot), 135, 338
"Lycidas" (Milton), 220, 226, 338

Madame Bovary (Flaubert), 75–76, 261, 336
Madonna, 265, 268–269
The Madwoman in the Attic: The Woman Writer and the Nineteenth-Century Literary Imagination (Gilbert and Gubar), 56, 320, 350
Mailloux, Steven, 10, 68, 303, 305, 306, 356
Male literature, 179–180
Mansfield Park (Austen), 76
Margins of Philosophy (Derrida), 346
Marxism, 8, 11–12, 16, 47, 64, 70, 101, 103, 116, 238
  resources for information on, 296, 314–315
Marxism and Form: Twentieth-Century Dialectial Theories of Literature (Jameson), 319, 353
"'Master Harold'... and the Boys" (Fugard), 175, 336
McGann, Jerome J., 100, 313–314, 332, 357
McLaughlin, Thomas, 15, 261, 296, 323, 357, 389
Meaningful interpretation, 136–137

"The Meanings in the Pattern" (Grahn), 141, 142, 337
Melville, Herman, 198, 325, 338
"Mending Wall" (Frost), 232–236, 336
The Merchant of Venice (Shakespeare), 91, 125, 330
Miller, Arthur, 65, 338
Millett, Kate, 47
Milton, John, 12, 14, 34, 118, 129, 219, 220, 224–226, 338
Minority writers, 13, 180
Minot, Susan, 135, 338
Minty, Judith, 14, 236, 358
"MMDCCXIIII/2" (Thomas), 141, 339
Modernism, 191
Moi, Toril, 63, 321, 358
Monarch Notes, 123, 124–125
Moral technology, 118
Morgan, Thaïs E., 2, 275, 302, 351
Morrison, Toni, 9, 25–27, 28, 35, 65, 191, 211, 333, 338
Morton, Donald, 5, 118, 317, 365
Movies, 128
Ms. magazine, 79, 80, 81
Multicultural perspective, 9, 13, 16
  flaws in traditional courses, 179–182
  media portrayal of minorities, 187
  need for, 182
  Othello as a springboard, 183–184
  resources for information on, 323–326
  works that stimulate, 184–186
Multiple belongings, 9, 33–34
Mumbo Jumbo (Reed), 192, 338
Music videos, 125, 128, 265
"My Last Duchess" (Browning), 168, 218, 335
"My Papa's Waltz" (Roethke), 167, 338

Narrative into essay, 39
Narrative of the Life of Frederick Douglass (Douglass), 192, 193, 325, 336
National Black Feminist Organization, 80
Natoli, Joseph, 4, 5, 6, 293, 296, 326, 358
Nelson, Cary, ix, 4, 260, 301, 321, 328, 358
Neo-formalism, 277, 286, 290
Neo-humanists, 273
Neo-New Criticism, 276
Neurosis, 50, 55
New beginning attitude, 19
New Criticism, 50, 60, 202, 204, 227, 286, 295, 296
  author, recognition of, 63–64
  close reading, 38, 62, 92, 93, 102
  coverage model in, 13, 199, 200
  decline of, 102
  and deconstruction compared, 14, 228–237
  dominance of, 227
  limitations of, 85
  literature and science in, 88
  and New Historicism compared, 89–90, 97, 99
  objectivity in, 6
  and psychoanalytic theory compared, 47
  and reader-response theory compared, 73
  textual form and, 6–7
New Historicism, 8, 11, 16, 71, 202, 206, 211
  arguments for, 99
  cultural amnesia as a precondition for, 85–86
  examples of literature taught using, 92–93
  and New Criticism compared, 89–90, 97
  organization of literature courses under, 92
  origins of, 86, 87–88
  reading literature, methods of, 92–93
  resources for information on, 313–314
  rise of, 85
New History (history courses), 86
New Yorker magazine, 110
Noncanonical works, inclusion of, 153
Nonmajors, courses for, 2, 8, 118–119, 123, 131–132, 179
Nontraditional students, 175
Nonverbal language, 15, 215, 266
Norris, Christopher, 329, 359
North, Stephen M., 359
The Norton Anthology of Black Literature, 86
The Norton Anthology of English Literature, 152
The Norton Anthology of Poetry, 223
Norton Critical Editions, 82, 83

Oates, Joyce Carol, 136, 338
Objectivity, 6, 62, 120, 151, 202
O'Connor, Flannery, 200
"Ode on a Grecian Urn" (Keats), 95–97, 337
The Odyssey (Homer), 13, 179, 182, 337
Oedipus Rex (Sophocles), 124–125, 309
Of Grammatology (Derrida), 294, 346
Of Mice and Men (Steinbeck), 65, 66, 339
Ohmann, Richard, 103, 316, 319, 359
"Old Woman Magoun" (Freeman), 30, 336

"Once More to the Lake" (White), 78, 110, 339
On These I Stand (Cullen), 336
Open texts, 259
Oppression, 159, 184
The Order of Things: An Archaeology of the Human Sciences (Foucault), 315, 348
Othello (Shakespeare), 125, 182, 183–184, 311, 339
Otherness, 28, 29, 159, 169, 175
Overturning, 241
"Ozymandias" (Shelley), 168, 339

Paper Dolls (Jackson), 141, 148, 337
Parameters of dissonance, 181
Parodies, 125
Parrington, Vernon, 103
Patriarchy, 127, 157, 165, 173, 182
p'Bitek, Okot, 79
Pedagogical imperatives, 2
Pedagogy of the Oppressed (Freire), 317–318, 349
Perestroika, 147
Personal experience, 167
Phallocentrism, 150, 153
Phenomenological criticism, 49, 296
Place, 166, 168
Plato, 203
Pluralism, 9, 13, 198
  model for, 203–204, 211–212
  need for course emphasizing, 202–203
Poetics (Aristotle), 128
Polite, Frank, 141, 148*n*, 338
Political struggle, 131, 144
The Political Unconscious: Narrative as a Socially Symbolic Act (Jameson), 353
Politics, 2, 20, 103
Popular audience, 77, 80
Popular literature, 253
Positions (Derrida), 346
Positivism, 4
Porter, Katherine Anne, 15, 266–267, 338
Postmodernism, 14, 15, 263–264
Poststructuralist theory 9, 14, 15, 16, 47–48, 63, 86, 190, 263, 268–270
  as a product of culture, 261–270
  resources for information on, 326–327
Pound, Ezra, 21, 34, 191
Power, 71
Pregeneric myths, 191
Pride and Prejudice (Austen), 72, 76, 78, 182, 184–185, 331, 335
Process, 75
Professing Literature: An Institutional History (Graff), 4, 119, 211, 262, 296, 351
"Prowling the Ridge" (Minty), 236, 338
Psychoanalysis and Shakespeare (Holland), 305, 352
Psychoanalytic criticism, 207–208, 211, 296
Psychoanalytic theory, 8, 10, 13, 16, 47–55, 115
  Dracula as an example of using, 50–54
  neurosis, 50, 55
  origins of, 47–48
  problems with, 48–49
  resources for information on, 309–312
  student resistance to, 52–53, 54
Pynchon, Thomas, 259–260, 338

Race, 20, 66, 88, 106, 109, 111, 120, 148*n*, 166, 169, 179, 183–184, 218, 296
Ragged Dick and Mark, the Match Boy (Alger), 252, 254–256, 257, 259, 335
A Raisin in the Sun (Hansberry), 65, 186, 337
Rank, Otto, 47
"Rapunzel" (Kicknosway), 141, 337
Rationality, 162–163
Raymond, James C., 297, 303, 360
Reader-as-created text theory, 48
Reader expectations, 75–78, 84
Reader-focused stage, 30, 40, 41–42
Reader-response theory, 8, 9, 10, 16, 60, 73–74, 211
  advantages of, 36, 45–46
  applications, 38
  combining personal and textual experience, 40–41
  reader-focused stage, 41–42
  resources for information on, 296, 305–309
  spontaneous reactions in, 109
  student resistance to, 36
  subject-focused stage, 42–43
  text-focused stage, 44–46
Reader's Guide to Periodical Literature, 83
The Reader, The Text, The Poem (Rosenblatt), 37, 306, 307, 361
Reading Capital (Althusser), 316, 340
Readings and Feelings: An Introduction to Subjective Criticism (Bleich), 308, 343
Real-life conditions, 216
Realism, 67, 83
Reception theory, 8, 10–11, 16, 73–75
  advantages of, 83–84
  chain of receptions, 75, 78–80
  integration of formal and social analysis, 75–78
  and reader-response theory compared, 73–74

socially formative nature of literature, 75, 80–82
Reed, Ishmael, 13, 191, 192, 338
Religion, 10, 109, 166, 218
Renaissance, 94, 314
Research institutions, 3–4, 294
Research papers, 69
Resisting readers, 12, 62, 111, 116, 152, 158, 166, 182, 202
Response/position papers, 120–121, 129, 172
Retrospective narratives, 65
Revising inner speech, 39
Rhetorical and discourse studies, 1
Rhetorical triangle, 74
A Rhetoric of Motives (Burke), 159, 344
Rhys, Jean, 54, 338
Rich, Adrienne, 360
Richards, I. A., 65, 71, 360
Robbins, Tom, 141, 338
Roethke, Theodore, 167, 338
Romanticism, 6, 206, 295
A Room of One's Own (Woolf), 79, 152, 208–209
"Root Cellar" (Roethke), 167, 339
"A Rose for Emily" (Faulkner), 226, 271
Rosenblatt, Louise, 9, 11, 37, 46, 102, 305–306, 307, 308, 309, 361
Rossetti, Christina, 152, 153, 158–159
Ryan, Michael, 239, 296, 299, 317, 327, 361

Said, Edward, 315, 329, 361
Scandal, 67, 68
The Scarlet Letter (Hawthorne), 29, 211, 297, 337
Schilb, John, 10, 11, 59, 67, 77, 162, 163, 304, 308, 361, 390
Scholarly journal articles, 125, 126
Scholar's Workstation Project, 271, 274
Scholes, Robert, ix, 157, 201, 217, 252, 296, 298, 314, 361
Selections from the Prison Notebooks (Gramsci), 337
Self, sense of, 165–166
Semiotics, ix, 78, 228, 262, 264, 296
Sexuality, 64, 66, 109, 158
Shakespeare, William, 11, 13, 14, 21, 34, 47, 49, 67, 77, 93–94, 125, 179, 182, 184, 202, 211, 242, 244, 339
Shared feelings, 216
Shelley, Mary, 153, 204, 206, 207, 208, 209, 339
Shelley, Percy Bysshe, 206, 209, 212, 339
Shikbu, Lady Murasaki, 182, 185, 339
Shor, Ira, 318, 362
"The Short Happy Life of Francis Macomber" (Hemingway), 111, 337
Showalter, Elaine, 152, 320, 362
Signifying, 13, 78, 84, 190–191, 226
The Signifying Monkey: A Theory of Afro-American Literary Criticism (Gates), 71, 190, 193, 226, 324, 350
Signs, power of, 264–265, 268–269. *See also* Nonverbal language
Sister Carrie (Dreiser), 67–68, 336
Situatedness, 75, 108
Sloan, Margaret, 80
Smedley, Agnes, 198
Smith, Bessie, 77
Social class, 3, 10, 20, 61, 64, 88, 106, 111, 166, 168, 179, 183–184, 218
Social context, 98, 175
Social relations, 131, 147, 148
Social Science Index, 83
"Song of Myself" (Whitman), 237, 340
Songs of Innocence and Experience (Blake), 268
"Sonnet 87" (Shakespeare), 93, 94–95, 339
"Sonnet 116" (Shakespeare), 242–243, 339
Sophocles, 12
Sosnoski, James J., 7, 15 , 271, 301, 330, 332, 362, 390
The Souls of Black Folks (DuBois), 191, 194, 195, 336
The Sound and the Fury (Faulkner), 271, 333, 336
Southworth, E. D. E. N., 339, 358
Speculative instruments, 65, 69, 71, 77
Speech acts, 226
Speech genres, 14, 175
beyond the classroom, 225–226
defined, 220
indispensability of, 224
in interpreting literature, 221–224
Spielberg, Steven, 76, 81
Spivak, Gayatri Shakravorty, 1, 239, 323, 327, 363
Spontaneous theorizing, 277, 282–284, 290
Stafford, William, 103
Steinbeck, John, 65, 66, 339
Stepto, Robert B., 189, 191, 195, 197, 324, 326, 348, 363
Stereotypes, 41, 42, 44, 265
Stoker, Bram, 50, 51–52, 339
Strickland, Ronald, 10, 11–12, 115, 150, 151, 317, 319, 363, 390–391
Strong/symptomatic reading, 122, 129
Structuralism, 285–286, 296
Student involvement, 9, 61, 277–282
Student librarying, 15

Study guides, 123–124, 125–126, 127
Subject-focused stage, 39, 40, 42–43
Subjective Criticism (Bleich), 308
Subjectivity, 11, 62, 111, 202
Subpopular audience, 77
Sula (Morrison), 65
Summer Institutes for Teachers of Literature to Undergraduates, 3, 302
Superreader, 74
Syllabus, 92, 120, 123, 151, 153–154, 165, 166–167, 196, 198, 202

The Tale of Genji (Shikbu), 13, 182, 184, 339
The Taming of the Shrew (Shakespeare), 125, 211, 339
Teacher(s)
  as adversary, 122
  as archivist, 120–121
  as authority figure, 6, 9, 76, 116–117, 120, 125
  as convener, 120
  as coyote midwife, 12, 165–172, 173
  as explorer, 143
  male *vs.* female styles, 173, 175
  as mentor, 12, 116
  as a student of students, 10
  as transformative intellectual, 149
  use of personal experience by, 167
Television, 126, 128, 265
Tennyson, Alfred, 268, 275
Terkel, Studs, 186
Text-focused stage, 39, 40, 44–46
Text, reader, author, history approach, 10
  arguments against, 60
  pairing canonical works with noncanonical works, 65–66
  relations among terms, 61–65
  works that stimulate inquiry, 65–68
  writing, uses of, 69–70
Textual Power: Literary Theory and the Teaching of English (Scholes), 296, 314, 361
Textual studies, 1, 62, 63–64. *See also* Close reading
Textual theory
  defined, 251
  lack of hierarchies in, 253
  liberating nature of, 260
Their Eyes Were Watching God (Hurston), 65, 71, 78, 191, 192, 337
"Theme for English B" (Hughes), 168–169, 337
Themes, 65, 205
Theorizing, 284
Theory body, 293
Theory innovation, 5
Theory movement, 1
  gaps between theory and practice, 1–2
  hostility toward, 2, 299
  impact of on classroom, 2, 7–8
Third World struggles, 64
"This is Just to Say" (Williams), 221–222, 340
Thomas, Brook, 11, 85, 206, 318, 363, 391
Thomas, Lorenzo, 141, 339
Three American Literatures (Baker), 341
To Have and Have Not (Hemingway), 271, 337
Tompkins, Jane, 246–247, 305, 306, 307, 318, 327, 363
Toomer, Jean, 79, 191, 325
Toward an Aesthetic of Reception (Jauss), 74, 313, 353
Transactional view of reading, 38
Treichler, Paula A., 4, 158, 173, 301, 319–320, 321, 322, 354, 363
"Trifles" (Glaspell), 175, 337
Trilling, Lionel, 47
Trouble Is My Business (Chandler), 252, 253–254, 256–257, 259, 335
Twain, Mark, 67, 68, 333, 339

Ulmer, Gregory L., ix, 9, 217, 254, 276, 298, 329–330, 364
Understanding Poetry (Brooks and Warren), 306
Unifying themes, 179, 181, 186
Unlearning, 253
Updike, John, 102
Up From Slavery (Washington), 339
Utopian literature, 176

"Variations on a Theme by William Carlos Williams" (Koch), 223, 338
Verbal icons, 11, 200
Verbal language, 262–263
A Vindication of the Rights of Woman (Wollstonecraft), 208, 340
Voloshinov, V., 148, 175, 215, 216, 218, 226, 364
"The Vulture" (Kafka), 22–23, 337

Walker, Alice, 11, 13, 65, 66, 71, 72, 77–78, 79, 81, 84, 103, 139, 182, 185, 191, 192, 193–194, 100, 339
Warren, Robert Penn, 288, 306
Washington, Booker T., 191, 197, 339

Weir, Peter, 336
The Well Wrought Urn (Brooks), 343
Welty, Eudora, 200
Wenders, Wim, 339
Wheatley, Phillis, 79, 190
White, E. B., 11, 78, 110, 111, 339
Whitman, Walt, 14, 237, 325, 340
Wide Sargasso Sea (Rhys), 54, 338
Williams, Raymond, 70, 315, 365
Williams, Robin, 127
Williams, William Carlos, 14, 221–222, 223, 224, 225, 346
Wilson, August, 139, 141, 340
Wimsatt, W. K., Jr., 307, 365
Winterowd, W. Ross, 365
Wollstonecraft, Mary, 208, 340
The Woman Warrior (Kingston), 103, 110, 338
Women in Love (Lawrence), 65, 338
Women's movement, 149
Women's studies, ix, 174
Woolf, Virginia, 21, 45, 79, 152, 153, 208, 209, 340
Word-processing programs, 287
Wordsworth, William, 153, 217, 218, 226, 298
Wright, Richard, 191, 192
Writing
  as a form of student inquiry, 69–70
Writing-across-the-curriculum programs, 91

Yeats, W. B., 65, 191, 268, 331, 340
The Yellow Wallpaper (Gilman), 53, 337

Zavarzadeh, Mas'ud, 5, 118, 130, 317, 330, 365

Editors

James M. Cahalan works at Indiana University of Pennsylvania, where he has served as Director of Graduate Studies in Literature and Criticism, and regularly teaches introductory undergraduate courses as well as graduate seminars. The idea for this book occurred to him when he was offering a doctoral seminar at IUP on literary theory for college teachers and could find no adequate book about teaching introductory literature courses in light of contemporary theory. Previously he taught at the University of Cincinnati, the University of Massachusetts at Boston, and Northeastern University. He is the author of *Great Hatred, Little Room: The Irish Historical Novel* (1983); *The Irish Novel: A Critical History* (1988); *Liam O'Flaherty: A Study of the Short Fiction* (1991); and numerous articles in such journals as the *Colby Quarterly*, *Éire-Ireland*, the *Irish Literary Supplement*, the *Journal of Teaching Writing*, and *Hemingway Notes*.

David B. Downing has taught, since 1988, in the English Department of Indiana University of Pennsylvania, where he regularly teaches introductory literature classes and the core doctoral courses in the history and theory of criticism and literary theory for the teacher and scholarly writer. Previously he taught for nine years at Eastern Illinois University. He is the editor of *Works and Days: Essays in the Socio-Historical Dimensions of Literature and the Arts*, and coeditor, with Susan Bazargan, of *Image and Ideology in Modern/Postmodern Discourse* (1991). He has published numerous articles in the areas of critical theory, cultural criticism, and American literature. In 1990 he organized and directed a conference at IUP on "The Role of Theory in the Undergraduate Literature Classroom: Curriculum, Pedagogy, Politics."

Contributors

Don Bialostosky has taught Romantic poetry and the history and theory of criticism at the University of Utah, the University of Washington, and the State University of New York at Stony Brook. He is currently professor of English and Coordinator of the Colloquium in Rhetorical Theory at the University of Toledo. His *Making Tales: The Poetics of Wordsworth's Narrative Experiments* was published by the University of Chicago Press in 1984, and he has published widely on Wordsworth, Mikhail Bakhtin, narrative theory, and the pedagogical and critical practices of English. He has books in progress on "Wordsworth, Literary Study, and Liberal Education" and "Dialogics and the Arts of Discourse."

David Bleich teaches in the English Department and the Graduate School of Education and Human Development at the University of Rochester. A leading figure in the teaching of literature since the early 1970s, and particularly a pioneer in reader-response theory and pedagogy, Bleich is the author of *Readings and Feelings: An Introduction to Subjective Criticism* (1975); *Subjective Criticism* (1978); *Utopia: The Psychology of a Cultural Fantasy* (1984); and *The Double Perspective: Language, Literacy, and Social Relations* (1988).

Patricia Prandini Buckler is assistant professor of English and Director of Composition at Purdue University North Central, a campus of 3,300 students in Westville, Indiana. She holds a Ph.D. in Rhetoric and Composition from the University of Louisville and has been teaching English in high school and college for twenty years. She believes firmly in making literature students write and composition students read. Buckler has published and presented numerous papers, and her research interests include the conflict between student privacy and collaboration in the writing class, the antebellum woman's scrapbook as autobiography, the essay, and the relationship between discourse and historical context. Her oldest love is Chaucer.

John Clifford is professor of English at the University of North Carolina at Wilmington, where he teaches literature, writing, and theory. In the summer he also teaches at the University of Pennsylvania's Graduate School of Education and at Northeastern's Martha's Vineyard Institute. He taught high school English for ten years in Brooklyn, New York, and worked for four years in the writing program at Queens College–CUNY before moving to UNCW in 1978. He was a National Endowment for the Humanities Fellow at the University of Southern California, 1980–81, in literature and literacy. Clifford studied literary theory with Louise Rosenblatt at New York University and wrote his dissertation for the Ph.D. in 1977 on collaborative learning and composition. He has written numerous articles and reviews on literary and writing theory and has edited a collection of essays on Louise Rosenblatt, *The Experience of Reading,* as well as coauthoring several other books, including *Modern American Prose: 15 Writers.* With John Schilb, he is currently editing a collection of essays on writing theory and critical theory for the MLA.

M. H. Dunlop earned a Ph.D. in American literature from The George Washington University and teaches at Iowa State University. An active scholar in American literature and culture, she has delivered papers on nineteenth- and twentieth-century popular forms at various regional and national conferences, and her essays on the darker sides of nineteenth-century American culture have appeared in *The Old Northwest* and *American Quarterly.* She regularly teaches courses on late-nineteenth-century American literature and on literature by and about women, and has used a course entitled "Introduction to Literary Study" as a site for considerable experimentation with texts and theories. Recently she has conducted grant-supported research on curricular development in undergraduate literature courses; she is pursuing ongoing interests in canon revision and in theorizing undergraduate study in literature and culture.

Thomas Fink, an associate professor of English at CUNY–LaGuardia Community College, has published articles on deconstruction in the *Publication of the Society for Literature and Science, American Letters and Commentary,* and the *Wallace Stevens Journal.* His criticism on contemporary poetry has appeared in *American Poetry Review, Twentieth-Century Literature, Modern Poetry Studies, Nouvelle Europe,* the *Minnesota Review,* and elsewhere. He has completed the first book-length study of the contemporary American poet David Shapiro.

C. Mark Hurlbert is an associate professor of English at Indiana University of Pennsylvania. He teaches courses in IUP's graduate programs in rhetoric and linguistics and in literature and criticism, and undergraduate courses in writing, literature, and English education. He also supervises student teachers, and he previously taught high school English for seven years in upstate New York. He has written numerous articles, and he is coeditor, with Michael Blitz, of *Composition and Resistance,* a collection of essays and dialogues on ideology and the teaching of writing and literature (Boynton/Cook, Heinemann). He is guest editor of a special issue of *Works and Days* on the relationship of theory and pedagogy, and is currently coediting, with Samuel Totten, *Social Issues in the English Classroom: Theory and Practice.* He and Michael Blitz are also writing a book-length study of ideology and the academy's rhetorics and the literacy demands these rhetorics make on teachers and students.

Phillipa Kafka, a professor of English and Africana studies at Kean College of New Jersey, has been teaching multicultural courses since 1977. She has published in the *CEA, Critic*, the *National Women's Studies Association Newsletter* (on Phillis Wheatley), and *Sage: A Scholarly Journal for Black Women* (on Marita Bonner). She is presently writing an article on Phillis Wheatley for the *NWSA Journal*. Forthcoming in *MELUS* is her essay on transforming the American literature survey.

Douglas Lanier has taught at Duke (where he developed an interdisciplinary humanities course for the Talent Identification Program), the UCLA Writing Program, and Allegheny College; he has recently joined the faculty of the University of New Hampshire. His research interests include Renaissance literature, the history and theory of rhetoric, and the development of authorship as a cultural institution. He has written on Jonson, Shakespeare, Marston, and Milton, as well as an essay entitled "In Defense of Jargon"; currently he is finishing a book on Jonson, self-fashioning, and authorship entitled "Better Markes."

Thomas McLaughlin teaches in the English Department at Appalachian State University in Boone, North Carolina. He is the author of the anthology *Literature: The Power of Language* and the coeditor (with Frank Lentricchia) of *Critical Terms for Literary Study*. He regularly teaches advanced courses in literary criticism and theory, as well as first-year introduction to literature courses, and his pedagogical and scholarly work has focused on integrating these two activities. He is currently at work, with Melissa Barth and James Winders, on a reader about issues of gender, race, and class.

Patrick D. Murphy teaches undergraduate and graduate courses in English at Indiana University of Pennsylvania, with approximately half of his teaching load consisting of lower-division introductory courses. At the graduate level he teaches critical theory and contemporary poetry. An associate professor, he is editor of *Studies in the Humanities*, coeditor of four books (including *Essentials of the Theory of Fiction*), editor of *Critical Essays on Gary Snyder*, and *Staging the Impossible*, as well as author of some thirty critical essays, including "Prolegomenon for an Ecofeminist Dialogics." The essay printed in this book is based in part on a paper delivered at the Re-Visioning Knowledge and the Curriculum conference held at Michigan State University in April 1990.

Mark S. Paris spent the last year teaching at Montgomery College in Rockville, Maryland, and has also taught at Marymount University in Arlington, Virginia. He also spent two years as a lecturer in the department of English at East Carolina University, Greenville, North Carolina, a four-year comprehensive institution. He received his Master's degree in English from Emory University in 1988. At present he is pursuing a doctoral degree in English at the University of California at Riverside. This is his first publication.

Pancho Savery is associate professor and Director of the Graduate Program in English at the University of Massachusetts at Boston where he teaches courses in African American literature and modern and contemporary

American and European drama and fiction. Recent publications include *Approaches to Teaching Ellison's "Invisible Man,"* the introduction to the 1989 edition of Saunders Redding's *Stranger and Alone*, and "Third Plane at the Change of the Century: The Shape of African-American Literature to Come" (in *Left Politics and the Literary Profession*). He is completing a book on Saunders Redding and serves as manuscript editor of *Radical Teacher*.

John Schilb directs the Freshman Writing Program at the University of Maryland, College Park. He has also taught literature, composition, and rhetorical theory at Loyola University of Chicago, the University of North Carolina at Wilmington, Denison University, and Carthage College. Especially interested in how literary theory and composition theory relate, he has published on this subject in journals such as *College Composition and Communication, Journal of Advanced Composition, Rhetoric Review*, and *PRE/TEXT*, as well as in the anthologies *Literary Nonfiction* and *Perspectives on Research and Scholarship in Composition*. He is coeditor of *Contending with Words: Composition and Rhetoric in a Postmodern Age* and *Writing Theory and Critical Theory*, both for the MLA.

Louise Z. Smith, the new editor of *College English*, teaches undergraduate courses in composition, tutoring, fiction, and nineteenth-century British literature, and graduate courses in nonfictional prose and in composition theory and pedagogy at the University of Massachusetts at Boston, where she formerly directed the Freshman Writing Program and now supervises graduate teaching assistants. She is coauthor with Emily Meyer of *The Practical Tutor* (Oxford University Press, 1987), and she is editor of *Audits of Meaning: A Festschrift in Honor of Ann E. Berthoff* (Boynton/Cook, Heinemann, 1988). Her work has appeared in *College English, Studies in Scottish Literature, Studies in Romanticism*, and other journals and books. Her essay on teaching Keats's poetry from the perspective of composition theory appears in *Teaching Keats*, edited by Walter H. Evert (MLA).

James J. Sosnoski is professor of English at Miami University in Oxford, Ohio, where he has recently been teaching student-centered courses following the principles outlined in his essay in this book. He has published articles on literary theory and criticism. He is the co-founder of the Society for Critical Exchange and was its executive director from 1982 to 1988. Having recently completed a book-length manuscript entitled *The Magister Implicatus: The Call to Orthodoxy in Literary Study*, he is now at work on another, entitled *Rethinking Theory*. In addition, he is the director of the Teaching in Electronic Schools Project (TIES), which is concerned with the development of telecommunicative and hypermedia courseware in cultural studies.

Ronald Strickland teaches general literature courses as well as upper-division and graduate courses in Renaissance literature at Illinois State University, having earned his Ph.D. at Syracuse University. He has published articles and reviews on Renaissance literature, literary theory, and pedagogy. He is currently working to develop innovative strategies for enhancing cultural diversity in traditional literature courses.

Brook Thomas teaches American literature at the University of California at Irvine. He has also taught at the University of Constance in Germany, the University of Massachusetts at Amherst, and the University of Hawaii at Manoa, where most of his teaching involved general education courses for nonmajors. For this essay he drew on literary examples from outside his specialty, something that teachers of introductory courses must always do. He is the author of *James Joyce's "Ulysses": A Book of Many Happy Returns, Cross-examinations of Law and Literature: Cooper, Hawthorne, Stowe and Melville,* and *The New Historicism and Other Old-Fashioned Topics.*

Lois Tyson received her Ph.D. in American literature and critical theory from Ohio State University in 1989. She is currently assistant professor of English at Grand Valley State University in Allendale, Michigan, and is working on a book on the intersection of ideology and psychology in twentieth-century American literature. She has taught a wide range of introductory and survey literature courses and is especially interested in the uses of critical theory as an interdisciplinary learning tool.

Barbara Frey Waxman is associate professor and Director of Graduate Studies in English at the University of North Carolina at Wilmington, where she has taught many courses at all levels. She has also taught at the University of Richmond, Virginia State University, and Brooklyn College. Waxman's publications include pedagogical essays on the politics of the literary survey course, a feminist approach to the issue of a black literary canon, a discussion of English instructors' social responsibilities and how teaching literature through the life-cycle can fulfill these, and an essay on using computers in the composition classroom. She has also written critical essays on works by Mary Shelley, George Eliot, and others for a variety of journals. Her book, *From the Hearth to the Open Road: A Feminist Study of Aging in Contemporary Literature,* has recently been published by Greenwood Press.